Sovereignty Suspended

THE ETHNOGRAPHY OF POLITICAL VIOLENCE

Series Editors: Daniel J. Hoffman, Tobias Kelly, Sharika Thiranagama

A complete list of books in the series is available from the publisher.

SOVEREIGNTY SUSPENDED

Building the So-Called State

Rebecca Bryant *and* Mete Hatay

PENN

UNIVERSITY OF PENNSYLVANIA PRESS

PHILADELPHIA

Published by
University of Pennsylvania Press
Philadelphia, Pennsylvania 19104-4112
www.upenn.edu/pennpress

Printed in the United States of America
on acid-free paper

10 9 8 7 6 5 4 3 2 1

Library of Congress Cataloging-in-Publication Data
Names: Bryant, Rebecca, author. | Hatay, Mete, author.
Title: Sovereignty suspended : building the so-called state / Rebecca Bryant
   and Mete Hatay.
Other titles: Ethnography of political violence.
Description: 1st edition. | Philadelphia : University of Pennsylvania Press, [2020] |
   Series: The ethnography of political violence | Includes bibliographical references
   and index.
Identifiers: LCCN 2019045157 | ISBN 978-0-8122-5221-7 (hardcover)
Subjects: LCSH: Nation-building—Cyprus, Northern. | Self-determination, National—
   Cyprus, Northern. | Turks—Cyprus—Social conditions. | Cyprus, Northern—Politics
   and government. | Cyprus, Northern—International status. | Cyprus, Northern—
   Foreign relations.
Classification: LCC DS54.95.N67 B79 2020 | DDC 956.93—dc23
LC record available at https://lccn.loc.gov/2019045157

In memory of Özer Hatay (1937–2013)

CONTENTS

PREFACE

It would be a great understatement to call this work a collaboration. Every observation, every idea, every argument emerged out of a shared experience and joint vision of what it means to live in an unrecognized state. The work began in the pleasure of recognizing similar ways of seeing and thinking about that experience and the sense that we could accomplish so much more by thinking about it together. That thinking began in 2006 when Rebecca received seed funding from George Mason University, where she was then teaching, to begin research for a project on governmentality and sovereignty conflicts. Her interest at the time was in how the institutional entrenchment of de facto states shapes the present of unresolved conflicts and constrains negotiations to resolve them. This led to exploratory research in Sri Lanka and Abkhazia, but as an anthropologist she found herself pulled back to the case that she knew best, north Cyprus.

By that time Rebecca had already written one book and was finishing a second about the island, but the collaboration with Mete began in 2007, when on a sabbatical in Cyprus they wrote their first journal article together. That article dealt with a subject that had long intrigued Rebecca, namely, the social forgetting of the 1963–1974 period, in which Turkish Cypriots lived in militarized enclaves and for five years were under siege. While that period was widely regarded as the most critical period in Turkish Cypriot history, there were no memoirs, books of oral history, or even stories or poems that described the period. While Rebecca had been intrigued by this process of social forgetting, Mete pointed out the reverberations of that period in the present, resulting in an article that reversed many standard interpretations of a time of Turkish Cypriot protest and political action in the early 2000s (Hatay and Bryant 2008). We saw that period of agency against Turkey and action in favor of reunification as one that referenced the enclave period, a period of both deprivation and strong solidarity. Building on that argument, we published a second article that asked what agency under the siege experienced during the first five years of the enclave period can tell us about constructions and simulations of sovereignty (Bryant and Hatay 2011). As a result of those two articles, we initially began this book as an exploration of state-building in the enclaves.

The state-within-a-state that developed then could not be explored, however, without going further back in time and linking Turkish Cypriots' minority status under colonial rule to a struggle for institutional representation and what we call sovereign agency that ultimately led to the creation of a de facto state. Our genealogical approach to the contradictions and paradoxes of life in an unrecognized state also suited us both, since we had each separately conducted historical as well as ethnographic research in Cyprus in the past and so knew that many of the contradictions and paradoxes that we encountered in everyday life had much longer histories. For example, the present-day discourse about becoming a minority and disappearing, which we discuss in our first article together, in fact had a much longer history going back to the late nineteenth century. The archival and ethnographic research specifically for this work took place over about seven years and continued through the three years of writing, although the research has been layered over time and builds on the accumulated body of our previous work. That body of work includes research in various archives in Cyprus, Istanbul, Athens, and London, as well as interviews and ethnographic research dating back to the early 1990s. It includes Rebecca's ethnographic and archival research for her second book on Cyprus, *The Past in Pieces: Belonging in the New Cyprus,* which took as its site a particular region of the island's north and the changes that it experienced after 2003, when the checkpoints that divide the island opened.

Tracing Turkish Cypriots' institutional drive over several decades, however, began a long road of new research that took us into the hitherto unexplored archives of the Turkish Cypriot Federation of Institutions (Kıbrıs Türk Kurumları Federasyonu) from the 1950s and Turkish Cypriot parliament minutes from the 1970s. It also led us to explore thousands of pages of newspapers from Cyprus and Turkey from the 1950s to the present. It meant dozens of interviews with persons involved in the unrecognized state's founding and in its political parties, especially persons engaged in the original distribution of properties after 1974. It meant around three hundred formal and informal interviews with persons displaced during the conflict and ultimately

resettled in the island's north, as well as a set of thirty interviews with journalists, union leaders, and civil society representatives about Turkish Cypriots' relations with Turkish nationals and with Turkey. All interviews and
almost all written sources used for the book were originally in Turkish, and
Rebecca was responsible for all translations from Turkish to English.

One of the most important sources, however, has been participant observation over more than a decade, during which we noted down anecdotes,
observations of friends, discussions in which we participated, and other
ethnographic material. These ethnographic examples appear in the text primarily as unattributed examples, both because the size of the community
means that it is very easy to identify persons through description, and also
because in long-term fieldwork one may observe interlocutors changing their
minds, positions, and political affiliations over time. Alternatively, people
may express in private views that they do not want publicly aired in ways that
would reveal their source. As should become clear throughout the book, such
contradictions are part and parcel of living with a state that is not supposed
to be one. Because we live at least half of the year in Cyprus, we also lived
with those paradoxes, and we watched our friends and family struggle with
them. We watched them grapple with how to build lives, plan for the future,
and negotiate their status as citizens of a so-called state. The shape of the present book eventually emerged as we realized that the contradictions and
paradoxes of life in an unrecognized state that particularly engaged us would
be best explored by focusing our attention on de facto state-building in the
post-1974 period.

We should also say a few words about how we wrote this book. In one
sense, much of the structure, framing, and narrative of the book fell to Rebecca, for whom English is her native language and anthropological theory
the currency of her discipline. However, things were hardly this simple.
Because we are married, the creation of this book permeated our daily lives
and interactions, becoming one of the ways that we lived together. We would
wake up and talk about ideas. We would take walks and hash out the structure of chapters. We would go on vacations and find comparisons. We would
run into someone on the street and come up with a new way of thinking about
the argument. A day did not pass without a new observation or a new concept entering our relationship. In that sense, this book has been inextricable
from our life together.

This was also to be expected when our backgrounds and the audiences
each of us had in mind are different. Rebecca was trained as a cultural

anthropologist and only arrived in Cyprus as a PhD student in the early 1990s. Mete, in contrast, was born on the island and grew up in the militarized Turkish Cypriot enclaves of the 1960s. His father was a well-known journalist, the longtime Cyprus correspondent for Turkey's *Hürriyet* newspaper, and many of the photos in this book come from his personal archive. Mete began his career in the field of tourism and management, reflecting the opportunities available to young men on the island in the early 1980s. As the reader will see, that job experience provided us material and insight into the workings of institutions that are relevant for this book. Within a decade, however, Mete was following in his father's footsteps by becoming a researcher, writer, and public intellectual.

These quite different backgrounds have meant that while Mete was more concerned with taking the analysis back to his community, Rebecca was more concerned with what this case has to say for other cases of unrecognized states and for the anthropology of the state. From the beginning of this project, then, the direction of our thinking was rather different: while Mete was concerned with finding concepts that would explain what we were seeing, Rebecca was more convinced that existing concepts did not really fit the case and that new ones needed to be invented. This created a highly productive synergy in which Mete insisted on certain concepts, such as liminality and enclavism, that he saw as fitting what we experienced ethnographically, and Rebecca was forced to rise to the challenge of showing why such concepts did not quite fit and trying to explain why.

As a writing method, however, it has been Mete's work as a journalist and public intellectual that has contributed as much to the shape of this book as Rebecca's more disciplinarily oriented insistence on form and framing. In his weekly research articles and twice-weekly columns in north Cyprus's *Havadis* newspaper, as well as in countless radio and television interviews, Mete has been able to test our interpretations and gain feedback for further developing the analysis. On the basis of this feedback, we have discussed, argued, refined, and sometimes gone back to the beginning. We have also, at times, seen our interpretations take root and develop discursive lives of their own, becoming part of public discourse about what it means to live in a so-called state.

In the end, this book represents only a fraction of what we wrote or have thought of writing on the subject, the condensation of a much larger, historically richer argument. As so often happens with large projects, the written products have multiplied and have varied audiences. One of those products is the present volume, while another is a single-authored ethnography that Rebecca is publishing about the post-2003 period, where the current book ends.

On a stylistic note, the book presented a grammatical challenge, forcing us to switch between the first-person "we" and a third-person perspective in which we use our names when we describe ethnographic incidents experienced by one of us. Throughout the book, we have emphasized the former and tried to minimize the latter, though the latter was unavoidable. In order to overcome this problem, we had to see the narrative voice of the book as a third voice, one that was part of our conversation but could stand back and write about each of us. We trust that the reader will also understand this voice in that way, as a composite narrator who emerges as the voice of our deliberations together.

For a large part of the twentieth century, toponyms have played an important part in signifying space in Cyprus as ethnic. Contests over toponyms began when British colonial administrators started replacing Ottoman names with British ones. For example, Arabahmet Sokağı became Victoria Street, and newly constructed roads were given the names of British rulers. Starting in the 1930s, struggles to claim space as ethnic began to mean changing Ottoman place names to Greek or Greek toponyms to Turkish. The former was accomplished through municipalities, which had the mandate to change such names and were mostly controlled by the majority Greek Cypriot community. Urban toponyms were Hellenized, so that, for instance, Cenktepe became Akropolis, and Bayraktar Meydanı became Plateia Venizelou, or Venizelos Square. In reaction to the Hellenization of urban space, the Turkish Cypriot leadership of the period decided in 1958 to choose Turkish language place names for villages and neighborhoods with Turkish majorities.

We explain this process in Chapter 2, along with the toponym changes that Turkified the landscape of north Cyprus after 1974. Although the Republic of Cyprus government has never accepted the 1958 toponym changes, in scholarship there is a tendency to view them as semi-legitimate, the result of an attempt to Turkify one's own environment rather than the result of ethnic cleansing and Turkification of a territory, as occurred after 1974. Nevertheless, in 2013 the Republic of Cyprus parliament criminalized the use of all names not officially accepted and recorded by the government of Cyprus. According to this law, "anyone who publishes, imports, distributes, or sells maps, books, or any other documents in print or digital form that contain geographical names and toponyms on the island of Cyprus other than those permitted, commits an offense punishable with up to three years in prison or a fine of up to 50,000 euros ($57,500) or both" (U.S. Department of State 2019; also Pancyprian Bar Association 2013).

Throughout this work, we have chosen to use the English-language versions of names of towns, cities, and regions, where these exist and are in common use. For instance, the name "Kyrenia" is in common use in English for a town that has been known in Turkish as Girne since the Ottoman period. Where common English names do not exist, we use Turkish names in cases of historical precedent. This includes both cases where names existed from the Ottoman period in the island and names that were changed by the Turkish Cypriot leadership in 1958. An example of the former is the village name Değirmenlik, which exists from the Ottoman period, and which is known in Greek as Kythrea. An example of the second is the village of Erenköy, which is known in Greek as Kokkina and acquired its Turkish name in 1958.

In addition, there are cases where we use Turkish and Greek names interchangeably, particularly when quoting Turkish-language sources or to indicate which names are in common use today.

*   *   *

Turkish is a phonetic language that is written in Latin script and pronounced as it is written. In most cases, pronunciation resembles English, with the addition of several letters:

c	Pronounced like *j* in *jam*
ç	Pronounced like *ch* in *cheese*
ğ	Soft g, lengthens previous vowel
ı	Pronounced like *e* in *the* or *u* in *duh*
ö	Pronounced like *e* in *her*
ş	Pronounced like *sh* in *shower*
ü	Pronounced like *oo* in *shoot*

Sovereignty Suspended

Figure 1. Divided map of Cyprus (CIA Factbook, Creative Commons).

Introduction

The Aporetic State

In early 2016, the World Economic Forum in Davos, Switzerland, welcomed the so-called president of the so-called Turkish Republic of Northern Cyprus (TRNC). A political leader with a left-wing past, Mustafa Akıncı had been elected several months earlier, triggering the start of a new round of negotiations intended to reunify the divided island. The cameras clicked as he shook hands with world leaders, and media heralded his appearance there with his Greek Cypriot counterpart, Republic of Cyprus president Nicos Anastasiades, as a step toward an elusive peace. Never mind that they had actually come to Davos to implore heads of state to fund what was starting to look like a very expensive potential solution to what many of those same leaders perceive as a middle-class conflict.

After all, Cyprus is a country that is not at war, and at the time of writing the island that has been partitioned for more than four decades seems to make international news primarily in travel magazines' reports on its beaches and, most recently, because of Greek Cypriot banks' laundering of Russian money. As far as conflicts go, Cypriots on both sides of the divide are relatively well off, and the recognized Republic of Cyprus (RoC), effectively confined in its scope to the island's south, is a full voting member of the European Union (EU). On both sides of the island, Cypriots have nice houses, decent cars, and good educations. Middle-class families take vacations to Italy and Thailand. As a result, while international actors have been active in diplomacy to help solve a conflict that is simply known as "the Cyprus Problem," they have been reluctant to pull out checkbooks.

Of course, the perception of well-being is deceptive, since all Cypriots have lived for almost half a century with the political, economic, and psychological consequences of an unresolved conflict and a divided island. Moreover, as citizens of an unrecognized state, Turkish Cypriots' ability to do well or to continue doing well is always improvisatory, as they constantly adapt to whatever limitations are being imposed on their ability to trade, study, and travel. Despite the conflict, citizens of the recognized RoC are able to plan their lives and the lives of their children with the assumption that they will continue to live in a recognized, EU-member state. Citizens of the so-called TRNC, however, live their daily lives with what they invariably call *belirsizlik*, uncertainty. That uncertainty arises from not knowing one's place in the world, from not being "seen" or recognized, and from the knowledge that the shape, form, and substance of their so-called state could be altered with a pen stroke.

For these reasons, the significance of the Davos visit as reflected in the local press was somewhat different from the international version. In commenting for Turkish Cypriot journalists, Akıncı would remark, "This is the first time that a Turkish Cypriot President has come here. Even if the world does not recognize the TRNC, the Cypriot Turkish people is an existence/presence (*varlık*). Everyone is aware of this. Everyone knows that there will be no resolution in Cyprus without the contribution of the Turkish Cypriot people and their chosen leader."[1] Akıncı alludes to the widespread perception that Turkey is an occupying and colonizing power in north Cyprus and that the unrecognized TRNC is its puppet or vassal. This widespread perception also has the consequence of erasing Turkish Cypriots as sovereign agents, so that Greek Cypriot leaders have often complained that their counterpart in negotiations should be Turkey, not the Turkish Cypriot (puppet) leader.

Akıncı instead asserts that the world has begun to see that Turkish Cypriots are present as a people and have their own will. The word that he uses, *varlık*, in this context means an existence, presence, or being. It is also a word that connotes, however remotely and in echo, what many Turkish Cypriots understand to be the source of the conflict itself, namely, the majority Greek Cypriot community's insistence for a large part of the twentieth century that it had the right to decide the future of the island as a whole. Turkish Cypriots called their fight, as a minority, to have a space that they could control themselves a *varoluş mücadelesi*, literally a struggle for existence, that was also a *varolma mücadelesi*, a struggle for being or presence. To say that the Turkish Cypriot people have a "presence" in Davos is effectively a reassurance that even if their state is not recognized, they have still made strides in the struggle for being.

The "president" appears to say here that they have lost the battle but won the war. His spokesperson, Barış Burcu, seemed to repeat this claim some weeks later, when he asseverated that with a solution Turkish Cypriots' status "would undergo a revolutionary change." "With a solution," he remarked, "we will take our place in the world as the equal founding partners of a recognized state. We will come under international law."[2] Right-wing commentators immediately attacked the statement on social media, arguing that they could not have status as individuals or a community but only as a state, and that in a federal solution the TRNC would be dissolved rather than recognized. Instead they would become only a constituent state of a federation—"a local administration, that is all" one commentator remarked. He asseverated that it would be "unacceptable to give up the 33-year-old, independent and sovereign state of the TRNC" for a constituent state that would actually lower their status.[3]

What this so-called president, his somewhat bumbling spokesman, and their acerbic commentators all share are sovereign anxieties, or an everyday concern to resolve the gap between the real and the realizable that constitutes what we call here the *aporetic state*.[4] In his brief book *Aporias*, Jacques Derrida poses the aporia, the space of nonpassage, in tension with the border, which he defines as that which one is able to cross even when one knows one should not. The aporia is in tension with the border, because it represents the point at which crossing is impossible despite there being no border to stop us. The aporia is "the difficult or the impracticable, here the impossible, passage, the refused, denied or prohibited passage" (Derrida 1993: 8). In contrast to the border, what is significant for Derrida about the aporia is that it represents an impossible possibility, a refusal or prohibition, that is both known and inexplicable, seemingly arbitrary.

In this book, the aporia represents the known distinction, present in de facto states from their very inception, between the *real* and the *realizable*. De facto states are those entities, such as the TRNC, that look like states and act like states but do not have the international recognition that makes them de jure, or states "in law." These are entities with well-defined and well-guarded borders, ones with developed political and bureaucratic systems that hold elections, give out identity cards, issue checks to civil servants and retirees, build roads, and distribute water. At the same time, their leaders are shunned, and the state is always in various stages of embargo and isolation. In the academic literature, scholars often refer to them as unrecognized or informal states (Isachenko 2012), while some have tried out epithets such as "quasi" to label them (e.g., Jackson 1990). Indeed, there is a lively discussion in the political science literature regarding what these states should be called and how to identify them when we see them. Most of these works begin by setting out criteria that such entities must meet in order to be classified as unrecognized or de facto (e.g., Harvey and Stansfield 2010; Kolstø 2000, 2006; Lynch 2004; Pegg 1998). For instance, one of the pathbreaking books in this field is Nina Caspersen's *Unrecognized States* (2012), in which she attempts to set out such descriptive criteria, including having control over their territory, remaining in existence for more than three years, and so on.

While these studies have helped to define a new subfield within international relations and have been essential for us in thinking about the case that we examine here, we begin from a different starting point. We begin not by developing criteria that will allow us to know a de facto state when we see one, but with the assumption that we already know a de facto state when we see it and to ask why that is and what it implies.

This book uses extensive archival and ethnographic research in one de facto state for two aims: (1) to ask what the case of de facto state-building can tell us about state-building as such; and (2) to use this case to interrogate the singularity of the "de facto." The first of these aims builds on a body of literature in political theory, international relations, anthropology, and geography that interrogates the social construction of the state and sovereignty through everyday discourse and practice. Indeed, sovereign anomalies have played an important role in developing that literature, which burgeoned when the violent breakup of the USSR and Yugoslavia, and the unexpected claims of many groups to self-determination, led to a proliferation of breakaway states (e.g., Cornell 2002a, 2002b; Kolstø 2000; Kolstø and Blakkisrud 2008; Meadwell 1999; Pegg 1998; Richmond 2002; also cf. Grant 2009). These states' inability to gain recognition for their claims to self-determination has been used as an example by scholars to question Westphalian sovereignty as a normative framework, indeed leading one scholar to refer to it as "organized hypocrisy" (Krasner 1999; see also Paul 1999; Strange 1999).[5]

Most important for this research, critiques of the Westphalian framework have included an important literature questioning the reification of both the state and sovereignty. One critic of the tendency to see sovereignty as a "thing" has instead described it as "a discursive framing of space, time, and identity"

(Walker 1996: 16). In this view the sovereign state arises through discursive claims and practices, both domestic and international, that simultaneously "perform" sovereignty and create it (see also Howland and White 2009). These descriptions echo Timothy Mitchell's earlier argument that we may see the state as a structural effect, "the powerful, metaphysical effect of practices that make such structures appear to exist" (1991, 94; see also 1990). Concomitantly, Cynthia Weber called sovereignty a simulation produced by the agreement of other states not to intervene in another state's affairs. She notes, "The identity of the state—the ways we understand this materiality of people, territory, government, etc.—does not pre-exist performative expression of the state, including sovereignty" (1998: 92). Among a certain influential strand of political theory, then, there seems some agreement that *acting like a state* brings the state into existence, is a kind of metaphysical trick that makes something that is really only an idea seem like a real thing in the world. This view is, moreover, backed up by an anthropological and geographical literature on everyday state practices (e.g., Corbridge et. al. 2009, Ismail 2006, Wilson 2016) and the prosaic state (Painter 2006) that is visible in the mundane (Thrift 2000).

Our own focus on state practices, then, is not in itself original. Moreover, a number of important recent ethnographic works take a performative approach to the state and sovereignty, particularly in sites where the borders and constitution of the state are contested (e.g., Reeves, Jasanayagam, and Beier 2014; McConnell 2016, Reeves 2014; Wilson 2016; see also McConnell and Wilson 2015). However, we note that all of this literature relies on the workings of already existing states, even if they are contested ones. These are administrations where the cogs and engines of administration are already running, even if not always so well, or even if their right to do so is called into question.

Our case, in contrast, is one of a territorial state being built ex nihilo in a space that had not previously existed as such and that had to be ethnically cleansed and resettled. Moreover, it was an administration being built in full knowledge that only a negotiated solution with the Greek Cypriot government of the Republic of Cyprus would bring recognition, or legitimacy for their new entity. *Realizing* one's state, then, was always a project for the future, deferred until after a settlement (see also McConnell 2016: 20–24). As we show throughout this book, these circumstances meant that Turkish Cypriots' relationships with both the time and space of their new "state" were aporetic from the beginning, always suspended in anticipation of "the solution."

Throughout the book, we ask what de facto state-builders were thinking as they crafted an entity that the rest of the world told them should not exist and would never have statehood. It is a state whose sovereignty is suspended from its inception, a state whose ultimate form, and the sovereignty that will presumably come with it, are indefinitely deferred. In terms of our first aim, then, de facto states shed light on the state as such through the ways that citizens desire, contest, need, and believe in an entity that they may simultaneously joke is only "made up" (*uyduruk*). They participate in politics, contest in courts of law, educate their children, and generally follow the rules of a state where important parts of their lives—having recognized passports and internationally recognized title deeds, for example—are on hold. In this sense, our first aim of thinking about what de facto states tell us about the state as such is intrinsically connected to our second aim, interrogating the singularity of "the de facto."

Throughout the book, we prefer the term "de facto" over other labels—unrecognized, quasi, and informal, among others—that describe these entities, as we find it to be the most analytically helpful in pointing us to the puzzle that these states present. This became clear when we first began looking at the TRNC and other similar entities ethnographically. We were struck by a tendency—prevalent throughout all aspects of everyday life—for others to label everything about such states "de facto." They have de facto police, de facto judiciaries, de facto civil servants, and de facto politicians. They issue de facto passports that they stamp at de facto borders. People living in such states are de facto citizens and subjects, and in popular descriptions they lead de facto lives.

As should be clear from these examples, the "de facto" is both a practice—something "in fact"—and an illusion—a denial of fact. Moreover, there appears to be a thin line between the term "de facto" as applied to such entities and the idea that they are "fake" or "pseudo." Certainly, what is known in the literature as the "parent state"—the state from which they broke away—invariably denies their legal existence and insists that they are frauds. In both official pronouncements and public discourse in parent states, the breakaway entity is a "pseudo-state," while all the institutions we just named become "pseudo"-entities: pseudo-police, pseudo-courts, pseudo-passports. In Cyprus, the use of the prefix *pseudo* is so widespread that it often becomes a source of humor even for those who use it, especially when they slip and speak of pseudo-roads and pseudo-populations. For instance, the Greek Cypriot owner of one hip café in southern Nicosia described to us how he set up an outdoor shower on the roof of his house, which was just on the edge of the buffer-zone area that divides the capital. When someone asked him if he wasn't embarrassed to shower naked on his roof so that people on the other side could see, he asked sarcastically, "What people? It's a pseudo-place over there, so they can't be real people!"

The subtle difference between the two descriptions is that the "pseudo" of course emphasizes falseness and pretending to be something one is not. It is a way for parent states not only to deny the legitimacy of breakaway entities but even to pretend that they do not exist in fact. The "de facto," in contrast, simultaneously acknowledges a "fact on the ground" *and* denies it. In this sense, the de facto may be seen as a form of apophasis, a rhetorical device in which the speaker explicitly denies that she is saying something while implicitly saying it. So when a reporter refers to "Russia's de facto war in the Ukraine," she is saying that this is a war in fact, even if Russia does not want to name it that. Similarly, when we speak of de facto states, we refer simultaneously to their existence *and* the denial of their existence. They are de facto precisely because they do but should not exist.

Paradoxically, then, the "fact" of the de facto depends on denials of its existence for its facticity. The de facto introduces an element of doubt, as though to say that there is a ruse being attempted, but we are not falling for it. At the same time, it acknowledges that *something* has happened, a performance convincing enough to merit being called what it claims to be, even though we know this cannot or should not be the case. It is in this sense that the disbelief expressed in the de facto also points to practices or performances that simulate what they claim to be. The de facto, then, simultaneously invokes a "fact"—the practices and orders that make up what we call a state—and a doubt, or a discourse around that fact. One sees this in the label *so-called*, a term that may be used to express one's doubt about something (a so-called doctor) or simply to express the name by which something is commonly known (the so-called Lover's Lane of this town).

As a result of this pervasive discourse of fakeness or pseudo-ness, citizens of such states from their genesis live their lives in *simultaneous* knowledge of their state's existence and its nonexistence. In interrogating the de facto, we show throughout this book how Turkish Cypriots go about their daily lives enacting the practices of states and citizens, but always in the simultaneous knowledge that their very real state is not a reality as far as the world is concerned. Moreover, as we will see in this book, the state's impossible possibility is not only visible in labels given to it by others, such as "so-called" or "pseudo," but is also written into its laws and visible in its practices. Statecraft develops through tactics that circumvent their own impossible statehood. Citizens plan their lives in anticipation of their state's potential (though unlikely) dissolution. Developing the concept of the aporetic state, we explore how states and lives are built around the possibility of the impossible.

Arriving at the Aporia

Akıncı's 2015 election was greeted with considerable excitement not only in north Cyprus but perhaps even more so in the international community and in the island's south. Many Greek Cypriots considered him a leader who had consistently worked for peace, and there were high expectations that the newly restarted negotiations would have a quick resolution. Those expectations in the south were primarily framed in terms of Akıncı's presumed ability to think independently of Ankara, even his willingness to stand up to Ankara, and the expectation that he would make more concessions than the previous right-wing president had been willing to make.

What soon became apparent, however, were the contradictions of Akıncı's position as a leftist who had always supported a federal solution to the island's division but who had also grown up with the Cyprus Problem and who, in his youth, had been an actor in the establishment of the so-called state. Akıncı was born in 1947, during the final years of British rule of the island, when symbols of Greek and Turkish nationalism were the divisive expressions of political aspirations. For the first three-quarters of the twentieth century, "motherland" nationalisms were unquestioned in the island: Christian Greek speakers had a "natural" affiliation with the culture and history of Greece, embodied in the Greek state, and their political leaders worked toward *enosis*, or union of the island with the "motherland." Before the island passed to British rule in 1878, it had been a provincial part of the Ottoman Empire, and in the early twentieth century, Turkish Cypriots still expressed a historical memory of their fall from a ruling community to a numerical minority when the island changed hands. When the empire's collapse after World War I resulted in a Greek invasion of Anatolia, a rout by Turkish forces, and establishment of a new Turkish state, Muslim Turkish speakers on the island embraced the secularizing Turkish nationalism of Mustafa Kemal Atatürk, who represented victory and modernity.

Akıncı was only in primary school when a popularly supported Greek Cypriot guerrilla organization, EOKA (Ethniki Organosis Kyprion Agoniston, or National Organization of Cypriot Fighters), took up arms against the British colonizers in 1955, with the aim of uniting the island with Greece. Greek Cypriot political leaders had expressed the desire for union with Greece for decades, and Turkish Cypriot leaders had always rejected that proposal. However, Turkish Cypriots were an 18 percent minority against an 80 percent majority that expected to be able to decide the fate of the island. After the first shots were fired in 1955, small bands of Turkish Cypriot men began secretly to organize the defense of their own villages. The first groups emerged as village gangs who armed themselves with hunting rifles and guns that they and their fathers had brought home from the world war. These gangs engaged in retribution and random acts of violence so that the civil conflict quickly escalated in 1956 and 1957. It was only when Turkish Cypriot leaders managed to draw Turkey into the dispute in the same period that organized resistance became possible. The gangs were brought under the control of the Türk Mukavemet Teşkilatı (Turkish Defense Organization), popularly known as TMT. TMT was, in turn, under the command of Turkish officers who had secretly entered the island at the request of Turkish Cypriot political leaders and who soon disciplined the gangs and made them fighters for the "cause" (Keser 2007, 2012; Kızılyürek 2016).

Those same leaders who drew Turkey into the emerging Cyprus conflict were simultaneously beginning to create a representative institution that looked increasingly like a protostate. For several decades, Turkish Cypriots had tried their hand at creating representative institutions, largely because they saw the wealthy, independent Greek Orthodox Church as the primary motor behind the success of irredentist Greek nationalism on the island. In the late 1950s, other previous structures merged into the Kıbrıs Türk Kurumları Federasyonu (Federation of Turkish Cypriot Associations), KTKF. Under the leadership of certain educated nationalists, particularly the KTKF's president, Rauf Raif Denktaş, the body worked to spread and enforce a "motherland" Turkish nationalism in the community through methods such as Turkifying toponyms, coordinating village education, and organizing parades and festivals on national days. The KTKF also worked to build a Turkish economy on the island by enforcing a "Turk-to-Turk" consumer campaign that punished persons buying from Greek Cypriots (Keser 2007), and it promoted nationalist values and physical ideals through plays and beauty contests (Bryant and Hatay, in progress a).

At the same time that this institutionalization was happening, however, the spiraling violence led to Cyprus's first conflict-related displacement. Groups who were minorities in their own villages and neighborhoods fled to areas where their own community was a majority, setting the stage for larger displacements that were to come.[6] Most of those displaced in the period returned to their homes after 1960, when the island was granted independence and a power-sharing constitution as the Republic of Cyprus. According to that constitution, Turkish Cypriots held 30 percent of the positions in the civil service. They also had fifteen of the fifty seats in parliament along with their own Communal Chamber, which handled civil affairs, such as those involving personal status, religion, and education. There was, in addition, a Turkish Cypriot vice president, and the Turkish Cypriot legislators had veto power over proposed legislation.

In 1963, when Akıncı was a high school student of sixteen, President Makarios, also archbishop of the Orthodox Church of Cyprus, proposed changes to what many Greek Cypriots of the period considered an unworkable arrangement. Turkish Cypriots walked out of the parliament in protest. Violence exploded, and the Turkish Cypriot minority retreated to armed enclaves. Over the course of the winter of 1964, approximately 25,000 Turkish Cypriots fled mixed villages and neighborhoods for the safety of those that were entirely Turkish. However, almost 90 percent of the community, or around 100,000 people, soon found themselves in enclaves.[7] Displaced Turkish Cypriots crowded into relatives' houses and other buildings, such as theaters, storage rooms, and schools, which were requisitioned to house them. The Turkish ghettos were put under a siege that would last for five years, though almost all continued to live in the ghettos even after Makarios unilaterally lifted the siege in 1968. During the 1963–1968 period, only those who had no choice attempted to cross through the layers of U.N. peacekeeping troops and Greek and Greek Cypriot military that surrounded the ghetto. Moreover, all men who could hold a gun became fighters, *mücahits*, and Akıncı took up his own weapon to guard his neighborhood in the port city of Limassol, in the island's south.

Absent their Turkish Cypriot partners, the bicommunal RoC was quickly transformed into a Greek Cypriot–controlled state. Immediately after Turkish Cypriots' withdrawal from the government, Greek Cypriot legislators unilaterally abolished the bicommunal nature of the state and so effectively impeded Turkish Cypriot legislators' return to their seats in parliament.[8] And in 1964, the Greek Cypriot leadership refused to allow U.N. peacekeeping troops to enter the island unless the United Nations received the permission of the Cyprus government, which at this point was controlled solely by Greek Cypriots. While questions were raised about what the "Cyprus government" meant at this point or how it was constituted, Turkish Cypriots' protests that they should be consulted as partners in the republic were disregarded. The state of the island was recognized as one of exceptionality, a suspension of the constitutional order, in which a state-within-a-state operated in enclaves while the recognized government of the island proceeded to run the republic without the partner community required by the constitution.

Turkish Cypriots very quickly re-created within the enclaves all the functions of a "real" state, complete with copies of the government offices of the state from which they had withdrawn. As early as 21 December 1963, when the first attacks began, the General Committee of Cypriot Turks (Kıbrıs Türk Genel Komitesi) was formed to constitute the infrastructure of the new administration. In coordination with TMT, the General Committee took over all the legislative and administrative functions of this new entity, employing the large numbers of civil servants who were out of work and whose positions the RoC had recorded as "abandoned." The administrative structure that was already in place put them to work distributing food, tents, blankets, and other supplies within the enclaves. By March 1964, Turkey sent its first package of monetary aid, and soon all heads of families began to receive the equivalent of 20 pounds sterling per month; working women were given half that amount.

In the following years, TMT gradually became a standing army that began increasingly to be concerned foremost with matters of security and that turned over other elements of enclave life to civilian control. By 28 December 1967, the Temporary Turkish Administration of Cyprus (Kıbrıs Geçici Türk Yönetimi) was declared "with the aim of gathering legislative, administrative, and judicial functions under one roof" through the aid of "Fundamental Rules" (Temel Kurallar). It should be noted that the first of these "fundamental rules" stated that "until the full implementation of all of the conditions of the 16 August 1960 Constitution of the Republic of Cyprus, all Turkish Cypriots living within the Turkish Areas will be under control of the Turkish Administration" (Plümer 2008: 157). In other words, the "temporary" nature of the Turkish administration was dependent on a return to the 1960 constitution. At the same time, this was a period when military service, until this time voluntary, became compulsory. The Turkish Communal Chamber, historically representative of the Turkish Cypriot community, and former Turkish representatives to the RoC parliament also joined forces under this new administration to form the Administrative Council (Yönetim Meclisi). On 21 April 1971, the Administrative Council then made a decision to lift the word *temporary* from the name, changing it simply to the Cyprus Turkish Administration (KKTC Cumhuriyet Meclisi, N.D.).

Starting in the late 1960s, young men such as Akıncı who had spent their youths studying in the day and guarding the trenches at night began receiving fighters' scholarships (*mücahit bursları*) to study at Turkish universities. This was how Akıncı went to study architecture at Middle East Technical University in Ankara, where, like so many Turkish Cypriots of his generation, he was influenced by the 1968 movements and leftist and antimilitarist ideas. He returned to the island in 1973 and settled in northern Nicosia. The city, the island's capital, had been divided into Greek and Turkish areas since 1956, although by the time of Akıncı's return, the barricades were open and Turkish Cypriots could pass to the "other side" to shop and work. Like all the other enclaves, however, the city's north remained under the control of the Cyprus Turkish Administration, and Greek Cypriots were unable to enter.

In 1974, at twenty-seven years old, Akıncı's entire life had been shaped by the island's political conflict. Moreover, for the previous decade, educated, politically engaged youth such as Akıncı had closely followed the periodic negotiations aimed at resolving the long-standing political impasse. Over time, the Turkish Cypriot position on how to resolve that impasse had shifted significantly, though all proposals contained one common element: the creation of a zone where Turkish Cypriots would have autonomy and authority. In the late 1940s, Turkish Cypriot leaders had proposed *taksim*, or partition, after their close contact with counterparts in Pakistan led them to model their own future on the division of the subcontinent. In the 1950s, this solution took the form of demands for "double union," or a division that would unite the newly created parts with the "motherlands" of Greece and Turkey.[9] By the 1960s, union with Turkey was off the table, and in 1964, Turkish Cypriot leaders officially adopted the concept of bizonal federation with Greek Cypriot partners, and this position was backed by Turkey. For most of those same leaders, federation was a continuation of their previous position of *taksim*, or division of the island, but the question was how to create a territorial federation in an island where populations were scattered.

The answer was provided in 1974, when EOKA B, a right-wing Greek Cypriot guerrilla organization backed by the junta government in Greece, attempted to overthrow President Makarios and unite the island with the "motherland." In response, Turkey launched a military invasion that divided the island and resulted in the flight of Greek Cypriots from the island's north, creating there a "safe zone" for Turkish Cypriots, who subsequently fled to that area.[10] As we describe in the next chapters, in very quick order Turkish Cypriots set about state-building, and Akıncı was one of the first leftists to enter the new state's Constituent Assembly. That assembly was tasked with writing a constitution that would form the basis for their first stab at state-hood, the Turkish Federated State of Cyprus (TFSC). This was the new entity whose name in its genesis already marked it as transitional, the first step toward a federation with a Greek Cypriot state in the island's south.

As those state-builders would soon learn, however, what they perceived as a military victory may have been a pyrrhic one. Even though they had stamped the new territory with "facts on the ground," those "facts" would remain de facto until they could convince their Greek Cypriot partners, possessors of a recognized state, to enter into a federation that would end the temporary nature of their own state's temporality. As Akıncı would learn during his own failed period of negotiations, this was no easy task. Rather, as one former civil servant put it to us, "As we were rising from people to nation, we got hung somewhere in the middle." They got hung in the gap between the state that they were building on the ground and the federation that they imagined. It was in this gap that the aporetic state emerged.

The State That Is Not One

"We were establishing a state, but as one leg of a federal state," Akıncı remarked to us in an interview a few months before he announced his candidacy for president. When we asked why he and other leftists did not believe in an independent Turkish Cypriot state, he answered,

> Because for so many years, even from our youth, we saw federation as a model for Cyprus. . . . This was the Turkish proposal, the Russian proposal, it was what the Soviets supported, *it was what was possible in Cyprus, what would be possible*, and what would rescue us from being a minority. What would rescue us from living as a scattered minority in a Cyprus Republic that had become a Greek Cypriot Republic. . . . We believed that this solution would bring peace to Cyprus. *We believed that this solution was the possible solution.* Apart

from that any other idea for a solution was not a solution for us. *We believed there could be no other alternative.* (authors' italics)[11]

Akıncı emphasizes that their support for federation was because it was "the possible solution" (*mümkün olan çözüm*) and there were no other options, referencing the external constraints put on independent statehood. Instead, a bizonal, bicommunal federation with their Greek Cypriot partners was the solution that even from the 1960s began to receive support from various members of the "international community" (a term to which we return in Chapter 6), a support that gained ground after the island's division. As a result, the state that they were building after 1974 was supposed to be a temporary or transitional one on the way to a permanent solution.

What Akıncı's remarks make clear, and what a large body of literature on the state and sovereignty supports, is that having a state is not only up to them and that "sovereignty . . . is an inherently *social* concept" (Biersteker and Weber 1996: 1). By granting or withholding recognition, "international society participates in the social construction of sovereign states" (6). Political theory and IR literature has long noted a gap between what is known as the declaratory view of sovereignty—"if it acts like a state, it must be a state"[12]—and the constitutory view of sovereignty, which says that a state cannot be one without the recognition of other states. This is another way of expressing the tension that we find between sovereignty's social construction through the recognition of others and the idea that the state is a performance or practice.

Indeed, despite a rather large literature on the social practices that constitute state-ness, there remains a tendency for the declaratory view of sovereignty to collapse into the constitutive view. Jens Bartelson remarks that while we may see the successful ability to project one's legitimate sovereignty claims through discourse as constituting a political and legal reality, "the benchmark of that success" is "nothing less than these sovereignty claims being recognized as such by other similar entities" (2013: 116). In other words, no matter how much one may perform state-ness, one does not perform in a void and needs an audience to see and recognize the performance as such.

Throughout this book, we take seriously this social nature of sovereignty and in particular the work done by recognition. We do this not to argue whether an entity such as the TRNC should or should not be recognized. We find that arguments around the necessity (or not) of recognition are too often trapped in ontological loops of trying to define whether an entity *is* a state or *is not* a state without recognition. Our concern, in contrast, is with the ways that people—both citizen of unrecognized states and others—treat the so-called state as a *real* entity with real effects on the world, even as those same citizens and international actors behave as though that entity cannot be re-a*lized*. We are very much concerned, then, with how the social nature of sovereignty—the geopolitics of recognition and its withholding—shapes everyday lives and their possibilities. As we show throughout the book, every-day geopolitics not only affects the ways that de facto state-builders strategize but also how citizens think about, plan, and manage their lives.

Everyday geopolitics, we show, defines what is *realistic* and what options are ruled out. As we will discuss, many Turkish Cypriot leftists such as Akıncı perceived federation as the realistic solution, the possible or *realizable* solu-tion. As we will show in Part II, Turkish Cypriot politicians of all ideological persuasions took an active, indeed enthusiastic, part in building and shap-ing the de facto *reality* that was their new state, founded on an ethnically cleansed territory. All of this state-building took place, however, under the shadow of an overarching hegemonic *realism* that said that this state would never become one.

We return to this hegemonic realism in Chapter 6, but we will anticipate that discussion here by quoting a remark that James Scott makes in one of his first works on strategies of resistance. There, in a discussion of hegemony, he makes a direct link between the hegemonic and the realistic. "From a much more modest view of what hegemony is all about," he remarks, "it might be said that the main function of a system of domination is to accomplish pre-cisely this: to define what is realistic and what is not realistic and to drive cer-tain goals and aspirations into the realm of the impossible, the realm of idle dreams, of wishful thinking" (Scott 1985: 326). In our terms, it is hegemonic realism that defines the aporetic border, the inability to cross from the real to the realizable. This hegemonic realism told Turkish Cypriot state-builders that however much the entity they would establish might look and act like a state, it would never gain acceptance as such from the "international com-munity."

Under the shadow of this hegemonic realism, then, the real is not realiz-able. But as we note above, this does not mean that the real is not perceived as real. Indeed, commentators often point out that even leftist leaders who support federation insist on the reality of the north as a space and a state. For instance, after a recent round of talks Akıncı objected to the insistence of his interlocutor, Anastasiades, that only the Republic of Cyprus would be transformed in the creation of the federal state: "It is known that we have differences on this subject. As far as they are concerned, there is only the Cyprus Republic, and [a new state] will be its transformation; because for them, the TRNC does not exist. As far as we're concerned, on the other hand, even if it's not recognized, of course there is a TRNC, and it will be transformed into a constituent state with a solution."[13] After this statement appeared in the news, many people commented on social media that there was no difference between this position and that of right-wing nationalists who insisted on the north's independence.

It should not be surprising if average citizens are not always able to comprehend the subtle difference between a so-called nationalist position that says that the real is also realizable, and a so-called peaceful position that posits the real as a temporary step on the way to conforming with a hegemonic realism supposedly in line with international norms. This is particularly the case in that so-called nationalist or conservative leaders have based many of their arguments for potential independence on the dominant international relations theory of Realism, which says that in an anarchic international system, nation-state interests will trump international law. From this perspective, then, the hope of recognition—of finally realizing state*hood* for one's already existing state—is bolstered by the knowledge that, in international politics, stranger things have happened.[14]

Of course, to call Akıncı's position nationalist implies that to be peace-loving the so-called president of a so-called state should disavow the entity that he represents. According to this peculiar position, for Akıncı to describe himself as anti-nationalist and peace-loving, he could and *should* engage in the battles of multi-party politics—spend months preparing a campaign, engage in rancorous debates with opponents, and win the so-called presidency in a second round—but in doing so should always hold in mind the non-existence of the state that he fought to lead. What the public confusion over Akıncı's statement should make clear, then, is that the aporia or gap between the real and the realizable—a "self-engendered paradox" (Aalberts 2018: 864)—generates further contradictions that shape the lives of de facto citizens.

Those ever-multiplying paradoxes and contradictions are at the heart of this book. And what we believe this example makes clear it that while our aporetic state certainly can tell us something about the practice or performance of the state as such, it is also a phenomenon that deserves to be explored on its own terms. We emphasize this point because some of the best recent work on sovereign anomalies has explicitly eschewed a study of those entities' exceptionality. Fiona McConnell, in her insightful ethnographic account of the Tibetan exiled administration, says that she follows "the argument that the 'exceptional' has something to tell us about the 'normal'" and that she wishes to expose "the contingent practices that underlie political power in so-called 'conventional' states" (2016: 5). Similarly, Yael Navaro's ethnography of our own case, north Cyprus, points to the so-called state's obviously made-up character even as she insists that an unrecognized state can provide a lens onto the "make-believe" aspects of state-making as such (Navaro-Yashin 2012: loc. 574). To that end, she rejects, indeed discourages, comparison with other de facto entities, viewing any attempt to delineate what such states may have in common as "a narrow reading of what an ethnographic lens onto a de facto administration can offer" (loc. 574). In contrast, we suggest that *not* making such comparisons leads to a narrow reading, as otherwise it is difficult to delineate what an analysis of a de facto state tells us about the state as such, and what it may tell us about living with non-recognition (see also Pelkmans 2013).

Certainly, Turkish Cypriots perceive their contradictory lives as exceptional or abnormal and long for what they call "normalization," *normalleşme*. *Normalleşme* is what is expected to happen after "the solution" rescues them from *belirsizlik*, a perpetual state of uncertainty. *Belirsizlik* can cover a wide range of ambiguities, from haziness or fogginess to dubiousness and being in limbo. In general, Turkish Cypriots use it to say that they do not know where they stand in the world or where they are going. *Belirsizlik*, then, is both temporal and spatial, both leaving them without a clear path to the future and turning the space where they live into a "black hole" in the international order.

Above, we quoted one of our informants as describing this sense of spatiotemporal entrapment (Jansen 2015) through the remark that they had become "hung somewhere in the middle" as they were "rising from people to nation." This description also applies to other unrecognized states, who are often called "states-in-waiting" (Caspersen 2012, Pegg 1998). Of course, citizens of de facto states are not the only ones to experience temporal "stuckness" (Hage 2009). Stef Jansen, for instance, has described Bosnians after the Dayton Accords as living in a Meantime defined by the yearning but not-quite expectation of someday having a "real" state (2015).[15] Fiona McConnell has written of the Tibetan exiled government as being in a state of extended liminality (McConnell 2016: 20–24). Permanent temporariness is also a recurring theme amongst refugee populations, who often flee with the dream of return, only to find their dreams suspended (e.g., Dunn 2018, Weber and Peek 2012). But while exiled governments or refugee populations are in a state of waiting in which temporary structures set up to meet immediate needs become increasingly permanent, the so-called state is one that was constructed and imagined as permanent but where its form and name were suspended until "the solution."

Along with that liminality, citizens of the Turkish Cypriot state also experience a sense of spatial entrapment resulting from their international status as a "pirate," "puppet," or "pariah" state. We discuss throughout the book how this sense of entrapment has changed over time, and the conjunctural factors that led to such changes. What is worth noting now, however, is that all of the descriptors (pirate, puppet, pariah, rogue, outlaw, etc.) that justify isolating these entities describe them in ways that cast them outside the international order. One of the main results of this, as we discuss in Part II, is that the so-called state lacks an International Legal Personality that would endow it (and by extension, its citizens) with rights and responsibilities in that order. Being outside the international order not only traps them in their so-called state as a result of embargoes and isolations but also makes them invisible to the rest of the world: this is the state that *should not* exist and so *cannot* be seen.

What distinguishes the spatiotemporal entrapment of de facto states, then, is what we describe throughout the book as invisibilization, and we examine the various acts of both the state and its citizens aimed at making them perceptible in the world. Ralph Ellison, writing of the position of African Americans in the United States, had described such a lack of perception: "I am invisible, understand, simply because people refuse to see me" ([1947] 1995: 3). Similarly, with unrecognized states, international bodies see you quite well but choose to ignore you. Moreover, as will become clear, no matter how much one shouts and screams at the world, international actors who refuse to acknowledge you simply turn their metaphorical backs. "'High visibility'" Ellison remarked, "actually renders one *un*-visible" (ii). The de facto state, too, is the one that *cannot* be seen, because seeing it would mean having to do something about it.

One of the most tangible ways in which this invisibilization or refusal to see is manifested in everyday life is in the use of quotation marks to describe everything referring to the so-called state and the people who live within it. The TRNC is the "TRNC," and it is not a state but a "state." Its boundaries are not borders but "borders," and those persons who live there and claim rights in the "state" are not citizens but "citizens." Quotation marks multiply exponentially, with a president who is a "president," members of parliament who are "MPs," mayors who are "mayors," identity cards that are "identity cards," and so on, ad infinitum. The quotation marks stand in for the more cumbersome prefixes "de facto" or "so-called," or the more pejorative "pseudo." The quotation marks allow one to point to a stubborn reality while at the same time behaving as though it does not really exist.

Quotation marks, then, simultaneously acknowledge something as real and say that it cannot or should not be seen as real. We may say, then, that the quotation marks circumscribe the aporia. They call attention not to the de facto itself but rather to those invocations of doubt that accompany descriptions of the de facto. Their use makes these entities appear to be phantasms (Navaro-Yashin 2012) or phantoms (Byman and King 2012), their reality dubious. However, this spectrality is not a quality of the entities themselves but a result of the hegemonic realism that persistently invisibilizes, including through punctuation.

Quotation marks, then, act as an aporetic border, circumscribing lives of persistent uncertainty, where permanence is a project for the future. As a result, as we describe in Part III, citizens of the so-called state learn to "manage" or to "get by" in their daily lives, finding ways around the quotation marks that contain them and the international order that excludes them. If the first two parts of the book, then, return to the beginnings of the so-called state to understand the aporias that were present in state-building from its founding, the final part of the book explores the resilient tactics that Turkish Cypriots have developed to go on with their lives. Excavating the contradictions and paradoxes of the aporetic state allows us to understand the sorts of citizens, subjects, and agents who manage a life in quotation marks.

Sovereignty Suspended

Observers often describe Cyprus as a frozen conflict, by which they mean one in which a relatively comfortable stalemate prevails, and people do not have sufficient incentives to change the situation (Adamides and Constantinou 2012). Decades may pass without significant progress toward a negotiated settlement, and each side has an interest in remaining entrenched in its position. That entrenchment means that the conflict is not the only thing that is frozen: Frozen conflicts also produce a wealth of solidified concepts, ones that are as ubiquitous as their meanings are obscure. Throughout this book, we interrogate concepts such as *status quo* and *facts on the ground* that are pervasive because they "capture something obvious but elusive and hard to put into words" (Stolzenberg 2009: 8–9). Two of the most important of these are *de facto* and *sovereignty*, and it is worth saying a few words in this introduction about how we use these concepts throughout the book. We earlier noted that the *de facto* is a description that, when applied to states, already contains within it a denial of its facticity that makes it aporetic. *Sovereignty*, on the other hand, is a concept that seems like a driving force in such conflicts, even as its meaning and content remain opaque.

While there is a large body of literature acknowledging that we really do not know what we mean when we talk about sovereignty,[16] it turns out that the concept of the de facto is in quite a similar position. Indeed, despite its claims to common-sense factuality, *de facto* turns out to be one of the most widely used but least examined terms in the social sciences. Because of this, we initially did not focus on the term itself but rather on the facticity to which it pointed. We tried to find the state's recognizable marks (Lombard 2012) and were particularly concerned with the *fait accompli*, the "accomplished fact," which creates a "fact on the ground" (Stolzenberg 2009) whose reality cannot be denied. We soon found, however, that at every step those realities *were* denied, and that this, rather than its facticity, was what made the so-called state de facto. As such, we comprehended that we were dealing with a term that on the one hand helped us attempt to pin down something that was widely perceived to be "real" and on the other hand concealed the paradox that it already denied the real's realizability.

We wandered around in the conceptual maze of the de facto for quite a few years before finding our own concepts to help us understand the paradoxes of living in a state that the world refuses to see. Throughout the book, we use the *factum* of the de facto to describe what it is that people point to as real when they use the term *de facto*, while we use the term *factitious* to explain the element of falseness that invocation of the de facto seems invariably to connote. The *factum* of the de facto points to those elements—the deeds, acts, or practices—that people see as real. Etymologically, the *facto* of the *de facto* is the ablative of the Latin *factum*, meaning a deed or act. We see the *factum* of the de facto as constituted by the practices and orders of state-building, pointing to what we acknowledge as state-ness when we see it.[17]

However, invocations of the de facto also contain an excess of meaning that points to falseness, suggesting that people performing the state are just faking it. We call this second-order level of discursive practice the *factitious*, a performance that emphasizes its own making. As such, it may at times appear factual, at times fabricated. The aporetic state is one where the performance of state-ness that gives other states what Timothy Mitchell (1991) described as a "powerful, metaphysical effect" is always already handcuffed by an acknowledgment of that factitiousness. As we will see throughout this book, it is a "state" where state-builders were quite serious about the tasks of statecraft even as they simultaneously acknowledged that they were just making it up. As we argue later in the book, it is at the level of the factitious that the conflict over the realizability—or not—of the de facto state comes to be played out.

Our approach to the "made-up" or so-called state, then, is one that takes seriously the role of factitiousness in everyday life and that ponders the paradoxes that emerge from it. In this sense, our approach differs significantly from what is otherwise the only other ethnographic work also to address the "made-up" nature of an unrecognized state, also focusing attention on north Cyprus. Yael Navaro's 2012 *The Make-Believe State: Affective Geography in a Post-War Polity* points to this state as a "phantasm," remarking, "The make-believe can be read as a play on the notion of the de facto: something that exists, but not really; an entity that has been crafted and erected phantasmically, that has been believed through the making or materialized in the imagining" (Navaro-Yashin 2012: loc. 570). Navaro's basic insight in that work is that the social construction of the state is not only imaginative but also material (loc. 257), an observation that is certainly in consonance with our own descriptions of how the material making of the so-called state was entwined from the beginning with its imagining.

Where we immediately part ways, however, is in what we noted above as Navaro's desire to make her case speak to the state as such and insistence throughout that work on the non-exceptional nature of her exceptional case. From the beginning of our work, we have been concerned instead with the particular qualities of de facto states that make them seem made up. What makes this particular state, or this *sort* of state, differ from other states such that it develops qualities of the unreal? Moreover, does it always have those qualities, or only at certain moments? And what sorts of everyday practices and ways of getting by emerge in response to those qualities? Furthermore, how do we understand the relationship between making and believing, and what does that relationship in this instance tell us about the relationship in similar cases, *and* in the social construction of the state as such?

The standard way of explaining the spectral nature of the so-called state brings us to our second opaque concept: *sovereignty*. The lack of sovereignty is the usual answer to the question of why this state is de facto. However, as the reader should understand by now, even invoking the problem of sovereignty obscures things more than it clears them up. Indeed, *sovereignty* is another pervasive but elusive concept, and one with its own venerable tradition of conceptual confusion. (Should sovereignty be applied to persons, to communities, or to states? Where is it located? How does one acquire it? What does or should it do?) When coupled together with the de facto—as in *de facto sovereignty*—one may struggle for years to emerge from the conceptual maze that is created. As a result, sovereignty is another concept that requires dissection in this book.

The book builds to a discussion, in the conclusion, of a particular understanding of sovereignty that we believe provides a new way to appropriate the term for anthropology. Looking ethnographically at what Turkish Cypriots want when they want the sovereignty they cannot have, we argue that what they express is actually a desire for *sovereign agency*, a way to be "present" in the world (see also Bryant and Reeves 2020). In the vernacular, this is articulated as *"bu memleketin efendisi olmak"* (to be the master of this country). In its older usages, *efendi* meant a master, lord, or seigneur, in other words, someone who controls a small fiefdom but also someone whose word is law. In addition, however, it has the connotations of a gentleman, someone worthy of honor and respect. To say, then, *"Bu memleketin efendisi olacağız"* (We will be masters of this country), is to say that one will be able freely to realize one's communal will and have that respected by others.

Indeed, from the beginning of the twentieth century, this minority community had tied the ability to have sovereign agency to being seen, acknowledged, and respected (see also Bryant 2004). The phrase *varolma mücadelesi*, discussed earlier, meant a struggle to be present or existent. More recently, many Turkish Cypriots have begun to describe this as a right to enact their "political will" (*siyasi irade*). All of these descriptions have resonances with Jessica Cattelino's ethnographically informed understanding of sovereignty as "lived experiences of political differentiation" (2008: loc. 2202), something that "is both built from and sustains collectivities" (loc. 2214). In other words, not only did a desire for sovereign agency arise from experiences of difference but the struggle to realize it defined them.

Over the course of the twentieth century, many Turkish Cypriots understood that this sovereign agency could only be achieved through representative, communal institutions that began increasingly to look state-like. However, having institutions that looked state-like did not mean that they were particularly intent on having a separate state. Rather, as the list of institutions in the Appendix shows, those institutions were conjunctural and improvisatory. Even the so-called state that they established immediately after 1974 was predicated on its future dissolution into another, federal state—one where, as Akıncı's speaker commented, Turkish Cypriots' status would be elevated, that is, where they would have a "presence."

We use the idea of sovereign agency to describe what political theorist Patchen Markell (2003) has articulated as an imagined form of effective agency or control in which one will be able to achieve what one wants when one wants it. Markell and others have described this as a desire that is always frustrated, because it relies upon misrecognition of "one's own fundamental situation or circumstances" (19; see also Epstein, Lindemann, and Sending 2018). Or as Charlotte Epstein observes, "At the core of all human agency lies an impossible desire to be recognised as the sovereign actor that one never quite is, even when one is a state" (Epstein 2018: 807). Here, the idea that sovereign agency is always impossible, "even when one is a state," again makes it seem as though the particular impediments to sovereign agency experienced in de facto states simply are one part of the misrecognition that characterizes all states. While accepting the fundamental conditionality of all agency, we contend that there are *also* specific forms of misrecognition that emerge from the hegemonic realism that says that a state such as that in north Cyprus cannot be one.

We have referred several times to the gap between the real and the realizable that we contend defines the aporetic state. What would it mean to realize the real? The concept of sovereign agency enables us to give the "realizable" substance, because clearly what the citizens of the so-called state find is missing and makes their "state" seem spectral is the ability to use it to act as effective agents in the world. And while full sovereign agency may always be unrealizable, whether as individuals or as communities, the inability to realize the state as a sovereign agent takes a particular form in de facto entities.

Specifically, we show throughout this book how Turkish Cypriots have been made into subjects of the international regime of power *only to the extent* that they have been denied sovereign agency. Within that regime, they have been cast either as "pirates" and therefore "outlaws" or as "puppets" and therefore without will. This leads initially to what we call, in Part I, the *aporia of perceptibility*, or the ways in which the practices and orders intended to make Turkish Cypriots perceptible to the world instead invisibilized them. Part II builds on these insights to focus on the *aporia of recognizability*, or how Turkish Cypriot attempts to make themselves recognizable made them unnameable. As state-building proceeded and the state became more entrenched, the distinction became ever clearer between the *reality* of a state, something recognizable in its state-ness, and the always present knowledge that it was an entity that could not be named, whose name would always be censored and surrounded by aporetic quotation marks. In Part III, however, the aporias of perceptibility and recognizability that were part of state-building from the beginning ultimately produced ways of "getting by" the international order. We discuss there what we call the *aporia of agency*, or an agency that is possible only to the extent that it is denied.

These, we argue, are the particular qualities of de facto states that make them seem made up. The circumstances that create these aporias also allow us to understand how such states differ from other states such that they develop qualities of the unreal. Discussion of these aporias allows us to explore those moments where factitiousness, or the constructedness of the state, disappears into the background, and others where it becomes urgently present. It allows us to trace out the sorts of tactics and practices that emerge in response to these paradoxes. Moreover, while our focus is the nitty-gritty of unrecognized state-building in a specific case, our preliminary comparative ethnographic fieldwork in Abkhazia and Transnistria leads us to believe that the story told here has wider relevance for other persons living with the paradoxes of being actors but not agents and performing a state that everyone else says is only faking it.

A Few Words on Writing

Much has been written about the Cyprus conflict, including by the authors themselves.[18] Some readers may be surprised to find that in this book the ongoing, frozen conflict is background but not the subject; indeed, Greek Cypriots very rarely appear in these pages. We see this as a reflection of our ethnography and of the ways that in a divided island particular life worlds emerge whose practices and orders make very contained references to the "other side" and its inhabitants. This is not to say that Greek Cypriots and the Republic of Cyprus are not present, but they tend to enter the picture at particular levels of discourse, especially in the realm of what we call the factitious. In other words, they enter the picture primarily at the point where the realization of the real is called into doubt because of claims to another real, and the way those claims are realized in the hegemonic realism of the international order.

Other readers may be surprised to find that Turkey and its government are not the main actor in our narrative. It is certainly the case that Turkish Cypriots' patron state has provided military and financial support since the 1950s. Indeed, there is a widespread assumption that Turkey controls north Cyprus, that the island's north is effectively a Turkish colony. This perception influences not only the actions of other governments but also scholarship about the island. The latter consistently repeats the assertion that in the immediate post-1974 period Turkey set about colonizing the north by bringing Turkish settlers and Turkifying it through destruction of Greek Cypriot cultural heritage, renaming of places, and the erection of new Turkish symbols. It is not that these things did not happen; they most certainly did. But rather, as we show in Part I, Turkish Cypriots either took the lead or actively collaborated in these actions. Instead of focusing on Turkey, then, we concentrate instead on the circumstances that make it impossible for de facto citizens to claim this agency: while charges of Turkish colonization render one invisible, claiming agency through acknowledging one's own role in the island's partitioning makes one unacceptable to the international community.

This is not to say that Turkey does not have a determining role in Cyprus, but rather to assert that charges of colonization are unhelpful in understanding how unrecognized states work, how they are able to have such longevity, and how their citizens deal with the state's exceptionality. While two of the following chapters address how Turkish Cypriots deal with Turkish citizens and with Turkey, our main concern in that regard is with explaining how it is that Turkey can have a large troop presence, can sustain the state through its financial support, can be the source of the island's largest migrant population and yet, as one friend is fond of saying, "Turkey may gnash its teeth, but it can't bite us." The pretense of statehood, their so-called "stateness," provides a buffer that, as we describe in later chapters, these de facto citizens have learned to "manage." This is managing in the sense of "getting by," the realm of tactics rather than strategies. While that buffer appears flimsy, it has proven surprisingly resilient in the face of military coups in Turkey, an increasingly anti-democratic Turkish government, and regional crises.

The persistent framing of Turkish Cypriot state-building as colonization is also a main reason why, despite the expansive literature on the conflict, very little has been written in English about the island's north, particularly for the period under study here.[19] Indeed, until the opening of the checkpoints in 2003, research in and on the north was highly politically constrained, and researchers consistently self-censored their language in order to avoid "taboo" words such as state, sovereignty, or border (minus the quotation marks) in relation to the entity in the island's north. Persons who attempted research in the north or with Turkish Cypriots risked being censured, particularly in the island's south. Academic conferences and public events were predictably marked by political grandstanding and rote condemnation of any attempts to understand political life in north Cyprus outside the framework of "invasion and occupation." In the early 1990s, when she crossed often from south Nicosia to its northern side, Rebecca experienced surveillance by Greek Cypriot police. Anthropologist Yiannis Papadakis describes similar experiences when he attempted fieldwork in the north during approximately the same period (2005).

In the years since the 2003 opening, the situation has considerably relaxed, and today there is much academic collaboration across the Green Line. Previous scholarly emphasis on the Cyprus conflict and focus on ethnonationalisms—their emergence, their historical narration, their continuation today—has given way to a more diverse set of research topics, including labor migrants (e.g., Trimikliniotis and Demetriou 2011); the island's religious and ethnic diversity (e.g., Varnava, Coureas, and Elia 2009; Constantinou and Skordis 2011); the environment and climate change; and the politics of resource extraction (e.g., Gürel, Mullen and Tzimitras 2013). Along with this post-2003 diversification and increased interactions of Turkish and Greek Cypriot academics in scholarly venues has come an acknowledgment that the "invasion and occupation" description of the island's north does not suffice to explain the complexities of politics there. Nevertheless, the sovereignty conflict that continues to divide the island also continues to constrain scholarship in surprising ways. One example, as we describe in our Note on Toponyms, was the Republic of Cyprus legislature's unamimous decision in

2013 to outlaw the place names that Turkish Cypriots use today and make their use subject to heavy penalty in the island's south. As a result, there remain important impediments to research that also constrain political possibilities. If one cannot have informed discussions, how can one hope to negotiate a "realistic" solution to the island's division?

The reader will notice that throughout the book we refer to "Turkish Cypriots" (Kıbrıslı Türk) or the "Turkish Cypriot community" (Kıbrıs Türk toplumu) to describe Turkish-speaking, nominally Muslim (though actively secular) persons who consider themselves indigenous to the island. In the past couple of decades, an active discussion has emerged in the island's north, and is reflected in academic literature, that questions the identity of this self-described community using a spectrum of possible identifying descriptors ranging from entirely Turkish (and associated with Turkey) to entirely Cypriot (and downplaying the Turkish side of "identity"). This heterogeneity of views on this community's "essential" or "real" identity means that our use of the term "Turkish Cypriot" cannot and does not refer to some essence that we take as definitional. Rather, we use "Turkish Cypriot" to describe that group of people and their descendants who answered the "call" of the so-called state: those persons who crossed the line, settled there, and refused to return to the south. Moreover, this refusal, which we discuss in Chapter 7, legitimized their so-called state as a space of safety. "Turkish Cypriot," then, refers to those persons who were intepellated by the hailing of the so-called state (Althusser 1971) and whose active participation in its political life served to ground and found it.

Throughout this book, we interrogate the ways that the community and its institutions were co-created in the act of making the so-called state. We find that much of what constitutes both the inside and the outside of community in north Cyprus has emerged as Turkish Cypriots enacted the practices and orders that make up what we call the site of the state. In this sense, community-building is inextricable from the nitty-gritty of (unrecognized) state-making. This will become clear throughout the book as we concern ourselves with the practices of displacement and resettlement that constituted the border; with the distribution of appropriated Greek Cypriot "resources" that constituted the economy; and with the conflicts over those resources that constituted politics and party divisions. We concern ourselves with Turkish Cypriots' complicated relationship with their "patron state," Turkey, and with Turkish citizens, and how that relationship was inserted into a political economy of loot. We call this work an ethnographic genealogy because we take our cues from problems present today in the lives of de facto citizens, but we show that the dilemmas and contradictions of those de facto lives can only be understood genealogically, by returning to the founding of their aporetic state.

Our story begins from this founding moment, when an island that had been whole was suddenly split, and the flight of populations to either side of the cease-fire line, and the ethnic homogenization that resulted, would create what we know today as the island's north and south. Our story begins, then, from the moment when the "north" began to emerge as a tangible, separate, if unrecognized space. It concerns how a "north" might emerge as "real" despite international condemnations, denials of its existence, and the belief of large numbers of its citizens that such a state was not realizable. Our story concerns what it means to have de facto lives, and even de facto dreams, always on the threshold between acknowledgment and recognition, between certainty and uncertainty, and between the state and its "so-called" mirror.

PART I

THE BORDER THAT IS NOT ONE

Figure 2. Turkish Cypriots wait in 1975 in the Akrotiri base, in Cyprus's south, to be transported to Turkey and from there to north Cyprus (Özer Hatay archive).

"THE DIVISION DIDN'T happen in 1974," our friend Filiz Naldöven tells us. "The division had already happened long before in people's minds." Filiz grew up in the island's south and was a university student in Turkey when the coup began in 1974. She also was a poet and writer and even as a child observed and noted down the behavior and conversations of her neighbors. She described one such neighbor to us, a woman who had spent part of her childhood in Kyrenia, in the island's north, because her father was a teacher. "She always used to talk about how one day she would return to Kyrenia," our friend said. "She made plans about it, talked of selling her property. When I asked her, she told me, 'But we'll all go there one day! We can't stay here.' That was the mentality then."

Indeed, by the time a line dividing Cyprus became a de facto border, the idea of a partitioned island had already established itself in the Turkish Cypriot popular imaginary. In the late 1950s, Turkish Cypriots began to write poetry and popular songs that anticipated the intervention of the "heroic" Turkish army and their own displacement. The political project of *taksim*, or partition, that emerged in the popular imagination of the period anticipated a separate space, one that in that initial imagining would be politically united with Turkey. By 1974, that imagination had transformed into a bizonal federation, but one in which a space would be created whose difference would be defined by its Turkishness: it would be the space where Turkish Cypriots should belong. This was the territory that was intended, in Mustafa Akıncı's words, to "rescue us from living as a scattered minority in a Cyprus Republic that had become a Greek Cypriot Republic." In other words, it was supposed to give this small community sovereign agency, to make them visible and perceptible as political actors.

Part I concerns the *aporia of perceptibility*, or the ways in which the very practices and orders intended to make Turkish Cypriots visible to the world, to give them *varlık,* or presence, increasingly made them invisible. Our story begins with the border that was not one[1]—the border that could only be a "border," a cease-fire line, but not the boundary of a "state." The preferred term in Greek Cypriot discourse is the Attila Line, a name that they gave to it after learning that the Turkish military had named its intervention Operation Attila (Atilla Harekâtı). The name immediately entered the international public imaginary; even the *Oxford Reference Dictionary* has an entry for it: "Attila Line: The frontier line dividing Greek from Turkish Cyprus following the Turkish invasion of 1974. The invasion, which was likened to the action of Attila the Hun, put into effect Turkey's scheme for the partition of Cyprus (the Attila Plan)."[2] The name is of course intended to elicit images of barbarity and the idea that the island had been slashed, as with a sword. The Greek Cypriot Public Information Office not long after 1974 began circulating maps of Cyprus in which a gash through the middle drips blood. Such images still circulate, especially on social media.

Yet this was also a line that, as we will see in Chapter 1, thousands of Turkish Cypriots risked their lives to cross. The line circumscribed a new area that they began popularly to call the "free zone" (*özgür bölge*), and where those crossing, or those already in the north, began immediately to use their experiences of enclave state-building to establish a functioning administration and, very soon, a multiparty, democratic political system. As one bureaucrat put it to us, "The idea was that 'we're in the north now.'" And even if many found the loss of their ancestral homes and the uncertainty of their new lives difficult in the first years, we show in the next chapters how they nevertheless began to adapt to new lives in a new land.

Ethnographically, Part I concerns the making of "the north" as a territory. The Turkish army had drawn a line where previously there had been none, and making a territory out of the space created there required a disentangling of people and movement of one part of the population to an area that had previously existed only in their imaginations. It required learning to belong to that place and also stamping it with the signs of belonging. Our story begins, in other words, with what Madeleine Reeves provocatively describes as "the messy, contested, and often intensely social business of making territory 'integral'" (2014: 6; see also Aggarwal 2004). For a de facto territory created *ex nihilo*, the question of how that territory acquires a sense of integr(al)ity and separateness—how, in this case, the world began to perceive Cyprus's north as a separate, de facto space—is the first one that needs to be asked.

The question also points us to the role of perception in territorialization. Territorial integrity is a perception of wholeness, the *sense* of a territory as whole—or what Carl Schmitt in his discussion of *nomos* called the "force-field of a particular order" (2006: 70). In the next three chapters, we are concerned with the ways in which a separate space known as "north Cyprus" emerged and acquired such a sense of territorial integrity, with its own "force-field" that made people begin to feel and sense that they belonged there.

Chapter 1 tells the story of de facto territorialization in the process of refugee settlement and the gradual "adoption" (*sahiplenme*) of this new territory by those who settled there. Territorial integrity, the sense of a separate space, particularly emerged in Turkish Cypriots' expectations of the new state that defined this territory—that the state assign them houses, clean up what remained from Greek Cypriots, and provide displaced persons with a livelihood in this new place. Chapter 2 then describes the building of a sense of integrality or separateness through the de facto Turkification of the landscape, such as putting up road signs and opening shops with Turkish names. Finally, Chapter 3 discusses the de facto polity, or those who had a right to belong in that space, that emerged in conjunction with the demographic engineering project that brought persons from Turkey to help inflate the population.[3]

Territorialization, Turkification, and the creation of a new polity all involved sets of practices that in turn created their own "force-fields" or effects. We refer to these as the *territory effect*, the *sovereignty effect*, and the *polity effect*, and we argue that it was through such effects that it was possible to recognize the de facto *qua* de facto. In other words, we are able to talk about an entity called "north Cyprus" because the territory effect creates a sense of territorial integrity; the sovereignty effect creates a sense of separateness, a space controlled by a sovereign people; and the polity effect creates the political inside and outside, what Jacques Rancière (2004) calls a "partition of sensibility." These effects, we claim, are what make "north Cyprus" stubbornly perceptible as a separate place with a separate people, even when the world says it should not exist.

As should become clear, this part of our story is much like other stories of state-building and points to what de facto state-making may tell us about the state as such. However, even as we describe these "facts on the ground," these emerging practices and orders, we show how this state-building was interlaced with aspects of the factitious. In our case, what Schmitt called "the ordering of the order" also always existed alongside the knowledge of its potential dissolution. Even as a new territory was emerging, Turkish Cypriot state-builders claimed that it was not a state but a "state," in other words, not a "real" state but a stepping-stone on the way to federation. Even as they tried to make themselves perceptible through Turkifying the landscape, they found themselves disappearing into a larger "Turkish nation." Even as Turkish Cypriot administrators were importing Turkish nationals as settlers to boost the population, the bonds of "kinship" with those Anatolian Turks were dissolving. As a result, the very ground on which state-building took place was itself aporetic—not an order but an "order," though one that as time passed looked increasingly "real."

As we will see, even as a sense of a perceptible, separate Turkish space in the north was emerging, the same practices and orders intended to make Turkish Cypriots visible to the world instead began to invisibilize them. The very attempts to make themselves visible *as Turks* that were at the heart of state-building in the period caused them to disappear behind claims of Turkish occupation or colonization—what one author calls "Turkey-fication" (Navaro-Yashin 2012) and another a "Turkish domestication process" that aimed at "transforming the occupied Cypriot space into a Turkish colony" (Ram 2015: 27).

The next chapters will show how such claims of Turkish colonization in which Turkish Cypriots have no agency obscure more than they explain because they can tell us little about the contradictory ways in which Turkish Cypriots have appropriated, adopted, and lived in the north as a space and a territory. Even more than this, however, such analyses of the north as a "Turkey-fied" space reproduce the very conditions of Turkish Cypriots' aporia of perceptibility. That aporia of perceptibility has meant making themselves perceptible through the signs and symbols of Turkishness—that is, making themselves visible *as Turks*—while at the same time finding themselves made invisible in the process through a sleight of hand that makes their own Turkification into a Turkey-fication and that turns their agency into a source of their disappearance.

CHAPTER 1

Building a "Border"

In late July 1974, Mete and his family disembarked from a ferry anchored off the Kyrenia coast and climbed into a military landing boat with their luggage. They had been on holiday in Turkey when the coup and invasion occurred, and Mete's father, a journalist, was anxious to return home. The Five Finger Mountains that surround Kyrenia were burning as they pulled into the harbor. From there, the family was loaded onto a bus with a military escort that would take them and other returning Turkish Cypriots across the mountains to their home in northern Nicosia. Along the way, they passed through the Turkish Cypriots' main mountain stronghold near the Crusader castle of St. Hilarion. Mete, then twelve years old, and his younger brother, then nine, had cried in Istanbul at the thought that they were missing the excitement of war, and they had urged their mother to let them all return together. But as the lines of tanks rumbled past and drowned their voices, and helicopters landed and took off in clouds of dust, the boys were silent and frozen by the reality of war.

Mete would later discover many other Turkish Cypriots who had arrived on that same ferry, either frantic to find families or eager to join the battle. One such man was Emin Çizenel, today an internationally known painter.[1] In July 1974, he was an art student en route from his studies in Vienna when the coup and Turkish invasion occurred. He invited us one day to his studio with its distant view of the beach that was the main landing point for Turkish troops when gunboats touched sand on 20 July 1974.

We went to visit to talk about his role in the immediate postwar period, a story that until then we had heard from him only in pieces. In 1964, Emin and his family had been displaced from a grape-producing village in the mountains of Limassol, in the island's south, and had taken refuge in his mother's natal town. Like other Turkish Cypriot boys, he took up a gun, attending school during the day and standing guard at night. When he completed high school, he did one year of compulsory military service as a fighter for the Turkish Cypriot Administration. At the time, Turkey was giving "fighters' scholarships" that allowed young Cypriot men who had completed their military service to study at Turkish universities. Emin won a highly coveted place at what today is Mimar Sinan University, Turkey's academy of fine arts. "When I went to the academy to study art, I left my gun and went to the best school in Turkey," he recalls. "Everyone's very civilized, very European, and three days earlier I've put down my gun."

In summer 1974, Emin had recently finished his master's degree in fine arts in Austria. Returning to Cyprus, he got as far as Istanbul, when he found that all transport to the island was canceled. When he finally arrived in Cyprus on the boat that brought Mete, he reunited with his younger brother in Nicosia and began looking for work with the new administration. Using connections, he went first to the man who had been appointed "foreign minister." "I went and said, 'I'm looking for work, help me.' He said, 'What branch did you graduate from?' I said fine arts. 'Ha!' he said. 'I have the perfect job for you!' He sent me to İsmet Kotak [then in charge of the Settlement Department]. İsmet Kotak said, 'Yes, I have a job that's going to make you very popular in public relations.' What was it? Refugee rehabilitation, but before that the inventory." The inventory involved taking stock of all Greek Cypriot property, at that time left empty. The inventory included houses and their furniture, workshops and their tools and machinery, shops and their stocks.

Below, we use the story of Emin's return to the island and incorporation into these new institutions to examine the territory effect, or the ways that emerging practices and orders produced a *sense* of a de facto territory. We are concerned with the initial emergence of order from postwar chaos and the way in which a new border slashing through a hitherto undivided island began to circumscribe a territory, with people who began to perceive that they "belonged" in it. This is what Carl Schmitt, in his controversial late work *The Nomos of the Earth*, describes as the founding of *nomos*, or "the ordering of an order." Schmitt describes land appropriation as the first act in founding the order of law.[2] But he also describes that ordering as a process not only of seizing land but of how that land becomes domesticated, cultivated, and transformed by human hands. To explain this process, Schmitt turns to the etymology of *nomos* in the Greek *nemein*, meaning both to divide and to pasture—in other words, not only to appropriate but also to take care or take charge. *Nomos* is what emerges when a people becomes settled, when it "turns a part of the earth's surface into a force-field of a particular order" (2006: 70; see also Vismann 1997). In this sense, territory emerges in the relationship between the arbitrary line demarcating territory and the lines drawn by the furrows that work the land and thereby make it one's own.

This "force-field" is what we call here the territory effect, the *sense* of a territory as a separate place where a certain people may belong. It is the territory effect that enables us to recognize something that we call the de facto—a "de facto territory in Cyprus's north." The "ordering of an order" that creates this force-field, this territory effect, is what we refer to here as de facto territorialization, or the practices and orders that settled people in new homes, encouraged their productivity, and generally gave them a sense that this was the space where they were supposed to be.

However, de facto territorialization also contained elements of the factitious. As we noted earlier, we use the factitious to refer to those "facts" that contain references to their own making. This makes them appear at times to be artificial in the sense of crafted, at other times in the sense of false or fake. At the same time that a territory effect emerged through de facto territorialization, a *"territory" effect* emerged through its factitious elements. While one might work the land and thereby make a claim to it, one might also know that one's title deeds are factitious. They are title deeds that have currency in one's own "state" but that are never fully realizable as "real" title deeds. While the "border" may appear real enough in daily life, where it simply acts to keep others out and circumscribe one's territory, one may simultaneously know that it is unrealizable, with one's territory constantly on the verge of dissolving into the recognized Republic of Cyprus, which claims sovereignty, or into the Republic of Turkey, without whose troops there would be no line in the first place.

While the territory effect creates a sense of a place as one's own, the "territory" effect creates a sense that the place can never really be one's own. These two effects, moreover, exist simultaneously—and in fact are encapsulated in the dual nature of the de facto, which is simultaneously an acknowledgment and a denial of something's existence. As a result, territorialization is always aporetic, both creating a visible and perceptible territory and always emphasizing its impossibility.

Building a Border

The towns and villages of the Kyrenia region have long stretches of flat land near the coast that in 1974 were covered with lemon orchards. Although there were houses dotted among these orchards, many of the homes swept up the mountain, also giving them a commanding view of the sea. This meant that at dawn on 20 July, people in these villages had only to look out their windows to see the lumbering gray warships threatening the horizon. Soon those ships' guns trained on them, and as helicopters buzzed and tanks rumbled onto land, many Greek Cypriots piled into cars and trucks and tractors and fled over the rough mountain roads, trying to find a way south, to an area beyond the bombardment. Many fled with only the clothes on their backs, "without even a handkerchief," as women often say. Although some men would later try to sneak back into the area to recover valuables and personal items, most would be unable to see their homes again for twenty-nine years.

Emin was assigned to inventory the two seaside towns of Lapithos and Karavas, in Turkish Lapta and Alsancak. Because these towns were particularly close to the Turkish landing point, in 1974 they experienced heavy fighting and were also bombarded by gunboats. It should not be surprising, then, that Emin says when he and four colleagues first arrived in the area they found a scene of postwar disaster: "There was no one, the dead bodies had still not been removed. Bam, bam, you knock on the doors, and you just go inside. People had left their belongings as they were. They just fled as fast as they could, without even taking shoes or children's clothing. There was food on the tables." In the midst of this horror, they were supposed to fill out forms that described sizes, types, and states of houses and the belongings left in them.

The forms that Emin used asked him to describe the state of buildings and list their contents. In industrial areas, the inventory included large and productive factories, while in tourist areas it included the contents of luxury hotels. And even as Emin and his team were surveying the area, there was already movement of people. The original Turkish Cypriots from Lapta, displaced in 1964, began returning, moving into the homes of their former Greek Cypriot neighbors because their own had been destroyed. Not long after, the administration sent groups of male refugees from the south who were part of prisoner exchanges to Lapta, where Emin assigned them houses. Although he encouraged them to get the houses ready for their families' arrival from the south, there were still bodies in the fields and Greek and Greek Cypriot soldiers hiding in the mountains. Instead, the men took their blankets to the town's movie theater each night, where they slept in rows on the floor. "Those poor people," Emin recalled. "They were going crazy. They had been sent without their wives and children, who were still in the south, and they couldn't get word from them."

Even as this movement into the town was occurring, some Greek Cypriots, mostly elderly, still clung to their homes. Others took refuge in one neighborhood of the town, which was eventually surrounded by Turkish forces, until they were evicted in late 1975. Although there are some scattered stories of kindness to these remaining, mostly elderly, Greek Cypriots, there were also reports of rapes and cruelty committed by Turkish soldiers and Turkish Cypriot fighters in the area.

In her important study of the making of the border between Pakistan and India, Vazira Zamindar (2007) describes the ways in which the movement of people to places where they were supposed to "belong," and the perception of others as needing to go, began to define the space on either side of what was an arbitrarily drawn border. In Cyprus, there was no geographical or demographic precedent for the line that sliced through the island. Apart from the large Turkish population of Nicosia, which had been divided since 1956 and where Turkish Cypriots were indeed concentrated in the city's north, there were more Turkish Cypriots scattered throughout the island's south than there were in the area that they eventually claimed as "theirs." While approximately 12,000 Turkish Cypriots from the south had already been displaced in 1963–1964 to areas of what became the north and had been living in insufficient and crowded conditions since that time, they were joined by another 45,000 Turkish Cypriots who had remained in their villages in the south until the events of 1974. And in order to achieve the project of partition and the concentration of this minority of around 115,000 persons in the north, approximately 150,000 Greek Cypriots, around one-third of that community's population, were displaced.

"It was through the making of refugees as a governmental category," Zamindar remarks, "through refugee rehabilitation as a tool of planning, that new nations and the borders between them were made" (2007: 231). And, indeed, in Cyprus we see how the perception of the north as a zone of safety

Figure 3. Cover of *Hayat,* the Turkish version of *Life*, with the title "In Cyprus, Turks Are Settling into Their New Homes." 3 October 1974.

and the momentum of flight to the north drew others. Emin's own family arrived in early 1975, after having been flown from the British bases[3] to Adana, in Turkey, and then brought by boat from Mersin, the way that Emin had also come. During those months there was a general flight of Turkish Cypriots from the island's south to the area north of the Turkish demarcation line. Some paid smugglers to hide them in trucks and tankers; some piled ten or twelve persons into cars and tried to make their way along back roads over the mountains. Several thousand persons walked over the mountains, while several thousand more fled to the British bases (Bryant 2012). Moreover, prisoner-of-war exchanges between the two "sides" in the fighting also took place to the two "sides" of the island: Turkish Cypriot prisoners were not sent back to their homes in the south but were exchanged to the north, while Greek Cypriot prisoners were sent to join their families who had fled south.

Indeed, it seems that for many Turkish Cypriots the flight toward the north, to the area behind the Turkish army's line of defense, was what Emin called "instinctual," especially as word of massacres spread. Indeed, one of the main triggers for flight was the news that quite early in the fighting, on 14 August 1974, all 89 males of the village of Taşkent (Tochni in Greek) in the Larnaca district had been rounded up and massacred. A couple of weeks later, Turkish Cypriots heard that a mass grave had been discovered in the villages of Murataǧa, Atlılar, and Sandallar (Maratha, Aloda, and Santalaris in Greek). The grave contained the bodies of 126 villagers, including many small children, all slaughtered on the same day as the Taşkent/Tochni massacre. Other individual incidents led to flight, such as the murder of three women and two small children from Limassol by a taxi driver who had been paid to take them to the barricades in Nicosia.

Given the chaos of those first months, and looking at that period in retrospect, it is difficult to know with what expectations people fled. Certain people we interviewed, especially those with large landholdings, claimed that they fled with the expectation that once things calmed down, they would return. For many, the first months appear to have been a period of uncertainty, as they were still separated from family members and unsure of what was to happen. Although the political project during this period was to establish a separate Turkish Cypriot state that would become part of a federation with the south, many people seem to have had little understanding of what the implications of this would be for them. Indeed, the declaration of the Turkish Federated State of Cyprus (Kıbrıs Türk Federe Devleti) in February 1975 did not seem to clear up uncertainty, since negotiations were continuing with Greek Cypriot leaders, and no one knew if a federation would be established or if the establishment of such a federation would necessarily imply that they would remain in the north.

The August 1975 Vienna Agreement began to change perceptions of the temporality of their displacement. In that agreement, leaders of the two communities consented to allow the reunification of families. To many Turkish Cypriots, this appeared equivalent to the Lausanne Treaty of 1923 that provided a mechanism for the exchange of populations between Greece and Turkey (Gürel and Özersay 2006). Although movement according to the Vienna Agreement was voluntary, all but 135 Turkish Cypriots chose to make their way to the island's north. Moreover, as we describe below, this same period saw an increasing institutionalization in the north, with a referendum on the new state's constitution and the first parliamentary elections.

Gradually, then, many people began to understand that this was to be a permanent, or at least a long-term, division. Emin, who was not on the island when the division happened, had no chance to see his village a last time. "It was cut like with a knife," he remarked. "Our lives were cut in two." At the same time, Emin is clear about what many people perceive as the gains of their displacement. While we often talk of the losses of refugeehood,

Figure 4. Prisoners of war arrive in a transport to the north (Özer Hatay archive).

a division such as happened in Cyprus is also predicated on gains: the gains of safety and independence but also material gains. In what many people described as the "drunkenness of victory" (*zafer sarhoşluğu*), what they had suffered, what they had been deprived, and desires for revenge combined with suddenly finding themselves in what seemed a world of plenty. "After the deprivation of the enclaves," Emin commented, "for the first time the Cypriot Turk found himself in this space that takes up almost half the island, in the midst of abundance, in a space so big they couldn't even distribute all of it, governing themselves, starting slowly to institutionalize."

The sense of the largeness, openness, and abundance of the north after the deprivation and abjection of the enclaves is repeated in many accounts of what it meant to leave behind their homes in the south. As we noted earlier, a "north" as a Turkish Cypriot space had long been part of the social imaginary, a place where they would be "free." For many people, a decade of confinement in ghettos certainly gave to what seemed the enormous space of the north a sense of freedom. One woman from the tiny hamlet of Alevkaya (Gr. Alevga) in the Tylliria region in the island's northwest had been trapped for a decade in the nearby village Erenköy (Gr. Kokkina), where they sought refuge. Nafia told us that since their transport to the north, she and her family had had very few thoughts about what they left behind: "Over there, four or five villages had taken refuge in one little village, and just think, we were there for ten years. We were in that tiny place. Of course, we liked it when we came here and could be free."

That sense of freedom was also expressed in words and phrases commonly used for their displacement and the new area where they settled. Following the Vienna Agreement, when the last remaining Turkish Cypriots were brought from the island's south, the buses that brought them were called "freedom transport" (*özgürlük nakliyatı*). Consistently, in writings, speeches, and the discourse of the period, people referred to the north as the "rescued area" (*kurtarılmış bölge*) or the "free area" (*özgür bölge*).

This freedom, however, was not only a freedom in contrast to the enclaves. It was also, as Emin implied, a new experience of institutionalizing that in the first instance depended on refugee settlement.[4] Settlement of refugees was a humanitarian issue, but in this instance the technocratic distribution of property and settlement planning were both intended as and perceived as the first and most urgent acts of a new state. In fact, the Settlement and Rehabilitation Department (İskan ve Rehabilitasyon Dairesi), as Emin remarked above, was the first "ministry" that emerged among the units that were being established. Moreover, the contradictions of the new "state" would emerge most clearly in the process of settlement, which depended in the first instance on the appropriation and distribution of "enemy" property and the passage of laws that regulated it. In Turkish Cypriots' submission to the authority of those laws, as well as the benefit that they received from them, a state and its territory were already in the process of formation. The *factum* of Turkish Cypriots settling and going on with their lives began to build a de facto border and create a space that was "theirs."

Settling the Land

Hakkı Atun is a small, neat man who calls himself a technocrat. Although he enjoyed several decades in politics, including a stint as the de facto state's prime minister, his first roles were in positions where his education as an architect and town planner mattered. In 1964, he became head of the Planning and Building Department of the Temporary Turkish Administration, then in charge of finding refuge for Turkish Cypriots fleeing their villages. His first job had been to take over an empty British camp, evacuated by the colonial rulers as they withdrew from the island, and use its warehouses and empty homes to accommodate the displaced. Beginning in 1968, when there was a lifting of the siege on the enclaves, they were able to buy prefabricated housing from a Greek Cypriot firm, using as a middleman a Turkish Cypriot who was in charge of procurement at the British bases. Later, they would begin to import prefabricated housing from Turkey, and ultimately, as they were able to bring building materials into the enclaves, they would begin to build their own housing. "The entire crafts industry was under our command," he recalls. They built 3,500 houses around the island during the period between 1968 and 1974, many of which are still in use today.

Because of this experience, in early 1975 Atun was made undersecretary of the Settlement and Rehabilitation Department, which began to oversee the operations of people such as Emin. When Emin arrived on the island in August 1974 and began his work on the inventory several weeks later, he was hired by the Turkish Administration of Cyprus (Kıbrıs Türk Yönetimi), which appointed its first "cabinet" in late August. Even as he was beginning his work with the inventory, the members of that earlier administration changed its name on 1 October to the Autonomous Turkish Cypriot Administration (Otonom Kıbrıs Türk Yönetimi), changing also the members of the "cabinet."[5] Only a few months later, on 13 February 1975, the name would change again, when the administration declared it the Turkish Federated State of Cyprus, a new "state" intended to become part of a federation then under negotiation with their Greek Cypriot counterparts. In contrast to earlier incarnations, that state had fifty members of a new Constituent Assembly that had been chosen not only from among the previous administration but also from civil society organizations, especially represented by the left. This was how the first leftists, such as Mustafa Akıncı, entered the parliament and aided in writing the new state's constitution. In June 1975, Turkish Cypriots would experience their first constitutional referendum, where the body of law guiding their new state would receive almost unanimous support. After that first act of a fledgling democracy, campaigns began preparing voters for their first multiparty election that would put forty members in a new parliament in June of the following year.

Even as thousands of Turkish Cypriots were struggling to make their way north, the process of institutionalization was proceeding at a rapid pace. "On the one hand," Atun remarked, "a constitution is being prepared, and we're moving toward an election. An election and a referendum are being prepared. A political party law is being written. On the other hand, refugees are being haphazardly settled."[6] This nascent state-building also meant that while flight from their homes may have been "instinctual," Turkish Cypriots' migration to the north was not only because of the push of fear. Rather, the first *sense* of territoriality emerged in the pull of a new zone that was beginning to take the form of a place *where they were supposed to be.*

By the time Atun became undersecretary of the Settlement and Rehabilitation Department, much of the inventory work had been completed, but Turkish Cypriots from the south were fleeing to the north apace. Ultimately, Atun's office would be responsible for making sure that 61,500 displaced Turkish Cypriots found adequate housing in the post-1974 period. In order to ensure this, one of the first acts of the new "state" was to pass laws expropriating all "foreign" property, hence making it available for easy distribution. "We're speaking of resources left by Greek Cypriots," Atun explained. Property expropriation and distribution and the settlement of refugees, then, became the primary ways in which the north emerged as a separate space that was also a territory built on the assumption, as Atun phrased it, that "we're in the north now."

The assumption that the north would be "their" space emerged in two ways: first, by labeling Greek Cypriot property as "already abandoned" and so there for the taking, and second, by finding ways to settle refugees that would encourage them to produce and look toward the future in this new land. These were, in the first instance, contradictory conditions, because while administrators such as Atun aimed to settle the refugees and immediately start them working to build the new state, the very fact of declaring Greek Cypriot property left in the north as "abandoned" seemed to many people to mean that it was there for the taking and so resulted in a "flurry of looting" (*ganimet furyası*) that interfered with the technocrats' plans. At that time, appropriating the "abandoned" property appears to have been viewed as a right of the victor. *Ganimet*, or loot, is *helal*, or allowed, in Islam, and in this case there was the additional element of revenge or reparation for what many people had experienced as the deprivation of the enclaves.[7] As a result, the technocratic language of "resources" that Atun uses disguised a much messier process by which a new space was emerging.

In her moving description of what Zamindar calls the "long Partition," she shows a similar process at work: "In discussions that ensued these homes came to be described first as 'abandoned' and then as 'vacant' and 'empty houses,' which could then be used for rehabilitation. The violence that accompanied this process of 'emptying' was thereby erased" (2007: loc. 839). We see in Cyprus not only the "legal" state control of all Greek Cypriot and Armenian property but also attempts to erase the traces of former owners and hence to ease the transition for refugees. Indeed, Atun describes how they attempted to clean up the villages, especially before the last refugees arrived, since "that post-war landscape is enough to make anyone wish the whole thing hadn't happened."

In the case of South Asia this process also depended on the classification of certain persons as "intending evacuees," that is, persons having the intent to leave and whose property could therefore be taken from them. In Cyprus, the "intending evacuees" were those Greek Cypriots who had not yet fled to the island's south, either because they were too old or ill to leave or because they clung to their property.[8] While they were not legally classified by the new regime as "intending evacuees," certain incidents indicate that not only did Turkish Cypriots expect them to leave but also saw them as having forfeited their right to property in the north.

For instance, around six hundred Greek Cypriots from the Kyrenia area were held for more than a year in the Dome Hotel, far beyond its capacity, so that people slept in the lobbies and corridors. For the most part, they were not allowed or did not dare to venture beyond those confines. While held there, however, they witnessed what was happening around them from the hotel windows. One later wrote that as early as August 1974 they saw the plunder of Greek Cypriot property taking place around them:

> Across from us, they were looting the house of Andreas and Fanis Katsellis, I saw them, the small cars were those of local Turks, the settlers had not yet arrived. In the barbershop opposite us, owned by the Ktoridis brothers, they took down the sign that read "American" and in its place put up one that read "Unal." It was a Turkish Cypriot woman hairdresser, the new "heir" of the Ktoridis brothers. Mustafa [a policeman that they knew] was ecstatic; his eyes were turning in his head; he felt like the king of the town. . . . Many men would pace on the balconies. Among them was Theocharis Savvas, who saw his own taxi driving in front of the Dome, driven by the stranger-robbers of our land.[9] (Spyrou 2004: 217)

In another incident that was described to us, a Greek Cypriot woman approached her house to try to collect photographs, only to be told by the Turkish Cypriot woman who had settled there, "No, it's our house now." Again, this process bears significant resemblance to the process by which Partition had divided South Asia. Zamindar notes, "An equation emerged in *muhajir* [Muslim refugee] opinion whereby Hindus were believed to be leaving (sooner or later) and so their houses were there for the taking" (2007: loc. 1460).

In Cyprus, not only houses were there for the taking, but there appears to have been a perception among some Turkish Cypriots that all property remaining in the north after the Turkish military victory could be considered "loot." Indeed, looting was an activity in which it seems almost everyone during the period participated (Bryant 2010, 2014a). In many cases, this was out of necessity, as they had fled their homes in the south with only a few belongings, and the houses where they settled had also been plundered. As a result, many people went to other neighborhoods or villages looking for beds and furniture.

However, it also became such a widespread activity that most people had or wanted to have some *ganimet*, some loot. As a twelve-year-old, Mete witnessed many persons from his own neighborhood, which had not been affected by the division, return from looting excursions with silverware, jewelry, and tablecloths. There were instances such as the boy who woke one morning to find that everyone in his village had gone on a looting excursion to the neighboring town or the woman who witnessed a man wrenching a suitcase from the hands of an elderly Greek Cypriot woman who was being expelled to the south. The administration used the Turkish army to impose punishment, and everyone in the period knew that a shaved head symbolized a "*ganimetçi*," a looter.[10] Still, the sense of entitlement during the immediate postwar period, along with the "drunkenness of victory," led to numerous excesses and the overlooking of such excesses in the pursuit of "booty."[11]

In an article that builds on Schmitt's insights regarding territory as a form of relationship that founds law, Andrea Brighenti remarks, "Territory plays a fundamental function of *naturalizing the ownership* of a given object, as it publicly declares it to be a property of the territory's pre-announced owner" (2006: 75). In the cases above, the sense of a new territory as "theirs," the space where they belonged, also appeared to naturalize objects and property within it as belonging to them. The second *sense* of territoriality, then, was a naturalization of all movable and immovable property in the territory as "theirs" for the taking.

Bureaucrats such as Atun describe the frustrations that this "drunkenness of victory" caused for those attempting to build a new state on these "resources." Because the administration saw the "loot" as resources, they used the Turkish army to prevent the plunder and wanton destruction of Greek Cypriot property, gathering movable property into what came to be popularly known as "loot depots" (*ganimet ambarları*) in Nicosia and Famagusta. Refugees could then apply to those depots according to their needs. In certain cases, the military also had to settle disputes over property, especially where squatters refused to give in to the new government's settlement schemes. In February 1975, for instance, the newly formed Constituent Assembly of the Federated State heard that soldiers had forced 450 such squatters out of property that was to be distributed to refugees.[12] In another instance, certain persons from one Paphos village still under attack in the south learned from scouts who traveled across the line to the north which village had been assigned to them by the new administration. Abandoning their co-villagers and their natal village's defense, they crossed the mountains and claimed the houses that they liked in the new location. As Atun described it, "We looked around, and some persons from Yialia, for example, more than a third of the village, had risked their lives to get to that village first and settle in the best houses. In that case, the ones who actually resisted, who remained and stood up for the village, were being punished. . . . A squad of soldiers attached bayonets to their rifles and emptied out all the houses. There wasn't any other way. After that we drew lots and distributed the houses. We went through things like that." What this example makes clear is not only the difficulty the newly forming administration had in maintaining order but also displaced persons' simultaneous submission to this order: one-third of the village of Yialia had already discovered the new village in the north to which their "state" had assigned them and had gone ahead to claim its houses.

One of the most basic assumptions at work, then, was that the new "state" had a right to expropriate Greek Cypriot property. This property came to be perceived as "already abandoned," just as any remaining Greek Cypriots were what Zamindar calls "intending evacuees." In addition to this, however, was the technocratic planning of settlement, which intended to encourage displaced persons to go on with their lives. Or, as İsmet Kotak, the first director of the Settlement Department, would insist in questions put to him in the parliament in 1975, they were not engaged in a "fight over houses" but rather were "planting people" (insan ekmekteyiz). The idea of "planting people" might be seen as the most succinct summary of Schmitt's nomos, and indeed, as we will see, many Turkish Cypriot legislators considered "planting people" to be the first and most important duty of the new "state."

The Order of Settlement

One of the strategies Atun's office used to "plant people" was to keep villages together as much as they could, attempting to settle entire communities from the south together in the north. In the case of small villages, the Settlement Department was fairly successful in this, even where they may have settled two or three villages together. The idea behind this was clearly to encourage displaced persons to put down roots, something one especially sees in contrast to Greek Cypriot policies regarding their own internally displaced persons (IDPs). In the south, in stark contrast to the north, displaced Greek Cypriots were settled individually, their communities scattered, as the politics of return made any suggestion of settling them together sound like a nod at permanence (see Bryant 2010; Loizos 1981, 2008; Zetter 1985, 1999).

Hence, while settlement policies are clearly implicated in the creation of nations and borders, what also becomes clear in the Cypriot case is that this was not only a matter of finding places and property for people but also about encouraging them to go on with the process of production. It was about encouraging them to use the furrow that Schmitt had observed turns space into territory and a line into a border. As we will see in later chapters, the reluctance of many displaced persons to invest their labor in the process of production because of the uncertainties of the immediate future became a sore point for politicians in the new state who viewed production as a necessity for state-building. "Planting people," then, was always perceived as more than a simple process of getting them settled in houses; it was a matter of encouraging people to invest labor, become productive, and thereby begin to think of their futures in their new land.

Knowing this, the young "guides" or "troubleshooters" such as Emin developed strategies to try to encourage settlement. The troubleshooters were new graduates from top universities in Turkey, most in technical subjects related to planning. Tamer Gazioğlu was such a guide, having recently graduated with a degree in architecture and urban planning.[13] He described how in the first instance they worked together with representatives of villages to try to reconstruct some semblance of village life in the places where they were settling: "So the villagers would tell us, for example, Hasan Efendi had a coffee shop, or so-and-so was our butcher, and we would reserve places for them, not officially, but we would say, 'We've reserved this for the coffee shop, the coffee shop owner will come.'" The hope was that the immediate opening of basic village institutions, such as a coffee shop, a market, and a butcher, would give a sense of normalcy and encourage villagers to get on with the process of production.

As we discuss further in Chapters 4 and 5, the settlement policies that the Turkish Cypriot administration initially employed were originally guided by social justice principles coming from Turkey. Politicians from both the right and the left were influenced by the social democratic government of Bülent Ecevit, the poet and politician who had ordered the invasion of Cyprus while he was Turkish prime minister. Because of the widespread admiration for him and his policies in Cyprus, there was general agreement that in the establishment of a new state the inequalities of the past should not be reproduced.

Under this social democratic influence, not only were industries and the tourism sector "nationalized," but the Settlement Department at first assigned housing according to family size and by lot. Villagers from a particular village in the south congregated on an assigned day in the village where they were to be settled. Houses had been numbered during the inventory, and lots were drawn regardless of what persons had left behind in the island's south. This was one of the tasks of the guides, and Gazioğlu explained the system that they used, which was implemented hurriedly:

> When it was decided that a village would be opened to settlement, we would go as a team—a technician, an engineer, and an architect. And we would go from house to house making a quick assessment of its characteristics. How many rooms? Is it modern? Mudbrick? What are its physical characteristics? Its location? And we would distribute them by lot among the arriving families. . . .
>
> We also categorized the families who were part of the lottery, so for instance, one with three children, or four children, or one child, or six children. We didn't pay any attention to what they'd left in the south or what they owned, they could be the poorest person in the village, if it was someone middle-aged with four or five children, they got a big, modern house.

A similar form of distribution was employed for businesses and land. Each family settled in rural areas received a house and agricultural land, while each family settled in towns and cities was given a house and shop or office.[14] Atun commented, "In the land distribution we also undertook land reform. So for those coming from the south or from Turkey, whether they had land or they didn't, we distributed enough resources so that they would have an annual income of £1,000, which at the time was about 36,000 Turkish lira. . . . The point was to be able to have that income." Although the impetus for such a land reform came from Turkey, there were also leftist voices within the newly forming government that wanted to see such a system implemented. One of the leading leftists of the time, Özker Özgür, for instance, referred in parliamentary minutes to a socialist system of distribution based on what he called the "brotherly share" (*kardeş payı*).

While many people benefited from this system, there were others who lost or claimed that they lost. Gazioğlu remarked, "For instance, a person who's sixty years old, seventy years old, and in his own village has two or three houses, lots of fields, a shop, and when he comes to this side his renter, let's say, gets a new, nice house, and that person gets something more modest. There were lots of complaints because of this." In fact, there were so many complaints that after some months the government passed a new law establishing a point system that attempted to assign properties on the basis of what Turkish Cypriots had left behind in the south. The system, however, was reportedly rife with nepotism, favoritism, and various forms of discrimination, including for political reasons.[15] It was also open to interpretation, especially as regards the value of land. Indeed, in 1976 one journalist from Turkey had observed, "After the [military] operation the most discussed subject has been the difficulties in the distribution of houses and land." He goes on to remark,

> In the interviews that I've had with average people, I've seen that their complaints on this subject have increased. No matter with whom I speak, they sigh, "Oh, sir, I had such a house, such shops, such properties in the south." I've seen very few people who were satisfied with what they had received. . . . The administration conducted a survey with Turkish Cypriots now living in the Omorfo (Güzelyurt) district in order to determine how much land they had left in the south. When they began to add up the total square meters based on the answers, the officials' eyes popped out of their heads, because the total added up to 1.5 times the total square meters of Cyprus as a whole. (Köklüçınar 1976 113–114)

What this observation indicates is not only the ways in which persons may have exaggerated the value of their lost properties but also the central role that property would play in individuals' experiences of displacement.

What these experiences additionally point to, however, is that if territory is about the relationship of land and law, this is a relationship that emerges precisely in its contestation. People not only submitted to the authority that assigned them properties; they also contested the assignment of those properties and *thereby claimed them as their own.* In Turkish the word is *sahiplenme,* meaning both mastering and adopting. The *sahip* is the master or owner, while *sahiplenme* is a process of becoming master of something through adopting and caring for it. This sense of "becoming master" through care emerges in descriptions of the process of settlement. According to Gazioğlu, for instance, the ongoing negotiations held open the possibility that displaced Turkish Cypriots would return to their homes in the south, making it hard for them to think of their futures in the north. He remarked, "In our office we saw this: no one said, 'It looks like I'm staying in this house,' and took up a brush to paint the doors and windows. The houses started getting run down. People just couldn't know what was going to happen with the political situation, and they were saying, 'Why should I spend money on a Greek Cypriot house?'" He notes, however, that this attitude gradually began to change: "As time passed and things began to develop, the village got a *muhtar* [village headman], the town got a mayor, and as these institutional structures emerged, people began to behave as though the system was theirs. . . . And when that system bothered them, they wanted it to be fixed. In other words, the system was accepted."

He says, "They behaved as though the system was theirs" (*sisteme sahip çıktılar*). In the vernacular, there is a complicated relationship between the phrase *sahip çıkmak,* to "become master" or adopt something, and a related phrase, *sahip olmak,* to be master or owner of something. While one can be the legal owner, or owner in name, of something, to be the "real" or "legitimate" owner or master also implies taking care of it, *sahip çıkmak* or *sahiplenmek.* What is interesting for our purposes is that the reverse is not true: one may "adopt" or "become master" of something without being its owner. Indeed, *sahip çıktı* or *sahiplendi* (s/he adopted, took care of it) is a phrase often used for someone who steps up to take care of persons or things that have been abandoned by those who should care for them.

The distinction is one between possession and belonging, between simply physically occupying a space and having a relationship with it. Andrea Brighenti persuasively argues that territory "represents the bridge-mechanism between the two figures of *possession* and *ownership*" (2006: 76; emphasis in original) insofar as it "anchors" ownership on what is possessed rather than on the owner. We would suggest, however, that the key word is not *ownership* but *belonging,* a word in which the relationship of things and people is clearer. In a territorial sense, while property may belong to one, that also depends on one's belonging in the territory. That sense of belonging constitutes "a territorial framework for interaction" (76–77), a framework that is both hegemonic and constitutes an "accepted and shared framework within which even conflict and dissent can be accommodated" (77). In this view, then, territorialization occurs in the emergence of a hegemonic framework in which one can claim and contest ownership precisely because one respects or rejects the ownership of others.

The emergence of such a hegemonic framework through territorialization is also clear in an example from Turkish Cypriot social psychologist Vamık Volkan, who has lived in the United States since the 1950s but returned to the island several times in the 1960s and 1970s. During those visits, he also observed the change that Gazioğlu noted above. Returning to one village that he had visited earlier, Volkan remarks, "Whereas three years earlier these people clung to their psychic investment in the places they had left and over which they still grieved, they now seemed heavily invested in the land on which they now lived. Their indifference to tilling the northern fields was gone, and now they had a keen interest in working them and in obtaining additional water to make them more fruitful. There were five men there who seemed to be in their thirties, and I sensed that one belonged to an opposition party" (1979: 144). Not only were they concerned to make the land that they worked fruitful, but by that time they had also become entangled in the politics of the new state, including its political parties.[16]

It was in this process of both submitting to authority and contesting that authority that something resembling a separate territory or "country" began to emerge in the island's north. However, even in its emergence, the territory effect was laced with the doubt inherent in the de facto: the knowledge that the rest of the world did not accept their claims and that ongoing negotiations could change the status quo. They understood, for instance, that although they had pieces of paper that gave them rights to property, and although these pieces of paper had currency within their own hegemonic framework, they gave them no realizable claim outside the boundaries of their so-called state. Indeed, there was an always present knowledge that the ability of territory to bridge possession and ownership was ultimately aporetic: that what they had created was not a territory but a "territory." Moreover, the question of whether or not that territory would ultimately make them owners rather than possessors was still one on hold for the future, when a negotiated federation would legitimate their new zone. While in everyday life, then, people went on with claiming, contesting, and planning as though the territory where they lived was theirs and the land they worked belonged to them, the territory effect was also overlain by a "territory" effect, or the ever-present knowledge that the rest of the world saw their title deeds as illegal, fake, or pseudo.

However, if the "territory" effect that was always an intrinsic part of the property issue could be bracketed in everyday life, there were other realms in which the aporia of territoriality was always palpably present. In particular, it was present at the border, that line that is supposed to delimit territory and separate "home" from "abroad," naturalizing the "inside" as a "domestic" space (Donnan and Wilson 1994, 1999; Malkki 1995). A large body of anthropological work has shown us how borders need perpetual upkeep and reinvention by means of social practices, because these lines of division are also ones of contact where identities can be both constructed and challenged (e.g., Alvarez 1995; Ballinger 2003; Bryant 2010; Darian-Smith 1999; Green 2010; Paasi 1998; Pelkmans 2006; Wilson and Donnan 2010). What if, however, the border that circumscribes one's territory and defines one's national "home" is aporetic—not a border but a "border"? What if the factitious is an intrinsic part of one's bordering practices from their inception?

Borders and "Borders"

"In those early days, I used to cross often," a Greek Cypriot friend, Maria Hadjipavlou, tells us one day. Just after 1974, she had returned to the island from London first as a journalist and then to work for the Public Information Office (PIO) for several years. "I would meet with colleagues from the PIO in the north, and I would come to talk to the negotiators. I would bring journalists from abroad, even from Greece. The phones were even working in those days, and I would call up colleagues in the PIO on that side. Things weren't closed at first the way they became," Maria emphasizes, underlining the slow process by which "crossing" became a remarkable feat.

In the immediate postwar period, the cease-fire line dividing the island remained relatively porous. Turkish Cypriots still trickled across the line for two years, while Turkish Cypriot butchers sold pork from abandoned pigs to Greek Cypriots via the British bases, and smugglers ran an active trade in stolen Greek Cypriot goods. One man whose father had been a smuggler and "antiques dealer" during the period described the way that they even sold valuable Greek Orthodox icons to Greek Cypriot collectors. There were also middlemen for those who dared to risk the sale of property, mostly that left by Turkish Cypriots in the south. The administration continued to buy certain supplies not available in Turkey at the time through suppliers in the south, especially critical items such as certain drugs for the hospitals. And in November 1974, one member of the Legislative Assembly complained that although cigarettes were being imported from Turkey, and although they would have wanted "our money spent on cigarettes to go to the Motherland and not to foreigners," English cigarettes smuggled across the dividing line ensured that Greek Cypriots were still making money.[17] He asked for a legal ban on foreign cigarettes.

Over the first decade of division, the border with the island's south gradually went from relatively porous to impassable. By the 1980s, crossing from south to north would require permissions that often were not granted, and someone crossing on nonofficial business became suspect, even with permission.[18] Not only did the cease-fire line dividing the island become increasingly impassible for Greek Cypriots, but the "so-called state" gradually implemented what John Torpey has called "state monopolization of the legitimate 'means of movement'" (1998). This took place first through the issuing of identity cards and passports and through the use of those to restrict movement both domestically and internationally. Starting in 1975, for instance, males of conscription age were impeded from exiting north Cyprus unless they had completed military service or could show exemption from it.

These seem to be the bordering practices of a territorial state: controlling who is able to enter and exit one's "domestic" space. A large body of social science literature on borders has described the ways that they emerge through bureaucratic practices that control mobility (e.g., Bigo and Guild 2005; Soguk 1999; Torpey 1999), dividing communities and networks and thereby truncating the capacity for work and trade (Lubkemann 2008a, 2008b). However, even as these bordering practices contributed to the sense of a separate territory, or to a territory effect, the sense of wholeness and separateness that we think of as territorial integrity was compromised from its beginning by its own conditionality. The border, in other words, was always already simultaneously a "border."

One found this in such practices as Turkish Cypriot border guards stamping pieces of paper rather than the passports of foreigners arriving in northern ports. One also sees it in the way that Turkish Cypriots continued to travel on expired RoC passports and in the way that the Turkish Cypriot administration extended those passports, first with the stamps of the Communal Chamber, a body set up in 1960, and then with the stamps of the Turkish

Federated State of Cyprus, an entity that declared by its name that it was a building block for a federation still to be established.

While the bordering practices taking place at the border emphasized that their administration was building a territory that would become part of a future federation, other bordering practices seemed to call into question where that "border" might lie. Because Turkish Cypriots living in the island's north were under economic embargoes, in order to overcome the problem of foreign capital flow the administration changed the currency from the Cyprus lira to the Turkish lira.[19] Despite the division, the government in the south continued to supply electricity to the north as a humanitarian gesture.[20] In the first years, telephones and mail also relied on facilities in the south. It was only gradually that telephones in north Cyprus were cut off from the existing telephone system and acquired a new international code, that of Turkey, as well as a new internal prefix. Similarly, in order to prevent mail from being routed through the south, Turkish Cypriots gradually adopted a new postal code: "Mersin 10, Turkey." For many people, this postal code became one of the most humiliating signs of their dependence on their patron state. It meant that as far as the world was concerned, their address was the same as a Turkish provincial city.

The adoption of Turkish money, Turkish telephone codes, and a Turkish postal code were meant to ease their isolation, but at the same time they had the effect of making the north appear to be a province of Turkey. As early as December 1974, the Turkish Cypriot administration established the Cyprus Turkish Airlines, renting a plane and hiring personnel from a British company. However, no direct flights were or are possible from or to north Cyprus, which means that from the very beginning of what was to evolve into a "national" airline, Turkish Cypriot planes had to touch down at airports in Turkey in order to make it appear that they had come from Istanbul or Antalya when they arrived in London. In addition, half of the new airline's shares were owned by Turkish Airways, Turkey's national fleet.

Moreover, even as the border within the island gradually became more impenetrable, Turkish Cypriots suddenly found that their northern border appeared more porous than they would like. They established a new quarantine office specifically to handle animals and plants coming from Anatolia, while an outbreak of cholera on a ship in the Famagusta harbor led to parliamentary discussions of how to quarantine persons.[21] Rabies was a particular concern, as it did not exist on the island. And as we discuss in Chapters 4 and 5, as Greek Cypriot factories that remained within the north began to rumble back to life, Turkish Cypriots needed both engineers and workers with the know-how to run them. Turkish Cypriots received training under Turkish supervision, but they also began to import labor from the closest and cheapest source available to them. By the 1980s, Turkish Cypriots were already beginning to complain about uncontrolled migration across the maritime border with Anatolia.

All of this meant that even as the planting of people created a "force-field of a particular order," a territory effect, that territory was aporetic from the beginning, constantly dissolving into descriptions of it as a province or colony of Turkey. In daily life, a "territory" effect was always already present alongside the territory effect, often disappearing in the everyday practices of working land and contesting ownership but reappearing at the border itself. In this sense, many of the factitious elements of maintaining territorial integrity—controlling borders, demanding identity cards, moving people—often appeared not simply as fabricated but as false. As we will see in the next chapter, this "territory" effect was nowhere more evident than in attempts to turn the space into something recognizably "theirs" through a process of Turkification.

CHAPTER 2

Mastering the Landscape

In 1974, Kyrenia was a small harbor town in the shadow of the Five Finger Mountains with a population of about 3,500. The majority were Greek Cypriot, but there were around 1,000 Turkish Cypriots, as well as around 300 non-Cypriots, mostly British nationals who had remained on the island after decolonization. During the Ottoman and British periods, the port had been plied by caïques and piled with the carobs they brought from remote coastal villages for export. The town had had a small tourism industry since the late 1920s, when a native son and returnee from America, Costas Catsellis, built in quick succession first the small Sea View Hotel and then the much larger Dome (Katsellis 2017). The former had been favored by British administrators for its roast beef and the latter with British tourists because it offered services close to what they found at home, but with a bar overlooking the sea (Catselli 1974).

Erdal Andız, a burly man who today is a retired hotelier, described to us his amazement when, as a young man, he found that he had been appointed the Dome's first postwar manager: "It was the Dome Hotel that for years, from our childhood, we had heard about, the one the English went to, a hotel that we always knew as full."[1] It was for many Cypriots a symbol of European sophistication, and its clientele consistently included British royalty, theater actors, and writers.

That sophisticated aura was abruptly dispelled when Turkish forces who entered the town in 1974 rounded up six hundred Greek Cypriots and held them in the hotel's confines until the Vienna Agreement of August 1975. As we described in the previous chapter, the hotel balconies became the site from

Figure 5. The Dome Hotel of Kyrenia in a postcard rendering from the 1970s (authors' collection).

Figure 6. Greek Cypriot prisoner being led by a Turkish soldier in Kyrenia.

which Greek Cypriot captives observed the changes taking place around them. The author that we quote in Chapter 1 wrote not only about the looting taking place in the town but also about other changes to the landscape. Next to the hotel was a small square that marked the beginning of the seaside promenade that culminated at the old harbor. The author remarked that as early as the beginning of August 1974, "Red flags began to wave in the square opposite the Sea View Hotel . . . while one day a bust of Kemal Atatürk was erected there" (Spyrou 2004: 217).[2]

The hotel's future manager, quoted above, described to us how by chance he was in the square on that day: "I happened to find myself there when they were playing the Independence March and raising the Turkish flag to install the Atatürk bust in the square. I can't remember a more emotional moment in my life. I had goosebumps, my eyes filled, but when I looked to the left and saw the way all the Greek Cypriots were watching from the balconies that looked out onto the street, it gave me a very strange feeling. 'I'm glad I'm not in their place,' I said to myself, and I felt suddenly torn." Another man who was fifteen years old at the time went with his father to the ceremony and also recalled the Dome prisoners watching from the balconies. Although he saw a Greek Cypriot boy he knew from the English School,[3] he refused to look at him. Instead, he says, they felt triumphant, joyous.

This chapter addresses both the de facto and the factitious changes in landscape that very shortly after 1974 made the island's north look, sound, smell, and feel like a separate, "Turkish" space. This involved a "dehellenization" of the landscape that was also a "Turkification," and we describe this process both as an everyday practice and as a political act. As much literature on the nation-state has argued, what distinguishes it from other state forms is that sovereignty is presumed to reside with and to be exercised by "the people" (e.g., Gellner 1983; Kohn 2008). In this view, "nation became a *political* term because it defined the people who were members of, and who held sovereignty within, a state" (Penrose 2002: 284). Moreover, in the past couple of decades, an increasing body of literature has moved beyond the taken-for-grantedness of a state's territory and instead has tried to unpack how territory is implicated in state-ness (esp. Branch 2013; Paasi 1996, 2009; Penrose 2002; Storey 2001; also Yiftachel 2002). One answer to this question is that how the people who hold sovereignty are defined is inextricably entangled in modernity with territoriality, both through the "emotive power of a group's attachment to the land" and through the *territorial* definition of identity (Penrose 2002). The emotive aspect of territory that evokes a sense of identity is usually explained through senses of being "at home" (Tuan 1975). Those senses of homeliness depend in turn on the histories and memories that support the familiarity of place (Lowenthal 1985), as well as myths that reproduce communal belonging and make a territory a homeland (Schöpflin 1997). As a result, the "particular tastes, smells, sounds and sights" of nationalism are claimed to "carry cultural values and personal memories" (Howes and Classen 2014: 65) and make national place through the "spatial socialization" of everyday or banal nationalism (Paasi 1999; cf. Billig 1995).

But what about a case, such as ours, in which a territory is created *ex nihilo* and where that emotive power of identification had to be created from the ground up? Even though almost half of the Turkish Cypriot community was originally from the space that became "the north," almost all had experienced extended displacement and enclavement. As a result, even those originally from the north had only iterative and partial relationships to that space as a place over the previous decade. Moreover, changes during the decade of their enclavement, and later the flight of Greek Cypriots from the north and the devastation of war, all meant that the space they found was not the place they had left. Perhaps even more important, however, none had known a space that they would come to call "north Cyprus," or simply "the north." As a result, the sort of "spatial socialization," "the process through which individual actors and collectivities are socialized as members of specific, territorially bounded spatial entities," had to be built anew (Paasi 1999: 4; also Yiftachel 2002).

We discussed in the last chapter the making of place as a "perceptual unity," one perceived as a territory (Penrose 2002: 279, citing May 1973: 212). This chapter concerns the ways that materiality mediated the building of a new, communal "home." Steven Feld has remarked, "As place is sensed, senses are placed; as places make sense, senses make place" (2005: 179). It is precisely the senses as a form sense-making, or giving meaning to place, we argue, that was at work in the transformation of the landscape into one that reflected "us." This chapter, then, concerns the process of making a territory sovereign, and more specifically the *sense* of sovereignty that emerges through imbuing a space with the traces and imprints of a "sovereign" people.

We argue here that de facto sovereignty as something perceptible emerges not only through the construction of territorial integrality but also through the construction of separateness that is at the same time a construction of belonging: the perception that this territory might reasonably be called the communal "home" of a particular people. We call this the *sovereignty effect*, or perception of a socialized space, a sense of the north as a place where Turkish Cypriots belong. In speaking of this as a sovereignty effect, we build on Jens Bartelson's important genealogy of the concept of sovereignty, where he argues that we cannot understand the concept without understanding territory, particularly the ways that sovereignty has always been conceptualized as a line of division: "Sovereignty and space are conceptualized in logical interdependence with each other right from the start" (Bartelson 1995: 30). This is so, he believes, because "sovereignty . . . furnishes the very divide between what is internal and what is external [to the state] with meaning, and thus with political reality for the agents themselves, whose identity in turn hinges on this division" (47). This is what we refer to here as a sense of separateness: the sense or affect of being in a separate space, and the creation of that space as one to which one belongs. We describe that here through its materiality, showing how the process of settlement, of "adopting" a space, was materially mediated and gave the landscape a sense of being "one's own."

In our case, however, we witness at the same time the emergence of what we call the *"sovereignty" effect*, or those various official and symbolic manifestations of a "state" that were also aporetic from the beginning. The "sovereignty" effect is visible in those insistent manifestations of sovereignty that also contain within them the roots of, and persistently call attention to, their own undoing. While the sovereignty effect is mediated by the materiality of settlement—Turkish coffee drunk in a coffee shop, a Turkish name replacing a Greek one on a barbershop—the "sovereignty" effect is mediated by the materiality of sovereign enactments—flags, statues, new toponyms. These factitious enactments of sovereignty employed fetishistic markers of difference that during this period were expressions of Turkish nationalism. Exploring the relationship between the factitious and the fetish, we show how this laid the groundwork for a later sense that these were someone else's gods.

In other words, while the de facto and the factitious were for many people virtually indistinguishable in this period, when symbols of separateness were also symbols of Turkishness, they would become important later, when their difference from Greek Cypriots *as Turks*—an unproblematic way of formulating their identity in the immediate post-1974 period—began to erode the sense of separateness that we argue is the key to understanding Turkish Cypriot desires for sovereign agency.

The Sovereignty Effect

Only about two months after Turkish troops landed on the island and a little over a month after what is usually called the "second invasion" in mid-August 1974 that secured the current partition line, schools in populated areas of the island's north began to open. In Lapithos, where, as we have seen, soldiers were still hiding in the mountains and some elderly Greek Cypriots still clung to their homes, the new school year opened once they cleaned out the large Greek schoolhouse that had been built in the 1950s in neo-Hellenic style. A woman who was nine years old at the time recalled for us the excitement the children had felt when they sat at real school desks after the makeshift tables they had known in the enclaves. In similar fashion, on the day that school opened that year in northern Nicosia, Mete and around two hundred schoolmates were marched in silence through the empty Greek Cypriot suburbs, where doors still stood open and dogs left by their owners wandered the streets,[4] into a newly built school building with spacious classrooms and laboratories that boasted a microscope on each desk. The staff had removed all Greek writing before their arrival, though they found Greek books and other materials, which they burned.

As we noted earlier, during the period when Turkish Cypriots were trapped in enclaves, life in the Greek Cypriot–controlled areas outside the enclaves went through a process of rapid economic growth and development that changed the landscape and enriched villages and towns (Strong 1999). Famagusta and Kyrenia quickly developed tourism infrastructure, while Morphou exported its oranges and Lapithos its lemons. Small industries sprang up. Almost all the houses that the guides labeled "modern" and distributed to young families were built during the period when Turkish Cypriots lived in ghettos. The factories with up-to-date machinery and the hotels with central air conditioning had all been constructed while Turkish Cypriots guarded their villages with guns. While Turkish Cypriot villages lacked electricity, the Greek Cypriot–controlled state built the luxury resort of Varosha, where millionaires and Hollywood stars such as Sophia Loren came to bask on the white sand.[5] Moreover, the invisibility of Turks during this period meant that much of the island outside the enclaves was thoroughly imbued with the signs and symbols of Greekness, as well as signs of a "modern" otherness.

We described in the previous chapter how the affluence that they found provoked contradictory reactions of envy, desire, and resentment and resulted in a "flurry of looting" so widespread that euphemisms emerged for it, such as *buluntu*, "found things" (see Yaşın 1976). At the same time, there was much destruction of anything symbolically Greek Cypriot or anything not usable. Some people preserved photographs and other items that they assumed would have a personal meaning, secreting them in suitcases and boxes under beds and on top of cupboards.[6] However, many people told us how they threw out or burned personal possessions that they found in the houses where they settled. Several women described to us collecting photographs, books, and letters in Greek and burning them in the streets or gardens.

At a larger scale, there was also devastation of or damage to statues and monuments, churches and cemeteries, and any Greek writing. In very quick order, the Greek alphabet almost completely disappeared from the island's north. Statues and monuments were torn down or replaced. Although in many cases, building new monuments would take time, the almost immediate destruction or even erasure of Greek Cypriot nationalist or historical symbols was also a way of erasing the Other's claim on the visible landscape.

Moreover, this on-the-ground "dehellenization" was also a de facto "Turkification." While, as we discuss later, there were also official policies that promoted Turkification, de facto Turkification was not part of state policy but part of the way in which people attempted to settle and go on with their lives. As shops and coffee shops began to open, their new owners removed the signs in Greek and replaced them with Turkish names. The many Greek flags that adorned official buildings, shops, and even houses were taken down and destroyed. Mete's brother, who was nine years old at the time, climbed into an abandoned Greek Cypriot barricade and removed a Greek flag, which he then tried to paint red and white, the colors of the Turkish flag. The troubleshooter Tamer Gazioğlu and social psychologist Vamık Volkan (1979), both quoted in the previous chapter, remarked that people did not immediately settle, did not immediately begin repairs on their houses. However, one exception to this was a phenomenon that many Turkish Cypriots recall from the period: that in very quick order the blue house shutters that against whitewash represented the blue and white of the Greek flag and that were prevalent throughout Cyprus in those years were immediately painted dark green or brown.

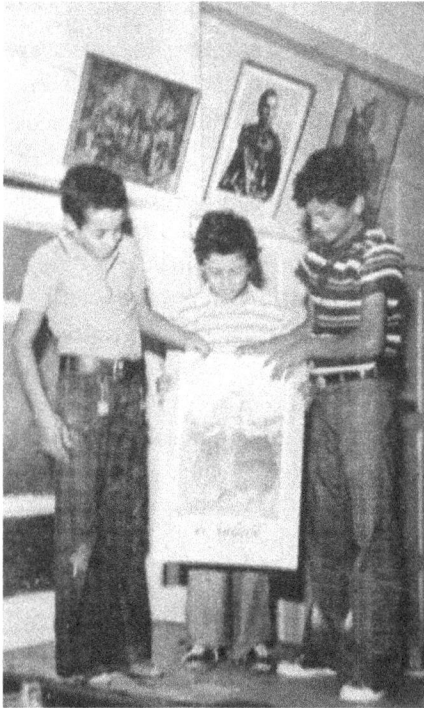

Figure 7. Children remove a photograph of General Grivas, the leader of EOKA B, from the wall of the house they have moved into, while other photos belonging to the Greek Cypriot owner hang on the wall (*Hayat* magazine).

But apart from this was the way that gradually the coffee shop, butcher, and grocery that Gazioğlu had seen as signs of village life began to open, taking their new owners' names, or sometimes the names of their former villages. People cleaned the houses where they had been settled, and gradually the *muhtar*s and mayors who had been transported from the south began their work. They began collecting and burning the rotten food and unwanted belongings that people had piled on the streets. Pigs and dogs ran wild in the postwar landscape, the former a continuing sign of the enemy's "pollution." Within a year, farmers were collecting and selling their crops through companies that employed large numbers of Turkish Cypriots and acquired new names. Within a few months after the cease-fire, empty Greek Cypriot factories rumbled to life with the help of experts from Turkey, and as we discuss in Chapter 5, these became both a foundation for the new state's economy and one of the main sources for manufactured goods. All of these factories acquired new names, and they produced goods for the Turkish Cypriot market or for certain markets that were willing to deal with them, such as Arab countries.

In other words, in the long process that we discuss in Chapter 1 by which people began "to behave as though the system was theirs," they also began to see these changes reflected in the plowed fields, tended orchards, stocked shops, productive factories, and children running home from school that reflected a new life in the places where they had settled. If this "dehellenization" was also a de facto "turkification," it was a form of place-making that was also a form of sense-making, in Feld's phrase (2005). The sense that there was a separate territory with a separate people in the island's north was created, to build on Timothy Mitchell (1991), from the powerful, metaphysical effect of practices that made such *separateness* appear to exist.[7] Indeed, if Cynthia Weber (1992, 1995) is correct that de jure sovereignty is premised on the principle of nonintervention, then de facto sovereignty might be seen as the structures supporting the "separateness" that underpins such a principle. The sovereignty effect, we claim here, emerges out of everyday practices, practices of *sahiplenme,* both mastering and adopting, that at the same time mark a place as one's own and that thereby produce the metaphysical effect of "separateness."[8]

In other words, the more Turkish Cypriots planted flowers in the gardens of their "temporary" houses, stocked the shelves of groceries with Turkish

Figure 8. Turkish Cypriot women clean the house they have just been assigned in the north as other family members wait outside (*Hayat* magazine).

goods, tended trees whose fruit would be pressed in nationalized factories, stocked school libraries with Turkish books, played Turkish music on the radio, and tried to sort out disputes over water to the land that they cultivated, the more the landscape around them began to look, feel, sound, and smell like it was theirs. Each of these small, everyday acts cumulatively produced a sense of having "adopted" a place, having made it one's own, and gave the reinforcing feedback effect of seeing this reflected in the landscape. Their children would later grow up in a landscape that they understood to be "theirs."[9] Hence, the materiality of adopting the place, making it one's own, or *sahiplenme*, mediates the relationship between people and territory, allowing us to *project belonging* and have it reflected back to us as a *right to belong*.

Of course, in parallel to this everyday adoption of the place where they had settled, and the gradual adoption of the system that they established there, they also went about imprinting the landscape with the official signs of Turkishness that were associated with the "motherland." While changed toponyms, large flags, and new statues were all part of the "official" Turkification of the landscape, they were also factitious, elements that emphasized their own making. In contrast to the everyday production of separateness, this territorialization that stamped the landscape as Turkish made reference to a state that was not their own. In contrast to the *de facto*, then, the *factitious* also became part of everyday sovereignty practice, but in ways that were neither predictable nor stable.

Enactments of Sovereignty

In 2014, on the fortieth anniversary of the division, a schoolfriend of Mete's, Uğur Karagözlü, wrote in the *Birmingham Press* about his experiences as a twelve-year-old when the invasion occurred. He was from Limassol but was visiting his grandparents in Lefke, the mining town to which they had been displaced a decade earlier. When Turkish troops landed on the island, Greek forces entered Lefke and held the town for the next three weeks. At the end of that period, Uğur writes, a group of U.N. soldiers came to their house to tell them that the Greek forces had left and the Turkish army was about to enter the town:

> My grandmother's immediate reaction was to hang two Turkish flags in front of her house. Thinking back what strikes me the most about

this was the fact that these people who had been kicked out of their
ancestral home by their Greek Cypriot neighbours in 1963 and were
forced to live as refugees—refugees in the proper sense of the word....
[In their shack] were two beds, a table, a couple of chairs and an old
radio. That was all they had but so it transpired they also had Turkish
flags. And they were not alone. The whole town was immediately
awash with Turkish flags.[10]

One of the centerpieces of Uğur's article is his twelve-year-old surprise that
his destitute grandparents—and indeed, it seems, everyone else—had Turkish flags stored and ready to be unfurled.

These secreted flags seem to have been common among both Greek
and Turkish Cypriots for a good part of the twentieth century. Historian
Nicos Kranidiotis, for instance, describes how his natal town of Kyrenia
joyfully responded to Greek prime minister Metaxas's rejection of collaboration with invading Italian forces in 1940. The context was a period of almost a decade in which flags and other national symbols had been banned
by the British administration because of riots against Government House
in 1931: "From every door, from every window, there sprang a flag, waving
proudly in the breeze. Suddenly, the little provincial town was immersed in
blue. The flags, which for so long had been waiting, folded with sweet laven-
der in drawers and chests, now once again fluttered in the morning air,
emblems of the yearnings and hopes of an enslaved people" (quoted in
Catselli 1974: 131). Cypriots in large numbers, then, seemed to possess the
flags of the "motherlands," hidden away to be unfurled at appropriate
moments.

Certainly, Turkish Cypriots had long had an attachment to the Turkish
flag, which during the enclave period they visibly displayed in all areas they
held. During that period, for instance, Turkish Cypriot fighters controlled the
crusader castle of St. Hilarion, which hovers over and is visible from Kyrenia. They stitched an enormous Turkish flag, which they hung between the
turrets of the castle, both taunting Greek Cypriots and asserting their own
presence there. Their fascination with the Turkish flag was also expressed in
other ways, such as naming their first radio station "Flag Radio" (Bayrak
Radyo) or that one of the most popular music groups of the period was "Flag
Quartet" (Bayrak Kuartet).

There could have been no more appropriate moment for the unfurling
of those flags than what the vast majority of Turkish Cypriots of the period

perceived as a military victory.[11] They had been "saved" by the "motherland," and that country's flags were immediately draped from the windows of houses and strung across streets. Turkish flags soon appeared on all official buildings, in village squares, in coffee shops and homes. Atatürk busts and statues multiplied. These were "official" signs but also in this period signs of victory and a way of planting a communal stamp on the landscape. These were intended as ways of making the landscape perceptibly Turkish.

In a multicountry, collaborative study of religious heritage, Robert Hayden refers to major religious sites as markers of contested dominance and discusses ways in which the location and size of churches or mosques, for instance, may be used to increase visibility (Hayden and Walker 2013; Hayden 2016).[12] Hayden develops a notion of *perceptibility* in relation to the built landscape, defined by buildings' audibility, size, and centrality, or the tendency to locate major religious sites in the center of villages, towns, and cities (Hayden and Walker 2013: 413). Our own notion of perceptibility is much broader than that of Hayden and his coauthor, who are primarily concerned with the architectural projection of dominance. Nevertheless, Hayden's work points to ways in which the *quality of being perceivable* may be projected in and tied to the materiality of landscape.

As we remarked in the introduction to Part I, one of the main ways in which this minority community expressed its desires for sovereign agency was in saying, throughout much of the twentieth century, that they wanted to be "put in the place of men/humans" (*adam yerine konmak*) (see esp. Bryant 2004; Bryant and Hatay 2011). One might paraphrase this as a minority group claiming that it is not *perceived* by the other, or the other not "seeing" them, not respecting them, not taking them into account as political actors. In order to claim sovereign agency, to be taken into account as a political actor, moreover, this minority community clung to the signs and symbols of Turkishness, particularly after the establishment of the Turkish Republic and its reforms intended to modernize and "civilize" them. Those were, moreover, the signs and symbols of a powerful "motherland" country that was dominant in the region. Commenting on the relationship of Turkish nationalist symbols to the struggle for visibility, one art historian, in a doctoral thesis on Turkish Cypriot monuments, remarks, "I suggest that these monuments' original symbolic 'work' lay in showing the realness of the Turkish Cypriot people, albeit in political form, who otherwise were being cast as non-real, or absent, within their own environment and within the wider conveyed images of that environment" (Adil 2007: 4).

Hence, in the period when Turkish Cypriots disappeared into the enclaves, effectively overlooked by a Greek Cypriot community that grew wealthier in their absence, the large flags were a way of making themselves visible. In the post-1974 period, flags multiplied as part of official policy but also with the collusion and encouragement of Turkish Cypriots, who wished to see this most visible sign of Turkishness. Flags were planted by the Turkish military in "conquered" villages and often on the highest point, which in most villages was the church's bell tower. At the same time, however, the flags that had been carefully folded into the drawers and chests of destitute refugees were unfurled on houses and strung across streets.

In similar fashion, while there were and are official representations of Mustafa Kemal Atatürk, the founder of the Turkish Republic, in offices and schools, much of the Turkish Cypriot populace adorned and continues to adorn homes, coffee shops, restaurants, and clubs with photos of the Turkish leader. Moreover, this intimate reverence for the leader goes back to the very beginning of the Turkish Republic: we know that people in Cyprus in the early 1920s were already hanging newspaper clippings and photos of the leader on their walls.[13] The art historian quoted above includes in his thesis self-reflexive passages that describe his own relationship with national symbols on the island. One of these describes how when he was a boy in the late 1950s, among the family portraits hanging on the living room walls were three other pictures: Adnan Menderes, then president of the Republic of Turkey; a photo of two Turkish generals who had commanded forces in Korea; and Atatürk in uniform.

> This picture was placed in such a way that the two walls forming the corner of the room created a frame of perfect symmetry for it. It seemed as if the gaze of that image of Atatürk followed you, no matter where you were in the room. Looking back, it seems that in our daily chores such images acted as constant mnemonic devices, reminding us that as a family we belonged to a larger Turkish family, the Turkish nation whose founder and father was Kemal Atatürk. This was not a matter that was ever explicitly discussed at home rather it was to be tacitly understood via presence of such images. It was a matter of symbolic belonging. (Adil 2007: 54)

Moreover, during the enclave period of the 1960s, he speculates, "this figure of Atatürk was an important part of the imagery used in the generating of a sense of national unity to meet the perceived needs of the time amongst the scattered Turkish settlements and enclaves" (55).

Along with photographs and drawings of the leader, there were also busts and statues that acquired a reverential quality. The first Atatürk busts had arrived on the island in the 1950s at the request of teachers in collaboration with the Federation of Turkish Cypriot Associations. Moreover, the arrival of these busts created great excitement in the populace, with villages and towns competing for the honor of erecting such a bust in the neighborhood square or school garden. This excitement reached its peak when the first full-size Atatürk statue arrived in the Famagusta harbor in October 1963 for erection in front of the Kyrenia Gate of Nicosia. This much-anticipated statue, preparations for which had begun immediately after the declaration of the Republic of Cyprus in 1959, traveled slowly in a caravan from the port of Famagusta to the capital, its route crowded by Turkish Cypriots throwing flowers and scrambling for a view. In the capital itself, thousands of Turkish Cypriots waited, hundreds of them having arrived the night before and erected tents. Even after the ceremony, the crowds did not disperse but instead remained until morning watching the statue with tears in their eyes (Sadrazam 1990: 99).

Moreover, many Turkish Cypriots who were able to do so carried with them to the north the original Atatürk busts that had been brought to the island in the late 1950s. Such villages as Stravrogouno and Vreça in the Paphos district dislodged the busts from their pillars in the village squares and carried them with their belongings across the line to be erected in their new villages. İsmail Bozkurt, a politician and writer from the Larnaca district, describes the concern some of his fellow villagers had felt for their Atatürk bust in the midst of a siege by Greek Cypriot forces in 1974: "There was a group of youths, who as much as their own security were concerned about what was going to happen to the Atatürk bust. Because they were afraid the Greek Cypriots might come and destroy it, they began secretly keeping watch over it. One night, taking advantage of the dark, they removed the bust and hid it. Although the whole village knew this, they said nothing."[14] Some weeks later, when it became clear that they would be evacuating the village and would be transported to the north, Bozkurt describes the way in which they concealed the bust to get it across the line: "No one was content to leave the Atatürk bust behind. However, U.N. Peace Force officials were searching belongings that were being transported to the north. There was also the high possibility of having to pass through a Greek Cypriot checkpoint along the way. With the cooperation of everyone, the bust was wrapped very well and hidden in such a way in the village bus that the U.N. officials would not see it."[15] This Atatürk bust traveled with them, then, to the village in the north to which they were assigned, and the villagers erected it in a small square across from their new municipal offices.

Like the hotel manager and the teenage boy who stood with tears in their eyes as they watched the erection of an Atatürk bust in the center of Kyrenia, or the flags concealed in drawers, here we see the emotional attachment of average Cypriots to certain symbols of Turkish nationalism. The practices of average Cypriots in relocating and displaying those symbols would play a large part in the "Turkification" of the north.

In the introduction to Part I, we noted that many authors portray this Turkification of the landscape as a form of Turkish colonization, or "Turkey-fication" (Navaro-Yashin 2012). Indeed, one book whose title summarizes this view is called *In Turkey's Image: The Transformation of Occupied Cyprus into a Turkish Province* (Ioannides 1991). As we also earlier remarked, however, claims of Turkish colonization in which only a few Turkish Cypriot leaders had any active role obscure more than they explain. Such claims cannot explain, for instance, secreted flags that flooded the streets or villagers risking their lives to take Atatürk busts with them to their new homes in the north.

Turkish colonization or "Turkey-fication" cannot explain, in other words, how Turkish Cypriots appropriated and lived in this space. Indeed, explanations of this sort reproduce the conditions of the aporia of perceptibility insofar as any attempts to make themselves perceptible and visible *as Turks* have also, in the process, made them invisible by turning their own Turkification into Turkish colonization. The very symbols and images that were to lead to their perceptibility become the source of their invisibility. Instead of being actors, they become extras on the set of their own history.

This transformation of symbols of identity into sources of invisibility makes those symbols important for demonstrating the way in which we use the concept of the factitious throughout this book and the work that concept is doing. The factitious is the fabricated, something that appears at one moment to be only human-made or manufactured but at other times to be "made-up" or fake. This duality of the concept becomes evident in its etymological and genealogical relation to the fetish, words whose roots are the same. As William Pietz brilliantly demonstrates, the fetish has an "irreducible materiality" that makes it both the bearer of meaning and something that always spills beyond the meaning attributed to it. "The fetish," he notes, "has an ordering power derived from its status as the fixation or inscription of a unique originating event that has brought together previously heterogeneous elements into a novel identity" (1985: 7).

Flags have often been labeled fetishistic, and in this case one could say that flags and Atatürk busts or statues had a fetishistic aura insofar as Turkish Cypriots clearly wished to acquire for themselves the qualities that they saw these symbols as representing—power, conquest, modernity, Turkishness. "The Turkish flag reflects the Turkish character as if by force of its colour and content," remarked one commentator, in a newspaper article discussing the use of flags on the island. "It is a conspicuously powerful flag not to be trifled with."[16] In this sense, flags may be seen as "ciphers" that encode many different values (Orr 2010: 505). It is also in this sense that Adil, quoted earlier, might refer to Atatürk's watchful eyes as those of the "father" who originated modern Turkishness, a "father" uniquely capable of creating a sense of national belonging in the context of scattered enclaves.

But as we know from other uses of the word *fetish*, it also contains a historical accretion of meaning inherent in the factitious that can imply the false or fallacious. This is its meaning in Marx's understanding of commodity fetishism as that which disguises the commodity's true source of value. One sees this here in the ways that, as Turkish Cypriots attempted to stamp the landscape with their presence *as Turks*, they appropriated the symbols of a state of which they were not citizens. While these symbols were unproblematic in this period, as we show in later chapters, it was precisely as Turkish Cypriots began to feel more at home in the new place they had created that the fabricatedness of these symbols came to the fore. While in this period such symbols appeared to give Turkish Cypriots visibility and increase their sense of having adopted the land where they had settled, in later years, as senses of belonging shifted, these symbols began to seem fabricated, fake, imposed.

Not only this, but as we discuss in Chapter 5, the particular "irreducible materiality" that these factitious symbols came to represent was that of "facts on the ground," a term used to indicate acts of possession or occupation that "are at least of questionable validity" (Stolzenberg 2009: 12). While fetishistic symbols such as flags and monuments, then, seemed to give to the landscape a "historically singular social construct" or "novel identity" associated with the "motherland," they were also always factitious to the extent that they emphasized their own making and so could seem at times constructed, at other times fake. This was the case because those very symbols always already emphasized the "Turkifying" of the landscape *as* Turkification, that is, always emphasized the need to transform it into a new territory. Moreover, precisely by emphasizing their construction, they also brought attention to the way in which, according to the "international community," calling such acts *faits accomplis* or "facts on the ground" already called attention to their illegitimacy and grounding in violence.

The contradictions of these factitious enactments of sovereignty were nowhere more present than in two areas that have often been used as paradigmatic examples of Turkification: the conversion of churches to mosques and toponym changes. While Navaro (Navaro-Yashin 2012) views the latter as the prime example of "Turkey-fication," Ram calls the former "an effective form of signification of the occupied territory as Turkish" (2015: 28). What we show below, instead, is that if these acts are paradigmatic of anything, they are paradigmatic of the aporia of perceptibility, the way in which Turkish Cypriots found themselves disappearing in the very agentive acts that declared their presence.

Inscribing the Landscape

One day, Mete's mother produced for us a typewritten list of place names, with various ones scratched off and others written in. "We sat up until late working on this," she sighs, insisting on refiling the list in the folders that she keeps from her days as secretary in the Ministry of the Interior. She explains how she and Ahmet Sami Topcan, then the *kaymakam*, or district governor, for Kyrenia, had hurriedly compiled this list of new place names in advance of the first parliamentary election, scheduled for June 1975. Turkish Cypriots already had experience with changing toponyms, since in 1958 the KTKF had undertaken to "Turkify" the names of villages that had Turkish populations but non-Turkish names (Bryant and Hatay, in progress). There are suggestions in parliamentary minutes that the initiative for the name changes had come from Turkey.[17] Similar toponym changes had been implemented by the Turkish government in "subdued" Kurdish areas of Anatolia (see Öktem 2005, 2009). Certainly, the initial list of names consisted of some suggestions from Turkish military commanders but also those from Turkish Cypriot district commissioners and village *muhtar*s.

Turkish Cypriot legislators were active in the selection of names, arguing that they needed to find ones that would "stick."[18] Following the first parliamentary election of the TFSC in 1975, the new parliament set up a special committee to review the name changes and make recommendations; these would be further discussed in a special session of parliament in December 1975.[19] The committee in charge of assessing the name list followed three principles: that names that had been changed in 1958 be retained; that places in which villages from the south had been settled in whole be given the southern village's name, including the post-1958 names;[20] and that certain villages and towns that already had Turkish names retain those.[21]

From the list of two hundred names, ten would be singled out to be rethought. The Constituent Assembly then voted individually on each of the remaining 190 names, all of which passed with a majority, often unanimously.[22] What is clear from the lively discussion that accompanied the voting is that lawmakers were primarily concerned with whether or not the names would stick or "whether or not the people living there internalize the name," as one of the leading leftists, Özker Özgür, phrased it.[23] The word that we translate here as "adopt," *benimsemek*, is literally "to make something one's own." In that process, Özgür, for instance, was not against changing even Ottoman names if that was what the new population of the village preferred.

In that regard, one of the founders of a leftist party, Burhan Nalbantoğlu, objected to names that phonetically resembled the previous ones, and he was in favor also of changing the names of cities and historical sites:

> Friends, we are changing village names. That is, we're Turkifying them in our own way. Given that we're Turkifying them, it's necessary for us to stay away from made-up names, or ones that derive from Greek or even Latin. Are we going to say, "Well, this was the Greek name, and there's a Turkish word that resembles it," and make changes on the basis of similarity and so go down the road of remembering? . . . My opinion is that if our main aim is to Turkify these names, there are sufficient Turkish names in our Turkish language for our villages, our towns, our cities. . . . So I want to make clear that I will not vote in favor of any names that are translations of Greek or have resemblances to the Greek or Latin.[24]

We see from this that members of the new assembly from both the left and the right were aware that what they were undertaking was a process of Turkification (*Türkleştirme*), though as Nalbantoğlu says, they were "Turkifying in our own way." Moreover, the debates in which they engaged concerned the best way to accomplish this so that people would adopt the names and through adopting the names also adopt the places.

Hence, although the initial impetus to change toponyms after 1974 apparently came from elsewhere, it was a process in which Turkish Cypriots in their villages and in the parliament participated and that they resisted and shaped, both at the time and through subsequent use. It was in the process of Turkifying in their own way, we claim, that Turkish Cypriots were constructing what we call a "sovereignty" effect, a sense of the territory as theirs that also contains elements of the factitious.

The "sovereignty" effect contains practices in which the subject takes a second-order stance toward the object, always already explaining it as a product of ideology. Or to paraphrase Slavoj Žižek (1989), we might say that they are aware that what they are doing is Turkifying, *but they do it anyway.* Not only this, but as will become increasingly clear in the next chapter, Turkish Cypriot state-builders were also aware that what they were doing was internationally condemned, as was made clear to them by U.N. Security Council resolutions and European Commission reports. In other words, their need or desire to demonstrate mastery over a territory through symbols of Turkish nationalism is aporetic from its inception, what Žižek might call a "deadlock of our desire" (1996: 207). For Žižek desire is inherently impossible—or, we might say, unrealizable—but we avoid confronting that impossibility because of the "illusory misrecognition of the inner 'hold' a figure of authority exerts upon us, that is, the notion that we are merely yielding to external coercion" (ibid.). In this case, the impossibility of Turkifying the island's north—unrealizable because of its international condemnation—appears simultaneously to unmask that practice as ideology (Turkification) *and* to mask it as Turkey-fication.

Ethnographically, this factitiousness emerges today in the way that many Turkish Cypriots know both the old and the new names and code-switch between them. There are, of course, certain names that have been forgotten, especially when Turkish Cypriots had no previous association with the village or found its old name difficult to pronounce. Other new names are simply favored, even by leftists who for political reasons today prefer the old names.

"We've gotten so used to the new names," one left-wing former bureaucrat told us, "that at this point I catch myself saying Güzelyurt instead of

Omorfo. Or I'll remember the Turkish name but can't for the life of me remember what the Greek name was."[25]

Code-switching involves deciding which name to use on the basis of an interlocutor's age, class, and accent, among other factors. For instance, one may use Vasilya with an elderly person but Karşıyaka with a youth unaware of its previous name. However, code-switching occurs primarily at the moment of political interpellation, an interpellation coded as one's stance on the "Cyprus Problem." This very common, everyday practice interpellates the speaker in a series of calculations that unmask this naming as ideology, either through leftists insisting on using the old names in what they see as an antinationalist stance or through persons on the right insisting on the opposite.[26]

What code-switching today encapsulates, however, is the anxiety of audience: the knowledge that for more than four decades since the island's division, international maps refused to use the new names, considering them an act of colonization or "Turkey-fication."[27] This failure to realize the reality of "facts on the ground" was always one risk of Turkifying "in their own way." Indeed, what makes these practices second-order or factitious is that they are always already viewed as "facts on the ground": stubbornly real in the face of assertions of their impossibility. They insist on a particular reality while at the same time incorporating the knowledge that this reality is denied by others.

Danilyn Rutherford has argued that "like social action more generally, the assertion of sovereignty unfolds before the eyes of imagined others; every bid for power entails a confrontation with audiences of various sorts" (2012: 4). These audiences, moreover, may often be spectral, "an ability to reframe a situation without actually appearing on the scene" (5). In this case, there were many spectral audiences, from "Ankara," the name that came to symbolize a whole military-bureaucratic complex; to the "international community," a formula that described those countries that might recognize them; to simply "foreigners," or those persons who might want to visit the island and leave their sterling.

And indeed, within a few years, despite the disapproval of the second category, the third category began to arrive, first in the form of British tourists who had some former association with the island, and by the 1980s in the form of foreign visitors curious about what was being billed as an isolated paradise. However, even as tourists from Leeds and Leicester blithely used the name Karşıyaka rather than Vasilya, this "reality" was underlain by the knowledge, on the part of Turkish Cypriots, that the "international community" viewed these name changes as a Turkification that was part of transforming the north into an occupied territory, that is, Turkey-fying it. The deadlock of desire described by Žižek is palpably present as the aporia between the real and the realizable that emerges in that moment of hesitation when, on the basis of one's interlocutor, one calculates and chooses which place name to use.

It is because of this deadlock of desire, we argue, that the aporia between the real and the realizable emerges within the factitious as absurdity. Žižek divides approaches toward the unmasking of ideology into the cynical and the ironic, arguing that while the cynic is out to expose the base coercive function of power, the ironist sees even coercion as a strategy disguising something else (1996: 205–207). In this case, however, as should become clear throughout the book, the factitious manifests and reveals the aporetic in the form of the absurd. Albert Camus had viewed the absurd as the true philosophical attitude toward the human search for meaning, exposing the necessity of searching for something that cannot be found ([1955] 2012). Here, too, the process of Turkifying takes place in a context in which one knows that this is not, in fact, possible—that the audiences at whom one aims, whether Greek Cypriots across the divide or the international community, will deny that this Turkification is possible or view it as a process of colonization.

Looked at in this way, it should not be surprising that in the moment of recognizing the deadlock of desire—in this case the aporetic nature of toponym changes—agency may be turned to subordination, adoption into ideology, and Turkification into Turkey-fication. The gap between the old and new names appears in the moment of hesitation as one decides which one to use and thereby reveals the anxiety of audience. It is in this gap between the old and new names that the aporia emerges as the absurdity of enacting agency at the same moment that one denies it. This absurdity would be nowhere more palpably manifest than in the treatment of religious heritage.

Stamping the Territory

In early 2012, then TRNC president Derviş Eroğlu, known as an uncompromising nationalist, was called to dedicate a newly built mosque in the border village of Beyarmudu, near Famagusta. In his speech, he stressed the importance of religious sites to Turkish Cypriots' perceptibility. "Especially in border villages, the erection of mosques and minarets sends messages to those who are observing us. Every mosque, every minaret is a stamp on the TRNC (*KKTC'ye vurulan bir mühür*)," he remarked.[28] The metaphor of the stamp implies indelibility as well as marks of the state. This nationalist president expressed a view of these structures as ways of securing TRNC territory, making it clear that whatever happened in the future, this territory would remain stamped with the signs of Turkishness.

Looking at the way that religious heritage has been used over time in Cyprus, however, we see that for at least a century Turkish Cypriots used it to make themselves more perceptible, more visible to particular audiences that in the first instance were their Greek Cypriot neighbors. As Hayden (2016) observes, religious sites stamp dominance on a landscape in a distinctive way, often through height and audibility. In Cyprus, throughout the British period the island underwent a phase of bell tower and minaret building, as Christians and Muslims competed for visible dominance in the landscape (Hatay 2011, 2015b). In the early part of British rule, Orthodox churches suddenly acquired bell towers, which they began to use for all sorts of audible public and political purposes. British records are filled with reports of bells being rung to gather villagers, and there are also many letters of Turkish Cypriot leaders for whom the ringing of bells spelled trouble (see Bryant 2004).

But Greek Orthodox were not the only ones attempting to make themselves visible: by the 1950s, most sizable Turkish Cypriot villages had attached minarets to their mosques, while others dreamed of having them. In his memoirs of life in 1940s and 1950s Cyprus, poet Taner Baybars eloquently describes the yearnings of the Turkish Cypriot villagers of Vasilya for a minaret and how one schoolfriend was constantly drawing pictures of the mosque with a minaret attached (Baybars 2006: 32). As early as 1957, colonial administrator C. F. Beckingham observed that Turkish Cypriots viewed minarets as community symbols: "Minarets are as conspicuous as church spires are in England and are a matter of pride to Muslim villagers who feel that they proclaim to the traveller the presence of a Turkish community" (1957: 169–170). He also reported, however, that because of the expense of building them, some villages had even considered using prefabricated minarets. Moreover, during this same period, there was frequently competition over the height of the bell tower and minaret in mixed villages, with additions being made to each in order to extend higher than the other (Hatay 2015b). And partly in order to compete with the ringing of bells, Turkish Cypriots began to amplify the call to prayer with megaphones even in the 1950s (Hatay 2015a).

Given these uses of religious sites to achieve a dominant position in the skies, it should not be surprising that converting churches to mosques and building new mosques or minarets became ways of stamping the landscape as Turkish in the post-1974 period.[29] Initially, this involved converting seventy-seven of the five hundred Greek Orthodox churches left in the north into mosques in villages where they had none or where the size of the mosque was not sufficient for the new population.[30] Converting churches into mosques kept buildings intact, but the methods employed involved cleansing the building of all its Christian symbols and artifacts, such as icons, crosses, and bells. It also involved "Islamizing" the structure, initially by adding a conical metal hat and loudspeaker on the belfry, covering the floor of the church with carpets, and placing a *mihrap* or altar facing Mecca. The Evkaf Office, in charge of religious foundations, was responsible for much of this conversion in the initial process of preparing villages for Turkish Cypriot resettlement.

Visibility, however, gained pace in the early 1980s, when villagers began demanding that tall minarets also be added to ensure that the structure appeared to be Muslim. Again, although the Evkaf Office in charge of religious properties funded these minarets, the need and initiative came from villagers themselves. A good example of the desire of villagers to use mosques for visibility was related to Mete by a friend, Okan, who had been displaced from a village in the Limassol district and who served on the mosque committee of his new village. In the mid-1990s, Okan joined a delegation that visited Rauf Denktaş, the former leader of the Turkish Cypriot community, to seek his support to build a mosque in the former Greek Cypriot village where they had resettled:

> When we went to visit Denktaş it was during the fasting days of Ramadan. Denktaş welcomed us at the door of his office and showed us where to sit. He later sat beside us and asked us whether we would like coffee or tea. Without thinking much, we all said yes for the coffee. Following our affirmation, Denktaş started laughing very loudly and asked us what kind of mosque committee we were that doesn't fast on Ramadan. He was right, none of us was religious but the reason for asking a mosque to be built was because the mosque was going to

Figure 9. The mosque of Paşaköy, formerly Assia, an example of the later addition of minarets to churches, which took place in the early 1980s (photo by Rebecca Bryant).

make our village look more Turkish and we, as refugees, would feel more rooted.[31]

However, Okan also added that it took them years after this visit and many other visits to other politicians and the Turkish Embassy to get the mosque built in their village. In other words, the villagers, who were not particularly religious, worked on their own initiative to build a mosque with a minaret in their village. In a similar way, attaching loudspeakers to the bell towers or minarets and blasting the call to prayer five times a day ensured an aural and visual dominance over the landscape.

In puzzling over why the secular Turkish state would enact a policy of "colonization" through "Islamizing" the landscape, Ram remarks, "It became an effective form of signification of the occupied territory as Turkish" (2015: 28). While we agree that this was a way of signifying Turkishness, we have shown that rather than a form of colonization it was part of Turkish Cypriots' long-standing desire for perceptibility. One may also see this in the way that according to a long-time official of the Evkaf Office, what villagers desired most of all were minarets, those visible signs of a "Turkish" presence. One former director of Evkaf remarked to us, for instance, that "the villagers always complain about the other village's minaret, but then they come to me wanting a minaret for themselves." Indeed, so much did they desire minarets that in certain cases where adding a minaret to a church was not feasible or affordable, the villagers would insist on attaching conical hats to the church's bell tower, making it look more like a minaret.

Again, the conversion of churches to mosques, addition of minarets, and transformation of religious sites to other uses was primarily a vernacular "Turkification" that was both a way of living with these remains and an attempt to increase their own perceptibility. It was a way of stamping the landscape as Turkish that had roots in the colonial period and was part of the process of adopting the landscape and making it one's own. However, this was also an obviously factitious process, one that made visible the mechanisms of its own making. A church with a minaret added to it is also one that constantly refers to the violent process of erecting it there. Even more, the addition of mosques and minarets to the landscape creates an irrevocability—not simply a fact on the ground, but a fact that according to international human rights conventions that protect religious heritage, cannot easily be changed.

The image of the church with a minaret attached may act as the symbol for the absurdity that we argue is part and parcel of the way that the factitious both masks and unmasks ideology. The church's minaret nevertheless stands in what Pietz calls its "untranscended materiality" (1985: 7), pointing at one and the same time to its reality *and* its impossibility. This is what we refer to as the "sovereignty" effect, or the effect that creates a sovereignty always bracketed by aporetic quotation marks. These scare quotes or sneer quotes, as they are sometimes labeled, emphasize the so-called, that something is not or cannot be what it claims or appears to be. However, as we remarked in the introduction to this book, such scare quotes have their own absurd exponential multiplication, potentially growing to encompass all around them. As we will see in the next chapter, this factitious absurdity would become most apparent in the process of boosting the north's population and controlling mobility that one parliamentarian referred to as "planting people."

CHAPTER 3

Planting People

Zehra was forty-two years old when she came to Cyprus from the town of Yozgat, in central Anatolia.[1] They had a good life, she says, growing fruits and vegetables in their fields in the summer months and selling them in Ankara, where they had a grocery. A decade before they emigrated, a tape had circulated among their neighbors, and on it a Turkish Cypriot woman described how her family had been killed. Zehra says she used to listen to that tape and feel anger and sorrow for the Turks in Cyprus, though she never expected that the conflict there would result in her son, who was a young military conscript in 1974, being paralyzed by a piece of metal penetrating his brain. He was treated in Ankara and after his recovery was given a house on the north Cyprus coast. He persuaded his parents to come as well, bringing his four siblings.

In those first years, she recounts, they would make the trip to Morphou early in the mornings and, like so many of the Turkish nationals who came to Cyprus during that period, they would work all day in the fields and orchards. "We suffered a lot," she remarks, describing how her second son died in the fields of heart failure at the age of eighteen.

A few months after their arrival, she and her husband requested their own house from the administration and were given one, though she says the only thing they found in it was a broken stove. "The army took away everything,"[2] she observed impassively. "They even took the windows and doors." They invested everything in the house, selling their properties in Yozgat to pay for their third son's wedding and gold for their two daughters when they married. Although her children were born in Turkey, all her grandchildren were born on the island. "I often ask myself if we shouldn't have stayed in Turkey," she remarks as she shows us the loom she uses to weave rugs on winter evenings. "I just want to live in peace."

In her story, Zehra describes a minimal knowledge of Cyprus before her arrival there, a knowledge garnered from a circulating cassette tape. While Turkey had become politically involved in the conflict in the 1950s, the Turkish Cypriot leadership recognized that public momentum would drive Turkey to intervene militarily. That momentum was slowly built through political mobilization in the "Motherland" but also through films, songs, and other techniques, such as circulating cassettes that reached the country's heartland. Still, in 1974, Cyprus was very far from the minds of most Turks and a country about which they knew little. The remoteness of Cyprus from the lives of village Turks is effectively portrayed by Turkish actor and filmmaker Yılmaz Erdoğan (2001) in his box-office hit film *Vizontele*, which ends with the arrival of the first television in Hakkari, on the Iranian border, and with it the news that one of the village boys has been killed in the 1974 Cyprus war.

This chapter addresses the movement and control of people through which the de facto polity emerged in this new space. This constituted the most obvious process of Turkification, in that it literally cleansed the north of non-Turks and planted other Turks from Turkey there. It was also the point at which the lives and futures of people in the north began directly to intersect with newly emerging state practices, discussed in the next chapter. Because over the past decade or so much has been written about the movement of people from Turkey to north Cyprus (see esp. Hatay 2005, 2007, 2008; also Akçalı 2007, 2011; Kurtuluş and Purkis 2008, 2014; Ramm 2006; Talat 2015), our discussion of this social engineering project only summarizes this literature and moves it in a different direction. In the previous chapter, in discussing the vernacular shaping of landscape and territory that we refer to as the sovereignty effect, we remarked, "The materiality of 'adoption' . . . mediates the relationship between people and territory, allowing us to *project belonging* and have it reflected back to us as a *right to belong.*" We show here how this projection of a right to belong produces the *polity effect,* or the effect that allows us to identify which persons belong and have rights in this state—in other words, allows us to identify the de facto polity. We discuss in this chapter how that right to belong was realized in the everyday practices of the state and how, in its realization, a polity effect emerged. If the sovereignty effect produced a sense of separateness, that separateness acquired an inside and an outside through the movement of people and definition of those who had a right to belong that was part and parcel of the emerging de facto polity.

In every standard definition of sovereignty, control of population is an essential element.[3] However, as Caspersen has noted, concern, even anxiety, over population tends to plague de facto states (2012: 84). Most have populations of less than one million—ranging from perhaps 72,000 in South Ossetia[4] to 500,000 in Transnistria[5]—and endured a historical trajectory in which claims to self-determination were tied up with claims to oppression by a hostile majority. Emigration of one's own population during the conflict, combined with immigration, especially from a patron state, once the conflict ends, produces in all such states what Caspersen calls a "demographic crisis" (2012: 84ff; see also Friedman 2015). In many cases, moreover, the sense of demographic danger (Hatay 2008) or demographic threat characterizes much of the history of the conflict. Elsewhere we trace the ways in which a fear of disappearing has characterized Turkish Cypriot politics over more than a century, going back to the island's initial transfer from Ottoman to British rule in 1878 (Bryant and Hatay, in progress b).

After territorial separation from a majority community, that sense of demographic danger or threat has generally transferred from the majority community in control of the parent state to the usually even larger population of the patron state on whom they are dependent. For instance, during initial fieldwork in Abkhazia in 2012, we heard from quite a number of civil society leaders and businesspeople that immigration from Russia—Abkhazia's bordering patron state—endangered their sense of the state as Abkhaz. One civil society leader remarked that there are constant complaints but that "Abkhaz don't want to sweep the streets or wait the tables. They want to run the country. Especially the fighters who say they fought so long to establish it."[6] As we will see in this and the next chapters, it has been precisely this desire to "run the country" and the right to do that established through sacrifice that would define what we refer to here as the de facto polity and its factitious mirror.

Our concern in this chapter is with the way in which "the political and social order of a people becomes spatially visible" (Schmitt 2006: 70). It was in the emergence of a governed space as *theirs*, we argue, that the polity effect emerged. As with the farmers who fought for their water rights, contestation becomes one of the most important elements of the sort of adoption that we claim is at the heart of territorialization. This "space of appearance," as Hannah Arendt (1958: 198–199) called it, is one in which "acting and speaking individuals disclose their unique 'who-ness' as distinct from others" (Dikeç 2012: 672). The polity effect emerges, then, in the process of creating a space for political contention and contestation and particularly in defining who has the right to contest and contend.

The polity effect creates the perception or sense that a group of people has the *right to belong*—those who will "run the country." Jacques Rancière has referred to this sense of differential rights as "the distribution of the sensible," which "establishes at one and the same time something common that is shared and exclusive parts." This distribution, he asserts, "determines those who have a part in the community of citizens" (2004: 12). We explore here how this polity effect emerged first through the movements of persons who for Turkish Cypriots exploded any idea of being part of a larger polity, namely, the Turkish nation.

Migration, suggests Radhika Mongia, has historically been the trigger for "the emergence of nationality as a staunch territorial attachment" (1999: 528). And indeed, immigration produced not only new imaginations of difference but also new attachments to north Cyprus as a contingently defined homeland. This has been accompanied by intense public discussion of and demand for new laws and regulations to control immigration, demonstrating Mongia's contention that borders, "premised on the notion of a nation as a territorially and demographically circumscribed entity" (1999: 528), emerge through efforts to keep certain groups at bay. We then explore the idea of a factitious polity, or a *"polity" effect*—the polity in which the relationship between order and orientation is always on the verge of its own unmaking.

The "Northern" Migrants

Zehra's story of their migration to the island places them at something of an angle to the schemes then available for settling migrants from Turkey. The first protocol reached between the Turkish Federated State of Cyprus and the Republic of Turkey immediately after the former's proclamation in February 1975 included an agreement to transport approximately 30,000 to 50,000 Turkish citizens to the island's north as part of an "agricultural work force" (*tarım iş gücü*). These Turkish nationals were to be given Greek Cypriot property and citizenship in the new state. As should be clear from the previous chapters, this scheme ran in tandem with the expulsion of Greek Cypriots, and in fact the arrival of this group of people that came to be known as settlers preceded the last evacuation of Greek Cypriots by several months.

At the moment that the protocol was signed, the motivation had been to increase the island's Turkish population and have a sufficient workforce to run the many farms and factories that were standing idle. Atun explained, "Some villages and agricultural lands were untended and empty. And at that time the worry and strategy was, 'Let's fill this place up as soon as possible.' . . . There was also a lack of know-how, people [Turkish Cypriot refugees] coming from a grape-growing area couldn't immediately become citrus producers. We needed time. So for that reason, we chose this path." There was a rush, then, both to empty and to fill the territory. There was an anxiety about the empty farms and factories, and as several bureaucrats of the time related to us, a desire to kick-start the local economy.

Moreover, the best-laid plans of technocrats such as Atun encountered difficulties in remote areas, especially the Karpassia (in Turkish, Karpaz) Peninsula, where Turkish Cypriots were reluctant to settle. Not only did the Settlement Department attempt to resettle villages together, but they also attempted to do so in places that resembled the villages they had left behind in the south. However, attempts to do so were often thwarted by Turkish Cypriots' urbanization over the previous decade, when many persons from rural areas had taken refuge in towns and cities and no longer wished to live in villages. Others saw their move to the north as a chance to improve their situation and so wanted to live in urban areas. As a result, İsmet Kotak, head of the Settlement Department, complained, regarding the settlement of the Karpassia, "Even when we've tried to settle villages from the south whose character is suitable, villages where they've worked with vineyards, where they grow Sultani grapes, those people insist on being settled in particular centers, in fact they're insistent and even resistant."[7] In other words, they overturned the best-laid social engineering plans.

As a result of this refusal, Kotak laments, "We find the majority of the Karpaz Peninsula abandoned to the Greek Cypriots," referring to the fact that not only were their social engineering plans thwarted, but after the end of hostilities around 10,000 Greek Cypriots attempted to remain in their villages there.[8] This was considered a strategic problem, as the peninsula is a long finger pointing toward Alexandretta, in Turkey's south. Even more important, however, it was a political problem, as it prompted international pressure on the Turkish Cypriot administration to allow Greek Cypriots to return to the peninsula. The return of the original villagers would, in turn, have reconstituted the peninsula as a primarily Greek Cypriot area. As a result, the administration was concerned with settling the Karpassia in order to maintain its claims to a separate ethnic zone that would form part of the federal state that they were then negotiating.

Earlier, the administration had tried putting out a call for the 30,000 to 40,000 Turkish Cypriots living abroad, especially in the United Kingdom, to return to the island, and they had offered them Greek Cypriot properties in the "free Turkish area." Although there were some who accepted the offer, their number was far less than the administration had expected. It is probable that settling in a postwar landscape, in a house seized from someone else, did not appeal to Turkish Cypriots who were settled in other countries. Some of those who did come were not satisfied with the houses they were offered and returned to their homes abroad. For this reason, the bizonal federation project was in danger, with 18 percent of the island's population holding 36 percent of its land. In order to protect their project of bizonality, social engineering was necessary—part of the project that Kotak called "planting people."

In late 1974, the Constituent Assembly met in a special, closed session to discuss the situation, and the members agreed on the necessity of increasing the population to 200,000. Although a few people in the assembly did mention that a transfer of population could present potential problems for them internationally, the decision for such a transfer was nevertheless approved unanimously. They had already unanimously passed a decision to give citizenship to men who had participated in the 1974 Turkish military operation.[9] After the assembly made the decision, they entered into an agreement with Turkey, which resulted in approximately 30,000 peasants being transferred from Anatolia under the categories "Agricultural Labor" and "Seasonal Labor" and settled in empty villages.

This transfer began almost immediately, with convoys arriving by late spring 1975, long before the last Turkish Cypriots had arrived from the south and before the last Greek Cypriots had been transferred there. One of the troubleshooters of the period related how he took one group of transferees from Turkey to the village where they were to settle, only to find that Greek Cypriots were still occupying it. In other cases, peculiar decisions were made in a rush. Atun, for instance, described how his superior decided to settle the first group of Turkish transferees in a section of the Famagusta neighborhood of Varosha. While most of that formerly Greek Cypriot neighborhood was at the time and remains cordoned off by the Turkish army, what Turkish Cypriots call "open Varosha" (*açık Maraş*) was selected as the site for the first settlement of Turkish transferees. Atun remarked, laughing, "They were nomads! In other words, this is how much enthusiasm there was, and how much of a rush they were in! . . . We said, we can settle the urbanized Limassol and Paphos refugees in this area, and that will relieve us of finding places for them. No! . . . So we had to disperse them, one part to Kyrenia, one part to Morphou, another part to Famagusta." After this initial decision, however, most Turkish nationals were settled in the remote and empty villages that Turkish Cypriots had rejected but that needed to be "filled" and where they would have minimal interaction with Turkish Cypriots in their daily lives.

In much writing about the Cyprus conflict, this group of Turkish nationals who were transported to the island in the period are called "settlers," a word implying both agency and power. The analogies are with settler colonialisms of various sorts, most obviously including Israeli settlers in occupied Palestinian territories. Writing about Israel, David Lloyd remarks, "What distinguishes a settler colony from an administrative or extractive one is in the first place the settlers' focus on the permanent appropriation of land rather than the political and economic subordination of the indigenous population." Moreover, "the expropriation of indigenous land" is necessary "for the express purpose of settling a permanent colonial population" (2012: 66).[10] In these assessments, one of the primary facets of settler colonialism is settlers' active participation in the remaking of a territory (see also Abdo and Yuval-Davis 1995; Moran 2002).

The difference in Cyprus was that these so-called settlers often had little knowledge of Cyprus, coming as they did from some of the most remote areas of Turkey. They were primarily farmers from Turkey's Black Sea and southeastearn regions, and many spoke Greek or Kurdish as their native languages. Others were nomadic shepherds from the Taurus Mountains of the Adana region. They were transferred to Cyprus because the Turkish state in any case needed or wanted to put them somewhere else. In some instances this was because of dam projects, in others because the state wished to settle nomads.

While the project itself may be viewed as a form of settler colonialism, then, the persons who have been called "settlers" might be more appropriately called transferees, or even "exiles" or "deportees," a direct translation of the Turkish *sürgün* that describes population practices employed first by the Ottoman and then by the Turkish states. *Sürgün*, which originally meant banishment or exile, was a preferred practice of the Ottoman and Turkish states for subduing opposition, including entire regions (Babuş 2006). The Turkish Republic also employed it as part of state-building, so that displacement through population transfer was an intrinsic part of constructing the Turkish state from its inception (Chatty 2010; Clark 2007; Gingeras 2011; Hirschon 2003). For the most part, then, these were persons who were trapped between the development projects of the Turkish Republic and the Turkish Cypriot state-building project.

In other words, displacing people as an essential element of state-building was not questioned in this period, and there was general agreement in the Constituent Assembly about how it should occur. In spring 1975, the Constituent Assembly was engaged in writing a new constitution and its laws, including a new citizenship law that everyone there seems to have agreed should include without question soldiers who had fought in the "Peace Operation." In those discussions, a number of parliamentarians remarked on something not found in the minutes, namely, an apparently implicit agreement that the population should double. One parliamentarian, Özker Yaşın, remarked that given that they have found it necessary to increase the population, and "given that this number has been thought of as 200,000," and also given that they have not yet reached that number, they should give priority to Turkish veterans of the 1974 war and to the wives and children of fallen soldiers.

Indeed, the citizenship law gave the extended families of the 498 Turkish soldiers killed in 1974 the right of TFSC citizenship (Günsev 2004: 195–212), although most chose not to come to Cyprus. The same citizenship law also allowed former members of the Turkish "Peace Forces" of all ranks and all Turkish soldiers who had served in Cyprus before 18 August 1974 to become citizens. As a result of this provision, some officers chose to retire on the island, setting up businesses or becoming managers of state-run enterprises, though most did not remain permanently. All of these military personnel were allocated homes and other "resources." Today, there is a Turkish Army Veterans Association on the island with around 1,200 active members, the majority of whom are married to Turkish Cypriots.[11]

Moreover, Yaşın closes his remarks by saying, "Of course, we will feel happiness and joy at having them by our side in the coming struggle, the upcoming economic war." As we discussed in previous chapters, the immediate postwar period was one of urgent state-building, the basis for which was the appropriation of Greek Cypriot "resources" and attempts to make them profitable. The main resources were industrial and agricultural, and there was a lack of what many interviewees called "know-how" to run the enterprises, as well as sufficient manual labor to make use of all the abandoned fields and orchards. They were concerned, then, both to "fill this place up" and to jump-start the economy that would also be the motor for the new state. As a result, the Constituent Assembly recognized the need to bring white-collar workers and technicians to help run the factories and manual laborers to work in the fields.

The white-collar labor force consisted mainly of technicians and administrators who arrived to help repair or build communication and transportation networks, an electricity plant, and the like. Some were also involved in capacity-building, helping to instruct and train Turkish Cypriots in tourism, textile manufacture, agriculture, and other industries. For instance, according to a former manager of Salamis Bay Hotel, then a luxury hotel in the Famagusta area, the Cyprus Turkish Tourism Enterprises, established in November 1974, brought cooks, managers, and other personnel from the Ankara Hotelier School to reopen the establishment. By the end of that year they were ready to receive guests and were able to host a large New Year's Eve party. After the establishment of the TFSC in 1975, those early white-collar workers remaining on the island were offered citizenship and allowed to bring their families (Ioannides 1991: 28–31). Some accepted the offer, and many today live in mixed neighborhoods in urban areas, often married to Turkish Cypriots.

Zehra's immigration to Cyprus lies at something of an angle to these schemes because her son was wounded but not killed in the war, so they did not qualify as a family of "martyrs." Instead, her son received property, and the rest of the family came of its own volition, thereby joining the large number of Anatolian Turks who arrived on the island as an agricultural labor force. The majority of these peasants came to Cyprus between 1975 and 1977. Mete's previously published research on the subject shows that between 1974 and 1981, a total of 21,851 citizenships were issued to Turkish nationals, the largest part of which was to these early transferees (Hatay 2005). Our interviews, however, suggest that the number of original transferees was larger than this and that a significant number of those eligible returned to Turkey without taking up TFSC citizenship. Many interviewees reported that their relatives who chose to return had been unable to adjust to the climate and agriculture, as when one elderly man from the Black Sea region watched the corn he had planted in the spring dry up in the summer or a rancher used to cows found himself chasing goats through the Cyprus mountains.

Hence, although this group is commonly called "settlers," these were set-tlers with no discernible ideological agenda and in many cases only a vague knowledge of where Cyprus was or what it would be like. Of course, there were those who made the journey because they apparently saw Cyprus as a land of opportunity and sought to reap profit from a postwar economy.[12] Turkish journalist Mehmet Ali Birand, who reported from Cyprus at various points during this period, later recalled that "of course during this period a flow from Turkey of thieves, shrewd businessmen, and criminals began in significant number" (Birand 1979: 86). The largest group, however, consisted of those who, like Zehra's family, would become an agricultural labor force.

As Yaşın notes above, the declared aim of the state-building project was to raise the number of ethnic Turks in the island's north to 200,000, a num-ber that administrators believed would justify the territory they held and al-low them to become economically viable. Kotak's metaphor of "planting people" expresses the expectation that their efforts would grow into a flour-ishing economy and state. However, there was an implicit assumption, re-peated on numerous occasions in the minutes of the Constituent Assembly, that these were "also" Turks and so would integrate easily with the Turkish Cypriot community.

Indeed, there were initially no protests against this facilitated migration scheme, which many people recognized as the only way to win what Yaşın called the "economic war." However, it quickly became apparent that the dif-ferences between peasant Turks and rural Cypriots were greater than any-one had anticipated. Indeed, in settling people from various parts of Turkey together, the administration quickly realized that the nationalist ideology of a single Turkish culture conflicted with realities on the ground. Hakkı Atun recounted the administration's first error, when they tried to settle Kurds and Black Sea people together in the same village.[13] Fighting between the groups meant that the administration had to resettle the Black Sea transferees. "And I remember I made a joke then," he recalls. "'Look,' I said, 'the infidel [Greek Cypriot] became a refugee, and he's crying in the south, and we're crying because we can't settle people.'" In this description, we see the attempt at dis-passion of the bureaucrat faced with a postwar landscape and the confronta-tion with people who do not conform easily to social engineering schemes. The people who were the subjects of those schemes had their own local cultures, their own internal hierarchies, and their own dreams and disappointments.

Even early on, Turkish Cypriots reacted to Turkish immigrants' rural background and lack of education, remarking on cultural differences such as dress and appearance. Anthropologist Sarah Ladbury, who carried out fieldwork in north Cyprus in 1976 and 1977, claims, "The mainlander is respected for his fighting ability, but not for his cultural ingenuity ('they saw the legs off tables'), commonsense ('after two years they still ride their bicycles on the right'), or Western ways ('they wear *shalvar*').[14] ... Even the religiosity of the mainlander is used in the process of ethnic delineation ('they build mosques before schools')" (1977: 320–321). Moreover, certain isolated criminal incidents involving Turkish immigrants, such as fights between neighbors or cases of men who were already married in Turkey wedding Cypriot girls, produced a coolness between Turkish Cypriots and the newcomers. The late Turkish Cypriot leader Dr. Fazıl Küçük wrote a series of articles in 1978 criticizing the "immoral behavior" of the settlers, saying that those from the East should be sent back because they were not "civilized" enough to stay in Cyprus: "Thus an 'Eastern sultanate' has been established in many villages. . . . The earlier those who have such bad manners and little civilization that they would even spit in the face of the policeman on duty are sent back to their villages [in Turkey], the earlier they could reach the freedom they desire, and Cypriot Turks and the people who settled on the island could live in peace. Those coming from the western provinces [of Turkey] are as unhappy as we are."[15] These initial criticisms, though, fell from the political agenda for many years, particularly because immigrants tended to be settled in remote villages where they had little contact with Turkish Cypriots.

Instead, most of the vocal criticism of the initial settlement policy primarily concerned the distribution of Greek Cypriot property. Turkish Cypriots resented the government's distribution of the "rewards" of the war, as many of the settlers received empty Greek Cypriot land and property in what appeared an indiscriminate way. Ladbury notes this relationship between the exaggeration of cultural "otherness" and other motivations: "Here the cultural differences between Cypriot Turk and mainland Turk, non-existent to the uninitiated observer, are emphasised and exaggerated by Turkish Cypriots in order to justify their exclusive claim to certain resources which seem to be both scarce and, at present, unjustly distributed" (1977: 318). We will return shortly to the claim that differences with Turkish nationals were exaggerated in order to advance an exclusive entitlement to resources, an observation that returns us to our reflection in the beginning of this chapter regarding the links between contestation, territorialization, and the creation of a polity.

In those eighteen villages where Turkish nationals were settled together with Turkish Cypriots,[16] the neighborhoods and houses that settlers occupy are identifiable as smaller and older than the more modern houses that Turkish Cypriots preferred. In some cases, that preference resulted in antagonism. In the village next to the one where Zehra acquired a house, a squabble over who would obtain particular Greek Cypriot properties led to a fight between settlers and Turkish Cypriots that required the intervention of the Turkish military (Ioannides 1991: 35). However, these outbursts of antagonism were exceptions, as only small pockets of Turkish nationals were settled together with Turkish Cypriots.

At first, the administration attempted to portray these Anatolian villagers to the international community either as Cypriots who had previously emigrated to Turkey and were returning or as seasonal workers. Of course, it would not be long before the truth would come out, and the settlement scheme would be internationally condemned as an attempt to change the demographic character of the island's north. That international pressure, coupled with rising internal opposition, led to the end of this facilitated migration in the late 1970s. Although immigrants afterward continued to arrive of their own volition, these were not part of a settlement scheme. A 1982 amendment to the housing allocation law also eliminated property privileges for immigrants arriving after that date.[17] In addition, because of the 1980 coup in Turkey and restrictions on exit from the country, immigration had by that time declined, and the number of immigrants acquiring citizenship significantly dropped for some time (see Hatay 2007: Appendix 1). A further amendment of the citizenship law in 1993 restricted citizenship rights to persons who had been resident on the island for at least five years.[18]

In much of the writing about this facilitated migration, both popular and academic, authors describe the population transfer as the most obvious act of Turkey's colonization, or "Turkey-fication," of the island's north. What should be clear by now, however, is that this transfer was initially an act of Turkish Cypriot state-building, intended to "fill this place up" and protect the principle of bizonality. We return to the effects of the projected bizonality in a later chapter, but for now we wish to note the unanimity of the Constituent Assembly's decision, a unanimity that included both older, nationalist leaders who may have harbored hopes of separatism and younger, leftist politicians, such as Mustafa Akıncı, who saw state-building as part of the federalism that would ultimately produce "peace."

The equal and indeed enthusiastic involvement of the left in the social engineering project of "planting people" in the new state comes out most clearly in the way that they surveilled implementation to be certain that principles of social justice, discussed in Chapter 5, were being followed.[19] A group of nine opposition MPs formed around their agreement on principles of social democracy, and they began canvassing the villages to track the process of settlement, whether of Turkish Cypriots from the south or of peasants settled from Turkey. For instance, one member of this group, Fuat Veziroğlu, expressed his disappointment with the slowness of the process: "The wives of soldiers who were martyred in the Peace Operation, some with two- or three-year-old children, have been waiting for months in the school garden opposite the barracks, in tin shacks with no heating, shivering on these winter days. These are the wives and children of those who spilled their blood for this land. . . . Every day they're sent like a football from one office to another. Every day they apply to the Settlement Department, to the Prime Ministry, to this ministry and that ministry, and they're given the runaround."[20] He goes on to complain that this treatment of the families of those who shed blood for them was creating a bad impression among their "coethnics" (soydaşlar) who had come from Turkey for the purpose of settling.

From the assembly minutes, then, it is clear that both left and right embraced a plan to Turkify the north through the planting of other people they perceived as Turkish. There was widespread agreement that they needed to increase their population, and there was considerable enthusiasm about using that population influx to create a thoroughly Turkish space as the basis for their state. The initial transfers were rushed, largely because of the panicked perception of technocrats and assembly members that the refusal of their own people to conform to social engineering plans left them vulnerable at the negotiating table. In discussions of a future federalism, how could they claim to keep certain areas within their new, "Turkish" zone if they could not even populate them? How could they make claims to equal representation in the new federal state if their population was only a fraction of the island's total? What would soon become clear, however, was that these "coethnics" would destabilize the relations with their mutual "mother"—which would also bear the brunt of decisions made by her island "children."

The Self That Is Not One

"I was just a child and with some friends, and we were speaking Romaika [Black Sea Greek] among ourselves," describes one man who arrived on the island as a young boy and later would rise to high religious office in the unrecognized state. He recalled his family's fear of this foreign land, with its eerie, empty houses and devastated landscape. One of the fears related by many settlers regarding this period was that Greek Cypriots—to them a faceless enemy—were hiding somewhere in the villages and would attack them. On the day that he describes, he was walking in the street of their new village, speaking Romaika with his friends, when they came across another group of boys. "I would later figure out that they were speaking Kurdish," he says. "But that day we heard the other speaking a language we didn't recognize, and we assumed they were infidels (*gavur*). We fought with each other because neither of us was speaking Turkish."

The story simultaneously shows the hesitation with which the transferees approached this postwar landscape and their marginality, as many belonged to ethnic groups that were denied recognition by the Turkish state. And while the settlement scheme had initially begun as an invitation to "coethnics" to help Turkish Cypriots "fill this place up," the quick realization that these were different sorts of Turks than they had expected—in fact, that many were not Turks at all but rather Laz, Arabs, Kurds, Turcoman, and Greek-speaking Black Sea peoples—led to not only a geographical but also a social and political marginalization. As described earlier, many helped to "fill up" areas of the remote Karpassia Peninsula, as well as certain border villages in the Mesaoria plain. Large numbers of these settlers became agricultural labor, being bussed to various parts of the island at seasons when they were needed. During the citrus harvests in the early spring, for instance, they would board buses from the tip of the Karpassia Peninsula in the island's far east and be driven to the Morphou area in the far west, a trip that at the time took about three hours each way. It was in one of those orange groves that Zehra's son's heart stopped.

By late 1976, almost all of these early settlers had arrived on the island, and the last Turkish Cypriots had been transferred from the south. By that time, moreover, it became clear that small numbers of the Greek Cypriots and Maronites who had been viewed as "intending evacuees" were in fact not intending to leave. While the Vienna Agreement of 1975 had provided for the transfer of populations to reunite families, it had also given certain guarantees to those who wished to remain on the "other" side. Although only 135 Turkish Cypriots chose to remain in the south, many because they were married to Greek Cypriots, several thousand Greek Cypriots and several hundred Maronites attempted to cling to their lands, although their numbers would dwindle as the years passed.

The Maronite community of Cyprus is a small Catholic community that has its roots in Lebanon but arrived on the island in the seventh century. When the Republic of Cyprus was established in 1960 with a power-sharing constitution along ethnic lines, the tiny Maronite community—along with the minority Armenian, Roma, and Latin communities—had to make a choice to "join" the Greek Cypriot or Turkish Cypriot communities. Only the Roma, who were predominantly Muslim, were placed under the Turkish Cypriot community according to the constitution, while the smaller Christian communities "became" Greek Cypriot.

As a result, not only Greek Cypriots but also Maronites remaining in the island's north were subject to harassment, surveillance, and restrictions on movement, although by most reports the situation of Greek Cypriots was considerably worse (Dayıoğlu 2014). The approximately five hundred Greek Cypriots remaining in the north by the 1980s were enclaved in the tip of the Karpassia Peninsula, surrounded by Turkish nationals who had been settled there precisely to protect the territory from demands that it be given back to what they anticipated would become a Greek Cypriot constituent state in the process of negotiations. It was in one of these villages that the man quoted above had been settled as a boy. Maronites, however, were confined to a set of villages on the Kormakiti Peninsula in the west, an area that had been Maronite since the twelfth century.

Both Greek Cypriots and Maronites had to receive permission to leave the villages where they were confined, although by most reports this was easier for Maronites. It was difficult for both groups to see their families in the island's south, and restricted educational opportunities in their own languages meant that families with children mostly dwindled away, gradually making their way south of the borderline. Although their situation would begin to change in the late 1990s, for at least the first two decades, these small communities effectively remained imprisoned within their natal villages.

We see, then, that even in the establishment of this new territory there were certain "others" who either had been invited to come or allowed to remain but who were not perceived as part of the de facto polity. These Others were not evicted from that polity but were literally marginalized within it, settled or allowed to remain in the two peninsulas, Karpassia and Kormakiti, through which most Turkish Cypriots never had to pass. Indeed, the Karpassia Peninsula is the one place where Greek Cypriots would live with Turkish speakers, though these would be settlers from Turkey, many from the marginalized groups mentioned above. Although a *modus vivendi* eventually emerged, perhaps aided by the fact that quite a number of the settlers spoke a form of Greek as their native tongue, the first years were reportedly quite difficult, and tensions eased only as children who had no experience of the war began to mingle together.

Although Turkish Cypriots knew of the plight of the remaining Greek Cypriots and Maronites, they effectively viewed these communities as leftovers—what Dan Rabinowitz (2001) calls "trapped communities"—and as such saw them as suspect. In terms of philosopher Giorgio Agamben, they became sovereign exceptions, persons subject to an exceptional regime. Although Maronites were able to cross to the south to see their families, and their families were able to cross to see them, this also put them under suspicion of spying and made them the objects of surveillance. While two Maronite villages became military zones, there was no principle of nationalizing Maronite property in the way that Greek Cypriot "enemy" property was nationalized. Nevertheless, Maronites were, like Greek Cypriots in the Karpassia, politically, socially, and geographically marginalized (Dayıoğlu 2014).

Although some original transferees from Turkey received property in neighborhoods of the Kyrenia area or in Mesaoria villages, they nevertheless often found themselves isolated from their Turkish Cypriot neighbors. Certainly, they were excluded for several decades from positions of power and from access to resources of the new state, especially coveted civil service jobs. While the remaining Christian communities were marginalized in enclaves, settlers were also both geographically and politically excluded from the center.[21] While Christians remaining in the north were leftover or trapped communities, the new settlers disturbed Turkish Cypriots' sense of Turkishness or of the north as a Turkish space. Indeed, illiterate peasants in *shalvars* were the "backward" Other to the Turkish nationalism that Turkish Cypriots had embraced. When Dr. Küçük said, "Those coming from the western provinces [of Turkey] are as unhappy as we are," he referred to those Westernized Turks—probably white-collar workers and some military officers—who had come to help jump-start the economy and were emblems of a "modern" Turkish nationalism. For that Turkish nationalism, the "backward" in the national self had always been its most important, and dangerous, Other (see Bryant 2004).

Both groups, then, were abjected, what Julia Kristeva (1982) describes as a process of exclusion from the self of that which is close but intolerable— what she calls "the me that is not me."[22] Their geographical marginalization was an abjection that made them unseen, and therefore unthought, parts of the newly developing polity. The enclavement of Greek Cypriots and Maronites and control of their movement meant that for more than two decades after the establishment of the so-called state, Turkish Cypriots would have little reason to encounter or think about these groups. The settlers, however, could not be entirely marginalized, as they had been given citizenship.

Instead, settlers produced an unsettling of identification, a new understanding of the boundaries of the polity. This was not, however, simply because they became a new Other, as some scholars have argued (e.g., Akçalı 2011; Navaro-Yashin 2006, 2012; Özsağlam 2003), but more complexly because they represented what Kristeva would call a "narcissistic crisis" (1982: 209). For Kristeva, the narcissistic crisis emerges in the struggle between language and ego, or what she refers to as the child's struggle between an imaginary father and imaginary mother in which the mother must be abjected in order for the child to emerge in language. Adapting Kristeva, we may say that it was precisely the encounter with the "real" children of the imaginary mother, the "Motherland," that led to an irresolvable narcissistic crisis in which their abjection of the base, or backward, in that imaginary mother seemed to mirror a sense that they themselves were abjected, or had never been that mother's child at all.

If a sense of separateness created the boundaries of a de facto territory, then, abjection within created the *polity effect*, defining the boundaries of who would have full rights in the new state, particularly access to the resources of that new order. Simultaneously, however, Anatolian settlers came to represent factitious constructions of difference, their presence being based on but at the same time exploding the idea that this community of persons grouped together in the north was a polity as Turks and hence part of the larger Turkish nation. Although they exploded this factitious idea of the polity as Turkish, however, the settlers' presence in the island *as Turks* was necessary in order to secure the de facto polity.

As a result, the presence of Anatolian settlers on the island produced a *"polity" effect* that contained its own absurd masking and unmasking. On the one hand, there was the factitious unmasking of the polity as a "Turkish polity in Cyprus" through the settlers' abjection; on the other hand, there was the masking of the settlers as "brothers" who had come to aid in the "economic struggle." So, while their presence in the island exploded the idea of all being "brothers of the same mother," at the same time it *could not* explode that idea precisely because the realization of this through the sense of separateness that emerged with the new polity was dependent on their presence on the island as Turks. For instance, when discussing the new citizenship law of the TFSC, one representative commented, "Greek Cypriots keep proclaiming that they're the government and Turks are a minority or a community. The only thing they use to demonstrate this is their outnumbering us. I hope that with the law we've just passed we'll soon reach a number equal to Greek Cypriots."[23] The polity, then, contained an aporia from its beginning, not only because Turkish Cypriots were Turks who could never fully become ones but equally importantly because the realization of their own claims to agency relied on the impossibility of that difference.

"Facts on the Ground"

Sovereignty claims, Danilyn Rutherford (2012) argues, are always performed before audiences. Certainly, various audiences, such as the United Nations, the United States, and the Turkish public, seem constantly to have been in the minds of Turkish Cypriot state-builders as they attempted to negotiate the ground between the de facto and the de jure. As we show in Chapter 4, quite complex discussions ensued in the Constituent Assembly, and later in the parliament, over how they might appropriate property and what sort of state-building they might pursue without creating legal complications in the future.

In contrast to the complex discussions and reports of the Legal Committee regarding property and statehood, it is particularly interesting that the international audience does not seem to have been a factor in the decision to boost the north's population. Rather, the way in which all discussions and directives regarding the transfer were kept confidential suggests that they knew all along that what they were doing would be unacceptable, but they did it anyway. Moreover, as we stressed above, political leaders from all ends of the ideological spectrum enthusiastically supported the idea, in fact so enthusiastically adopted it that the parliamentary minutes are filled with references to a population of 200,000—their proclaimed goal, meaning a boost of another 85,000 persons. In an unrelated discussion from September 1975, for instance, leftist leader Özker Özgür remarked in passing that "two hundred thousand people live within this state's borders,"[24] thereby confusing their professed goal with the reality.

Although international audience was not a factor in the decision to transfer populations, this does not mean that Turkish Cypriot political leaders were not keenly aware of it. They simply did what many people caught in such a bind would do: they obfuscated and lied. For many years, authorities in the north refused to address claims of demographic engineering, asseverating that they made no distinction between their citizens in terms of place of birth and refused to provide the relevant data (Ladbury 1977: 318–319).[25] A good example of such denial comes from the TFSC's former minister of foreign affairs Vedat Çelik, who in 1975 sent a letter to U.N. secretary general Kurt Waldheim complaining that

> The allegation that there is a massive immigration of Turkish nationals from Turkey to Cyprus with the purpose of changing the demographic character of the island within a pre-planned partition project is not only completely contrary to the truth but also a distortion of the actual facts. All that is taking place is that skilled technicians and workers are being imported from Turkey on a temporary basis as "guest workers" to meet the immediate needs of the economy. . . . There is no question of these people acquiring Cypriot citizenship or taking up permanent residence in the island.[26]

Çelik also claimed that the majority of persons who migrated to north Cyprus after 1974 were Turkish Cypriot returnees who had left the island during the British period due to Greek Cypriot social and economic pressure or during the intercommunal conflicts of 1963 to 1974 (Ioannides 1991: 3).

The absurdity of this situation was that just as everyone knew that the Turkish Cypriot administration was obfuscating and even lying, the Turkish Cypriot administration also knew that everyone knew this. Despite the efforts of the Turkish Cypriot side to downplay the claims of a population transfer, even the press in Turkey picked up the issue. In 1976, for instance, then president Rauf Denktaş was angered by interviews published in Turkish newspapers and remarked, "When we say to the world, 'By God, we didn't bring immigrants from Turkey,' we're saying, they're not immigrants, they're [temporary] agricultural workers. But what does our press do? They go and get statements from the immigrants themselves that start with, 'You see, I came here as an immigrant . . .' with the idea that they're going to criticize us, but in fact they're providing information for the U.N. and the Greeks" (Köklüçınar 1976: 83).

Such attempts to conceal the extent of the initial migration had the effect of undermining the credibility of any information Turkish Cypriot authorities supplied on the issue (Ioannides 1991: 18–23). Ultimately, it would even undermine their credibility with their own constituents (see Bryant in progress). Indeed, the lack of information produced speculation, and the assumption was that the number of settlers must be quite large if the administration took such pains to hide it. In a 1992 study, for instance, figures for the numbers of settlers given by various Turkish Cypriot political party leaders ranged from 17,000 to 60,000.[27]

This peculiar obfuscation—this lie that everyone knew was a lie—makes more sense if we see it as based on a cynical Realism, one that simultaneously asserts the irreversibility of some "facts on the ground" even as it recognizes the need to deny them or to mask them as something else. Žižek observes that in the contemporary cynical attitude, "ideology can lay its cards on the table, reveal the secret of its functioning, *and still continue to function*" (1996: 200). In the case at hand, it seems that this peculiar lie that was already laid on the table, or fiction that was always already unmasked, was the simultaneous masking and unmasking of the de facto itself, that species of the real that is always already a denial of its own existence. It was precisely through the lie that everyone knew was a lie that Turkish Cypriot leaders unmasked the international community's inability to do anything about it.

All of this meant that even as the planting of people created a "force-field of a particular order" that we might call a de facto polity, that polity was aporetic from the beginning, constantly dissolving into descriptions of it as a province or colony of Turkey. It was in the process of planting people, of inflating the polity in order to ensure bizonality and strengthen one's hand in negotiations, that Turkish Cypriots encountered the impossibility of defining that polity, as their attempts to do so began to appear not simply fabricated but false. This was where, in the "ordering of the Order," the "inconsistencies and splittings" that "allow the edifice of Order to maintain itself" (Žižek 1996: 3) were present from the very beginning. Schmitt's "force-field of a particular order," then, relied from its foundation on elements that we have called factitious. The extent to which Turkish Cypriots perceived those factitious elements as factual or fabricated appears to have depended in large part on the extent to which they believed that they were able to control their own fate through the institutions of a so-called state.

PART II

ENACTING THE APORETIC STATE

Figure 10. Protests of U.N. resolutions against the so-called
state (Özer Hatay archive).

It has passed its constitution, completed free elections, chosen its parliament, and formed its government. There is no doubt about this. But it is not yet a State, only its name is State. It is hard for it to trade with other states. It is difficult for it to establish transportation possibilities. No one recognizes its passport. Foreign planes cannot land at Ercan airport, and foreign ships cannot approach its ports. The state does not even have its own money. Everything happens, but by finding a solution, or a work-around. In other words, this State resembles a pirate State. How long can this situation continue? Undoubtedly piracy must have an end. (Bil 1976: 4)

OUR FRIEND CENGIZ was a child in the 1950s, in the time of the Federation of Turkish Cypriot Associations (KTKF), the proto-state that represented Turkish Cypriots' first real attempt at institutionalization. He had just entered high school when the intercommunal conflict in 1963 displaced his family to a neighboring village, where they spent the next ten years in makeshift housing. Cengiz became a fighter in the state-within-a-state that administered the Turkish Cypriot enclaves, in the late 1960s taking up a scholarship for former combatants (*mücahit bursu*, literally fighter's scholarship) at a Turkish university. He was working in Ankara when the Turkish military offensive happened, and by the time he could return to the island, the entire space of Cyprus had been transformed.

When his family arrived in the north, he remarked, their experience of the enclaves made it seem an enormous space, with its new houses and factories and hotels. It was for them, he says, "a place of abundance," one that "even sharing out among themselves we couldn't use up." He goes on to observe,

That community began to see itself as a group that was starting to administer itself, starting to institutionalize. And suddenly they established a state. Actually, it's very interesting. In the rest of the world guerrillas fight independence wars to establish states. The Kurds, the Sandinistas, the Basques. Here all of a sudden a state happened. But because Cyprus's conjunctural situation has always been read differently, and because we always read it differently, this strange—that is, we couldn't find a name for anything. . . . They say, "country." "Our country." I can't ever digest that word, I can't make it fit. We just couldn't make it work.

Of course, Cengiz's own experiences of Turkish Cypriot institutionalization over the two decades leading to 1974 suggest that when he says, "Suddenly they established a state," he does not refer to a lack of preparation for statehood.

Rather, when he asserts that "all of a sudden a state happened," he refers to the fact that having an independent state, with its own borders and territory, had simply never been on the agenda. The "reverse reasoning" and "exciting situation" Cengiz refers to is the way that even as they were planning for a federal state that would reunite north and south, they were engaged in creating the north as a "country." However, when Cengiz says, "I can't digest that word, I can't make it fit," he refers to the way that their own sense of belonging in that place was also aporetic from its very beginning. At the same time that this "country" was emerging, people seem to have been acutely aware that they could not and should not expect an independent state. "Cyprus's conjunctural situation has always been read differently," Cengiz remarks. Because of this, he suggests, "We couldn't find a name for anything" (adını koyamadık hiç bir şeyin). Were they a state or not? Were they a country or not? Was the land they worked to be theirs or not?

Part II concerns not being able to find a name for anything, or what we call here the *aporia of recognizability*. We build on Judith Butler's observation that "one 'exists' not only by virtue of being recognized, but, in a prior sense, by being *recognizable*" (Butler 1997a: 5). In this book, when we use the word *recognizability* in reference to a state, then, we mean it both in the usual sense of "capable of being (legally) recognized" and in the Butlerian sense of a recognizability that is prior to that. The latter is what we have called the *factum* of the de facto, something that we identify as state-ness, or the "reality" of a state. It is, however, recognition that would *realize* that, making it a *real* state. This is why even nationalist Turkish journalist Hikmet Bil would observe, in the epigraph above, that the entity he found in north Cyprus was "not yet a State, only its name is State."[1]

The aporia of recognizability, then, emerges from the distinction between the *reality* of a state, something recognizable in its state-ness, and the always present knowledge that "only its name is State," as Hikmet Bil commented in the epigraph, because it was not an entity that would ever be realizable. In its unrealizability it is the state that cannot be named, the state whose name—that which is supposed to represent it—remains unspeakable and censored. Butler's remarks, above, regarding recognizability occur in a discussion of naming, in which she observes that "to be addressed is not merely to be recognized for what one already is, but to have the very term conferred by which the recognition of existence becomes possible. One comes to 'exist' by virtue of this fundamental dependence on the address of the Other" (Butler 1997a: 5). Butler writes specifically of names, particularly racial and other slurs, and her concern is with the power of words to wound. But what of the case in which naming is impossible, always already foreclosed? What if one remains unnamed and unnameable?

Part I showed the construction of "the north" as a separate space and how a de facto territory emerges as a perceptible entity, despite all efforts to deny its existence. Part II describes ways in which the practices and orders that emerged in that space took on the characteristics of what we identify as state-ness. In particular, we are interested in the "where" of the state—what Timothy Mitchell described as the state-society boundary, or the production of "the uncertain yet powerful distinction between state and society" (1991: 85). Our concern is with the "mesh of practices and orders" of "people, artifacts, organisms, and things" (Schatzki 2002: 123) that enable the "where" of the state, or its site, to emerge.

The next chapters describe the practices of statecraft, the building of an economy, and the declaration of sovereignty that allow us to identify the site of the state. Throughout, our puzzle is not simply or even primarily identifying what would allow us to call an entity a state but rather asking how it is that we may recognize state-ness when we see it but still be unable to use that word to describe it. What is puzzling is the unpronounceability of the word *state* in regard to de facto entities, the denial of the name through the use of aporetic quotation marks ("state").

What we call the aporia of recognizability is what stifles language, makes one unnameable, turning something that we identify as a state into a "state" and its ministers into "ministers." The aporia produces something that even nationalist Turkish journalist Bil remarked "resembles a pirate State." The "pirate state" is, of course, one very common way of describing entities that exist outside the Westphalian order of recognized, sovereign states.[2] Interestingly, however, such states are usually simultaneously cast as puppets of other, larger states who are their patrons. As we discuss in Chapter 6, this "puppet/pirate dilemma" is a symptom of the aporia of recognizability,

presenting Turkish Cypriot state-builders with the choice between an attribution of no will and one of too much will or the wrong kind of will (see
Ahmed 2014). We argue there that the aporia of recognizability is one in
which the very acts that make them visible and perceptible take away the
sovereign agency that would come with recognition.

Our focus on recognizability rather than recognition also allows us to address the issue of audience—particularly the "international community"—
in state-building. While it should be clear that audience was always on people's
minds and that the "international community" determined what Cengiz
called the "conjunctural situation," state-building was happening in any case,
but people living in the island's north had to find ways around that "situation." Bil's definition of the "pirate state" was one in which "everything happens, but by finding a solution, or a work-around." In practical terms, then,
enactments of statecraft often contained their own factitious elements, in
which one realized the functions of a state that was "managing" or "getting
around" the international order.

It is in the "work-around," the tactics of "managing" or "getting by" in
the international order, that we find again the question of will—of wanting
the "wrong" thing or wanting it in the "wrong" way, such that one's agency
is impeded at every step. Moreover, as we shall see, this hampered or handcuffed will and the acknowledgment of that will's impossibility was already
part of the so-called state from its inception. This is what Mustafa Akıncı
meant, in the introduction, when he remarked that for leftists of the period,
federation was "the possible solution. Apart from that any other idea for a
solution was not a solution for us. We believed there could be no other alternative." Here we find the usual distinction drawn between domestic and
international, or between internal and external, sovereignty (see also Dunn
2009: 224; Kapferer 2004; Kapferer and Bertelson 2009) collapsing in the
recognition that Cyprus's "conjunctural situation" did not allow them to
expect independence or recognition. That distinction collapses when the
"work-around," or the discursive rejection of their statehood—acknowledgment of what is "possible," or "the conjunctural situation"—is built into
the very practices of the state itself.

Indeed, while the entity that emerged bore all the marks of state-ness, allowing it to be labeled a de facto state in the first place, *it was through being
recognized as a "state"* rather than as a *state*. When Cengiz says, "We couldn't
find a name for anything," it is a way of acknowledging the aporia that stifles
language, in which de facto separateness and state-ness are couched in a

rhetoric of repudiation. As we shall see, discursive disavowal of what one wills becomes part of the everyday tactics of enacting the de facto state, part of the "work-around." So to say, "We couldn't find a name for anything," is a way of expressing that life may go on within quotation marks, but it is a life in which one has to behave *"as if."* However, behaving *"as if"* is not the same as behaving *as if*: while the latter suggests disbelief, the former suggests an appearance of disbelief. While the latter suggests that one accepts the "conjunctural situation" that makes a state impossible, the former suggests that one accepts that one must *appear to* accept that conjunctural situation. It is this distinction, as we will see, that defines the difference between the factitious as false and the factitious as crafted.

CHAPTER 4

The So-Called State

In the mid-1950s, Mete's mother bicycled every day from their home immediately outside Nicosia's walls to attend St. Joseph Lycee, a Catholic girls'
school run by nuns. Her father, a messenger for the British commissioner of
Nicosia, paid the tuition for her and her two sisters by working a second job
as a barman at the Nicosia Club, an elite sports club of the sort that British
administrators established in other colonies. The nuns taught her French and
English, and she learned Greek from her interactions with the other students.
Her language skills would serve her well at graduation, when she was offered
a civil service job in the newly established Republic of Cyprus. She began in
the currency department but was quickly assigned to the car registry office
because it was close to her home. She also married immediately after her graduation, and Mete was born two years later.

When the intercommunal violence of late 1963 began, "the next day the
Greek Cypriots didn't come. I phoned, I went and looked, there were one or
two people there." Within about a week, her Greek Cypriot colleagues had
packed and moved the entire office to southern Nicosia, the "Greek side." She
spoke to her supervisor: "I said, should I come, too? He said 'no, *kyria*
Müzeyyen. I have your telephone number; if everything is safe, I'll phone
you.' That telephone call never came."

Instead, like other Turkish Cypriot civil servants of the RoC, she was
quickly incorporated into the institutional structures that immediately sprang
up in the enclaves and that soon took the form of a state-within-a-state. She
was first assigned to the Settlement Office, where Hakkı Atun had worked,
and for several months she assisted with finding housing and clothing for displaced persons. The establishment of the RoC had given Turkish Cypriots

their own Communal Chamber (Cemaat Meclisi), as well as representatives in the parliament. Within their armed ghettos, the Communal Chamber and parliamentary representatives quickly reconstituted in a type of enclave parliament, and soon both Mete's mother and one of her sisters were working as secretaries there. She remained there after 1974, when the Turkish Administration of Cyprus evolved first into the Autonomous Turkish Cypriot Administration and then, in February 1975, into the Turkish Federated State of Cyprus. In this period, she initially joined the Ministry of the Interior, and among her other tasks in that period was compiling the paperwork and maps for the debates over toponym changes that we discussed in Chapter 2. After the TFSC's first election in 1976, she would be recruited to become secretary to its first prime minister, a post in which she served for two years until a change of government. Afterwards, she went to work in the administration of Cypruvex, a state company in charge of packaging the oranges picked by workers such as Zehra and her family, described in Chapter 3.

We give this example for what it shows us about the utterly unexceptional ways in which average persons, with their needs and expectations, were incorporated into the emerging structures of a new state. These are persons who have lived with the state, who expect a state, who have in mind the "idea of the state" (Abrams 1988) and what it should be. These are persons who have in mind how those structures should work and who criticize them when they do not. Contrary, then, to a strand of anthropological and sociological literature focused on resistance to the state (especially influenced by Scott 1976, 1985; cf. Vincent 1978)—or as the title of one classic text has it, "society against the state" (Clastres 1977)—these are persons for whom the state is desired and normalized, indeed one of the primary ways in which one produces "normal lives" (esp. Jansen 2014, 2015; also Fehérváry 2002; Greenberg 2011).

This chapter explores statecraft, a form of enacting the state whose practices form what Timothy Mitchell called the the "state/society boundary" (1991). As Mitchell notes, this boundary "is not a simple border between two free-standing objects or domains, but a complex distinction internal to these realms of practice" (1991: 85). That boundary defines the "where" of the state, what we have called the site of the state, which emerges through such expectations of what a state should be and do. We describe here how Turkish Cypriots in the immediate post-1974 period set about enacting the state through the bundle of practices that constituted statecraft, or the art and practice of governing, with its materialities, structures, and institutions. "These processes," notes Mitchell, "create the effect of the state not only as an entity set apart from society, but as a distinct dimension of structure, framework, codification, planning, and intentionality" (1991: 95).

We build on other recent ethnographic works that have similarly described the ways in which practices materialize the state, appearing to give it a "reality" and to distinguish it from society.[1] However, we also show how the practices of statecraft are performed for an audience that expects and anticipates the state, and in situations such as war expects and anticipates the (re)creation of the state as an externality, something separate from society. This is the sort of externality that, in north Cyprus, people expected to provide for refugee settlement and to provide jobs for civil servants who had lost them because of the conflict. We have earlier called what they were doing "enacting the state," where enacting is what J. L. Austin (1955) would call an illocutionary act, or a saying that is also a doing, something that creates what it declares. A judge pronouncing sentence or a couple taking wedding vows are instances of saying that are also doing or enacting. In order to achieve this illocutionary effect, however, there must be an audience that understands the speech act and accepts the authority of those who perform it. We will discuss in Chapter 6 the truncated nature of this illocution when it came to international audiences. This chapter addresses the expectations of those persons used to living with the state, those persons whose acceptance of one's statecraft are necessary to the creation of the state's externality, what Mitchell (1991) called its structural effect. We will see the ways in which the state emerged as a structural effect precisely through Turkish Cypriots' expectations of the state's intervention.

Something that might be called a state began to emerge in north Cyprus in the way that local politicians and bureaucrats conducted business that both they and others defined as belonging to "the state." Turkish Cypriot state-building is particularly interesting for looking at the emergence of a state-society boundary, or the state as an externality, not only because of its aporetic nature but also because the size of the polity makes it easy to think of such state-builders as "playing at" state-making. As we noted in Chapter 3, de facto states tend to have tiny polities, and the Turkish Cypriot state's population at its inception was around 60,000 Turkish Cypriots already in the north and later around 140,000 after the flight or exchange of 55,000 Turkish Cypriots from the south and the transfer of about 25,000 Turkish settlers. The size of the polity meant that the "state effect" could never be quite the "powerful, metaphysical effect" that Timothy Mitchell argues allows the state as such to appear to exist as a structure (1991: 94).

This does not mean, however, that people do not perceive, act in, act against, and long for something that they think of as "the state." We take much of our material in this chapter from the thousands of pages of transcripts of discussions and debates in the initial Constituent Assembly that was to write the new state's constitution and later from the assembly of the Federated State. What makes this material of ethnographic interest is partly our personal knowledge of the persons involved—some of whom are friends, others of whom are persons that Mete knew through his parents—making it possible to see, for instance, how their views and discourse about the state may have changed over time.

Equally important for us, however, is that everyone knows these persons or at least has ways to reach them. In other words, the size of the polity and the importance of kinship, village, and neighborhood networks mean that the verticality and encompassment of state institutions (Ferguson and Gupta 2002) are compromised from their inception. As a result, in studying these transcripts, we do not take them at face value or understand them as the distant pronouncements of elites on the fate of the masses. Rather, we read them while putting often rather vibrant personalities to names and while having in mind the trajectories of these persons' lives and careers.

What we see from this period is how the structural effect of the state emerges not only through performance but also through expectations of what that performance should be and critiques of the performance when it does not live up to expectations. In the assembly minutes, what comes through strongly is legislators' performance according to the norms of what they took to be good governance and statecraft, through their performances creating institutions and institutional histories that constituted the state's structural effect. In the process, they also enacted an externality, defining the boundaries of the state as separate from the society that they saw themselves representing.

Of course, these practices of state*craft* are never entirely separable from the problem of state*hood,* the concern of Chapter 6. State*hood* relies not only on expectation but also on validation, and particularly the willingness of external actors to see one as a state, that is, to recognize it. Jansen (2015) draws a similar analytical distinction between what the state does and should do (state*craft*) and what the state is and should be (state*hood*). Although he notes that concerns with what the state does or should do often slip into discussions of what the state is or should be, invoking its legitimacy or questions about it, Jansen tries to hold this slippage at bay to investigate what people long for when they long for a functioning state.

While Jansen's novel approach is focused on average citizens' reified category of "the state" and what it does or is, however, our concern is with institutions that are still being built and with what people think they are doing when they build them. What we find there is a distinction between the *recognizability* of a state as externality emerging through the practices of statecraft and an always present consciousness that *realizing* the state, that is, statehood, was not entirely up to them. The impossibility of statehood or having a "real" state was reflected, for instance, in the ways that legislators constantly planned for that state's potential dissolution. That potential dissolution was reflected in the refusal to give title deeds to property and in fine distinctions that they tried to draw between "nationalizing" (*devletleştirme*) assets and "expropriating" (*kamulaştırma*) them. It was reflected in legislators' insistence that their state was one leg of a potential federal one, even though that potential federal entity depended on Greek Cypriots accepting a federation—a potentiality that has not been realized at the time of writing.

As we will describe here, then, even as Turkish Cypriot representatives and bureaucrats set about enacting the state, that is, both acting like a state and realizing the practices of one, they were confronted with the factitiousness of those enactments, which we will call *"state"craft*. In those enactments, then, the de facto emerged in the practice of statecraft, which mostly entailed the distribution of Greek Cypriot "resources" and the debates around their distribution. However, at the very same time, the factitious emerged in the locutions, obfuscations, and instances of fudging statehood—what we call *"state"craft*—where the presumed immanent dissolution of their state was always felt.

Enacting the State

In February 1975, only six months after a cease-fire was declared, the Constituent Assembly (Kurucu Meclis) of the new Turkish Federated State of Cyprus assembled in a yellow stone building facing the central square of northern Nicosia to begin writing the new state's constitution. During the period of the Temporary Turkish Administration of Cyprus, established in 1967, the Legislative Assembly had incorporated the fifteen elected Turkish Cypriot members of the RoC parliament and thirty elected members of the Turkish Cypriot Communal Chamber. The latter was one of two ethnically defined bodies set up within the RoC constitution to address the educational, cultural, and civil affairs of the two communities. All of the members of these chambers were nationalists of various stripes, having become politically active at a time when the main issue on the communal agenda was resisting Greek Cypriot demands for union with Greece.

When the new Constituent Assembly convened for the first time in February 1975, however, that body included not only the nationalist leaders who had predominated in the Communal Chamber and parliament but also representatives of unions and associations, thereby embracing an opposition. For instance, Fatma Sezer, the only female member of the assembly, was the secretary of the Pharmacists' Union, which selected her to represent it. Others joined as representatives of the Physicians' Union, the University Graduates Union, and similar organizations. Many of these representatives were young leftists educated in Turkey, and two were members of the left-wing Republican Turkish Party (Cumhuriyet Türk Partisi, hereafter CTP), which had been founded in 1971.

These relatively young representatives, most newly returned to the island, participated in the assembly with their own visions of what a democratic state should be. We discuss at length in the next chapter the opposition politics that emerged during this period. What is particularly interesting for us is that even leftists who today are critical of the so-called state recall the excitement of that time, when the "freedom" of having their own space also meant for them democratic freedom from the dictates of what they had come to call the BEY regime, an acronym that stood for the three parts of the enclave administration: the military commander, the Turkish embassy, and the Turkish Cypriot administration itself (Bayraktar, Elçilik, Yönetim). For instance, Fatma remarked to us, "Look! Until then there was no democracy, there was the Denktaş regime. For the first time there would be a constitution. For the first time a different kind of council was forming. It was the kind of democracy we were longing for!"[2] It appeared at the time, even to the left, that the way to realize the longing for a particular type of politics was through a space and a state that would be "their own."

As a result, the left engaged enthusiastically and vociferously in debates over the new state's constitution and, as we will see later, was quite concerned with the problem of the state's foundation. Even as legislators assembled in early 1975 to discuss the foundation of their new state, negotiations to establish a federation of two ethnically defined constituent states were ongoing between Turkish Cypriot and Greek Cypriot leaders. At the time, their Greek Cypriot interlocutors offered other alternatives to a bizonal federation, such as a cantonal one composed of several rather than only two constituent states. Even in the midst of uncertainties about the form their state would take in the future, however, offices were being established, representatives were sent to foreign countries, transports of people arrived from Turkey, and state-building proceeded apace.

The assembly debated a constitution that finally passed at referendum more than a year later, in the spring of 1976, and in the summer of that year there were hotly contested elections. Even as all this was going on, however, the state was being enacted through practices of statecraft. As we see from the example of Mete's mother's career, there were already institutions in place on which the new state could be built, and those institutions simply continued within their "new freedom borders" after 1974. Despite this, however, we see ways in which legislators were distinctly concerned with the new state's establishment or foundation, with how to make it a "real" and effective state.

We see this initially in the way that they gave this new entity the name Turkish Federated State of Cyprus (Kıbrıs Türk Federe Devleti) in anticipation of a negotiated solution in which they would join in a federal state with Greek Cypriots. The name, in other words, was intended from the beginning to deny a desire for independence by suggesting that they saw themselves as a constituent entity of a federal state that did not yet exist. The federal state, they understood, was the "possible" state, the only state that would be a "real" one. At the same time, they were quite aware of the "reality." For instance, early on in the assembly's discussions, businessman and legislator Ali Süha remarked, "It is a reality and a fact that after the 20 July Peace Operation our community attained new opportunities. *This Community established an administration, it established a State, whatever its name may be* (*Adı ne olursa olsun, bu Toplum idaresini kurmuş, Devletini kurmuş*), and it is now in the process of making the organs of that state and the functions of that state work properly" (authors' italics).[3] The phrase we have translated here as "whatever its name may be" (*adı ne olursa olsun*) could also, in this context, be translated as "its name is irrelevant," or "whatever name we may choose for it," implying that whatever name they gave to it at that time or would give to it in the future, the "reality" was that there was an administration and a state. As we will see below, this aporia between the reality of the administration or state that they had founded and the impossibility of naming it would ultimately be reflected as a distinction between the practices and orders of something that could only be called a state and those practices and orders that demanded that they behave as though it was not one.

This structure or order emerged first in the departments (*daireler*) that were a continuation of the previous Autonomous Turkish Cypriot Administration period, departments that immediately mobilized qualified men and women for the tasks of settlement. Moreover, even before something that could be recognized as a state emerged, local administrations began to operate. In places where there had been Turkish populations who remained in place, such as Nicosia and the walled city of Famagusta, there were already municipalities that, especially in the case of Famagusta, quickly became responsible for aiding in the settlement of refugees. The movement of refugees into areas with existing infrastructure appears to have been a smoother transition than into those areas that had been emptied and devastated by the war.

One example of the problems of this transition and the demand for local services is provided by Özker Yaşın, a writer and poet who had also been a member of the Autonomous Turkish Cypriot Administration. As early as November 1974, he complained in the Legislative Assembly that while refugees in other areas had begun to return to some semblance of normal life, this had not yet been possible in Morphou (in Turkish, Omorfo, later Güzelyurt), which in his description was still palpably devastated:

> I am saddened to identify that even though considerable time has passed, this city still has not returned to a normal life like in the other rescued areas. Because Omorfo still has no municipal organization, the city is unfortunately swimming in filth.... I went around Omorfo's shopping area with the responsible person there [authors' note: probably a "guide," but possibly the district administrator]. I saw that there was a very discomfiting smell in the city, and I asked the responsible person what that smell might be. The answer that I got was this: "Unfortunately, we have no municipality. We have no municipal organization. Trash is not being collected, and even worse, in many of the houses that have not yet been assigned to refugees the refrigerators have not been cleaned. What you smell is rotting meat." ... It's necessary for a municipal organization immediately to begin work.[4]

In certain areas, the garbage was unbearable, and Vamık Volkan described his own visit to villages where the trash presented a health hazard. According to him, this garbage was the detritus of the housecleaning that took place as Turkish Cypriots moved into formerly Greek Cypriot homes and discarded those things that they did not want to keep (Volkan 1979: 131–132).

Very quickly, local administrative structures were put in place and tied to district administrators (*kaymakam*). In villages that had been resettled together, the existing *muhtar*, or village headman, ordinarily became the *muhtar* of the new village. This became more complicated in towns and villages with more than one displaced population, and in those cases *muhtar*s and mayors were provisionally appointed until elections could be held. In some cases, towns moved with their entire municipal apparatus. In November 1974, for example, the same month as Yaşın's complaint, İsmail Bozkurt, representative from Larnaca District, quoted in a previous chapter, raised questions about his own constituency from the İskele (Scala) district, resettled in Trikomo, which they immediately renamed Yeni İskele (New Iskele):

> Larnaca's municipal organization, with the exception of the municipal council, was transferred to Yeni İskele intact. The municipal offices and municipal market have begun working. But so far there has been no clarification of the municipality's legal status. The mayor and municipal council have not been appointed. Is this simply neglect or slowness, or is there no intention of establishing a municipality in Yeni İskele? . . . If a municipality is to be established in this heir of Larnaca, Yeni İskele—and its establishment is unavoidable—is there thought being given to extending the existing village borders in order to provide Yeni İskele with opportunities to grow and develop?[5]

He continues by complaining that so far the municipality had been given only one garbage truck and was in need of at least one more, plus other vehicles for transporting meat and emptying sewage.

Bozkurt's questions concern the legal status of a de facto situation, as well as the possibility of extending village borders in anticipation of future growth. It is here, then, that the site of the state begins to emerge as the ground on which the needs of persons who are used to living with the state are met. In the introduction to Part II, we mentioned Theodore Schatzki's definition of the site of the social as a "mesh of practices and orders" of "people, artifacts, organisms, and things" (2002: 123). Here, we see states as such social orders, encompassing displaced municipal councils, displaced and also looting villagers, piles of discarded Greek Cypriot belongings, garbage trucks and garbage men, a newly established municipal market that needs to transport meat, the new name given by villagers to their new village, the perception of cramped municipal boundaries, the Communal Chamber building that now held a legislative assembly, and the solemn assembly before which the discussion above transpired. Such sites or arrangements are the ground—both literally and figuratively—on which the de facto state emerges.

However, we also see the state here not only as a social order, an arrangement of people and things that hang together around human practices, but also as an effect that penetrates physical sites, creates territory, and becomes part of the domain in which we conduct our daily lives. We see, in other words, the relationship between the affect created through such inextricably entangled interrelationships and the state effect that emerges through practices. Potholes in roads and the odor of hot asphalt to repair them, fallen trees and the noise of chainsaws as crews cut them, and uncollected garbage and the trucks that rumble into the neighborhood to collect it are some of the ways in which the ground of our own lives is enmeshed with the site of the state.

The materiality of the state's effects is itself a subject with a recent anthropological literature exploring, for instance, such infrastructures as water, electricity, and roads (e.g., Anand 2015; Chaflin 2014; Chu 2014; Coleman 2014; Harvey and Knox 2012; Schnitzler 2013; Yarrington 2015). Infrastructures have become a subject of particular interest to political anthropology in recent years for what they demonstrate about the "materiality of state-effects" and the ways in which they "invoke both the presence and the absence of the state" (Harvey 2005: 131). However, the state may also be materialized in the production of standardized state products (Dunn 2008) or in the ways that the state is euphemized (Jauregui 2014; Pierce 2006) or impersonated (Reeves 2014) by its representatives. Certainly, garbage trucks and asphalt impress on us the presence of the state or in their very materiality create a state effect.

The comprehension of such acts as instantiating the state itself depends on a "vision and division" of the world (Bourdieu 1999) into orders that are specifically recognizable as "state-like." However, much of this literature remains in agreement with Penelope Harvey's writings that the state materializes through these projects and products because of "its intrinsic externality (and the consequent experience of absence), and its simultaneous pervasive presence in people's daily lives" (2005: 130). This view of the state as intrinsically an absent externality appears closely related to an older political anthropology literature that focuses on "society against the state," that is, "the state" as something always already outside of "us." Rather, we show that the state effect is *simultaneously* the appearance of the state in its materiality *and* people's expectations of the state. In our case, the state effect that separates the state from society and thereby produces the "where" or site of the state emerges not so much through the imposition of an externality as through the desire for and expectation of such an externality.

Akhil Gupta has described how the experience of Indian villagers with local bureaucracy enables "a certain construction of the state that meshes the imagined translocal institution with its localized embodiments. The government, in other words, is being constructed here in the imagination and everyday practices of ordinary people" (1995: 389–390). Gupta's concern is with what Madeleine Reeves has called the "impersonment" of the state, or the way in which local officials may come to stand for a distant and impersonal state (2014: 13). Jansen (2015) has suggested an important corrective to the idea of a distant state through his call for ethnography of "hopes for the state" visible in a desire for "gridding." Jansen takes the term from James Scott, who used "grids" to understand how the state "sees" people through standardized measures (Scott 1998). Through turning *grid* into a verb, Jansen attempts to make the term *gridding* into one that is "multilayered, dynamic and plural" (2015: 70).

Insofar as it is metaphorical and descriptive, however, the term *gridding* still implies state "capture" and making persons legible through standardized devices. We find it more useful, more descriptively helpful, to see statecraft as producing what Schatzki calls a "teleoaffective structure," in other words, acquiring its externality through both the affect of structure produced through practices and through the ways such practices are oriented toward ends.[6] By emphasizing this combination of ends-oriented activity and affect, it is possible to see how the state's state-ness, its externality, is bound up with *what we already expect the state to do.*

The affectivity of the state effect that emerges through materiality, in turn, is directly tied to teleology. It was not only that rubbish was being collected, electric cables were being installed, and roads were being built, but also that such governing practices interpellated persons in the state through planning and providing for their present and future there *and* through the fact that they waited for and expected it to do so. Yaşın had concluded that it was the lack of such local organization that prevented the people assigned to Omorfo from settling in and continuing with their lives. And in Chapter 1, we quote a guide who described the uncertainties and difficulties that refugees had in settling until such structures began to emerge. The guide had remarked, "As time passed and things began to develop, the village got a *muhtar*, the town got a mayor, and as these institutional structures emerged . . . people began to behave as though that structure was theirs." Such structures, then, had the dual effect of encouraging refugees to settle and get on with their lives and to adopt the place and the order that ordered it.

We see this understanding of statecraft and the role of the state quite early, in the records of the Constituent Assembly that deal with the settlement of refugees and the creation of a new economy. Only a couple of weeks after the complaint about the stinking refrigerators, Özker Yaşın again rose to the podium to complain about the state's aid to resettled villagers in his region. He gives the example of one village, where he says refugees were generally happy with the houses where they had been settled: "However, today, despite twenty days having passed, the refugees settled in that village have not been able to recreate a life like the one they had and have not managed to bring the village to life because of various delays and paperwork. They're becoming depressed." The MP then describes sitting in a coffee shop in the village and asking an elderly villager about his situation. "I received this reply: 'We've moved into a beautiful house. The house has very nice furniture. But for twenty days we're sitting here, and neither the house nor the furniture is filling our stomachs.' I know this villager as someone who loved to work in his fields and orchards and olive groves. But he was in depression because of not being able to find work for twenty days." Yaşın proceeds to observe that although supplies of food had been found in the village, these were not properly stored and distributed and that fruit trees were drying up because it had been difficult to persuade people to water the trees if they do not know that they would later be able to pick the fruit. Although there were fields that could be plowed, "the villagers are saying, okay, I want to plant this field. But he's worried, saying, 'After I've planted it and the crop has grown, will I be the owner of this crop or won't I?' For that reason, he goes and sits in the coffee shop, lazily passing his time, and the village life that we want to develop is not happening. . . . Measures need to be taken to ensure that villages will come to life within at most a week after people settle in them, measures that will transform those settling in the village from being consumers into being producers."[7]

It appears at first quite striking that Yaşın expects villagers immediately to recreate a semblance of normal village life after their traumatic displacement. This expectation, however, clearly derives from his association of social and productive activity with the imprint of the state. In one sense, Yaşın expresses a theme to which we will have opportunity to return later: that the uncertainty of the future of their "state" produced an uncertain state of affairs. For Yaşın, however, this is a matter of poor planning and administration and a failure to keep in mind the role of the state in transforming villagers into producers. Yaşın is here providing both a working definition of the state-society boundary and a rule for the practice of statecraft.

In some quite obvious sense, then, "the state" emerges where people say it does: if villagers wait for garbage trucks to collect their rubbish and if they refuse to plow fields until they have been assigned specific plots, then this is the space opened up for the de facto state, the state that people in practice define as separate from society, with structures that provide for rubbish collection and cadastral surveys. The state-society boundary emerges in the space opened up by rotting meat in refrigerators and unpicked fruit filling ditches. The de facto state, the state recognizable in its state-ness, in turn emerges through such practices, through what we summarize here as statecraft, or the art and practice of governing, of enacting the state.

Rescuing the Community

As we remarked in Chapter 1, both the flight of Turkish Cypriots from the south and the intense process of state-building make it clear that in the immediate postwar period Turkish Cypriots from both the left and the right, young and old, perceived the establishment of their own space in the north as "freedom" and the state they were building as a representation of that freedom. This was reflected in the language of the period, as Turkish Cypriots popularly called the north the "rescued area" (*kurtarılmış bölge*) or the "free Turkish area" (*özgür Türk bölgesi*), called their passage to the north a "freedom journey" or "freedom migration" (*özgürlük yolculuğu* or *özgürlük göçü*), and described their arrival in the north as "embracing freedom" (*özgürlüğe kavuşmak*). The transports that would eventually bring the last Turkish Cypriots from the south in late 1975 were named "freedom transports" (*özgürlük nakliyatı*).

For a certain segment of Turkish Cypriots, especially the young and educated, this freedom meant not only freedom to enact their political will together but also democratic freedom from the dictates of the BEY regime. Fatma Sezer, whom we quoted earlier, had been part of the 1968 generation in Turkey and was one of the leftists who opposed the entrenched regime. She described the period as one of the excitement of a new beginning: "People had started fleeing from the south and coming north. I had two older brothers in Limassol. I wanted them to come immediately—something was going to be established. *And democracy would come.* . . . The 'rescued area' (*kurtarılmış bölge*) wasn't just rescued from the Greek Cypriots. We were rescued as the Turkish community! We were rescued as the Turkish community, and the left came in" (authors' italics).[8] Fatma emphasizes the desire for change, the opposition to the entrenched regime, but also that they opposed the regime through the democracy that they were founding.

What is interesting here for us is that despite ongoing negotiations and the uncertainty about the future produced by them, there were no voices at the time decrying the establishment of an entity that could only be described as a state. While the left would later become critical of the state for reasons we will explore, as Fatma expressed it, "In those days of course, none of the leftists were thinking, 'O God, Turkey came, there was an operation, and it was not in our favor.'" Indeed, all seemed to agree with Ziya Rızkı, one of the members of the old guard, when he declared the proclamation of the federated state "the crowning achievement of the freedom struggle that we have won and a happy decision that the Turkish community has longed for for years."[9]

As we will see, there were intense debates about the shape that the state should take, but there were no questions about the right of Turkish Cypriots to establish their own entity in the "rescued area" (*kurtarılmış bölge*) or about their right to do so on Greek Cypriot property. Instead, in debates that stretched over almost a year, we see a process of constitution-making that was self-consciously a practice of statecraft. We see this in the quote from businessman Ali Süha at the beginning of the chapter, when he remarked that the community had established a state and was "now in the process of making the organs of that state and the functions of that state work properly." Beginning with their early state-building exercises in the 1950s, Turkish Cypriot political leaders had used the language of the Durkheimian progressive corporatism that served as the ideological foundation for Turkish state-building (Parla and Davison 2004; on Cyprus, see Bryant and Hatay, in progress a). Moreover, this organicist view of parts working in concert within the body of the state had infiltrated the language of the Republican People's Party (CHP), the party founded by Mustafa Kemal Atatürk that also served as the model for the main Turkish Cypriot opposition party, the CTP.

One sees these influences, for instance, in the way that an early leader of CTP, Naci Talat, adopted the manners of what he understood to be a statesman while outlining what he took to be the proper forms of a state: "The movement toward good state governance begins to the extent that the competencies of a state are divided among its various organs and these organs work together in concert. We have founded a new state. We're a young state, and we must give importance to these fundamental subjects. If the legislative and executive organs, and the executive and judicial organs cannot function in concert . . . disorder will ensue in the state administration. . . . We must not forget that we are the highest organ in the operation of the state."[10] Such expressions and discussions of statecraft fill the records of the Constituent Assembly, whose members were intensely concerned with the methods and manners of statepeople and the organization and function of the state.

In the beginning of the chapter, we referred to statecraft as the art and practice of governing, but we also noted that its motor was the *enactment* of the state, both acting like a state and realizing the practices of one. Statecraft in both of these senses necessarily depends on abstractions and models, on what we might think of as "the idea of the state," and what is clear from the numerous expressions of fealty to Atatürk and his principles that fill the records of the parliamentary minutes, is that the closest and most obvious model was that of the Turkish state. While almost all of the bureaucrats of the new state had been trained under the British administration, they had also grown accustomed to the improvisatory and less-than-perfect administration of the enclave regime. Moreover, as many persons involved in the administration in that early period commented to us, they lacked the "know-how" to get their new state running. As a result, according to Atun, "Experts came for instrastructure. For water works, roads, government buildings, telephone communications. That is, it was with the cooperation of Turkey. . . . *After all, they have a thousand years of experience as a state*" (authors' italics). The idea that Turkey has "a thousand years of experience as a state" is usually referred to in historical sociology as the "state tradition," a concept that emphasizes the culturally specific practices of statecraft, as well as the expectations of persons used to living with the state (e.g., Pomper 2012; on the Turkish state tradition, see Heper 1976, 1985).

Moreover, it is quite clear that the Kemalist principles on which all legislators agreed were fundamental to their imagination of the new state. This included particularly *devletçilik*, derived from the French *étatism*, or statism, understood as state control of economic resources but also providing for state intervention in the economy (on *étatism*, see Painter 2006).[11] This had been one of the basic principles of the state established under Kemalism in Turkey, which like many modernizing states of the period undertook multiyear programs of planned development. In this sense, the models from which they worked also conformed to Michel Foucault's observation that in the modern state, political economic knowledge is the foundation for governmentality (2007: 108). Or as one commentator on Foucault remarked, "To govern properly, to ensure the happiness and prosperity of the population, it is necessary to govern through a particular register, that of the *economy*" (Dean 2010: 28–29).

Certainly, we saw in the previous chapter and in Özker Yaşın's remarks how state-builders in north Cyprus were concerned from the beginning with production as a means of "planting people" and establishing the state. Turkish Cypriot legislators, and those who would become legislators, were strongly influenced by ideas of social democracy learned from Bülent Ecevit's Turkey of the 1970s. "Democracy, it was argued, was now intrinsically tied to considerations of economic and social development" (Ciddi 2009: 40). Although the Constituent Assembly was composed of members of the "old regime" alongside young leftists who had recently graduated from Turkish universities, there was surprising unity around the idea of social democracy.

Those principles, in turn, were the principles of social justice that ultimately were written into the federal state's constitution. Indeed, the constitution was quite a progressive document that asserts as its first article that "the Turkish Federated State of Cyprus is a secular Republic that is constituted on the principles of democracy, social justice, and the rule of law." It encompasses wide freedoms and at the same time defines the state as responsible for social order: "The state removes all political, economic, and social obstacles that restrict the fundamental rights and freedoms of the individual, and do not accord with the principles of personal tranquility, social justice, and the rule of law, and the state prepares the necessary conditions for the development of the person's moral and material prosperity." Moreover, throughout the document, the state is given numerous responsibilities for the welfare of its citizens. In the clause dealing with the "right to work," the document provides the following directive: "The state will support work and protect the worker through social, economic, and financial measures that ensure that workers live decently and have security in their work lives; and it will take measures to prevent unemployment."[12]

Indeed, the idea of social justice as a foundation for the new state appears to have been widely accepted even before the formation of the Constituent Assembly, in other words, before the young leftists entered the assembly and had a voice. On the same day as Yaşın's complaint about idle villagers, Fuat

Veziroğlu, one of the "old guard" who would later align himself with young leftists, rose to remark that if achieving social justice was their goal, they would need to be very careful in its planning: "This period, which could be called the founding period, is the most important period in the life of a state. Because it is only if the foundation is sound that the structure of the state and the other branches can be constituted soundly. *On paper, the ideal state is a constitutional state based on social justice.* But in reality achieving this is not easy, it's quite difficult, and arriving at such a state, that is, *a constitutional state based on social justice*, is something that will require quite a bit of time and hard work" (authors' italics). Veziroğlu observes, however, that whatever their hopes and ideals, the practice until that point had been less than desirable:

> As a community, we see that we're not in an atmosphere of establishing a state that respects the law, that is, a constitutional state, but we observe instead that there's the air of an arbitrary state (*Hukuka saygılı bir devlet, daha açıkçası bir hukuk devleti kurma havası içinde değil, bir keyfi devlet kurma havası içinde gözükmekteyiz, toplum olarak bu günlerde*). . . . While we're establishing the foundations, if we get ourselves used to bad habits from the perspective of democratic principles, and if we make it possible for the people also to adopt these bad habits, we will all suffer from the consequences as a community later.[13]

Veziroğlu's observations about "bad habits" would be prescient, as we show in later chapters regarding the nepotistic practices that would come to infiltrate all aspects of Turkish Cypriot political life. And during this period leading up to the Constituent Assembly, there was already worry that they were founding an "arbitrary state" (*keyfi devlet*), where the word *keyfi*, which we translate here as "arbitrary," might also mean "anything goes." The sense of arbitariness connoted by *keyfi* is one that is tied to the moment, to short-term tactics and to the word's root of *keyif*, or enjoyment and pleasure. The implication, then, is that rather than establishing a "constitutional state based on social justice," as this lawmaker had repeated three times earlier, instead they were playing at state-building, creating an "arbitary state."

Indeed, throughout the minutes of the Legislative and Constituent Assemblies one sees warnings that the representatives must *act like* statespeople— that despite the size of the community and knowing each other well, they cannot simply play at state-building but must recognize that their behavior in the period of "state foundation" would be important in setting the tone for later. Apart from this clear sense of enacting the state, or putting it into practice as they acted like statespeople, was also the oft-repeated call to take seriously the importance of *foundation*. Apparently, this was to be a new beginning, a new era, and in that foundation legislators influenced by Ecevit's social democratic principles and Marxist political economy tied democracy to social justice, in other words, put the economy at the heart of statism.

If, as we have argued, the site of the state begins to emerge as the ground on which the "natural" needs of persons who are used to living with the state are met, the foundation of the state itself appears to be the capacity to meet those needs (Foucault 2007). Because of this, the vast majority of the thousands of pages of parliamentary minutes devoted to questions of governing concern how the economy would and should be managed. Ali Süha, the businessman quoted at the beginning of the chapter, observed in that same speech, in response to leftist colleagues, "It does not mean that one has established a state just because one has a parliament, and a government that can implement its directives. For that, one must determine what sort of state it is, its economic form and philosophy. . . . What is the economic philosophy of the state? This is the important thing."[14] Indeed, leftist colleagues who had learned Marxist-Leninist philosophy in Turkey brought these discussions back to Cyprus, making debates about political economic philosophy central to quotidian decisions about management. And although Süha defended a mixed economy rather than full nationalization, he also espoused the principles of social justice that were the basis for most speeches made in the parliament during the period.

Parliamentarians were also quite aware that their attempts to bring freedom and social justice to their people at the same time were unusual for postcolonial states, where one was often stymied by the other. In his study of the writing of the Indian constitution, for example, Uday Mehta remarks on the irony that while many postcolonial rebellions were spurred by the conditionality that colonizers so often placed on demands for national freedoms, the material conditions of the postcolonial period and the demand for social justice meant that the implementation of certain freedoms was often delayed in the postcolonial period as well. In states such as India, Mehta comments, "The nation and its freedom, following independence, was a project for the future" (2007: 17). Social uplift and national unity become conditions for the achievement of a freedom that is always on the horizon, a distant destiny.

What made it possible for Turkish Cypriot parliamentarians to discuss and plan with great fervor *both* political freedoms *and* social justice was the fact that they had come into possession of an excess of what Hakkı Atun had called "resources," meaning Greek Cypriot properties of all sorts. These included not only houses and lands, but equally important for their state-building exercise, these included factories, hotels, and workshops that could form the basis for a new national economy. It was the incorporation of these resources into the heart of statecraft that would ultimately create the aporetic state.

Legalizing Liminality

"Just think, an operation happened, and after that operation we were left with a whole world of facilities!" These are the words of Mustafa Akıncı as he described to us the attitude of the young leftists at the time. He continued,

> We're talking about 1975, when I was twenty-seven years old. What is the psychological state of young people? Young people want to achieve something, they're full of excitement, and we were people who had finally come together in one place after [Turkish] Cypriots had lived for so many years scattered. And of course we had a leftist vision . . . and we were a young generation that of course was opposed to the BEY regime. In other words, we saw this movement from a closed period to an open period as an opportunity to free ourselves from that dictatorial mentality and achieve a more democratic structure, and of course with all the opportunities that fell into our hands after 1974, we saw it as the first chance for the Turkish Cypriot community to bring itself into existence economically (*ilk defa kendi kendine var etme olanağı olarak gördük*).[15]

Despite opposition to the BEY regime, then, there seems to have been a general understanding that the transformation of the Republic of Cyprus into a Greek Cypriot state after 1963, and the extreme inequalities of wealth between the two communities that resulted from that, justified Turkish Cypriots' capture of "a whole world of facilities." It was through the use of those "resources" that Turkish Cypriot leaders of all political persuasions imagined that their community would emerge as an economic and political actor.

As a result, assembly members of all political persuasions excitedly debated the opportunity to realize the social democratic dream of a state that can provide the economic prosperity of its citizens. The centrality of the "re-sources" they had acquired to this vision can be seen in the thousands of pages of Constituent Assembly minutes that address subjects having to do with the distribution of property, the management of new industries, and the disposal of items that had come into their possession, such as automobiles. Indeed, in early 1975 many more hours of discussion were taken up with the issue of how to distribute the 20,000 cars that had fallen into their hands than with any disagreements about the philosophy of the constitution itself.

In this period those who aligned themselves on the political left and op-posed private property saw this as an opportunity to enrich the community as a whole through establishing "national industries" out of appropriated fac-tories and workshops. Mustafa Akıncı, for instance, remarked on the excite-ment of the period for young leftists, the sense that they would contribute to building something new: "Toward the end of 1974 I became the head of the METU [Middle East Technical University] Graduates Association, and . . . this association would give its views about things like industrial holdings. We would develop proposals about what might be done with them. . . . These kinds of associations were trying to have an influence, trying to propose things, and for that reason it was an exciting period. A new era . . ." As we discuss at length in the next chapter, the medium-sized and larger factories that they had acquired, as well as the tourist facilities that fell outside the closed city of Varosha, appeared to these young leftists as a type of primitive socialist accumulation, the economic ground on which they could experi-ment with a socialist economic model.

Despite the fervor with which legislators pursued the ideal of social jus-tice, we see from the minutes of the Constituent Assembly that legislators from both the left and the right were also intensely aware of the potential legal consequences of what they were doing and the possible impact on a negoti-ated settlement. This is quite clear, for instance, from a session in April 1975, only nine months after the island's partition, in which the Constituent As-sembly debated an article on property appropriation that one of their legal advisers recommended including in the constitution that they were writing. The recommended article was apparently based on a similar article in the Turkish constitution, which outlines the conditions under which property may be appropriated by the state and the terms of compensation. While the Turkish law gives the state ten years in which to recompense owners for their property, the representative of the committee, Ümit Süleyman, recom-mended immediate compensation. This was something that he argued was more practical but also in line with the RoC's laws, indicating that there was already thought being given to how to harmonize laws in the event of a federation.

Of course, the Turkish law addressed state appropriation of its own citizens' property. In the debate that followed in the assembly, however, members tacked back and forth between discussion of the future needs of their state, such as expanded roads and government offices—in other words, the sorts of future state-building that such a law would normally foresee—and discussion of their unusual, liminal situation, in which much of the property that would potentially be appropriated had Greek Cypriot title deeds. This was especially the case because at the same time, they were in the midst of nationalizing and thereby de facto expropriating the various tourism facilities, factories, and workshops that had been left in the north by fleeing Greek Cypriots. One of the leaders of the left, Özker Özgür, observed that since they were in the midst of negotiations to establish a federal state, eliminating the clause, present in the Turkish law, that spread payment over ten years would open the door for Greek Cypriots immediately to demand payment: "A war has occurred in this country. And quite a lot of Greek Cypriot property remained in the Turkish side. And we're attempting to establish the federal wing of a federal republic. Now if we do what these colleagues have suggested and reduce the ten-year period to nothing, what will happen if, while we're discussing the constitution of a federal republic, Greek Cypriots come to us and say, 'You have a law, and as a state you've nationalized these properties, you've appropriated them. In that case, give us the money for them'?" His concern was partly financial, partly a matter of giving what they were doing an air of legitimacy. By providing for immediate compensation, he asks,

> Will we not be putting dynamite under the foundation of the state, this state that we're founding? And if we were to give the state a longer time period for this appropriation business, as we're seizing Greek Cypriot property would we not give our actions more legality? And thinking about the future, would we not save the state from a great expense? . . . As the state is sequestering the Greek Cypriot properties left in our area, it should be in a legitimate way, and one that will give its actions legality in the future rather than undermine the state or be the cause for economic depression.[16]

The dual concerns expressed in the last sentence of the state's legality and its economic viability were ones that legislators continually tried to balance, as they saw the need for economic planning that presented them with the problem of ownership of the means of production.

Some members of the old guard, especially, objected to this line of argument. Şemsi Kâzım, a representative originally from Paphos, for instance, remarked, "One of our colleagues spoke of Greek Cypriot properties. Certain Greek Cypriot properties will be dealt with as the Federal Republic is being established and will be an article that will constitute the core of an agreement. I don't believe, however, that any Greek Cypriots will want money from the Federal State saying that their property left here was 'expropriated,' and this article doesn't foresee that."[17] For this legislator, then, the issue of Greek Cypriot property was not covered by the article but rather was suspended until a federal state could be negotiated.

In response, Özker Özgür rose again to emphasize his original point, this time using the words of someone he otherwise considered an archenemy, Rauf Denktaş, the longtime leader at the head of the BEY regime:

> Mr. Denktaş has a particular opinion. He says, "In this assembly, while you're making laws, while you're putting articles into the Constitution, always remember that we're in a transition period, and keep in mind the colleagues who will have to take forward the negotiations while a federal republic is being established, while that framework is being established. Don't make laws and regulations that are going to make things difficult for them." I disagree with a lot of Mr. Denktaş's views. But this view I share. This is really a spot-on assessment. We're in a transition period. And we need to be very careful while we're making laws to ease things for those colleagues who will have to negotiate a federal republic framework. . . . There will be agreements, and this, and that. But what will happen if one of them comes up and says, "You've put such an article in your constitution. In that case, give us the money for our fields, give us the money for our houses, give us the money for our factories"?[18]

What becomes clear in this passage is that while all were working to establish the state and agreed on their right to use Greek Cypriot "resources" in order to do that, this state was also temporally hampered by its own liminality. In other words, they were not simply establishing a state but were establishing one that they wanted to be a strong component of a federal state and in which the laws that they were making also would have another audience, other readers, who could use them to their own advantage.

Even as they were writing the constitution, then, a distinct disjuncture emerged between the demands of statecraft, which required state and economic planning and implementation, and the ambiguities of statehood, always suspended because they were in a "transition period." The Turkish word *geçiş*, which we translated as "transition," literally means "passing" or "passage," and so in Turkish there is an even greater stress on its relationship to the periods of passage that Victor Turner (1987) had described as liminal, suspended at a temporal threshold. As a result, even in this early period, statecraft and statehood came to be separated by a temporal disjuncture. There was, on the one hand, the time of governmentality, in which days roll on and life continues in the form of state planning, factory motors churning, the sale of oranges, and as we will see in the next chapter, union disputes and strikes. Simultaneous with this, on the other hand, was the time of statehood, in which time is suspended in anticipated resolution of the Cyprus Problem.[19] This was the time in which "nationalization" might be distinguished from expropriation, and one might debate the tactics that would allow one to take property without paying for it. While the former emerges from the de facto state and the demand for state organization and practice, the latter emerges from the always present possibility of that state's dissolution or at least its transition to another form.

Here, then, we encounter the crux of what we have called the paradox of the de facto: that the de facto always already contains its own denial. While that denial is most obvious in the factitiousness of their statehood, it appears already in the materiality of statecraft, which quite obviously *does* exist even as it *should not*. Those practices of statecraft that always contain elements of obfuscation we call *"state"craft*, to emphasize state-builders' perpetual awareness that what they are creating is not a state but a "state." The absurdity of this aporetic position would become particularly clear in the "nationalization" of the Greek Cypriot "resources" that would become so intrinsic a part of statecraft that, as we will see in the next chapter, political divisions would emerge on the basis of their use. These so-called ideological divisions, in turn, would come to mask the source of those "resources" in violent dispossession.

CHAPTER 5

The Political Economy of Spoils

"In those days, the real story was that we became the owners of the hotel where we had been a doorman and the factory where we had been a guard." These are the words of Erdal Andız, a burly man who often speaks in tongue-in-cheek metaphors. Today he is the head of the Casino Owners' Assocation, but in 1974 he was an upper-level administrator in the tourist trade and we quote him in Chapter 2 as the first post-1974 manager of the Dome Hotel. He went on to work in other tourist enterprises and as an administrator witnessed the transformation of Greek Cypriot "resources" into Turkish Cypriot "national assets" (*milli servet*):

> The first time, we spilled the soup on ourselves. The second time we also spilled it. But the third time we learned not to spill it. The first factory we went into, we stole the engine. The second time, we broke the engine. The third time, we got it running. I remember, in the metal-pipe factory, they were making a large pipe, larger than they had before, and they were working until three in the morning. The man who now owns the factory and an engineer were there. And when that pipe came out of the machine, they were crying. You know how when you score a goal in football and run off and celebrate? That's how they were hugging each other.[1]

The metal-pipe factory was part of the large state company Sanayi Holding, which incorporated fifty-eight of the workshops and factories that fell into the new state's hands after the war.[2] Although there had been a liberal minority opposed to the idea of state-run factories, the large majority in the

Constituent Assembly followed the statist program of Turkey and insisted that "nationalizing" the factories was the only way to create an economy based on the principles of social justice discussed in Chapter 4.

One man who was in charge of sales for Sanayi Holding remarked, "After 1974, Sanayi Holding was established with the idea of adopting/appropriating (*sahiplenmek*) the small and large production facilities, workshops, and similar production areas that had been left from the Greek Cypriots, protecting them, and contributing to the economy by putting them into production."[3] A representative of the Revolutionary General Work Union (Devrimci Genel İş Sendikası, or Dev-İş) described the period in less neutral terms: "There is no company that has been established in any country in the world that was as lucky as that one. Think about it, people had established these factories, and everything was ready in them, from the raw goods to the products themselves to the sales mechanisms. And these factories, while they were working, really did almost completely solve the employment problem in the country."[4] The language used by these two men is that of "luck" or "chance" (*şans*), noting that the production facilities were "left by the Greek Cypriots" (*Rumlardan kalan*), the latter being the most common way of expressing how they came into possession of these properties. Because this is also the way that one would describe an inheritance (*bubamdan kalan*, for instance), to say that it was "left by" Greek Cypriots acknowledges that the property was built by others but allows "abandonment" to elide with bequest or legacy.

This chapter describes the creation of a national economy and emergence of democratic politics out of the ruins of war. Until the island's division, politics in this minority community had been dominated by a nationalist leadership with ties to the Turkish government and military. In the 1960s, leftist movements grew in Turkey, influencing Cypriot youth who studied there. Returning to the island in the 1970s, these young leftists began to enter politics, for the first time producing a viable alternative to the conservative nationalism under which they had been raised. Opposition politics had floundered during the hardship of the enclave period, when the state-within-a-state organized military resistance and distributed Turkey's economic aid. It was only after division, in the midst of the abundant "resources" left by Greek Cypriots, that a real opposition was able to emerge. Like so many leftist movements, those in north Cyprus also took the state to be their site of struggle and the economy to be its ground.[5] As a result, political contestation and multiparty politics would emerge in north Cyprus through struggles over the state's control of the economy.

Just as the state has a site, then, politics has a *ground*, both literally and figuratively. The literal ground of politics is the material basis for the emergence of political struggle: the properties of various sorts that had fallen into the new state's hands and had become "national assets." Debates over the best economic models and policies that occupied and exercised legislators throughout the first years took for granted the "resources" on which that national economy would be founded. Indeed, as we will see, *the ground of politics emerged precisely at the point where Greek Cypriot property became "resources,"* where "abandoned" property became the foundation on which to build a national economy.

The figurative ground of politics might be compared to the figure-ground distinction in perspectival painting. Just as size in a painting allows us to perceive something that is actually in two dimensions as having three, that is, being closer or farther away, so in this case a similar representational trick enabled the perspective of political ideology and defined the basis of political struggle. This figurative ground emerged through a leftist struggle against the nationalist old guard, whom leftist Turkish Cypriot leaders described in Marxist terms as using nationalism and conflict to propagate social and economic inequalities. Political struggle was intended to correct those inequalities. However, we describe below how this struggle to secure the socially just distribution of property took place by obscuring or masking the "real" ground of politics, namely, the "facts on the ground," or the seizure of that property through violent dispossession. We argue that the invisibilization of the state's economic foundation was the site in which citizens were interpellated into a founding act of violence.

The ground of politics, then, encompasses both the conditions of possibility for the emergence of political struggle and the particular field of concern that gives to that struggle its terms and meaning. Ethnographically, we focus in this chapter on the emergence of multiparty politics out of a political economy of spoils. We do this for two reasons. First, while much writing on the state in north Cyprus has focused on nationalism and the nationalist right,[6] the left was quite vocal in the practice of statecraft and in calling upon legislators and bureaucrats to behave like the representatives of a "real" state, as we saw in Chapter 4. In other words, through their participation as an opposition party, the left contributed to the indirect reification of the state, at the same time attempting to shape the state project in their own image. More-over, this indirect reification happened not only through the participation of leftist politicians who wanted to shape the direction of the state but also through the participation of farmers in villages and workers in factories who joined leftist parties and thereby became invested in the new state. Indeed, the emergence of a very active multiparty political system in the island's north has been one of the signs often used to support claims to the "de facto-ness" of the state—in other words, one of the primary ways in which one recog-nizes the state's state-ness.[7]

Second, it was through the active participation of the left in shaping the economic policies and distribution networks of the north that the violence of appropriating property as a founding state act came to be disguised through forms of distribution. In the discourse that the left developed quite early to describe its "ethical" distinction from the right, those in the old guard were *ganimetçiler* (looters) or *hırsızlar* (thieves). This referred to the presumed in-equalities of the distribution process that at the same time invisibilized the violent founding act of appropriation. In turn, certain members of the old guard complained that their leftist colleagues were transforming a state-building project of "planting people" into a "fight over houses." In other words, the right's concern with legitimating "facts on the ground," or giving legitimacy to a state founded on dispossession, turned into a squabble with leftists who sought to overturn the ground of politics, or the right's control of resources. This "distribution by dispossession," in turn, would put leftist politics in an awkward position in relation to the proposed federal state that they saw as the only peaceful solution to the island's division.

The Cinema of Dispossession

In the late 2000s, a group of young, educated Turkish Cypriots, all born well after the island's division, formed the Baraka Cultural Center (Baraka Kül-tür Merkezi) in protest against what they saw as the watered-down leftism of the main leftist parties. Using theater, dance, and music, Baraka attempted to turn Marxist critique to the specific problems of Cyprus. In 2013, at a time when Turkey's aid packages had become conditional on privatization, they produced a nearly two-hour documentary chronicling the rise and decline of Sanayi Holding. Based primarily on extensive interviews with persons who worked in Holding, as its employees commonly called it, the documentary aimed both to critique the neoliberal economy that had led to Holding's privatization in the 1990s and to demonstrate that contrary to much of the discourse at the time the film was made, Turkish Cypriots were not lazy but in fact could be hard workers when they saw the benefit of their work.[8] The film, then, documents an important period in Turkish Cypriot state-building with the specific aim of showing how persons could be attached to and dedicated to a state enterprise.

The film gives much information about how the industries that constituted Sanayi Holding were organized, who was employed in them, and how factories rumbled back to life after the destruction of war. For instance, one mechanical engineer explained how new university graduates learned to put their theoretical knowledge to practical use: "Ninety percent of the engineers and technical employees working at Holding had not been employed in production before. . . . They read the documents left by Greek Cypriots, they read the catalogues, and with their own efforts they managed to learn something, and they brought what they learned to life. . . . When there wasn't any know-how, know-how was created."[9] It was a period when Turkish Cypriots for the first time entered into large-scale production and when they experienced the satisfaction not only of creating a national economy but also of producing products that, in their descriptions today, made the Turkish Cypriot community largely self-sufficient.[10] A man who had been in charge of both domestic and international transport for these products used an appropriately Fordist analogy: "First of all, there was discipline. And second, if we were going to make the analogy with a Lego, everyone had their own duties. The worker who carried the raw materials to the cauldron, the worker who took care of engine maintenance, someone who pushed the button that started production, another person for quality control, others who did bookkeeping, export, sales—it's when you unite all of these that a product emerges. . . . And everyone experienced the joy of that production."[11]

For the anthropologist, such interviews are of interest for what they tell us about how people remember that period today. Even taking into account how the concerns of the present shape memory, however, there are certain themes, such as pride in production, that are repeated often enough to suggest that they give some insight also into the atmosphere of the period. Echoing Andız's description in the opening of the chapter, almost everyone interviewed for the film described the sense of solidarity, pride, and excitement in the production process. Similarly in her study of socialist state-building in Vietnam, Christina Schwenkel found that "the labor of infrastructure and of working toward a better future made the memory of participation in socialist modernization deeply emotional and transformative" (Schwenkel 2018: 115).

Indeed, like the solidarity of the enclave period that we describe elsewhere (Bryant and Hatay 2011; see also Dzenovska and Arenas 2012), persons who worked in these state-run industries in the 1970s look back on the time as one of friendships developed around the excitement of work. One woman who began her career as a laborer in a women's stocking factory, Serap Çorap, which was part of Sanayi Holding, remarked, "The friendships that we established at Serap Çorap—what can I say? I can't see friendships like that today, that is, really from the heart."[12] In Schwenkel's study, as well, for retired electricity workers, "the smokestack remained across time a powerfully affective force in their lives, one constitutive of the very materiality of their solidarity" (Schwenkel 2018: 121; also Muehlebach 2017).

Others described the pride that they took in their work, the long hours that they invested, and the excitement of the period. The sales manager quoted above, for instance, recalled, "I didn't pay attention to working hours, and all my colleagues were the same. . . . We didn't have any idea of working 8:00 to 5:00. We would work 8:00 to 25:00! There were plenty of times when we worked until midnight."[13] Many others similarly described the long hours that they willingly worked, implicitly contrasting that with a contemporary notion of a state employee as one who simply puts in his or her hours without caring about the work being done. One engineer remarked, "Going and working at Sanayi Holding was a matter of inclination or desire (*gönül işi*). . . . I mean, we would go to Sanayi Holding flying."[14] Expressions of pleasure in the process of work take up considerable time in all the interviews.

There are other contemporary indications that the immediate post-1974 period was one of excitement, the excitement of establishing something new. Certainly, this is reflected in the records first of the Autononous Turkish Cypriot Administration's Legislative Assembly and then of the TFSC's Constituent Assembly, where minutes recorded that legislators worked every day of the week and that sessions continued until late in the night. The excited speeches of the period show that legislators were caught up in the exhilaration of establishing a new state, as they argued with each other about the best way to achieve democracy and social justice. Indeed, throughout our own interviews as well, even persons today critical of the TRNC described the thrill of state-building in that period.

Regarding Sanayi Holding, one of the words most frequently used is *sahiplenme*, which we defined before as both adoption or belongingness. For instance, one man we interviewed who had been a young bureaucrat at the time insisted, "There was an excellent sense of proprietorship (*sahiplilik*). [They just wanted] Sanayi Holding to work, to produce. . . . There was a sense of ownership/investment (*sahiplenme*). . . . Even talking about it now I get excited." He repeatedly uses the word *sahiplenme* to refer to the sense of ownership, proprietorship, and investment that led to a desire to produce. Recent ethnographic research on infrastructure has shown how these collectively owned materialities "can become the metonymic sites for wider social discussions of participation and responsibility—that is, can become meaningful for the very definition of a collective" (Coleman 2014: 460). They become meaningful in this way, moreover, because of "their very collective crafting in the imagination as emblematic of the state and the political community itself" (461).

Certainly, in both the immediate post-1974 period and in collective memory of that period today, Sanayi Holding comes to stand for both the state and the political community. In recollections of that period, employees of the new state-run industries describe becoming the "heirs" of a ready-made industrial sector that just needed labor power and "know-how" and how they worked long hours with much energy in the interests of turning "national assets" into a working national economy. The producers of the Baraka documentary explicitly describe it as a film of "production, solidarity, and resistance"[15] and say that their goal was to show "that in the past we were producing and that we were intentionally separated from production" by the forces of neoliberal privatization, particularly coming from Turkey.[16] In this imagination, the productivity of the early state-building period comes to represent something fundamental about the political community itself.

By now it should be clear, however, that for all of its empirical and ethnographic interest, this film made by a radical leftist organization never once touches on what one might otherwise consider the most obvious form of exploitation: the accumulation by dispossession that made Sanayi Holding possible. When the representative of the self-described revolutionary trade union, Dev-İş, quoted in the introduction, mentions their "inheritance," he frames it in terms of luck: "There is no company that has been established in any country in the world that was as lucky as that one." He acknowledges, "People had established these factories," even as he allows the anonymous "people" (*insanlar*) to euphemize the specific dispossession of former neighbors.

We quote this recent film, then, not only for its empirical and ethnographic interest in documenting a period of significant social change but also for what it tells us about the left's capacity to critique the accumulation by dispossession that founded the economy of the north. Like their predecessors, the young people born after 1974 who founded Baraka have a well-developed critique of imperialist colonization of the island. And like them, there is no place in that critique, or in their nostalgia for a preneoliberal period, for the Greek Cypriot owners of the factories, workshops, hotels, and other establishments that became the basis for a new "national economy." One might expect that a leftist critique could argue, with some revolutionary fervor, for the necessity of dispossession when it freed the workers from their chains. But no such critique is forthcoming; indeed, it seems that for the young people making the film, the Greek Cypriot dispossessed owners never even came to mind.

What, then, allows for this masking of the violence of dispossession? What allows that violence to be turned to "chance," "luck," and "inheritance"? What allows for an "adoption" or proprietorship so thorough that its sources are masked? This foundational dispossession that grounded politics in its disappearance brings us to the heart of a debate about what Walter Benjamin called the state's lawmaking violence (1996: 240). In a discussion of Hannah Arendt's 1969 critique of Benjamin, Paul Ricoeur describes that which constitutes power as having the status of the forgotten, "a forgetting of that which constitutes the present of our living-together" (2010: 25). What is forgotten, for Ricoeur, is the *foundation*, forgotten not in the sense of a lived past but rather of that which is constitutive and therefore unseen. Ricoeur appears at first to be thinking of what Bourdieu calls "symbolic violence," those relations of domination that are always euphemized and disguised (1979).

However, Ricoeur goes on to argue that this foundation is occasionally visible through "signs" or "traces," and by "stubborn substitutes, which, while creating a veil [*ecran*], refer by default to this fundamental constituent" (2010: 26). Signs or traces would be, for instance, those moments of political upheaval when the actual constitution of power is laid bare. Substitutes or veils, however, are those explanations—particularly the explanation of domination—that seem to stand for power while never explaining it. "The real knowledge of power," Ricoeur remarks, "is almost exhausted in the suspicion that domination is not the true foundation of power" (2010: 27). In other words, even a theory of symbolic violence that explains relations of domination does not ultimately explain why we submit to them.

In north Cyprus, we may see how a particular foundation, the appropriated lands and factories that constituted the ground of politics, was thoroughly forgotten precisely at the moment that it became the condition of possibility for a new state. "Facts on the ground" were magically turned into the ground of politics. Ricoeur provides us with a clue to how this happens in his remark that the constitution of power is based on "forgetting of that which constitutes the present of our living-together." For Turkish Cypriots, the possibility of living together in a space carved out *ex nihilo* depended on the state providing them with the means to do that. However, the state providing them with those means depended on cleansing the territory of others. In this case, it seems that divesting ourselves of responsibility for lawmaking violence is an important part of the sovereign exchange that constitutes the state's forgotten foundation, that is, the ground of politics.

That sovereign exchange transformed the thanatopolitics (Agamben 1998; Mbembe 2003; Murray 2006) of the enclave period into a politics of victimization in which the claims of victimhood secured "rights" that would become both the basis for citizenship (see Chapter 7) and new political struggles. Those "rights," moreover, were secured in the sovereign exchange that traded individual victimization for the communal victimization that legitimated their so-called state. In that sovereign exchange, the material basis of those rights claims—that is, Greek Cypriot property—was transformed into "assets."

The left's entry into politics, then, simultaneously invisibilized "resources" as national assets and turned the "fight over houses" into an ethical struggle. The veiling or masking of the violence of dispossession, indeed its disappearance, would be effected through a particular politics of distribution that fed on the ressentiment that many people felt toward what we have referred to as the old guard: those nationalist leaders who had led the struggle and in the process had suppressed all opposition.

Distribution by Dispossession

On the third anniversary of the island's partition, the federal state's presidency, along with the education ministry, prepared a book entitled *In the*

Third Year of Freedom: TFSC. With a publication date to mark the start of the Turkish military intervention on 20 July, the book presents a comprehensive overview of developments in the new state, from the workings of the parliament and its legislation to the activities of various ministries and departments under them. We see, for instance, that under the Energy, Natural Resources and Tourism Ministry's Department of Geology and Mines "alongside geological field studies to create a geological map of the TFSC, there is ongoing study to find industrial raw materials, building materials, and stabilized materials, and research on raw materials for cement" (Kıbrıs Türk Federe Devleti 1977: 85).

We also see that around 40 million Turkish lira had been spent on two main road-building projects, while the Ercan Airport opened to civilian traffic on 3 February 1975. The newly created Cyprus Turkish Airways, a joint venture with Turkish Airways, would fly 1,048 flights in 1975 and 1,320 in 1976, while in the same month as the opening of the airport, the Girne harbor welcomed ferryboats coming from Turkey. The Famagusta harbor in the east and smaller Gemikonağı harbor in the west had already opened to international cargo traffic in September 1974. At the same time, the administration was replanting trees burned during the war, repairing water mains, and installing telephone lines. Journalist Keith Kyle, who visited the island during this period, observed that the new territory carved out in the north "contained most of the country's cargo-holding capacity in the port of Famagusta, the great majority of its tourist industry (65 percent of existing tourist accommodation and 87 percent of the hotel beds under construction), half the agricultural exports, including 75 percent of the citrus fruits, and nearly half of its industrial production" (1997: 20).

Before 1974, the three major economic sectors for the Cyprus economy had been agriculture, mining, and tourism, with a fourth, nascent industrial sector. Apart from some employment in mining and a small trade in agriculture during that period, these sectors had excluded Turkish Cypriots, who had been trapped in enclaves. After 1974, the international Cyprus Mines Corporation withdrew from Cyprus and left its mines derelict. This left tourism, agriculture, and light industry as main sectors, the latter two of these enhanced by new access to packaging and shipping facilities from which Turkish Cypriots had previously been excluded.

In 1960, in the year the RoC was established, only 24,000 tourists visited Cyprus, most going to the mountains. By 1974, however, beach tourism was booming, and Famagusta, in the island's east, made up 54 percent of tourist capacity.[17] In parliamentary minutes, we find legislators repeating that given the difficulties of transport to the island, postwar tourism would take time to develop. *In the Third Year of Freedom* declared, "In this period, from the viewpoint of our community, the most important subject is the industrial facilities in our region being protected, taken under wing (*sahiplendirilmesi*) and quickly put to work" (Kıbrıs Türk Federe Devleti 1977: 117).

The grouping of factories and workshops that constituted Sanayi Holding was to become the cornerstone of that new economy. Formerly Greek Cypriot factories and small enterprises acquired names such as Aba Parke Fabrikası, which made stone tiles, and Doremi Kozmetik Fabrikası, which produced cosmetics. The union leader quoted in the opening of the chapter noted that many of the products were oriented toward the tourism market, and "all the beds and mattresses and windows and I don't know what else were made there." Apart from furnishings for hotels, though, there were factories making chocolate, cookies, and candies; seven others making all kinds of plastics, from baskets to buckets; workshops knitting women's stockings and others producing shoes; and a whole range of agricultural and manufacturing products, from tractors to steel wire.

In the Third Year of Freedom notes that the development of a Turkish Cypriot industrial sector was particularly important because "despite the Turkish Community, which received second class citizen treatment, being one of the founding elements of the Cyprus Republic, it had been prevented, as in every other sector, from benefitting from state opportunities" (Kıbrıs Türk Federe Devleti 1977: 117). However, these early state-builders soon discovered that because of their previous exclusion from industry, the community lacked what all of our interviewees consistently called, in English, "know-how." Acquiring that know-how in the most effective way required them to bring experts from Turkey, where national industries were developing apace. Engineers and administrators arrived in the hundreds, many of whom would later marry Turkish Cypriot women and settle on the island. Their arrival also made it difficult to separate the direct influence of Turkey in this period from its indirect influence, the latter palpable not only in the form of Turkish "know-how" but also in the way that legislators touted Turkey as a model and described the "nationalization" of "resources" as the only way to achieve what one legislator in Chapter 4 called "the ideal state."

As we will see in the next section, the left appeared to view the "resources" at their disposal as a type of primitive socialist accumulation whose appropriation was taken for granted as a necessary step in the establishment of a new state. Indeed, at the very same moment that all of the institutions described in the anniversary book were being constructed, leftist politics emerged in the island's north within those very institutions. This happened as the left attempted to rectify previous wrongs and defend workers' rights using Greek Cypriot "resources" and the distributive mechanisms of the state. We see this from the very beginning of that state and its "national economy," when young leftist organizers returned to the island and encouraged unionization. Indeed, one characteristic of the period was the prevalence of strikes, when young leftists mobilized workers in the new "industries." The first post-1974 manager of the Dome Hotel, for instance, explained how the workers of the hotel went on strike before it even opened its doors, in protest against a temporary manager. And Sanayi Holding workers recall today how they agitated for shorter hours, higher pay, and facilities such as child care.

Indeed, at the same moment that Turkish Cypriots were establishing a "national economy," unions proliferated and labor actions multiplied. There had been a small number of unions before 1974, the most politically active being the Cyprus Turkish Teachers' Union (KTÖS, Kıbrıs Türk Öğretmenler Sendikası). However, leftist leaders quickly divided the new organizations into "yellow unions," those close to the administration, and "red unions," those with a "revolutionary" agenda. In response to a question in the Constituent Assembly, Naci Talat explained what the left meant by yellow and red unionism. Yellow unionism, he said, "does not only mean being on the side of the employer. It does not only mean being on the side of the patron." Instead, it intends to divide workers: "Under the guise of liberal democracy, attempts are being made to tear workers apart, to make them pawns of political games, to put them in conditions resembling slavery."[18]

It should become clear in Chapter 7 that the size of the community, methods of distribution, nepotistic networks, and high rates of unionization (both "red" and "yellow") made it highly unlikely that workers would have been put "in conditions resembling slavery." What this statement shows, however, is the introduction of a leftist discourse that divided the community into the oppressors, or those who would want to be oppressors, and the oppressed (*ezenler ve ezilenler*). In this new discourse, victimization was no longer simply that of Turkish Cypriots by Greek Cypriots but was that of Turkish Cypriots by the old guard. Moreover, the ground of struggle was the state itself.

The left, then, "unmasked" the corporatist politics of the old guard as a "guise of liberal democracy." However, because the left's critique was one based in political economy, *the wrongs of the past could only be righted through the economy, which in turn could only be established on the "resources" that they had acquired.* One needed the means of production in order to create new relations of production. One needed a base in order to create a new superstructure. It was in this sense of founding a new order that Greek Cypriot "resources" became a type of primitive socialist accumulation.

It was in this context, then, that victimization—for the left encapsulated in a discourse of the oppressor and oppressed—became what Žižek (1989) calls a "quilting point," a place to pin the ideology of social democracy to the actual circumstances of ethnic-based dispossession. Victimization became the way that the left would quilt together the otherwise seemingly contradictory elements of violence and equality, dispossession and distribution, that would constitute its approach to state-building.

Ideology as Mimicry

The history of the left among Turkish Cypriots is a brief one. Starting in the 1930s, small pockets of Turkish Cypriot laborers and intellectuals found themselves in sympathy with the workers' movement then growing in the Greek Cypriot community. However, as a minority community that for several decades felt under threat, the nationalism of Turkey, the country viewed as their protector, dominated the public sphere. Moreover, when in the 1950s the Greek Cypriot workers' party, AKEL (Anorthotiko Komma Ergazomenou Laou, or Progressive Part of Working People) supported the fight to unite the island with Greece, Turkish Cypriots supporting the party were viewed as traitors, and three were killed by TMT. As a result of this suppression, as well as the isolation of the enclaves, where even radio contact was limited, it should not be surprising that there was little discussion of or information about other ways of looking at their situation besides those shaped by Turkish nationalism. Although many people report that as youth in the enclaves they followed and were affected by the 1968 generation, including its music and dress, they nevertheless had few means to come to ideological terms with what was happening in the world.

Lack of communication in the context of the enclaves meant that many young Turkish Cypriot women and men who put down their guns or left their families for the first time to go and study in Turkey knew almost nothing of the intellectual trajectory that young people there were taking. Many people who would later become active in leftist politics while students in Turkey described their confusion when they left the enclaves and arrived in that country's cities, where they found a heterogeneity of political voices and views. A doctor and former minister of health, Eşref Vaiz, remarked to us in an interview that he was shocked when he arrived in Turkey to discover that there were alternatives to the nationalism under which he had been raised. When he arrived in Ankara, he explained, the Turkish Cypriots with whom he was rooming demanded that he declare his political position:

> For days on end we argued about "who am I?" I had an identity crisis. I went to university, and there were different camps, different groups. Those on the right sat in one place, those on the left in another place, fractions, in the teahouses, and everywhere. In the "who am I?" discussion, I would say, "I can't be a communist. Communism is bad." And my housemates would say, "Well, you can't be a fascist nationalist." And I would say, "Why? What's bad about nationalism?" And they would answer, "It's bad! If you're a nationalist, you'll be a fascist."[19]

Under the influence, then, of their "big brothers" and "big sisters" in Turkey, young Turkish Cypriot students began to study Marxism and socialism and to discuss how these might be applied in Cyprus.

On their return to the island, the most appropriate political home for these students was the Republican Turkish Party (CTP), founded in 1971 on the model of Turkey's Republican People's Party (CHP). While the party in the 1970s followed Turkey's CHP in adopting a social democratic platform, there were members of the party who were concerned with how to apply ideas from Turkey to the specific context of Cyprus. However, when young people returning from Turkey gravitated toward CTP, they began to pull the party in a more strictly ideological direction. Öntaç Düzgün, today a businessman and newspaper editor, remarked, "In that period there was a very shallow ideology and an ideological language that consisted of fifty memorized words." He and his friends would teach Leninism and Stalinism in the villages, he recalled. We commented to him that by that time Stalinism was long out of fashion in the Soviet Union itself, which by the late 1970s was undergoing changes and upheavals. "But in Turkey at that time there were no real sources of information," he explained. "And our generation didn't know English. The leftist publications were mostly concerned with Lenin and Stalin. Occasionally we would have access to some publications coming out of Bulgaria and the Soviet Union."[20]

Like the closed context of the enclaves, then, the problem of language had isolated these young leftists from major debates of the 1970s taking place in the Soviet Union and the English-speaking world. Moreover, in an interesting replication of enclave discipline, Turkish Cypriot leftist students in Turkey tended to keep to themselves, in their own dormitories and houses, and to marry among themselves, often with persons chosen for them or suggested to them by the movement leaders.[21] Although there were female comrades, whom the left in Turkey desexualized by calling "little sisters" (*bacı*), the movement was highly masculinized, one of its main symbols being a certain shape of mustache that distinguished them from the right, which had its own mustaches (see Durakbaşa 1998; Ertürk 2006).

The movement, then, while bringing a new critique of Cyprus's condition, was hierarchical, nondemocratic, masculinist and ideologically stuck in the period of Stalinism. Today, in looking back on that period, many of those who participated in the movement are able to reflect on how it set the tone for the way that the left in Cyprus would later develop. Ahmet Gülle, who studied medicine in Turkey and would much later become minister of health in the TRNC, described a structure that appeared to exchange one form of unquestioning conformity for another:

> As a part of the Turkish Cypriot Community, which had not developed its own democratic principles and structure, which had been severely affected by conditions, they accepted these ideas and ideologies without sufficiently debating or questioning them, and without creating truths appropriate to their own conditions. . . . Because in the organizational structure there was not a sufficiently democratic way of structuring things, . . . and models that were insufficiently democratic, there were attempts to create a single type of person loyal to a single ideology. Those who thought differently were either pressured, or ostracized, or thrown out. (Öncül and Düzgün 1999: 212)

As we will see below, one of the main effects of this loyalty to a single ideology was a deterritorialized discourse that had little to say about the "real" material conditions of state-building in the period. It was a discourse that focused on the realization of socialist ideals but was founded on a political economy of spoils.

Our use of the term *deterritorialized* refers to the ways in which a discourse emptied of constative meaning and unanchored to actual material conditions can acquire new meanings in the process of its reproduction. Alexei Yurchak (2006), adopting Gilles Deleuze and Felix Guattari (1987), uses *deterritorialization* to understand the ways in which, in the late Soviet period, authoritative discourse was emptied of meaning so that what remained was the "hegemony of form." In our case, however, we instead confront a deterritorialized discourse that is useful precisely because it veils or disguises the inherent contradictions of one's material conditions. In this sense it is closer to the example given by Lata Mani, who argues that because of the irresolvable contradictions of globalization—in her case, the desires of an Indian middle class to dress, work, and behave globally while living in cities with infrastructure crumbling partly as a result of globalization—the success of globalization depends on the attractions of "a deterritorialised discourse of globality (being global, feeling global, looking global, acting global)." This deterritorialized discourse, in turn, "relieves one of the burden of having to engage the actual material realities in which one undertakes to enact this new form of being and belonging" (Mani 2008: 42).

In other words, post-1974 Turkish Cypriot leftist politics offered—indeed, was trapped in—a critique of imperialism and the oppressive capitalist caste that undermined any possible critique of the "primitive socialist accumulation" that gave them the resources on which they would build a new state. As we will show, the old guard—those the left considered its right—worked from a relatively neat formula that subsumed the act of appropriation under the acknowledged violence of state-building. In other words, it explicitly acknowledged the appropriation of Greek Cypriot property as law-making violence. In their formula, individual victimization was subsumed under communal victimization, which in turn justified the establishment of a new state. Negotiations over a federal solution, in this view, should revolve around whether or not Cypriot history justified Turkish Cypriots' claims to want a separate space. With the intervention of the leftist "fight over houses," however, individual victimization was introduced into Cypriot politics as a means of receiving distribution.

As we will see in the next two sections, the invisibilization of spoils as "resources" during this period happened for four reasons. First, the subsumption of those "resources" under nationalized companies meant that they were everyone's and no one's, their future hanging on the future of the state that could potentially be dissolved. Second, those "resources" initially appeared to the left as a type of primitive socialist accumulation on which a socialist model would be built. Third, however, in the end those "resources" became the most important means for the left to establish a political base in the community. Unlike other aspects of state-building during this period, then, the left's oppositional stance regarding these "resources" did not concern the legitimacy of their use but rather how they were to be used. And fourth, as a result, unlike the origins of the state itself, the origins of these resources came to be masked or veiled by ideology.

The Politics of Dispossession

When the new state held its first election in summer 1976, it was the first time that the community had experienced a serious political contest. The panic of the established political leaders in the face of serious opposition may be seen in a remark by Hakkı Atun, who was directly involved in the foundation of the "old guard's" first political party: "Look, it's a newly founded state—it passes to full democracy! The opposition is stronger than the government! And how! Actually, for the conditions of the time I can say that we were a very mature community, I can claim that. And there wasn't opposition only on the Settlement Law, there was NOISY opposition on EVERY subject. 'Such-and-such offices have victimized [people]!' Whether true or not." The opposition was split in this first election into three parties,[22] and the newly founded party of the nationalist establishment, the National Unity Party (Ulusal Birlik Partisi, or UBP) garnered nearly 54 percent of the vote and thirty of the new assembly's forty representatives. From this early period, there were accusations that UBP maintained its hegemony through the dispersal of goods, jobs, services, and rights to property (see also Sonan 2014). Members of the establishment were entrenched in the bureacracy and the economy in ways that would have made this relatively easy.

According to the voluminous publications on the matter in the opposition press, the main tool that the establishment party used to garner votes in that first election was opening the doors of the "loot depots," those warehouses described in Chapter 1 where Greek Cypriot movable property was stored. There were reports in one newspaper, *Halkın Sesi*, that ministers' wives were canvassing villages, asking what villagers needed, and delivering those goods from the state warehouses (Sonan 2014: 137). Corroborating these claims in the present is no simple task, but given the extent of the claims, as well as the later form that politics in the north would take, it is clear that from its inception political contest in north Cyprus was built on distribution of "resources": politics quickly became a matter of how, when, and to whom those resources would be distributed and accusations that other parties were distributing resources unfairly.

In response to the old guard's use of its entrenched mechanisms, the left was not slow to develop its own nepotistic system, using union-run cooperatives to establish an alternate banking system giving loans to workers, as well as supermarkets where workers could benefit from monthly credit (Şafaklı 2003). Moreover, the proliferating unions were tied to parties of all ideological bents, and those from both the left and the right became mechanisms for distributing favors, expecially jobs and worker's "rights."

The extent of this distribution may be seen in the example of the Dome Hotel. Because the hotel was part of the state sector, managers were often forced to take on extra personnel before elections by the government-appointed board members, who wished to promote their own party. When Mete was its manager, he at one point was informed that he was going to need to hire ten new people on the payroll. He replied that it was a crazy request, since he did not need that much personnel. In order to try to stop it, he went to the union leader, a member of the left-wing CTP, and told him that if it happened, the right-wing UBP would also want its people employed. He then went away for three days of compulsory military service, and when he returned found ten new employees at the hotel. The union leader told him that he had been in negotiations and had worked it all out: five men for CTP and five for UBP. This is only one example of the ways that, by the end of the 1970s, unions had multiplied into all aspects of the labor force, allowing both left- and right-wing parties to distribute jobs as favors before elections.

As we remarked earlier, the old guard's approach to the properties that formed the basis for distribution was straightforward. In the expropriation of properties, the concern was to make their appropriation and distribution the responsibility of the state, a responsibility that was everyone's and no one's. However, as we observed earlier, it was the left's distrust of the old guard and view of them as oppressors that led to discourses of corruption and unfairness through which ideas of the "entitlements" of distribution came to be articulated. One sees this in the beginning of the state, when much of the business of the Constituent Assembly was taken up with addressing accusations of unfair and corrupt distribution. For instance, Ekrem Avcıoğlu, representative from Nicosia, consistently complained that persons working in the Settlement Department had given homes and shops to their friends and relatives, that they had filled their own homes with loot from the depots, and that they had taken the best cars. These, at least, were the rumors circulating among the people, he claimed. This legislator, then, asseverated that the "real" victims had become victim again to the predations of an administration focused on loot rather than its responsibilities.[23]

These and hundreds of other similar complaints in the assembly show us how politics takes place through victimization and its rectification. Indeed, *politics was founded on the material basis of rights claims.* As we remarked in the introduction, politics emerged at the point where appropriated Greek Cypriot property became "resources." The invisibilization of those resources occurred at the moment when politics emerged as a struggle over the "rights" (and "wrongs") of distribution. Those "rights," moreover, were secured in the sovereign exchange that traded individual victimization for the communal victimization that legitimated their so-called state. This brings us back to our interpretation of Benjamin's "lawmaking violence," which according to him "divest(s) the individual, at least as a legal subject, of all violence" (1996: 241). In a Schmittian interpretation of that divestiture, we may see this original forgotten, founding act as a "constitutive historical event—an act of *legitimacy*" where law and order coincide in land appropriation (Schmitt 2006: 73). What we argue, however, is that this happens through the relationship between political economy and sovereign exchange that was always visible in the right's more explicit statism, where their appropriation of territory and land was always already justified by communal victimization.

This problem becomes clearer if we return to a theme from the previous chapter: uncollected rubbish. Psychoanalyst Vamık Volkan had witnessed this same accumulation of rubbish described earlier in the chapter, which he called "the most common link to the Greeks." Piles were often gathered in village centers. "I was present when an official from the Turkish administration in Nicosia begged the village fathers to burn the rubbish in their village, emphasizing the fact that it was unsanitary and might spread disease. 'All it will take,' he pointed out, 'is a match and a can of gasoline to rid yourself of this ugly presence.'" While Volkan observes that the villagers agreed with the official, they "continued to point out to me items in the pile such as broken toys or children's books written in Greek." Volkan described being moved by what he saw as an inability to complete their mourning, which he attributes to "the guilt they felt at replacing the Greeks who had owned these simple family belongings, now rubbish" (1979: 131–132). As we noted in Chapter 2, however, Volkan found during a return visit to the village three years later that the melancholic moment had passed, and the villagers appeared to have completed their mourning.

Moreover, as we saw previously, while some refugees were reluctant to burn belongings or clean out the refrigerators of abandoned neighboring houses, they demanded such services from "the state." We would suggest that in addition to Volkan's individualist attribution of suspended mourning, it may also be possible to see in this refusal the birth of the social, where "the social" comes to stand for common victimhood, common struggle, and a refusal to face guilt individually. One may also understand the villagers to be saying, "I'm not individually the one responsible for this; we're responsible for it together. So let it be the state that takes care of it." It is such common suffering, after all, that justifies creating a separate region and self-rule.

It is here that we may find the ground of politics, Ricoeur's forgotten foundation, "a forgetting of that which constitutes the present of our living-together" (2010: 25). The justification of appropriating land and territory through communal victimization enabled the *project* of the state, as articulated by members of the legislative assembly and others in the period. This was a project that was careful, for instance, first to "nationalize" property and then to distribute it, in other words, to make that act of founding violence an act of the "state." This state project, realized as a form of statism, quickly ran aground on a populist politics born out of dissatisfaction with forms of distribution. While the project of the state was one in which the social engineering project of a separate space was justified by communal victimization, populist politics threatened to undermine that project by reducing persons to victims of "such-and-such offices."

Such a project was articulated most clearly in the Legislative Assembly by İsmet Kotak, head of the Settlement and Rehabilitation Office—an office that had been accused by opposition politicians of various forms of corruption. Kotak took the podium and first challenged his critic, Avcıoğlu, to point out a single person in his family who had benefited from his position. He then proceeded to articulate a vision of the state-building that they were undertaking during this period, and of the political difference that would ultimately emerge as one between the right and the left:

We have gone through a war. *A brand new country is being made. We are in the process of planting people from the south and from outside Cyprus in this soil (Biz, Güney'den ve de Kıbrıs dışından insanları ekmekteyiz, yeniden bu topraklara).* I want to bring your attention to this. It's a dream to expect that at the same time factories will begin working, and tourism will begin working, despite all the propaganda against us. . . . However, I want to make clear that in the villages we do not have a problem or we've had about eighty percent success. I would recommend you to visit our villages in appropriate areas, we can visit them together, and you can see what efforts we've made, and you can tell us our mistakes there, and we'll do our best to correct them. *I want to repeat again and again that we do not see this subject as a fight over houses (Biz, konuyu bir ev kavgası olarak görmediğimizi tekrar tekrar söylemek isteriz).* (authors' italics)[24]

Kotak, then, emphasizes the state-building effort and its limitations in the context of war.

In Kotak's remarks we can see the frictions implicit in Turkish Cypriot statecraft from its genesis: while the business of the de facto state was "sowing" or "planting" persons in a new territory, a populist politics was founded as a "fight over houses" (*ev kavgası*). The former depended on the legitimation of "facts on the ground," or the politics of dispossession, which Nomi Stolzenberg describes as a new state of affairs that cannot be undone: "When we say that facts on the ground 'cannot' be undone, we do not mean that they 'cannot' be undone in a literal sense. (Of course, they *can* be undone; all it takes is physical force, as the [2005 Israeli] pullout from Gaza boldly demonstrated). Rather, 'cannot' is a normative term, referring to political and moral 'impossibilities.' This is both the core idea and the basic mystery of facts on the ground" (2009: 22). Planting people is a way to create a new "sense of normality," where as time passes, and children and grandchildren grow up in these new places, reversing the status quo becomes inconceivable. As a result, a by-product of physical possession is the emergence of "some combination of considerations counseling against the dismantlement of facts on the ground—some kind of 'normative force field'" (24).

While "planting people" was about establishing the legitimacy of "facts on the ground," leftist parties opposed the hegemony of the old guard and their monopolization of the resources that constituted the ground of politics. Of course, both these understandings are established on the distribution of "resources" and as such are justified through Turkish Cypriots' victimization. Because death and victimization justified claims of statehood, statecraft and thereby the state-society boundary also came to be defined by victimization: the state becomes the institution that both rectifies victimization and distributes on the basis of it. Moreover, it was the emergence of political contest on the basis of distribution that transformed violence into victimization and Greek Cypriot property into "resources."

The Symptomal Kernel

Around the same time as the documentary film about Sanayi Holding was being made, well-known center-left journalist Hasan Hastürer wrote a column about the fate of the company. He places that fate in a historical trajectory that appears to take away Turkish Cypriots' productivity and economic viability in order to make them dependent on Turkey. "It was never desirable for us to stand on our own two feet," he claims. "In that case, we wouldn't have listened to orders." This dependency was created, he asserts, through the bribe of spoils: "After 1974 the Greek Cypriots' spoils remained. Both Turkish Cypriots and people coming from Turkey shared these spoils."

However, it becomes clear a couple of paragraphs later that he means by this only individual spoils, not the properties remaining that would have allowed them to be self-sufficient: "Could the Cypriot Turk have founded an economy that would have allowed him to stand on his own two feet? He could have 100 percent. The variety of the light industrial infrastructure left behind by the Greek Cypriots (*Rumdan kalan*) didn't exist in Turkey in that period. If that production had been structured with an economic mentality and sold on the Turkish market, we certainly would have created a productive community."[25] We see here the division between *ganimet* as spoils, something that was used to pacify the community and ultimately to corrupt it, and "infrastructure left behind by the Greek Cypriots" as what could or should have been the foundation for a self-sufficient community. We see, in other words, the distinction between a presumably unjust distribution of resources—the political victims and victimizers—and the forgotten or invisibilized "facts on the ground" that turned Greek Cypriot resources into "national assets."

What we have argued is that the founding of a state on dispossession was possible because of the sovereign exchange that traded individual victimization for a communal victimization that justified the establishment of a new state. The invisibilization of that dispossession, however, was made possible precisely because of a party politics that veiled or cloaked it in ideology. One sees this very clearly, for instance, in a September 1975 gathering of the Constituent Assembly, when they listened to a government adviser explain the problems they had encountered in running one large hotel that had previously been owned by a foreign corporation with mostly American shareholders. They did not yet have the tourism and management "know-how" to run such a hotel, the adviser explained, and he recommended that since its legal owners were not Greek Cypriot, the hotel should be returned to them in order to facilitate tourism. One of the leaders of CTP, Özker Özgür, passionately objected that this was directly against their political and economic goals: "While we're waiting for the establishment of a national economy, the decision to turn over our hotels and establishments that we won with blood and loss of life to the giant corporations of a country that is still implementing an embargo against the Motherland should be a source of consternation for all patriots."[26] Blood spilled—or in this case, the blood of martyrs kneaded into the soil—was what, in the nationalist rhetoric of the period, created a country (Bryant 2004: 190–216). Indeed, one of the best-known nationalist phrases, often inscribed on martyrs' memorials, is "What makes flags flags is the blood on them, and when someone dies in the name of a land it makes it a homeland" (*bayrakları bayrak yapan üstündeki kandır, toprak, eğer uğrunda ölen varsa vatandır*). In the particular rhetoric used in this discussion, these were "establishments that had been entrusted to us by our martyrs" (*şehitlerimizin bize emanet ettikleri tesisler*).[27]

In later decades, this nationalist discourse would be emptied of its constative meaning and take on what Yurchak (2006) calls a "hegemony of form," and one that, as we explain in Chapter 8, would often be used even by nationalists themselves for strategic purposes. This has led certain researchers, in looking back at the period, to associate this rhetoric of blood and martyrdom with the position of longtime nationalist leader Rauf Denktaş that "what had been taken in blood could not be given back at the negotiating table." However, the parliamentary records and newspapers of the period show that this rhetoric was not only a discourse of the old guard but was also prevalent among the self-declared left as a way of describing a type of primitive socialist accumulation, a "national economy" and "community property" that "has been won with blood and loss of life," specifically "the blood of our Fighters and Soldiers." What is remarkable here is not the thanatopolitical discourse of blood and soil, loss of life, and gain of land, which were the common ways of expressing the "facts on the ground" in this period. What is remarkable, instead, is that Özgür already expresses this as a national economy that grounds political struggle.

Interestingly, it was certain persons from what would come to be labeled "the right," that is, persons from the older establishment, who often pointed out the flimsy foundation of claims to a "national economy." One of these was businessman Ali Süha, whom Özgür labeled a "city aristocrat" or "bourgeois" (kent soylu).[28] In response to a similar argument put forward by another party leader, Süha would invoke the Realism of military conquest in opposition to the Marxist "real conditions of production" referenced by his colleagues: "Friends, do we have the foundational industry that Mr. Fuat Veziroğlu says we do? In other words, did this community sit down and establish industry and manufacturing by planning? Or is it just chance that the army, when it was going to pass through here instead suddenly passed through there, and it left you five or ten factories, and you present these five or ten factories like they're national industry and you're crying out in worry that this national industry will be given over to the private sector?"[29] Süha's leftist colleagues accused these members of attempting to deny workers' rights and destroy the "national economy" through privatization. Süha, in turn, aimed at an unmasking, an exposure of "national industry" as spoils.

Süha does this, moreover, through a series of questions, questions that Slavoj Žižek would label "indecent" because of their "drive to put into words what should be left unspoken" (1989: 179). It is noteworthy that none of Süha's opponents took up his challenge, which went to the heart of the leftist statebuilding exercise and especially its later association with federalism. As we have seen, while the right emphasized the community's victimization at the hands of Greek Cypriots as a justification for appropriating the property on which they would found the new state, the left would have a much more confused approach to that violence. As a result, the founding violence that the right tended to keep in full view would be subsumed by the left under their own attempts to "contribute to the democratic development of that constitutional order," as one former prime minister, Ferdi Sabit Soyer, phrased it.[30]

In a discussion of what he calls the "inconsistencies and splittings that allow the edifice of Order to maintain itself," Žižek observes that the aim of the critique of ideology is "to extract this symptomal kernel which the official, public ideological text simultaneously disavows and needs for its undisturbed functioning." He continues by observing that "the three main political-ideological positions" rely on "such an unacknowledged and unavoidable supplement": "The 'Right' finds it difficult to conceal its fascination with the myth of a primordial act of violence supposed to ground the legal order; the 'Centre' counts on innate human egotism . . . ; the 'Left,' as has long been discerned by perspicacious critics from Nietzsche onwards, manipulates with *ressentiment* and the promise of revenge ('Now it's our turn to . . .')" (Žižek 1996: 3). If we apply Žižek's remark to our case, it appears at first that the right's fascination with violence is the same as the sovereign exchange that founds the political order. Certainly, the right in north Cyprus was very concerned with *foundation*—but then, as we have shown, so was the left.

Rather, as multiparty politics emerged in Cyprus, the right's invocation of violence would develop as an arbitrary distribution of property and privileges aimed at nothing more than maintaining its own hegemony. The left, in contrast, would aim at "righting wrongs," at retribution for that arbitrary distribution. It is in this struggle over the ground of politics, however, that the "facts on the ground"—the founding of the state on Greek Cypriot dispossession—becomes disguised, masked, forgotten, or invisibilized. It is in this sense that what emerged as ideological differences become what Ricoeur (2010) refers to as substitutes veiling power and Žižek calls symptoms of power, where "attitudes which are officially opposed and mutually exclusive reveal their uncanny complicity" (1996: 3; see also Abrams 1988). We have seen here how the left's "contribution to the democratic development of a constitutional order" disguised the crack in its edifice that was the invocation of violence. What we will see in the next chapter is how an "uncanny complicity" emerges in demands for a federal state established on an initial partitioning.

CHAPTER 6

Federalism as Fetish

As one drives from the southern city of Larnaca toward the capital of Nicosia one sees it most clearly: the so-called TRNC's so-called flag, painted on the Five Finger Mountains the size of four football fields. Until recently, it was the world's largest flag, and some say that it is visible from space.[1] Certainly, it is highly visible from south of the cease-fire line. For more than two decades, from the time of its creation in 1987, it only annoyed Greek Cypriots across the line during the day. In 2001, however, some enthusiastic Turkish Cypriot nationalists formed a committee and raised money to light the flag at night.[2] Since 2003, it has been illuminated in a light show every evening, the flag disappearing into darkness and then gradually reappearing, first as the star and crescent of the Turkish flag, and then with the horizontal lines at top and bottom that distinguish it as the Turkish Cypriot flag.

"The fact is that the flag on Pentadactilos [Five Finger Mountains] dominates the Nicosia skyline too much," remarked one commentator in the south's main English-language newspaper. "After all it is just a protest flag that asserts a state without inspiring its realisation and fails as a flag."[3] The protest, in this assessment, is an assertion of presence in the face of a world that would deny it, a "fact on the ground" that is simultaneously unrealizable. As one comment on the above article suggested, it is "like a dog urinating on a lamp post to identify its territory." Even more than this, for many Turkish Cypriots it has become what a friend called "an expression of our nonrecognition complex"—a symbol that fails even as it succeeds and succeeds even as it fails.

We use the absurdity of this successful failure as an entry point to the ultimate enactment of the state, what is intended to be the ultimate act of

Figure 11. The TRNC flag on the Pentadactylos/Beşparmak/Five Finger Mountains (photo by Burçin Keleşzade).

sovereign agency, namely, the *declaration* of statehood. The flag on the mountain appeared four years after the TFSC's parliament voted unanimously to declare it a sovereign state, and the flag itself was intended as a symbol of that sovereignty. In ideal terms, declaring statehood is an illocutionary act, one that births a child to whom one will give a new name. This act is, indeed, intended as one of the main enactments of sovereignty: the capacity to name oneself and have that name recognized by others. Judith Butler asserts that the ability to name is considered one of the most original acts of sovereign power, the ability "to do what he or she says when it is said" (Butler 1997: 16). What is interesting in the case of north Cyprus is that a debate has existed there since the declaration of the "sovereign" TRNC in 1983 that revolves not around state-building or around the existence and reality of a state, but around the meaning of declaring or calling it such.

One can see the problem more clearly in the successful failure of the enormous flag. A couple of years after the flag's illumination, one friend decided to capture the light show on film, creating an ironic, one-minute video set to ska music. In the caption explaining the Youtube video, the filmmaker asks, "Is the world's largest flag a symbol of our existence, or of our nonexistence?" The video shows the flag lighting up against a darkened city, demonstrating how it is "illuminated at night to show off despite frequent electricity cuts." The caption concludes, "Here we have the TRNC's tragicomic story."[4]

Like the church with the minaret attached, explored in Chapter 2, there is something absurd about this flag that insists too much. Much of the problem with the flag is that it is aimed at an audience that denies it, and this makes it what the newspaper commentator above called a "protest flag," though one that the commentator also claims "fails as a flag," presumably because it does not symbolize effectively in the way that a flag should. Its ineffective signification is certainly clear when citizens cannot figure out if it symbolizes their existence or their nonexistence. Moreover, the newspaper commentator quoted above continued, "The flag would have no place in a federal Cyprus in which the Turkish Cypriots are represented and participate fully in its governance," suggesting that even as the flag asserts their presence, it simultaneously serves as a reminder of the refusal of others to see them or take them into account.[5]

The successful failure of the flag opens up a discussion of the failed performativity of the TRNC's declaration and allows us to explore the inherently social nature of sovereignty (Biersteker and Weber 1996: 1), or the way that states as well come to exist by virtue of a "fundamental dependency on the address of the Other" (Butler 1997: 5). This became clear in 1983 in the immediate international condemnation of the TRNC and subsequent unpronounceability and censorship of its name. In the case of this name, it is not only that one uses aporetic quotation marks (the "Turkish Republic of Northern Cyprus" or "TRNC") but rather that any invocation of the name must be buffered with layers of refusal, emphasizing that it is self-declared and unrecognized. The flag on the mountain defies this refusal, asserting a fact on the ground that to date no other state has tried to alter. It *insists*—and many would say that it insists too much. It insists on making one see it, taking that insistence to the extremes of a daily light show. But as our friend's invocation of a nonrecognition complex suggests, it simultaneously calls attention to their presence *and* to its denial.

In this book's introduction, we quoted Ralph Ellison remarking, "'High visibility' actually renders one *un*-visible" ([1947] 1995, ii). Referring to his own "invisibility," Ellison brings attention to what he called "a peculiar disposition of the eyes of those with whom I come in contact." These were, he claimed, "their inner eyes, those eyes with which they look through their physical eyes upon reality" (3). While the physical eyes see you, he says, the "inner eyes" deny you. "It is sometimes advantageous to be unseen," he observes, "although it is most often rather wearing on the nerves" (3). More-over, he remarks, "You ache with the need to convince yourself that you do exist in the real world, that you're a part of all the sound and anguish, and you strike out with your fists, you curse and you swear to make them recog-nize you. And, alas, it's seldom successful" (4). It is precisely in this sense of waving fists at the world that the flag succeeds in making Turkish Cypriots visible only to the extent that it calls attention to the ways in which they are not recognizable. While the physical eyes of the "international community" see, their inner eyes refuse to see.

In the case of the church with the minaret, which stood for the aporia of perceptibility, we might say that the physical eyes of the "international com-munity" engaged in a form of misrecognition, viewing such "stamps" on the landscape as "Turkey-fication." The flag, however, comes to stand for the apo-ria of recognizability, which we claimed in the introduction to Part II "is one in which the very acts that make them visible and perceptible take away the sovereign agency that would come with recognition." The flag does this by asserting a state-ness that appears to others as "state"ness.

The successful failure of the flag, then, is that rather than becoming a sym-bol of their state, it instead becomes a sign of what in conflict contexts is known as the Status Quo.[6] While *status quo* usually means simply "the ex-isting state of affairs," in conflict contexts it is used to point to certain "facts on the ground" that are illegitimate and so *must* change and yet are resistant to change. Even the Wikipedia entry defining *status quo* uses the case of an-other de facto state, Taiwan, to show how, even if the world insists that a status quo should be temporary, the lack of alternative solutions means that it often goes on indefinitely: "For example, Taiwan's political status straddles the line of a sovereign state in its own right and a non-sovereign area of China. Neither a full declaration of independence nor a forceful incorporation of the island into China is considered ideal by both parties at the current stage. Thus being 'pro status-quo' in this case generally means 'wait-and-see.'"[7] In addi-tion to "wait-and-see," though, the Status Quo in conflict situations could also be described as "wait it out," the assumption being that, as Hikmet Bil re-marked, quoted in the Introduction to Part II, "piracy can't continue forever."

In such contexts, then, Status Quo takes on another connotation of a stub-born stasis, simply digging in one's heels. The stubbornness of this stasis is often encapsulated in negotiators' descriptions of one side or the other in the conflict as "intransigent," that is, unwilling to move from the Status Quo. Dig-ging in one's heels, in turn, is a form of refusal (McGranahan 2016; Simpson

2014) that is an important part of the "myriad psychological and social effects unleashed" (Stolzenberg 2009: 9) by the phrase. This is a refusal of the de facto state to give in or give way, no matter the embargoes and isolations placed upon it. In our case, it meant a refusal of Turkish Cypriots to return to their homes in the south and insistence on remaining together in a separate space. In this sense, too, the flag could be seen as a sign of the Status Quo: "a dog urinating on a lamp post to identify its territory," marking it in a sign of refusal to give back or give in.

As a phrase, then, Status Quo does considerable work in capturing "something obvious but elusive and hard to put into words" (Stolzenberg 2009: 9) regarding the stubborn irresolvability of certain conflicts. However, like the term *de facto*, the Status Quo also contains a paradox, namely, that just as the Status Quo is resistant to change, so the "existing state of affairs" that it describes is illegitimate and so *should* or *must* change. The status quo is presumably a temporary situation on the way to a lasting solution, despite everyone accepting that it is a temporary situation that could go on forever.

Here, too, the flag is useful to think with. The flag, like the Status Quo, is abnormal—abnormally large, abnormally taunting—and so constantly points to the need for "normalization" (*normalleşme*), what would give them a "normal" state and normal lives. Most people seem to understand that the flag will need to be removed from the mountain in the event of a negotiated settlement. In the case of such a settlement, however, normalization would give them a flag that would be "seen" with the "inner eyes" of the international community even when it is a normal size. Normalization would give them a name that could be pronounced and a flag that could become the symbol of that state.

In the next pages, we use the 1983 declaration of the TRNC as a moment through which to explore the Status Quo, normalization, and the aporia of recognizability. In particular, we are interested in the question of nameability, having a state whose name can be pronounced—and by implication a flag that can be flown. The discussion will take us on a brief excursion into international law, or more specifically into what Stef Jansen (2009) refers to as "everyday geopolitics." Our interest is not in parsing the fine details of international law—as Turkish Cypriot leaders were often wont to do—but rather in seeing how international law, the politics of recognition, and what we have called the hegemonic realism of the "international community" led to particular contradictions in the enactment of political desires.

This will require an excursion into the idea of the international community itself, which until now we have tended to place in quotation marks. We have done this, as we will show, because it is a term without a referent: "There is no generally agreed understanding as to what the term means, but it is clear that the international community is presumed to possess agency, the ability to act in the world" (Brown 2001: 87). The fact that the term has no referent, however, does not prevent it from having efficacy in everyday life. Indeed, it is the "international community" that is both the audience and arbiter of claims to statehood, defining in an entirely contradictory way both the hegemonic realism that says the flag on the mountain can never be acceptable and the Realism of *realpolitik* that refuses to do anything about it.

Declaring and Naming

Every December, various institutions in north Cyprus print agendas for the upcoming year, which they distribute to members, clients, and supporters. Even in an age when many people rely on their mobile phones for keeping track of appointments, agendas remain a popular New Year's gift. One institution that has made a tradition of printing agendas is the Cyprus Turkish Teachers' Union (Kıbrıs Türk Öğretmenler Sendikası, or KTÖS), which has a membership of several thousand and a list of many more supporters, meaning that their calendars make it into a significant number of homes in the island's north.

As 2016 was drawing to a close, KTÖS made headlines when it took the opportunity of the calendar to write what they considered an alternative history. That history was in the agenda's margins, where the union commemorated dates not on official calendars, such as the murders of leftists mentioned in the previous chapter, or gave alternative interpretations to official holidays. One such official holiday is the anniversary of the founding of the TRNC. The state that we have discussed in previous chapters was the Turkish Federated State of Cyprus (TFSC), an entity that existed for a bit more than eight years, from its declaration in early 1975 to its transformation in 1983 into the TRNC (in Turkish, Kuzey Kıbrıs Türk Cumhuriyeti). The declaration of the latter was intended as an act of self-determination, but it was a truncated self-determination to the extent that the state was immediately condemned by the United Nations and remains unrecognized by any state besides Turkey.

The text of the agenda read, "15 November 1983: In agreement with the generals of the 12 September [1980] Military Coup in Turkey, Rauf Denktaş made a move that put our communal existence in jeopardy and destroyed all our international relations. The TRNC was declared. National holiday." The public reaction to the calendar was swift, with some demanding that teachers who were members of the union declare where their loyalties lay, either to distance themselves or support the union's statement.

One of those who immediately demanded an explanation from the union was Kudret Özersay, an international law professor who at the time of writing is the minister of foreign affairs. On his Facebook page, Özersay inquired, "In the education that you will give to new generations, are we going to ask them to stand up for our communal existence (*toplumsal varlığımıza sahip çıkmalarını isteyeceğiz*) by ensuring that they see their own state as an institution that endangers that existence?"[8] He asked, in other words, how the union of teachers paid by the state might nevertheless see that state as a liability.

The calendar and reaction to it point to a debate that has existed since the TRNC's declaration around naming, the central illocutionary act of the state in which state*hood* is declared. Until that time, the name "Turkish Federated State of Cyprus" indicated that they were establishing what should be the constituent state of a federation. What is peculiar is that even from the moment of the TRNC's declaration, leaders then, too, vociferously claimed that they were not secessionists. They were always open to federation. As a result, while the TFSC might be seen as a state acting like a "state"—that is, a state that accepted its so-calledness in dealings with the international community—the TRNC became a so-called state based on a presumed independence and sovereignty that was open to dissolution.

In one way, we might see this as reflecting the distinction, drawn by Jean Baudrillard, between dissimulation and simulation: "To dissimulate is to feign not to have what one has. To simulate is to feign to have what one hasn't. One implies a presence, the other an absence" (1981: 3). In our case, we might say that Turkish Cypriot state-builders used the TFSC to dissimulate, pretending that what they were building was not a state but a "state." The transition to the TRNC then appears to be a simulation, in which they pretend to have a statehood that is denied to them by nonrecognition. However, as Baudrillard emphasizes, the matter is not so simple, because "to simulate is not simply to feign." If I pretend to be ill, he says, I reproduce in myself the symptoms of that illness, thus threatening "the difference between 'true' and 'false,' between 'real' and 'imaginary'" (1981: 3). In other words, to simulate statehood also produces its symptoms.

To invoke simulation here, however, returns us to almost three decades of debates in political theory over the nature of the state. These debates suggest that sovereign nation-states are not "real" structures but rather are "the ontological effects of practices which are performatively enacted" (Weber 1998: 78), "the powerful, metaphysical effect of practices that make such structures appear to exist" (Mitchell 1991: 94; see also Biersteker and Weber 1996; Walker 1993). Cynthia Weber (1995), for instance, has argued that the state is always a simulation, dependent on the principle of noninterference to produce borders and territorial integrity. In a later article, she draws on Judith Butler's discussions of performativity to show how the state itself is produced through performances that are also gendered (Weber 1998). But if the state is already a simulation, what does this tell us about the so-called state, the state that is faking it? And what does the so-called state tell us about the applicability of theories of simulation and performativity to the construction of the state?

"The TRNC's founding in 1983 was the day we closed our doors to the world." This was the brief response of one Facebook follower to Özersay's comments regarding the teachers' union calendar. Indeed, responses were swift, and most seemed to argue that the union's negative evaluation of their so-called independence was pretty much on the mark. "We're talking about a community that has been made completely dependent on Turkey," one commented, "that has been completely shut off from the world, that both qualitatively and quantitatively is being led toward extinction. . . . The beginning of this paradigm was the establishment of that institution called the TRNC."

The current belief that the TRNC's declaration was intended to isolate them and make them more dependent on Turkey contrasted greatly with discussions of the time. The declaration of their so-called independence was preceded by extensive debates in the local press and society regarding what their independence would or would not bring. While there was a groundswell of support for the move, even the declaration of independence and sovereignty was hemmed in by simultaneous declarations that this was not secession and that they were open to federation. This created a lasting state of *belirsizlik*, a word of broad scope that can mean uncertainty but also lack of clarity or ambiguity. That state of uncertainty or ambiguity had existed in the TFSC period but took on new dimensions after 1983.

Ahmet, a schoolteacher who had just returned from his studies in Turkey in 1974, remarked to us on this uncertainty:

> And all of a sudden the republic was founded. I can only speak for myself, but a person gets this feeling like, "Is this place now *mine*? Should we see the future like this?" The message was that Cyprus was divided and we should get used to it. The island was divided. Because the discourse was like that, the joyful speeches in parliament and so on. And at the same time this couldn't go on forever, because Cyprus's international situation and that system that protects it has ways of ensuring that an act like that couldn't continue forever. In other words, again an uncertain situation, really!

Ahmet invokes here "Cyprus's international situation and that system that protects it" (*Kıbrıs'ın uluslararası durumu ve onu koruyan o sistem*), hence gesturing to that undefined entity that we usually call the international community. It was precisely because of this system, he notes, that the defiant act of establishing a state only created another situation that was *belirsiz*, uncertain or ambiguous, particularly regarding its status in the world. Moreover, according to Ahmet, this ambiguity emerged where even language fails: "In the constitution there's this thing that says this state is open to joining a federal Cyprus republic. For that reason nobody thought the TRNC was permanent—that is, everybody really knew that it wasn't going to work just to say, we've taken it, it's finished, and we're establishing a state here."

And indeed, the new so-called republic was swiftly condemned with a U.N. Security Council resolution against it. The resolution calls on "all States to respect the sovereignty, independence, territorial integrity and nonalignment of the Republic of Cyprus,"[9] suggesting that the TRNC resulted from an abrogation of those treaties in an act of secession. For this reason, in his speech before the United Nations Security Council where then president Rauf Denktaş defended the TRNC's declaration, he rehearsed the events of 1960 and the way in which the Republic of Cyprus had become an entirely Greek Cypriot entity despite its conception as a bicommunal state based on power sharing. Denktaş referred to the Security Council's expressions of concern regarding developments in the island's north before commenting in an agitated way, "I hope you are equally concerned that one part of a bicommunal government has for twenty years robbed the other part of all its rights and has not given them back and does not intend to give them back because they get all these confirmations from you that they are the legitimate government of Cyprus."[10]

Interestingly, Denktaş was a British-trained barrister, and he surrounded himself with other lawyers who were prepared to argue the intricacies of international law. One of their strongest arguments, emphasized again and again, was that the government of the RoC was *itself* de facto, existing in violation of the constitutional order, and that in any case the recognition of that government was only another instance of the arbitary and politicized way in which recognition was granted in the "international community." "You say that you consider the Turkish Republic of Northern Cyprus invalid," Denktaş remarked in the same speech. "You considered China nonexistent for thirty years, Eastern Germany nonexistent for twenty-five years. It doesn't matter. They are here with us, and I greet them with respect."[11] In other words, while Denktaş and his cohorts made legal arguments for the legitimacy of their state based on abrogation of the Republic's constitution, he also invoked realpolitik to remark that in any case political recognition is a matter of judgment and interests.

Indeed, Turkish Cypriot legal experts would consistently argue that even if the TRNC received no political recognition, this did not make it "illegal." In an article published in the *International and Comparative Law Review* two years before the TRNC's declaration, international lawyer Zaim Necatigil, one of Denktaş's advisers, argued, "Initially, the judiciary in the various countries generally took the view that a government or State not recognised de jure or at least de facto by their State should be regarded as non-existent. Nowadays this view has been almost entirely abandoned, and rightly so. De facto and de jure recognition are—and increasingly so—governed by political considerations which are irrelevant to the questions that the courts have to answer" (Nedjati 1981: 411). As Turkish Cypriot leaders and lawyers would argue again and again, nonrecognition made them neither illegal nor nonexistent, while questions of recognition were ultimately "governed by political considerations."

On this point, comparative legal scholar Yael Ronen, who compares the TRNC with other illegal regimes, appears to agree, remarking that while the U.N. resolutions give the appearance that the obligation of nonrecognition emerges from violation of the 1960 treaties, or possibly secession, the violation of those treaties, "if such took place, does not give rise to a universal obligation of non-recognition" (Ronen 2011: 66). What was unlawful, Ronen concludes, was the use of force on the part of Turkey, even if it was fulfilling obligations under the 1960 Treaty of Guarantee that made Turkey, Greece, and the U.K. protectors of the RoC's constitutional order. "It is not clear," she remarks, "that the Treaty of Guarantee allows the guarantor powers to intervene on behalf of only part of the population" (66). Moreover, even if it did allow that, "it cannot override the peremptory prohibition on the use of force in the UN Charter" (67). She continues by suggesting that even if the Treaty of Guarantee implied consent to use of force, it did not prohibit revoking that consent at a later date.

The peremptory prohibition to which Ronen refers is "the well-established principle that territory cannot validly be acquired by an unlawful use of force" (2). This principle constitutes what is known as a "peremptory norm" (*jus cogens*, or "compelling law"), a set of nonderogable norms from which arise *obligatio erga omnes*, or the obligations that must be recognized and enforced by all states to each other. Peremptory norms are binding but also notoriously debatable, both in substance and in derivation (Schmidt 2016). One commentator notes that "there is no scholarly consensus on the methods by which to ascertain the existence of a peremptory norm, nor to assess its significance or determine its content" (Bassiouni 1996: 67), and he describes the derivation of such norms through practice. In a nutshell, just as peremptory norms emerge from international legal practice, so the implementation of *obligatio erga omnes* relies on the interpretation of the "international community" that such a norm has, indeed, been violated. The United Nations was invoking such an obligation when it called on all states to deny recognition to the TRNC.

As we discuss below, wily Turkish Cypriot lawyers who understood the malleability of norms and the arbitrary way in which they were often applied attributed their own ambiguous status not to a situation of their own creation but rather to the way that they fell between the norms of the international system. They were aware, as one author writing about practices of recognition argues, that the recognition of either states or governments depends "to a significant degree on normative judgments by international actors." While recognition may be, or ought to be, "governed by criteria more principled than *realpolitik* . . . legal and moral criteria will only shape and perhaps circumscribe practices of recognition; it will rarely, if ever, dictate them" (Sloane 2002: 114). Hence, Denktaş's invocation of the changing status of such states as China and East Germany. Hence also his reference to the de facto-ness of the RoC, which had "robbed" them of their rights.

On the one hand, Turkish Cypriot leaders would consistently and untiringly argue that the establishment of their zone of safety was a matter of self-defense and that the RoC was not and could not be the legitimate government for the entire island because it had been established as a bicommunal republic. These arguments seemed to suggest that they sought legitimation for their separate state. On the other hand, however, they constantly invoked a desire for a federation—in other words, for a solution acceptable to the international community. In his U.N. speech, for instance, Denktaş declared, "We are not seceding. We are not seceding from the independent state of Cyprus, from the Republic of Cyprus—IF the chance would be given to us to establish a bizonal federal system. But if the robbers of my rights continue to insist that they are the legitimate government of Cyprus, we shall be as legitimate as they, as nonaligned as they, as sovereign as they in the northern state of Cyprus, but we shall keep the door wide open to reestablishing unity under a federal system" (emphasis in original).[12] The ultimate goal, according to this summary, was a federation that could only be established between two equal partners.

The contingency of Denktaş's remarks is clear. They are not secessionists but federalists, but they may be driven to secession by the "robbers of their rights." It is certainly not coincidental that in Denktaş's proclamation he does not refer to territorial integrity—one of the four elements of statehood ("sovereignty, independence, territorial integrity, and nonalignment") of the RoC that the United Nations had called on all nations to respect. He says that they will be legitimate, nonaligned, and sovereign, but the issue of territory is held in suspension as the very basis for the federal solution that was still to be negotiated.

What is noteworthy here is the high likelihood that Denktaş and other right-wing Turkish Cypriot leaders of the period had in fact no interest in a federation but saw it as a stepping-stone to recognition, in the event that negotiations failed (see esp. Kızılyürek 2005: 65–89). This opinion was borne out in the negotiations that he commanded for almost forty years, in which there was a push for greater separation of the communities that made the envisioned federation look a lot like a confederation. All of this was in contrast to those on the left who viewed their declaration of independence as a way to force Greek Cypriots' hands—in other words, viewed "independence" as a stepping-stone on the way to federation.

In both cases, however, what we see is the crucial role played by the figure of a future federation in deflecting from the stubbornness of the Status Quo, that is, from the "facts on the ground" that were altering the de facto situation. One could avow the temporariness of one's situation even as the Status Quo became more and more stubborn and permanent. Or as legal adviser Necatigil remarked to us, "Recognition isn't anything. Possession is sometimes as good as ownership." Returning to the example of the flag on the mountain, we can see how it proclaims precisely the idea that possession is "as good as"—by which Necatigil presumably means "as effective as"—ownership. After all, the flag dares someone to take it down, and no one has ever tried.

What will become clear is that by declaring their fealty to federation, secessionists could become federalists, but also federalists could become secessionists, as the whole possibility of a federation with two constituent states was built on the violent partition through which the north was created. As we will see, federalism would ultimately become fetishized precisely because of the way that it enabled both secessionists and federalists to accept the reality of partition—the Status Quo—while denying its violence. The discomfort produced among many Turkish Cypriots by the flag on the mountain is that, as a sign of the Status Quo, it is a constant reminder of the violence that gave them possession without ownership.

State and Status

> A visitor to the north of Cyprus cannot avoid noticing a change
> from the dynamic pace of life in the south. . . . This should not be
> misunderstood. The economy may be stagnant but North Cyprus is
> neither lethargic nor depressing. There is in fact a great sense of
> relief from the tensions and miseries of living in enclaves and a
> determination by the people to make a go of their own society.
> Although it is a small community and, except for the law courts
> (which were located in the Turkish section of Nicosia) it has had to
> build everything up from the beginning, the apparatus of govern-
> ment is in place, there is a lively multi-party politics which went on
> unhindered during the period of military government in Turkey and
> reasonable press freedom. There is no doubt either that the
> declaration of independence of November 1983 was very popular.[13]

These words of veteran Middle East journalist Keith Kyle, who covered Cyprus in the period, hint at the relative success of state-building in the island's north, as well as its sense of separateness, managing, as it did, to maintain multiparty politics and a free press even during the clampdown on free speech and dissent in Turkey during the military regime of the early 1980s. He also refers to the popularity of the TRNC's declaration, which passed unanimously through the parliament after a rancorous debate that lasted several months.

Indeed, the parliament rose to its feet to vote unanimously and enthusiastically for the declaration, and when the news that the vote had been taken leaked out, a crowd began spontaneously filling the streets outside the parliament building. The vote took place in the evening, and the following morning, 15 November, *Söz* newspaper, the voice of the same teachers' union that published the agenda, printed a long article calling on their Greek Cypriot counterparts to recognize the new state. Its extensive headline read in part, "Independence was declared! Good morning, Republic of Northern Cyprus! . . . Hello Southern Cyprus! Your little brother came into the world yesterday and greets you with respect!"[14] The same newspaper also printed a proclamation of the teachers' union that called on Greek Cypriots to recognize the TRNC "in order to contribute to the formation of a Union of Cyprus Republics."[15]

For the reader in the present, what Ahmet described as "the joyous speeches in parliament," or the gushing headlines calling on Greek Cypriots' recognition, appear self-deluded, especially given the United Nations' swift condemnation of the act and previous threats that such a condemnation would be forthcoming. Although Turkey recognized the TRNC within twenty-four hours, other initial nods came only from Bangladesh and Malaysia and were immediately quashed by the U.N. resolutions. Ahmet had claimed something that debates leading up to the declaration confirm: that "everybody really knew that it wasn't going to work just to say, we've taken it, it's finished, and we're establishing a state here." One must ask then, what on earth were they thinking? If such a large proportion of even those who supported the declaration knew that they were facing swift international condemnation, what exactly were they trying to accomplish?

The political conjuncture for the declaration was a frustrating one, and much of the rhetoric around the declaration reflects that. Beginning in the early 1980s, the RoC, in partnership with Greece, began to swing the Cyprus Problem from the negotiating table to the international level, eventually resulting in a 1983 U.N. Security Council resolution calling for the withdrawal of all "occupying forces" on the island. For many Turkish Cypriots of the period, this move was interpreted as an attempt on the part of Greek Cypriots to force their negotiating partners' hand through use of their recognition as the government of the entire island (Billuroğlu 2012: 69–70).

It was in this atmosphere, and given the failure of talks over almost a decade, that the TFSC's parliament during that summer debated and passed a resolution supporting Turkish Cypriots' right to self-determination. This then began a months-long debate and speculation about whether or not a declaration of independence was imminent. Indeed, on Denktaş's return to the island from meetings in New York in October 1983, tens of thousands waited for him in northern Nicosia's main square, while a group of fifty-one associations presented a manifesto in which they reiterated their support for a bizonal, bicommunal federation but insisted on the immediate declaration of an independent state.[16] And numerous newspaper articles of the time discussed the excitement then coursing through the community, remarking that the public "has no more patience with the delays in declaring the North Cyprus State."[17]

Even in the midst of public enthusiasm, however, there were still many who questioned what declaring a sovereign state really meant. Moreover, the issue was not cleared up for them when Denktaş, on his return from New York, greeted the crowds' cries of "We want an independent state!" (*Bağımsız devlet isteriz*) with an ambiguous response: "We are independent. We are independent under the roof of our state [*Bağımsızız. Devletimizin çatısı altında bağımsızız*]. It is written in our constitution that we are a Republic. In this situation, all we have to do is put a new name on it."[18] Even before this confusing statement, there was much discussion in the press about what independence and self-determination meant because of the proclamation of their right to self-determination earlier that summer. After this, however, discussion intensified around the question of what a *declaration* of independence would actually change. What did it really mean to "put a new name" on their state?

Indeed, in the run-up to the vote in parliament, much of the discussion centered on what it meant to be independent, *bağımsız*, literally "without ties." And in these discussions, two themes consistently intersected at the point where a declaration of their independence seemed inevitable: the first is what we have referred to as sovereign agency, while the second—inevitably linked to the first—was the state as status. The issue of sovereign agency emerged again and again not only in nationalist proclamations of their right to self-determination but even more clearly in the left's discussions of the need to demonstrate independence from Turkey, to show to the world that they were not simply an illegal occupation. The state as status was part of a historical trajectory of institutionalization discussed earlier that seemed inevitably to lead to the need for a sovereign, independent state in order to achieve political equality with their Greek Cypriot partners.

In political terms, the right was mostly unified around what they viewed as a declaration of independence from Greek Cypriots—in other words, separatism. There were those among them who saw the move as a way to gain more independence from their patron state and those who saw it as a way finally to fulfill the dream of *taksim,* or uniting their separate part of the island with the "Motherland." For the right, however, that distinction clearly took second place to their enthusiasm for declaring that they were no longer simply a federal state-in-waiting but a "real" state that dared to declare itself as such. For the right, what was important was insisting on their equality as a founding community of the RoC that should be treated as an equal partner at the negotiating table rather than simply a puppet of an occupying regime.[19]

Indeed, in his speech before the U.N. Security Council after the TRNC's declaration, Denktaş based their need for a sovereign state on Greek Cypriots' refusal to see them. "We believe that declaring our state will aid in the process of negotiation. Because this emphasizes the reality of equality that until now has been denied, not taken into account, viewed as comic, or forgotten in the negotiations."[20] It is noteworthy that Denktaş draws an implicit distinction between "having" a state—something that he already noted was a reality—and "declaring" it as such. If they had previously been dissimulating by pretending that their state was a "state," declaring the state, *giving a name to it*, was the act intended to make them perceptible, to say to the international community, "We are here."

The very act of naming their state, then, was intended as an act of sovereign agency. However, even this statement of a man considered to be a staunch supporter of self-determination seems to equivocate when it comes to the final form that state will take, seeing the TRNC's declaration as a way to make them agentive actors at the negotiating table. Moreover, as we argue in the conclusion, the uneven and uncertain path of Turkish Cypriots toward "state"hood shows us that while the state may appear to be the only form for the realization of political desires in the contemporary world, this does not always mean that those who use the language of the state and its sovereignty necessarily aim to have a sovereign state.

One sees this in the way that the left was more divided in how the goal of sovereign agency could be accomplished. For an important section of the left, especially that led by CTP, the only way to acquire such a sovereign personhood was through the internationally acceptable solution of a federation. In an interview in the mouthpiece of CTP immediately after the U.N. Security Council resolution in May, Alpay Durduran, leader of the social democratic Communal Liberation Party (TKP), explained, "The right of self-determination is a general concept that means a community taking decisions that will affect its own fate. This cannot be limited only to the declaration of a state. How can a community use its right of self-determination? It can use it in a democratic environment, in a democratic community. This is possible in a separate state, it's possible in a federation, and maybe for small communities that are spread out, it's possible in autonomous administrations."[21] Durduran suggests, then, that there are other, more realizable ways to achieve the sovereign agency that they seek.

Durduran went on to remark that contrary to what certain political leaders hoped, defying the wishes of the international community would not make them more recognizable as they wished, but rather made them unrecognizable as sovereign agents. Durduran argues that in the past, through a denial of desire for a separate state and adherence to federation, they had managed to convince the United Nations that the state but not the government of the RoC was legitimate. In other words, by treating their own state like a "state," they had managed to show that they were forced into such an undesirable position by the actions of their Greek Cypriot partners in the RoC. However, Durduran remarks, Turkish Cypriots' reactionary politics "has brought us again to the position of being an administration, and has made the Greek Cypriot administration into the Republic of Cyprus government."[22] In other words, demands for a "real" state only showed their secessionist hand and made them not equal partners in the RoC but rather secessionists running a "pirate," or "puppet," state. What is remarkable in this, and something to which we will return, *is the way that dissimulation— pretending that their state is a "state"—becomes a form of agency.*

For other members of the left, however, the only way to escape from their "puppet" status and acquire real independence was through a declaration of independence. This view was represented most forcefully by the teachers' union's *Söz* newspaper. At that time, the newspaper gathered together writers who were the most vociferous in their critiques of Turkish Cypriot dependence on Turkey and how that dependence erased them as actors. One columnist, Sabahattin İsmail, wrote, "As long as the Greek Cypriot side is recognized as a State, and we are viewed as an insurgent community, the Greek Cypriot side doesn't have much need to reach an agreement with us. . . . Parallel to this, we say that as long as there is no agreement, as long as we continue to get poorer, as long as our political isolation continues, North Cyprus will become more tied to Turkey economically, politically, socially and culturally."[23] While the assertion of the need for equality overlapped with a large strand of the right, it was the desire to free themselves from dependence on Turkey that separated them as supporters of the declaration.

Another writer in the same newspaper, B. Mahmudoğlu, also made clear that simply declaring their state would not in itself give them the perceptibility they desired; they also needed to show that they had their own political will—in other words, that they were not simply a puppet state: "Until today we've changed our sign three times but the world has never counted us as human (*dünya bizi adamdan saymadı*). . . . It doesn't matter how much we refuse to see that we're completely dependent on Turkey, or how much we deny that we're a puppet and show state, or however much we try to close the gap with demagogy, we're as visible as an ostrich, and the world is aware of this." The author argues that the only way to establish a healthy relationship with Turkey is to "explain openly our desire for independence," and rather than wasting their patron state's money, instead use it to establish a healthy economy that will allow them to stand on their own feet. He hints, then, at Turkish Cypriots' possible source of agency, while also suggesting that they have not been convincing in their attempts up to that point. With such a demonstration of sincere desire, he concludes, Ankara "would not insist on the Cypriot Turkish people remaining without status, *just a pile of stateless humans who don't know themselves what they are*" (*Kıbrıs Türk halkının statüsüz, ne olduğunu kendi de bilmeyen devletsiz bir yığın insan durumunda kalmasında ısrar etmez*) (authors' italics).[24]

The idea that without a state they are "a pile of stateless humans who don't know what they are" is a very strong reflection of what Ralph Ellison had described as the self-doubt of one's own existence that comes when others refuse to see: "You wonder whether you aren't simply a phantom in other people's minds. . . . You ache with the need to convince yourself that you do exist in the real world" (1995: 3). However, the state was not only about making them perceptible but also making them recognizable, that is, giving them status. What Mahmudoğlu means by "status" becomes clearer in İsmail's further observation that Turkish Cypriots of all political persuasions are quite obsessed with the question of equality, but no one seems to know what they mean by it. After reviewing different expressions of equality, İsmail declares, "The concrete meaning of equality is EQUALITY OF STATUS, that is, that the Cypriot Turkish Community is not a minority but is one of the main two communities of the island. And just as Cypriot Greeks have the right to found their own state, we have the right to found a separate state. And this right must be recognized."[25] Or as another commentator in the same newspaper remarked, "This is not 'right-wing' or 'left-wing,' it is the people's most fundamental problem of HUMANITY. To be able to live like humans. . . . For peoples, governing oneself in the first instance means having a STATE."[26] The state, then, was to give them status, to transform them from "a pile of stateless humans who don't know what they are" into people who are "able to live like humans." All the authors quoted above appear to accept that the state represents "status par excellence," something that "allows its possessor to advance and get by in the world" (Constantinou 2004: 1). Indeed, in Latin the word *state* derives from *status*, as in "a station, position, place, way of standing, posture, order, arrangement, condition."

However, the condition of possibility for their transformation into humans was also what prevented them from being recognizable to the world and so left them in a state of "abandonment" (Agamben 1998) by the international community: namely, the violence with which they had resisted and founded their "state." We have earlier discussed the desire to be "put in the place of men/humans" that led Turkish Cypriots to take up arms in what they called a struggle for existence, a *varoluş mücadelesi*. What became clear by this time, however, was that the attempt to achieve status through the state and thereby make themselves perceptible ended up making them unrecognizable. Their "struggle for existence" had come to undermine their struggle for being or presence, their *varolma mücadelesi*, by creating "facts on the ground" and an unnameable Status Quo.

Perceptibility, Recognizability, and the "International Community"

Without recognition, do you have a state or not? Can you claim to exist when no one sees you? These questions occupied surprisingly large parts of the public discussion of what it meant to declare their state. "Independent State! Independent State!" cried one columnist.

As though we're not independent, as though someone's holding us. . . . In fact, we already possess a simulation/phantom of an independent state (*görüntüsel olarak bağımsız bir devlete sahibiz*). The Turkish Federated State of Cyprus, with its legislative branch, its executive branch, its judicial branch is already an enormous power. A reality.

But I still say it's a simulation/phantom. Why? Because this business isn't as simple as a nation saying, "I've founded an independent state." It has to get other states to recognize/know it (*tanıtmak gerekir*). It has to get them to recognize/know it so that it will be clear that it's an independent state.[27]

On the one hand, the *reality* (*gerçek*) is that they possess an "enormous power" (*koskoca bir güç*) with all its institutions. It is, in other words, recognizable in its state-ness. On the other hand, that reality is *görüntüsel*, the adjectival form of *görüntü*, a word that may mean an "image," a "semblance," a "simulation," or a "specter" or "apparition."

The author here seems to gesture to the state as simulation, though clearly not in Baudrillard's (1981) sense of simulation as a representation of an absence. *Görüntü* may also mean a "specter," though there is nothing to indicate that the author is pointing to some kind of haunting (Derrida 1994; cf. Navaro-Yashin 2012). Rather, the author presents us with something that most closely resembles Ralph Ellison's "Invisible Man," who avers that because others refuse to see him, "you wonder whether you aren't simply a phantom in other people's minds." "Like the bodiless heads you see sometimes in circus sideshows," Ellison remarks, "it is as though I have been surrounded by mirrors of hard, distorting glass. When they approach me they see only my surroundings, themselves, or figments of their imagination—indeed, everything and anything except me" ([1947] 1995: 3). Like the feeling of invisibility at a party where no one knows or acknowledges you, we see in the invocation of specters or phantoms that the gap between the real and the realizable has a *realizer*—someone who knows, sees you, and makes you visible. This is what Butler (1997a: 5) referred to as the "fundamental dependency on the address of the Other." That realizer or other in this instance is "the world," or what is otherwise referred to as the "international community," that undefined body of actors who, like the crowd at a party, have a mysterious ability to determine one's sense of solidity or spectrality.

Even in the international law and international relations literature that attempt to define the "international community," however, there is a distinct frustration with the way, as an entity, it eludes the analyst's grasp. One international law scholar, for instance, remarks with exasperation, "Jurists have posited that the international community as a whole is equivalent with 'the civilized world,' 'the conscience of mankind,' morality and public policy, 'basic human values,' and 'more inclusive' than a state. Each associated referent leaves the signification of this ultimate referent of legal analysis up in the air. More often than not, like obscenity, the jurist assumes that we shall know it when we see it" (Conklin 2012: 135–136). In international relations the term hardly fares better: "Nowadays, international community is omnipresent in discussion of international politics and, as a rule, it carries a heavy normative, teleological, and political baggage. . . . Furthermore, international community is endowed with nearly fully-fledged agency, as any random Internet search for phrases such as 'international community acts; feels; believes; intervenes; can or cannot' would testify" (Roschin 2016: 179). And when an issue of *Foreign Policy* asked scholars from various disciplines to weigh in on the term, one denounced it as "the false community composed of an inchoate global majority and organized ruling elites" (Bello 2002: 41).

A significant part of the confusion lies in distinguishing whether the term refers to "a generic international community of states or possibly to a unitary actor called the 'International Community'" (Ellis 2009: 9). On the one hand, in other words, the term represents the "collective moral and ethical opinions of states" (Ellis 2009: 10), or "the shared universal values founded in international law and mainly borne by international organizations" (De Guevara and Kuhn 2011: 136; also Kovach 2003). These values must be implemented by individual actors, and it is never a given that states will adhere to those values at the expense of their own self-interest. Indeed, "as the implied set of 'universal norms' is not necessarily agreed upon by all, the concept is often used to construct them in the first place" (De Guevara and Kuhn 2011: 139).

On the other hand, the International Community is a reified construct, and although "there is no generally agreed understanding as to what the term means, it is clear that the international community is presumed to possess agency, the ability to act in the world" (Brown 2001: 87). While reference to "the international community" may define those who are part of a community of states, "the paradox is that actors can only be excluded from 'the international community' in the moral sense, while legally and structurally they remain part of it" (De Guevara and Kuhn 2011: 137). De Guevara and Kuhn are thinking of this inclusive exclusion in the Westphalian sense, referring especially to "rogue" or "failed" states, that is, those cases where states but not governments are recognized or where recognized states are sanctioned. "Rogue" states, for instance, may exist on the edges of the international system while remaining a part of it to the extent that they maintain their statehood and sovereignty (Beck and Greschewski 2009).

In the case of unrecognized states, however, we may see this inclusive exclusion working in another sense, where the unrecognized states view themselves as part of the "International Community," the reified moral actor, while excluded from the "international community," or the society of states. The International Community in this sense comes to represent "the world" into which their state had been born and in which it seeks to become an International Legal Personality. The International Legal Person is the "bearer of rights" in the "international society of states" (Bartelson 2013: 114).[28] It is by becoming such an International Legal Personality that the *reality* of their state—the child that has been born into the world—becomes *realizable*, that is, acquires a name that the international community can pronounce. Until that moment, their name is always placed in quotation marks or prefaced by *so-called* or *pseudo*. We remarked in the Introduction that the quotation marks define the aporia; the quotation marks also make them appear ghost-like, spectral, pseudo, and therefore always at the point of disappearing. What would give them solidity would be to acquire an International Legal Personality, turning them from specters into persons.

What prevents them from acquiring such a Personality, however, is the set of principles known as peremptory norms that define the hegemonic realism of the international order. As noted in the introduction, we take our understanding of hegemony from James Scott's early remark that "from a much more modest view of what hegemony is all about, it might be said that the main function of a system of domination is to accomplish precisely this: to define what is realistic and what is not realistic and to drive certain goals and aspirations into the realm of the impossible, the realm of idle dreams, of wishful thinking" (1985: 326). We remark in the introduction to Part II that labeling de facto states either puppets of other regimes or pirates outside the international order points to a certain willfulness, a desire for something that is not "realistic" in Scott's sense. In her brilliant excursion into what we mean when we speak of certain persons, particularly women, as willful, Sara Ahmed observes, "Thinking through will is an invitation to think about force differently. Force can take the following form: *the making unbearable of the consequences of not willing what someone wills you to will*" (2014: loc. 1246;

emphasis in original). Placed alongside Scott's early definition of hegemony, we see that hegemony in these definitions takes place through self-censorship, through the denial of desires, and even through the denial of a desire for those desires. It makes those desires "unrealistic," "idle dreams," that is, unrealizable.

The hegemonic realism that determines their "conjunctural situation" or what is "possible," then, is one that makes certain dreams appear impossible and makes unbearable the consequences of willing wrongly. Rather than seeing hegemony as something that goes without thinking (Comaroff and Comaroff 1991: 24–28), the automatic response to the Althusserian policeman's hailing, Scott suggests that we may hesitate in turning, wanting to resist but knowing its impossibility. In this way, the turning itself becomes not a demonstration of hegemony but rather a performance of it that over time is a repeated and iterative form of submission (Butler 1997b: 106–131; see also Butler 1990). It is a performance of submission to a "reality" that also constructs that reality, much in the way that submission to the presumed will of an International Community also constructs that reification.[29]

What, however, if the policeman never hails you? What if, in fact, the policeman refuses to hail you, refuses to see you, watches your antics but refuses to intervene? Ralph Ellison again is relevant here: "It is sometimes advantageous to be unseen," he remarks, reflecting what we discuss in Chapter 9 as an enjoyment of exceptionality, the possibility of falling through the cracks in the world order. However, Ellison also comments that "it is most often rather wearing on the nerves. . . . You ache with the need to convince yourself that you do exist in the real world" ([1947] 1995: 2). This is why, as Hikmet Bil remarked in the epigraph of the Part II introduction, "Undoubtedly piracy must have an end," and as we will see in Part III, the pirate/puppet dilemma produces desires for "normalization." This makes particularly pertinent Butler's observation that the Althusserian scene of interpellation is not only one of coercion but is also "a strange scene of love," what she called the formation of the subject "through the passionate pursuit of the reprimanding recognition of the state" (1997b: 128–129). The state's reprimanding recognition, then, is like the beloved master who tells one that certain dreams are left unpursued for one's own good, since you would simply be chasing idle fantasies.

While Butler, Althusser, and indeed it seems all theorists writing on hegemony are concerned with "the state"—that reified abstraction produced through our submission to it—we see from the case of an unrecognized state that "the state" is not the only hegemonic power whose reprimanding recognition one may passionately pursue. Just as the reified State may be embodied in the policeman and his hailing, so the reified International Community may be embodied in the U.N. resolutions that condemn one or the diplomats who place one's name in quotation marks. Similarly, when Mustafa Akıncı says, "We believed that [federation] was the possible solution" and that "there could be no other alternative," or when Ahmet claims that "everybody really knew that it wasn't going to work just to say, we've taken it, it's finished, and we're establishing a state here," or when Denktaş declares before the United Nations that they were not really secessionists, what they point to is what Ahmet called the "international situation and that system that protects it." What they point to is the way in which their own goals and aspirations are driven into "the realm of the impossible, the realm of idle dreams, of wishful thinking." What they point to is the way in which their state that should give them status instead becomes an unnameable Status Quo.

Normalizing the Abnormal State

In 2009, a member of the European Parliament representing the RoC brought a question to the European Commission regarding the flag on the mountain. The questioner asked, quite simply, if the commission was aware of the flag and Greek Cypriot sensitivities regarding it. She asked how the commission intended to intervene, given that the flag "constitutes an unprecedented daily provocation to the people of Cyprus, in particular Greek Cypriots" and "recalls the tragic events accompanying the Turkish invasion and the continuing slavery of the northern part of Cyprus, thereby wrecking any attempts to cultivate a climate of confidence-building between the two communities." Moreover, the flag "constitutes a hostile action which forms part of Turkish endeavours to make the occupied territories of Cyprus Turkish."[30]

The reply of the commissioner, then Ollie Rehn, was that the commission was aware of Greek Cypriot sensitivities on the subject and "would welcome any initiative of the Turkish Cypriot community to remedy the situation." The commissioner's conclusion, however, was that "the issue once again highlights the urgent need for a rapid solution to the Cyprus problem."[31]

Condensed in this question and its reply are many of the problems of a temporality in suspension, the idea that the magic wand of the Solution will bring about a new era when giant flags on mountains do not taunt and when the violence that they symbolize has been rectified. What is condensed in the question and its reply is the way that, even as the flag fails as a flag—that is, fails as a symbol of a state—it works very effectively as a sign of the Status Quo, constantly pointing to the violence of partition. Indeed, insofar as the flag is a sign of the Status Quo, its very in-your-face insistence condenses and stands for that violence. Moreover, both the frustrated tone of the question and the connotations of reprimand in the answer point to the way in which, through its insistent signification of the Status Quo, the flag also points to temporal "stuckness" (Hage 2009), to the stubborn stasis, a situation that *should* change and yet *does not*.

As will become clear in the next chapter, however, for Turkish Cypriots the flag's successful failure also comes to represent the aporia in another sense: as the unrealized or unrealizable state, the state that has never fully become one. The video of the flag at night comically points to this, showing the illuminated flag against the blackout of a city darkened by electricity cuts. In Chapter 7, we describe the ways Turkish Cypriots bemoan the failures of their state, or the ways that the lack of a clear future, the lack of planning, led to a lack of an entity that seemed sufficiently state-like. Or as Mustafa Akıncı himself would remark in a newspaper interview, "We couldn't seem to institutionalize. And that structure that couldn't institutionalize gradually started rotting."[32] Indeed, for at least the past two decades, it has been quite common to hear Turkish Cypriots complain, as did one right-wing union leader, that "we engaged in a struggle to save ourselves but couldn't engage in a struggle to establish ourselves." Because of this, he remarked, "We've become a community just waiting for peace."[33]

"Peace," also known as the Solution, is supposed to bring normalization, when time will flow in a normal way and flags can be a normal size. However, "peace" had been imagined and understood since the 1960s as a federation, precisely because federation had become the "acceptable," the "realistic," and the "realizable" solution, the one to which the International Community had given its approval. Any dreams of independence were always cast as wishful thinking, not "realistic"—although that did not prevent many people from speculating, in a realist way, that eventually the international community would get tired of bicommunal negotiations and simply recognize them. As a result, the figure of federation becomes fetishized as that which contains and condenses desires for the state.

We remarked in Chapter 2 that flags are often described as fetishistic, condensing multiple events and symbols in a unique identity. In this case, however, we see how the flag that fails as one stands not for the state but for the Status Quo, while the figure of federation becomes fetishized as that which condenses state desire (Aretxaga 2000; Taussig 1992). "Fetishists," Žižek remarks, "are not dreamers lost in their private worlds. They are thorough 'realists' capable of accepting the way things are, given that they have their fetish to which they can cling in order to cancel the full impact of reality" (2009: 65). "Realism," in this case, would be de facto citizens and statebuilders accepting that the world will not recognize them, while still clinging to the hope of recognition in the form of a federal solution that allows them "to cancel the full impact of reality."

As should be clear by now, however, the figure of the federal solution actually plays a greater role than that, and we have clues to its meaning in Baudrillard's later discussion of the fetish, which he helpfully distinguishes from the simulation as an "abstract prosthesis." "It's meaningless in itself," he remarks, "but it takes the place of everything. Of everything that cannot take place" (Baudrillard and Noailles 2007: 16). Federalism, indeed, becomes such an abstract prosthesis, in which the impossible exchange of violence and territory that established their state is crystallized.[34] Federalism becomes the always unrealizable and singular way to realize that impossible exchange, the solution that *should* be realizable and yet *cannot be*.

It is in this sense that, like other fetishized objects, federalism is both a "reality"—or the possibility of a "real" state—and a symbol made to stand for "normalization." Federation was the "realizable" solution that at the same time turned what was otherwise the legitimization of partition into the only "peaceful" solution. In the case of the flag, the federal solution that would remove it from the mountain would turn their Status Quo into a state, giving them an equal status and turning the violence of possession into the legitimacy of ownership. Peculiarly, then, the equation Federalism = Peace would founder on the contradiction that Federalism = Partition. The contradictory formula Peace = Federalism = Partition, in turn, may be used to express what Žižek calls "the deadlock of desire," where the real that emerged as a product of that deadlock was the literal ground on which their state was founded. As we will see in the next chapter, this was accomplished through inserting distribution based on victimization into a politics of spoils.

PART III

THE APORETIC SUBJECT

IN EARLY FEBRUARY 1975, a provisional Ercan Airport had opened to civilian traffic. For thirty-five years, the main airline that would fly commercial flights to the north would be the Cyprus Turkish Airline (CTA) (Kıbrıs Türk Havayolları [KTHY]), a joint venture of Turkish Airlines and the Consolidated Fund of the Assembly of the Turkish Cypriot Community. Although 50 percent of the airline was owned by Turkish Air, Turkish Cypriots tended to call it their "national airline." Despite embargoes and isolations, CTA was able to land in airports in the United Kingdom and other parts of Europe after touch-down stops in Turkey, hence bringing planes emblazoned with the name of "their own" airline into metropolitan capitals. In 2005, during the semiprivatization of Turkish Airlines, CTA's shares were sold back to the Turkish Cypriot government, making the airline for the first time an entirely Turkish Cypriot–owned enterprise. By that time, however, there was much competition in the form of new, private airlines flying to north Cyprus and many Turkish Cypriots choosing Larnaca Airport, in the island's south. Within five years CTA had declared bankruptcy, a result not only of the new, competitive environment but also of overstaffing and mismanagement.

The airline's collapse left a wound in the community and a sense of increased helplessness for many people. We had often flown the airline at the height of its activity, in the 1990s, when the border with the south was still closed and routes to the north were limited. In 2003, as a result of protests that we describe in the Conclusion, Turkish Cypriot leaders would decide to open the checkpoints, producing a new social, economic, and political environment on the island (Bryant 2010; Hatay 2007). The 1990s, however, were still a period of isolation, though as we explain in Chapter 9, this was an exceptionality that contained its own form of enjoyment. It was a period when tourist brochures still sold the island's north as an "untouched paradise," and a sui generis system had developed based on kinship and networks that gave to the north a sense of intimacy. That intimacy, moreover, was intensely experienced on Turkish Cypriots' one airline, where boarding a plane in London or Istanbul always had the atmosphere of boarding a village bus taking you home.

While we believed we were not the only ones with this perception of the airline, we decided in 2017 to test this theory by asking Mete's nearly five thousand Facebook friends what they missed about the airline.[1] The immediate flood of around two hundred responses confirmed the perception we had had ourselves that, as one friend put it, "Whatever the TRNC is, that's what CTA was. . . . But it was still ours." Indeed, what stood out among the responses was the overwhelming expression of loss of something that "was ours." "Despite its mistakes and its faults," said one friend, "I miss it being ours." Another said he missed "it being Cypriot, it being ours."

A number of friends expanded on this theme. "I miss everything about it," said one woman, the mother of an important politician. "It was like my hand, my foot, my energy, my breath, my wings. It was my identity that was valid in the world. It was my family, and when I was in trouble they found a solution. . . . It was what I trusted. . . . They smiled and made me smile. . . . For this reason I won't ever forget or forgive those who bankrupted it." All seemed to agree with one friend who wrote, "What I miss the most is the feeling that it tied me to my homeland, that it was a bridge with my homeland." Some cited the flight attendants being acquaintances or the airline's announcements being in the Cypriot dialect. Others remembered the sandwiches with *hellim*, a Cypriot cheese, and Bixi Cola, a Turkish Cypriot imitation of Coca-Cola. Others missed being able to take excess baggage without paying. Or for one, who had been a university student in Turkey, what he missed was "the sensitive people who enabled a student who hadn't been able to get to the airport on time still to make it to his exam by opening the plane doors and pulling out the stairs again even after they had boarded all the passengers and closed the doors, saying 'We have a student who has to get to his exam.'" What many missed, then, was the familiar and even familial intimacy, the sense of "being ours," that we argued in previous chapters began with "adopting" (*sahiplenmek* or *sahip çıkmak*) and that as we show in the next chapters in practice emerged from exceptionality and through "managing" or "getting by" (*idare etmek*) in the international order.

If Part I concerned the *aporia of perceptibility* and Part II the *aporia of recognizability*, Part III addresses the *aporia of agency*, or becoming agentive agents only to the extent that one's agency is handcuffed. While the previous chapters have described the de facto and factitious elements of the so-called state, focusing on the early years of state-building, Part III concerns how Turkish Cypriots have lived with, contested, and manipulated that state as both citizens and subjects. For this reason, this section examines the effects of living with a de facto state over time, while the particular ethnographic focus is the 1990s, or around two decades after the island's division.

As the next chapters show, the aporias of perceptibility and recognizability that were part of state-building from the beginning ultimately produced ways of "getting by" the international order. We demonstrate in Chapter 7 that not only were distribution mechanisms founded in victimization and became the primary way to acquire "rights," but those mechanisms made victimization into a form of constrained agency. It was agency to the extent that victim-citizens of the new state exchanged their individual victimization for that of the state, simultaneously justifying the existence of the state in the first place and disguising their own act of refusal: refusal to compromise, refusal to return to their homes in the south. The problem, however, with a rhetoric of victimization is that it appeared to make them into passive martyrs rather than active agents. As victims, then, they became persons to be "saved," and it is this paradox of the citizen as someone who acquires agency through victimization that we argue in Chapter 8 would shape relations with their patron and would-be "motherland," Turkey. In Chapter 9, however, we outline ways in which helplessness may itself become a form of agency, and powerlessness may have a disguised power.

Moreover, it was precisely through creating a space where one was "getting by" that a sense of place as one's intimate space emerged. As many people responding to our question about Cyprus Turkish Airlines expressed, it was precisely because of its irregularities and exceptions that many loved it. Smoking in the first rows, waiving excess baggage, and even stopping a plane's takeoff to allow a student on board were cited alongside *hellim* sandwiches and airline attendants who made announcements in Cypriot dialect as "the feeling it gave us that it was from us," as one summarized. As Turkish Cypriots' first and only international institution, the so-called state's representative in the sky, it had an intimacy of exceptionality and imperfection. It has been precisely this bond of imperfection—what one academic and politician called "the brotherhood of the underpants"—that we will see in the next chapters may give enjoyment to exception and agency to helplessness.

CHAPTER 7

Victim and Citizen

"People don't believe that you can get a job without pulling strings," a young party leader commented to us one day. We were drinking tea and eating a sesame-covered pastry called *simit*, both imports to the island from Turkey. Although the left-wing party to which the young man belongs emphasizes Cypriot as opposed to Turkish identity, members of the party also study in Turkey, take holidays at Turkish resorts, enjoy Turkish music, and partake of Turkish food and drink, especially the aniseed-flavored liqueur *rakı*. As a result, it only struck us as amusing in retrospect that we consumed Turkish tea while listening to complaints about Turkish Cypriot corruption that also made reference to Turkey's overweening influence on the island and the ways the right utilized Turkey to stay in power.

"I got a call one day from a man who wanted me to help him get a job for his daughter," our friend recounted. It turned out that the young woman had taken an exam in application for one of two open teaching positions. "We've tried to institute a new system, but no one believes it works," he complained, referring to certain attempts by his party to reform a nepotistic order. Indeed, even though his own party has used that order as much as any other, many people continue to blame the first ruling party for the entrenchment of nepotism on the island. Moreover, they view that party as consistently having been backed by Turkey. Our friend explained to his caller that in the new system the top two scorers on the exam would be given the positions and that there was really nothing he could do.

Nevertheless, several days later the man called again. "He was ecstatic! He said, 'We're expecting you in our village this Sunday. We're going to sacrifice a lamb in your name.' I said, 'What happened?' He said, 'You know what happened! My daughter got the job.'" Our friend asked how the young woman had done on her exam, and the father told him that she had come in second. "'So that's why she got the job!' I told him. The man just laughed. 'Everybody knows you can't get a job that way!' he insisted."

This friend's amusing complaint about the ubiquity of nepotism, as well as his invocation of the belief that only nepotism can get things done, is hardly an unusual one. Indeed, Turkish Cypriots consistently complain about corruption and the necessity for nepotistic ties in order to get simple things accomplished. Whether it is speeding up a passport application or a title transfer, receiving social security benefits, or simply getting proper health care, Turkish Cypriots find themselves employing an array of kinship and friendship relations in daily life. Securing a job in the civil service for oneself or one's kin requires a careful calculation of clientelistic relations and party affiliation. While jobs are more likely to be distributed immediately after an election, one has to put one's bet on the winning hand or play one's options. It is not uncommon for people to switch parties frequently in order to guarantee civil-service positions for children.

Turkish Cypriots complain about this system, and yet they are instrumental in its reproduction. In fact, it often seems that they would not have it any other way. In this sense, it resembles the discourses around corruption in Nigeria described by Daniel Jordan Smith, who remarks, "People frequently condemn corruption and its consequences as immoral and socially ruinous, yet they also participate in seemingly contradictory behaviors that enable, encourage, and even glorify corruption" (Smith 2007: loc. 255). Unlike Nigeria, however, "corruption" as we speak of it here is not dominated by the monetary exchange of bribery or by the extortion, swindling, and exploitation that appear to permeate the Nigerian state but rather by "a moral economy dominated by an ethics of reciprocal exchange" (loc. 1093). It is such an ethic that Smith argues ultimately underpins higher levels of corruption in Nigeria, as "all strata in Nigeria, except the very lowest, are invested in, and in some measure benefit from, the accumulation and distribution of public resources through informal private networks" (loc. 1152).

In north Cyprus, we show here, informal networks are not only an inroad to access the state or a way to navigate the state. Rather, the state is practiced as a set of informal private networks (see also Witsoe 2011). These are networks that one must use to acquire one's portion of the distribution of public resources, but they are also simply the face of the state. When one goes to a public office or when one makes decisions about parties and candidates, one looks first for people who are in some fashion related to one. Personalizing encounters is the key to getting served. At the same time, the divisions of clientelism and distribution are embedded in party politics. Our friend's narrative above is a complaint about nepotism, but it also has another undercurrent: the assertion that his party has attempted to rectify a corrupt system implemented by a right-wing regime close to Turkey.

And this points us to the main difference between north Cyprus and other nepotistic systems of governance: from the beginning, the state that emerged in the island's north was itself a client of a larger patron—what in the literature is called a "patron state"—that often intervened in its operation. Patron states are those protective powers that provide military, diplomatic, and financial aid to an unrecognized entity that they want to preserve. So, while Armenia is Nagorno-Karabakh's patron and Russia supports the breakaway states of Transnistria, South Ossetia, and Abkhazia, Turkey became both the facilitator and guardian of the state in Cyprus's north. This has included both stationing around 25,000 troops on the island, supposedly for Turkish Cypriots' protection, and providing hundreds of millions of dollars of economic aid each year.[1] As we discuss in the next chapter, the protecting wing of their patron would ultimately begin to seem crushing. What we explore here, however, is the way in which the Turkish state's patronage inserted itself into a local clientelistic system that began to define the state.

Our story in this chapter is about the *de facto citizen*, the bearer of the "right to have rights" (Arendt 1968: 267–302) who nevertheless questions her ability to enact her political will. In this and the next chapter, the idea of "political will" (*siyasi irade*), so often invoked by Turkish Cypriots to talk about their own agency or lack thereof, helps us understand Turkish Cypriots as political actors, both citizens and subjects of the de facto state. As we will see, "political will" comes to stand for democracy, as in holding free and fair elections, but it also comes to stand for agency, as in the capacity to act upon the world. We discuss the de facto subject and her agency in the next chapters; for now, we focus on the demands of democracy in a de facto state.

We argue here that nepotism becomes the way in which subjects are interpellated in the de facto state, through the distribution of "resources" on the basis of victimhood. And here it is necessary to emphasize the size of the community, where personal connections corrode attempts to establish authority. In Louis Althusser's famous example, the citizen on the street who turns around when a policeman shouts "hey, you!" is interpellated into an ideology that legitimizes domination (1971). In north Cyprus, however, not only is it difficult to imagine that a policeman would shout such a thing; it is even more difficult to imagine that a Turkish Cypriot on the street would respond to that shout with any seriousness. Insofar as the police have authority, it is because they are part of a command structure that ties them to the Turkish military.[2] But there are numerous tales of kebabs for prisoners, warnings rather than arrests, and looking the other way.[3]

The impersonal "hey, you!" would be likely to create curiosity and a sense of affront rather than "hailing" in Althusser's sense. The phrase that would be more likely to "hail" Turkish Cypriots is the more personal *"be, gardaş"* (hey, brother), a phrase one hears every day and that "hails" the speaker by invoking cultural intimacy, egalitarianism, and moral obligation. The "citizen," we argue here, is also a "brother," a locution that obviously invokes community but that is constituted through particular relations to property and politics. It is through the "brotherly" distribution of property—through what one left-wing politician of the early post-1974 period called "the brotherly share" (*kardeş payı*)—that politics operates. However, that fraternal distribution was legitimated by a victimhood that became both the source of a new political economy and the ideological foundation of the state.

As a result, we argue, the distribution of goods was not only an expectation of the nepotistic order *but was the primary way in which the de facto citizen emerged*. The de facto citizen, as we describe her here, is someone who appeared as bearer of that constellation of rights and entitlements that specifically depended on victimhood, partition, and enclavement. If the de facto state arose in the process of displacement and resettlement, the de facto citizen emerged in the networks of distribution that would define the political.

The "Brotherly Share"

"Unfortunately, the Greek Cypriots didn't leave behind social housing, where all the houses were a standard type," a friend of ours jokes as we discuss the period after 1974.[4] "Everyone was used to the ghetto life, to that equality. Everyone was getting their paycheck from the state, and everyone was living in the same sort of conditions. After 1974 it became a free-for-all, with all those houses and the state controlling them. 'Why did he get that and I got this?' That's where politics after '74 started."

Our friend was sixteen years old in 1974, but his father was a small tradesman who included him in the business; and so he saw firsthand the sorts of dealing that went on after the war. He witnessed the transformation from the enclaves in which a very small group of traditional elites who owned significant amounts of property clung to their positions while average citizens became dependent on the state. "People got used to getting their salary from the state. They got used to that equality." In the post-1974 period, in contrast, "Suddenly everyone was running after what he could grab. And there was a small, insignificant group of traders who snatched up the right to import certain things. We had one man who got rich from importing cigarette lighters. The world's first plastic lighter fortune! Another got rich from blankets, another from Pyrex. Because their right to import came from the Trade Office, people began to assume that only people close to the government could get rich."

In addition, the ideological "planting of people" articulated by İsmet Kotak had turned into the "fight over houses" that he had deplored. "Think about it," our friend says. "Take someone like Orhan Kâhya, one of the richest men in Limassol, and suddenly the man who worked for him has a wealth of property." Complaints by large numbers of Turkish Cypriots that they had not received the equivalent of their property in the south, he explains, inevitably led to changes in the original system. In 1977, the Chamber of Deputies began a long discussion of how to rectify the situation that eventually resulted in the Settlement, Land Distribution, and Equivalent Property Law (İskan, Topraklandırma ve Eşdeğer Mal Yasası), popularly known as İTEM, intended to enable the unilateral "exchange" of property. Under the law, commissions were established to calculate the value of property that citizens had left behind in the south and the value of property that they had been given or could potentially be given in the north. Turkish Cypriots displaced from the south renounced their claim on their properties there, giving up the titles to their lands in the south in exchange for equivalent properties in the north. This exchange was unilateral because it was enacted only in the island's north and was considered illegal by the Greek Cypriot owners of that property, displaced to the south. As a result, the Turkish Cypriot state began to resemble a large real estate company, while for about three decades Turkish Cypriot leaders would insist in reunification negotiations on a global exchange of properties.

Our friend, who later became a businessman with many land dealings, commented, regarding the system created by İTEM,

They said, let's create a system so that we won't create problems for the future. And they created *such* a system—it was too perfect! The packet system. Everything will be transparent, who's applied will be transparent, everyone's case will be examined one-by-one, the property, the property's value. . . . *Such* a system was created, so that for instance you'll apply to get points, and the points you get will be publicly displayed, and everyone will see how much you got. Don't look at today! The system was fine; there were just problems in the implementation.

Our friend insists that the rules of the system were "perfect" and encouraged transparency. However, the system turned out to be much too slow: "So when you apply to that system, a packet of properties will be announced, six months will have to pass, you go to the settlement office, and you'll say show me the properties. Everyone's got to know and see the properties. . . . At the same time, you hear that on the Greek side a property has sold for a million sterling, and the same property is selling on this side for ten thousand lira. You left a vineyard in Mallia and got a plot in Kyrenia, and the vineyard in Mallia is worth five times as much." Ironically, property prices in the south rose because of the demand created by the same Greek Cypriot refugees whose properties in the north appeared to be losing value. This encouraged Turkish Cypriot refugees to demand even more property in exchange. And in the nascent party politics of Cyprus's north, the public's anxieties over the distribution of properties emerged as the single most important arena in which one could garner votes.

As a result, accusations of graft were rife, even as politicians outdid each other in their attempts to give citizens their "rights." For instance, longtime right-wing politician and former president Derviş Eroğlu proposed what came to be known as the DBT system, a way of speeding up the process by which property was acquired. Our businessman friend remarked, "What happened in the meantime? The DBT system: Immovable Property with Valuation Certificate (Değerlendirme Belgesiyle Taşınmaz Mal). The system was this: you go, and they rent a plot to you if you have points, and you settle there. In other words, you bypass the system. And all of a sudden, the prime ministry, the Settlement Department, the parties were all filled with people saying, 'I'm in a hurry.' They did an accounting, and they had to announce thirteen more packets of properties to meet the demand." In the new multiparty system, political struggles were carried out over how much and how quickly to distribute "resources" to the public.

Given that Turkish Cypriots had left approximately 500,000 *dönüm*s of land in the south and had acquired 1.5 million *dönüm*s in the north, one would think that "resources" would amply fulfill demand.[5] This soon proved not to be the case. It had long been a principle that the families of those killed in the conflict would have priority in receiving property. However, others who had not lost property but were conflict affected began to claim their right to material compensation. In addition to points for properties left behind in the south, former fighters began to demand compensation, and a new point system developed to reward them for years served. As a result, someone born and raised in Nicosia, who had not been displaced and owned original Turkish-titled property, could nevertheless acquire points that he could use in exchange for a Greek Cypriot house or a plot of land.

At least one person warned that although "resources" were plentiful, they were not endless. "The resources were diminishing," Hakkı Atun recalled. "In fact, at one point the former fighters—and everyone from seven to seventy was a fighter—it was said, let's give the former fighters rights. As the person who knew this business best, I was saying, we don't even know if the resources we have are going to be enough for the equivalence exchanges, we can't do a real accounting, and now where is this coming from? Denktaş Bey says, 'You're right, Hakkı,' but then when pressure comes, he accepts it. That's how politics works!" Atun attributes injustices in the system, then, to the desire for short-term political gain.[6]

What we see in this system is that the citizen emerges as someone who has the right to "resources" as a result of her victimization, while "the people" emerges as that body that demands justice in distribution. Certainly, a long line of political thinkers, starting with Friedrich Engels, has seen property as one of the key nodes for understanding the modern state, where property comes to stand for the individual's relationship to the state. In the hypothetical social contract, we guarantee our safety and that of our property through renouncing our rights to do whatever we want. In a liberal, democratic nation-state, the individual enacts her political will in a sovereign exchange, including giving up the right to enact violence and take whatever she wants, while acquiring that will as a citizen. As Partha Chatterjee remarks, "Property is the conceptual name of the regulation by law of relations between individuals in civil society" (2004: 74).

In the polity that emerged in north Cyprus, in contrast, persons gained the rights of citizen in their status not as individuals but as victims. That polity emerged out of and was justified by Turkish Cypriots' victimization, both individual and communal. While carving out a separate territory was justified by communal victimization, property both represented individual victimization, through standing for what one had lost or fought for, and was the compensation for that victimization. The interesting contradiction that emerged, then, was between a discourse that "we all have suffered" and attempts to implement "rights"—often at the expense of others—on the basis of individual victimhood. As a result, struggles over property became the site where the tension between communal and individual victimization unfolded, as well as the site where Turkish Cypriots were made as citizens even as they made the state.

The latter happened in large part because while Turkish Cypriots did inherit land registry documents in the island's north, the property regime itself was one that they made up, improvised, and sustained through use. If in recognized states the relationship between individuals and the state is mediated by a property regime, this is so because the guarantee of rights in property is also a way of defining sovereign territory and the limits of the state. In a de facto state, however, citizens are aware that while their property regime works within the confines of their "borders," it is not—or at least *is not yet*—recognized by the world as a legitimate property regime. In fact, it is in the question of property that the de facto state always seems most palpably at the point of unraveling.

Indeed, as previous chapters have shown, Turkish Cypriots were aware from the beginning of their so-called state that title deeds had a temporality tied to future negotiations. Those future negotiations, moreover, aimed at a bizonal federation that looks very much like the one that has existed in the island's north since 1974. However, any claims to a separate state—and therefore to retaining the property that people received—depended in turn on the most central aspect of biopolitics, the management of population. Simply put, the state's claims to sovereignty and territory rely on citizens staying put, or at least on their not returning to the south. In propaganda to the world or in negotiations with Greek Cypriot partners, Turkish Cypriot leaders may point to the fact that only a handful of Turkish Cypriots remain in the island's south as proof that Turkish Cypriots have been victimized in the past and have security concerns in the present. In other words, the continuing refusal of Turkish Cypriots to return to their villages in the south despite numerous inducements becomes proof of their need for a space of their own.

Our businessman friend parenthetically described this situation when talking to us one day about the property issue:

As we approached 1975, there was a real estate boom on the Greek Cypriot side, because of crowding. And our biggest fear at the time was, "Lord, let's not have 5,000 to 10,000 people remaining on that side." Because today if we have any kind of case, the most important factor is that all the refugees moved from the south. In other words, God forbid, if something had happened and 20,000 out of the 50,000 had said, "No, we're not going"—and some did take this attitude. If something like that had happened—thanks a lot to Sampson,[7] he really helped us out here—if 10,000 to 15,000 Turks had remained, the situation could have been much different, we could have had a very different situation. We would have exploded the whole bizonality thing, we would have dug our own grave.

Our friend made this remark while trying to explain why, in 1977, Turkish Cypriot leaders were induced to write a new law on property, despite their own qualms about its international legality. In other words, he directly links a law that would allow Turkish Cypriots to pass Greek Cypriot property to their children to retaining Turkish Cypriots in the north and thereby maintaining claims to sovereignty.

What we see here, then, is that if Turkish Cypriot citizens have the "right to have rights," that right is based not in law but in victimization. What gave Turkish Cypriots rights in the new state, and most important, what gave them property, was not the law itself but their victimhood. While the law was rewritten to acknowledge that, Turkish Cypriots are more aware than other citizens of the factitiousness of the law, the fact that it will not be enforced by any other state and moreover that *it remains intact only as long as they themselves remain.*

Victimhood, then, performs a dual function here. On the one hand, it produces a reliance on the state, in the sense that you have crossed the partition line with nothing and must rely on the state to give you what it has. But on the other hand, you know that the state relies on your victimhood for its own legitimation, that your continuing presence in the north is what demonstrates communal victimization and so maintains the state. In this sense, you both collude in the appropriation of Greek Cypriot property *and* wash your hands of it, allowing the state to offer you the inducement of property in order to remain but at the same time recognizing that it is your own victimization, the fact of remaining, that legitimates this order.

What emerged, then, is what we might call a thymapolitical state (from *thyma,* or *victim,* in Greek) in which victimhood became currency in a political economy of spoils. The politics of victimhood is built on both physical and emotional suffering and loss. The distribution of "resources" to refugees very quickly resulted in demands that others who were not refugees but who had also suffered, especially martyrs' families, former fighters, and landless peasants, also receive rewards. Indeed, it soon turned out that everyone had suffered in some way as a result of the previous decade, and the government found ways to translate various forms of suffering into points, property, and positions. As one might expect, this was a system open to corruption, as well as competition, and in a small society where personal relations imbue every transaction, nepotism regarding distribution of state resources soon became the way that both politics and government were conducted. The prevalence of social democratic ideals, as well as a highly developed egalitarianism that combined with limited capitalist penetration, meant that civil-service jobs and distribution of political favors became a significant "asset."

Yurttaş and *Gardaş*, Citizen and Brother

In 2012, after having taken extended leave from her U.S. position to teach as a visiting professor in north Cyprus for more than two years, Rebecca prepared to take up a new post in London. During the time that she taught in Cyprus, the university made regular social insurance and providence fund payments to the state, and upon her resignation from the position, she had the right to the accumulated money in the providence fund. As she was taking a position abroad, she had a right to take the funds immediately. However, the university's human resources administrator informed her that it would probably take some months to get the money, as the ministry was practically broke and was trying to delay payments. "Just give them your overseas bank account number, and they'll send it to you eventually," the administrator suggested.

The university was a new one, and Rebecca suspected that at that point any faculty leaving the school had been foreign, not Turkish Cypriot. In other words, she suspected that persons who had tested the system previously had little understanding of how the system "really" worked. She decided, then, to drag Mete along to follow up on the paperwork herself. What ensued was a series of nepotistic performances that were necessary to overcome obstacles to the implementation of what, on paper, was a legal right.

The Social Insurance Office in Nicosia is a relatively modern-looking building, though its interior resembles so many other government offices:

crowded rows of wooden desks, stacks of yellowing folders, and a large number of personnel who seem to have little to do. Indeed, it is often difficult to know at what time to come to the office, since personnel arrive late after taking children to school, disappear for lunch breaks, and leave early to pick up children. On the day that we arrived, a woman whose function was apparently receptionist, as there were no files on her desk, was stereotypically painting her nails. She sat behind a glass panel, but it was easy enough to ignore the panel and simply enter the room. We told her our business, and she pointed to the desk behind her, which was piled with files.

"Your file is with her, but she's gone for the day," the receptionist told us. The time was about 11:00 a.m.

Mete began a series of loud complaints about the workings of bureaucracy in Cyprus, intended to be heard by the rest of the room. A few employees who were chatting in a corner looked up from behind stacks of paper, but they seemed to take the barrage in stride. The secretary recommended that we return the next day, which we did, only to find that the woman attending to the case was in the office that day but had stepped out. This time, Mete simply said, "In that case, we'll talk to Kemal Bey," and we trotted up the stairs.

A secretary in a tidy office with only a telephone on the desk guarded the entry to Kemal Bey's domain. Mete gave his name, and we waited only a few seconds before the thickly paneled door swung open and Kemal Bey welcomed us with smiles. "*Napan*, Mete?" (What's up, Mete?) he asked, patting Mete on the arm. We entered an office as large as the crowded room downstairs, but instead of battered wooden desks, it was filled with executive office furniture: plush leather chairs, a machine-made Oriental rug, a large desk with a black leather top. Kemal Bey offered us coffee, asking about Mete's father, a journalist, and brother, a businessman. They talked about people they knew, complained about the current government, and finally came to our case. "We're not asking for anything that's not our right," Mete explained.

Kemal Bey picked up the telephone and requested the file, which quickly appeared on his desk. He explained to us how his office was in financial trouble, because the bankrupt northern Nicosia municipality had taken money out of his office's funds to pay its own bills and had not yet put the money back. "We're waiting for Turkey to step in," he smiled in a self-deprecating way. "Once we get a payment from them, we'll start disbursing our own funds."

"We're leaving the country soon," Mete explained, and Kemal Bey promised to do what he could. Within about a week we received the funds in our account.

Having worked for several years in Egypt, a country known for its inflated bureaucracy, Rebecca was familiar with overstaffing of the civil service as a government move to reduce unemployment, at least in appearance (Wahba 2002). Egyptian friends complained about their low salaries, averaging at that time around 300 Egyptian liras, or about $100, per month. Most tried to make money elsewhere, but they kept their government jobs because of their security. Similarly in north Cyprus, it is common to find certain government employees, especially teachers and doctors, offering lessons and holding clinic hours in the late afternoon and evening. And like in Egypt, the prospect of a second salary that is often more lucrative than the first encourages doctors to spend as little time as possible at the state hospital and teachers to demand fewer teaching hours. Unlike in Egypt, however, civil service salaries in north Cyprus are quite high: in 2018, salaries ranged from around $900 to $4,400 per month.[8] Moreover, inflated numbers of civil-service employees and high salaries are something that north Cyprus shares with the south of the island, which in its 2013 financial crisis cut government salaries and benefits as an austerity measure.

Indeed, bloated government bureaucracies are a feature of many postcolonial countries, as are the stories of lazy bureaucrats and egregious abuses of the system (Anders 2010; Lodge, Stirton, and Moloney 2015). What makes the case of north Cyprus unusual is the combination of party politics, what Turkish Cypriots call "achieved rights" (*kazanılmış haklar*), and the presence of an external patron.

As we mentioned above in the discussion of property distribution, there was considerable dissatisfaction with the way that refugees had been settled in the north, and many people perceived that persons close to the administration had received favors, becoming—as our friend suggested above—Pyrex and plastic lighter kings. Moreover, property distribution reform was slow, and there was a bubbling anger in the community about this. As a result, most people date the first important political turning point to 1981, when anger turned into a real challenge for the community. As a friend of ours who began as a socialist and eventually moved to the right of the political spectrum explained it, the nepotistic system took root when Denktaş attempted to quash a major party contender that appeared in the form of the Communal Liberation Party (TKP):

There were all these brilliant young people, and many of them had
TMT [Turkish Defense Organization] background. Denktaş saw that
they were going to win, because people were furious! I was a soldier,
and they wouldn't let us vote because *all* of the soldiers, all of us, were
going to vote for TKP. Do you know what it meant to be a UBP [Na-
tional Unity Party] member then? There was a kid called Apo. His
brother-in-law or uncle or something was the mayor of Karavas. He
would say to me, "My friend, my friend, how are you so rich and you're
not with UBP?" In 1981, being with UBP meant being a thief, a free-
loader, mafia, you see what I mean?

In response to this serious political challenge, Denktaş, as president, took
upon himself all authority for hiring and firing in the government service.
Immediately, he created three thousand new jobs, and he won the election
with a little more than 50 percent.

Our friend remarked, "There was this anger, and to ease that—at the time
what was the biggest thing? Finding your child a job. And when Denktaş gave
jobs to 3,000 people, that anger disappeared." In a polity of less than 150,000,
3,000 jobs is a significant number. "We learned this business, and from
1981 to today, whenever a candidate goes looking for votes, everybody
wants a job."

Indeed, today in north Cyprus, election periods are the time when much
hiring is done and public works are accomplished. Many people have come
to accept that potholes will be filled, roads paved, and streetlamps repaired
only before election periods. Constituencies and families often vote in blocs
in order to assure candidates of delivering certain towns or districts. One assumes that villages with good roads and sidewalks are close to particular
parties, while the pre-election period is one when jobs for children are lined
up. One architect friend who lives in the Kyrenia district claims that his village is "an interesting laboratory." "During election periods," he says, "people
start dividing up by family. Evening dinners, lobbying, everybody gets a job
lined up. It's unbelievable!"

Whether believable or not, it appears to be typical: one summer in our
own village, we went for a week without receiving any water. This happened
to be immediately after a municipal election, before which we had taken advantage of the timing to appeal to the mayor for repairs to our road. They
had begun the repairs but then left things unfinished and in a state of dusty
disarray when money ran out immediately after the election. At the time of

our water shortage, our shepherd neighbor Elham passed by on his motor scooter, herding his flock. Our village was a mixed one before 1974, and Elham is from one of the original Turkish Cypriot families of the village and has significant networks. We complained to him about our lack of water and told him that the municipality had blamed it on a malfunction in the distribution system. Elham laughed.

"That's what they say, but what really happened is that they replaced the boy who had been doing the distribution with another boy just a month before the election," he explained. "It was his paternal uncle's son, but still they replaced him for political reasons. Of course, he doesn't know what he's doing. They should at least have kept the other one on for a while so he can see how the system works."

Whether Elham's information was correct or not, it points to another aspect of the nepotistic system about which everyone complains but which no one knows how to address: the way that party politics have undermined any pretense of meritocracy in the civil service. As another friend who was a young civil servant in the 1980s explained, the original three thousand hired to secure Denktaş's election in 1981 acquired their jobs with no regard to their qualifications. When the time came, they were later passed over for promotion. Many of those who were passed over in this way joined opposition parties, thereby ensuring that when the opposition came to office, the "injustice" of their failure to be promoted would be righted. In order to achieve that, in the late 1980s many of the older bureaucrats were pushed from their positions into early retirement.

Moreover, in the early 1980s the three main political parties signed what came to be known as the "Three-Way Agreement" (Üçlü Kararname), which opened the way for the *müşavir* system. A *müşavir*, or "adviser," was someone who had previously been in a high-level bureaucratic position but lost it when his or her party was no longer in power. These "advisers" would continue to receive the same salary that they had received in their previous appointment but without having an actual position. The system did not become active until 1994, when there was finally a change of government from the long-ruling UBP. Once activated, the *müşavir* quickly became the most desirable appointment in the north Cypriot civil service.[9] One acquaintance, for example, was a *müşavir* from 1995 to 2016, receiving the salary of a high-level bureaucrat while at the same time running his own company. When he retired from the civil service at the age of fifty-five, he began to receive around €2,500 per month retirement income, in addition to a €100,000 retirement bonus (see also Barışsever 2007). In other words, this system ensured that recipients of some of the highest government salaries today have not actually worked in an office for many years.

As a result of this accretion of practices, almost anyone with whom you speak today will complain that the civil service is politically staffed with persons who are not qualified, not interested in their posts, and generally just getting by. As one high-level administrator put it,

> It used to be that there were bureaucrats in Cyprus who had been trained during the British Administration, and those bureaucrats did their work, and they had a work ethic and seriousness. . . . In 1994 we signed the three-way agreement, and even office managers became political appointees. When we did that, the civil service was politicized. Today if there are eight thousand people working in the civil service, six thousand are from UBP and two thousand from CTP. From among these people, when CTP comes to power, the people from UBP sleep, and when UBP comes to power, the people from CTP sleep.[10]

Or as a former schoolteacher who is active in civil society described it,

> Actually in those days [before the politicization of the civil service] the government offices were really good. . . . That is, those bureaucrats from the earlier period, they were really administrators, they would do their job properly, without paying attention to who you are or where you came from. The political situation slowly eliminated them. . . . Everything was about who you knew or were related to, if you go the hospital you can't even get seen if you don't know someone. . . . After all the nepotistic relationships entered the picture, everything turned into cliques. So you have this party's people, and this party's administrators, and the three-way decrees, I don't know what else, everything got totally messed up![11]

This portrait of corruption literally corrupting the state is not an unusual one. Indeed, assessments of the nepotistic state as effectively rotting are widespread and have led some people to a play on the state's name: rather than Kuzey Kıbrıs Türk Cumhuriyeti, they say Kuzey Kıbrıs Torpil Cumhuriyeti— the Nepotistic Republic of Northern Cyprus.

In recent years, a small body of anthropological literature has emerged, especially from India and parts of Africa, that attempts to come to terms with the relationship between corrupt governing practices and claims to democracy. The ethnographic examples tend to be taken from postcolonial states with entrenched hierarchies of caste and class, in which uses of networks and what Chatterjee (2004) calls "paralegality" are ways of leveling the playing field and getting things done (see also Smith 2007; Witsoe 2011). Chatterjee draws a useful distinction between what he calls "civil society," or the elite realm of law governed by ideals of human rights, and "political society," or the ways in which people actually experience the state as it is mediated through networks and various associations. One anthropologist of India, commenting on this distinction, remarks that it "destabiliz[es] dominant social scientific frameworks such as 'state-society' and 'good governance' approaches" (Witsoe 2011: 75). This returns us to Timothy Mitchell's observation that modern politics is essentially about producing the line of difference between state and society (1991: 95). If, however, Chatterjee and Witsoe are correct, the essence of postcolonial politics is precisely the blurring of this line of difference.

It should be clear from the above that the state-society boundary in north Cyprus is, indeed, highly blurred. Unlike India or Nigeria, however, north Cyprus is a strongly egalitarian society with little tolerance for hierarchical behavior or rising stars (for similarities with Greece, see Herzfeld 1985). In this regard, everyday social interactions differ significantly from those in Turkey. While the hierarchies of age and status that structure social life in Turkey remain important in the Turkish Cypriot community, their significance is blunted by familiarity and familiality. Indeed, the highly hierarchical nature of Turkish social relations has often brought persons from Turkey into conflict with Turkish Cypriots, especially on the island itself. One benign instance of this was related to us by a Turkish professor who came for the first time to the island as dean of one of the many universities. She confessed that the egalitarian nature of social relations had shocked her at first, appearing to her as disrespect. "I walk into the building and the guards at the entrance don't rise!" she exclaimed. "It took us quite some time to get used to that."

We will return to the friction in Turkish-Cypriot and Turkish social relations in the next chapter, as it provides a context for other social relations while also needing to be contextualized. As we write elsewhere (Bryant and Hatay 2011), the enclave period, with its wartime solidarity, was the era in which this egalitarian ideal was most fully realized. However, it continues to manifest itself, for instance, in a sometimes vulgar familiarity, the use of informal language, and a tendency to rein in rising stars. The latter is what one legal scholar, leftist party leader, and former prime minister, Tufan Erhürman, has called "the brotherhood of the underpants" (*don kardeşliği*).[12] This refers to the way that whenever someone achieves something out of the ordinary—receives an award or honor, gets a promotion or good job, or is mentioned in the press—people often demean their accomplishment with the phrase, "I knew him when he was running around in his underpants." The phrase is a way of asserting equality and reining in any pretense to accomplishment beyond one's peers.

What this egalitarianism also means is that despite rifts caused by party politics, in almost all cases personal relations trump ideological or party differences. Not only are families often internally divided, with parents and children voting for different parties, but these differences can also be used in the interest of family or group solidarity. For instance, a young member of a left-wing party may still find his parents using his uncle, a former TMT leader, or his mother's former classmate, the wife of a party leader, to get him out of jail or get him a job. Moreover, as we discuss in previous chapters, differences in party politics tend to be blurred except in relation to the Cyprus Problem—how to interpret the past and how to imagine the future—and by implication in relation to Turkey.

If this so-called state is ideologically based in victimization and in practice run through with nepotism, the combination of shared experience and "fraternity" also gives the state an emotional or affective intimacy. Michael Herzfeld (1997) has eloquently described the concept of cultural intimacy, in which a "we" emerges precisely through those historical and symbolic aspects of ourselves that we enjoy among each other but do not want outsiders to remark upon. And while that certainly exists here as well, it might be more accurate to describe this "fraternity" as a form of *social* intimacy summarized above as a "brotherhood of the underpants." This implies, in an affectionate way, that we have a past and shared experiences but also that "we all know each other's dirty laundry." It is in this way, we suggest, that the de facto state is also experienced: as a fraternal intimacy that simultaneously gives shape to community and is defined by its experiences. It is through the very act of using networks to achieve one's goals that the state becomes one's own.

The Half-Lives of Victimhood

The headline reads, "I want my right," and the story underneath it tells the tale of one K.E., heir to a large number of property points. His father had been a landowner in the town of Polis tis Chrysochou, in the island's south, and on the family's relocation to the north, the father had shared his right to exchanged property among his four sons. Three had taken the points and exchanged them for Greek Cypriot properties in various parts of the north. The fourth, now an elderly man, had held his points for several decades and at the time of the article was attempting to use them for a plot of land in a seaside town on the island's north coast. He explained that until a few years earlier he had been living in social housing in Nicosia but that his wife had become ill and could no longer climb the stairs. They had moved to a house his son had built in the same seaside town where he was searching for appropriate exchange property. But the son, who had been living and working overseas, had begun to hint that they would like to return to the island, and the father wanted to build his own house to enable his son's return.

K.E. claimed that along with the 250,000 exchange points inherited from his father, he had also earned 300,000 "fighter's points" (*mücahit puanları*). Moreover, he remarks, "I'm also a wounded veteran of 1958, but at the time I had the mentality of 'sacrificing one's life for one's country,' and I didn't register myself then. At the same time, I'm someone who participated in both the first and the second peace operations [in 1974]. As someone who's served his country this much, I've asked for a plot of land that's my right in return for my points, but for years I haven't been able to get one."[13] The fact that a bit more than forty years after the island's division, an elderly Turkish Cypriot would still be seeking what he sees as his "right" in the form of property, as well as the fact that the newspaper would still see fit to publish this story of what K.E. calls "injustice," demonstrates both the continuing appeal of a rhetoric of unrecompensed victimhood and a view of the state as the site of an exchange of personal sacrifice for other forms of gain.

A friend of Rebecca's was just putting down a newspaper with the article about K.E. when Rebecca arrived at her house one day for coffee. Oya was a refugee from the island's south who had been studying in Turkey in 1974 and returned late to the island after completing her degree. Because her father had died some years earlier and her mother was ill, making their own claim to property fell to Oya, who had at various times explained to Rebecca the difficulties that she had in getting adequate compensation because of her left-wing political views. But rather than sympathizing with the subject of the article, Oya dismissed K.E.'s claims. Indeed, despite not knowing K.E. personally, she gave Rebecca a detailed counterreading of the article, asserting that his plight could not possibly be as dire as he portrayed it.

Oya's alternative genealogy of K.E.'s story read against the grain in the case's details. Although Oya accepted the right to justice in the form of property compensation, she immediately pointed to historical clues that she thought "anyone" should understand. For instance, K.E. describes sacrifices made over about two decades, starting in at least 1958 and continuing through the 1970s. However, "everybody knows," Oya asserted, that such sacrifices are associated with particular forms of politics and the distribution that went along with that. So, being a *gazi* from 1958 signals that the wronged man was at that time a member of TMT, and his being wounded also suggests that he was actively fighting during the period. This also means that he would likely have been in his early thirties in 1974, when he claims to have participated in both phases of the Turkish military intervention. If so, and given his active participation in the fighting, it is also likely that he had some rank in the standing army that TMT had become.

Moreover, after 1974, TMT came to be primarily associated with the ruling party, UBP, despite the fact that many former TMT members joined opposition parties. While many men who joined TMT in the 1950s did so in the belief that it was the only way to protect their families, as we noted earlier, it also later became a mechanism for imposing hegemony on a captive population. After 1974 and the destruction of the BEY system, those former TMT members who were incorporated into UBP were the ones who were also close to Rauf Denktaş and his adherence to Turkish nationalism. As a result, the ruling party became associated with what became known as "the spirit of TMT," referring to Denktaş's utilization of TMT to monopolize violence in the 1950s and 1960s.[14]

In the case of K.E., Oya suggested, an association with the ruling party may have meant access to social housing in the capital. She could not know whether or not that was the case—but then speculation about the networks of others and strategies to impede use of those networks is an important part of the way that nepotistic systems work. In any case, Oya remarked, "as you know, the government distributed the titles to social housing in the 1990s, so he can't be all that desperate." Although Oya still accepted that he should get what was due to him because of what he had left behind in the south, she dismissed the idea that he was suffering. In other words, one may simultaneously perceive the man's appeal to justice as it is understood within the particular system developed in north Cyprus and also know that his situation is unlikely to be that of a man who has been entirely deprived by the system against which he complains. Moreover, the article describes the way that K.E. claims to have been caught between the various changes of government of recent years—what Oya summarized as "not knowing whose ass to lick."

There are several points here that are important for our purposes. The first is that, as the quote at the beginning of the chapter notes, the economy of spoils continues today not only in repercussive aftershocks but directly as a nepotistic politics of distribution. Distribution, then, remains as relevant today as in 1974, even if what is distributed is not always property. The second point is that party politics has emerged less as a divergence of ideology than as a grouping of nepotistic blocs. Both ideological party trends and the language and discourse of the parties has tended to come from elsewhere, particularly from the language of politics in Turkey, but the actual practice of party politics is one of favors gained, given, and exchanged. This is why the former teacher referred to previously remarked that "after all the nepotistic relationships entered the picture, everything turned into cliques. So you have this party's people, and this party's administrators, and the three-way decrees, I don't know what else, everything got totally messed up!" K.E. himself appears prepared to use whichever party networks are necessary to get things done.

As a result, in K.E.'s complaint, the "rights" of the citizen and the practices of nepotism exist side by side. He rather clearly suggests that if his legitimate claim has fallen between the nepotistic cracks, it is because the changes of government mean he does not know which networks to employ. He appeals to the Turkish Cypriot public, using the language of what Philip Abrams (1988) referred to as "the idea of the ideal state," in this case the state that should give him his "right." That right, in turn, is based on a calculation of victimhood and its recompense. If he is unable to get that right, it is because of what the state has become in practice.

However, it would be incorrect to see this only as a complaint about a party system rife with nepotism; we have suggested that it would also be incorrect to think that Turkish Cypriots read it this way. Rather, as we will see in Chapter 9, Turkish Cypriots tend to take great pride in exposing the tactics and strategies of other Turkish Cypriots through counter-readings that employ local knowledge, as Rebecca's friend Oya had done. Moreover, this is local knowledge that emerges in Turkish Cypriots' intimate encounters with the institutions of their own state. This is the "brotherhood of the underpants" writ large, employed to explain not only people one personally knows but also others that one may never meet—although one could easily meet them with a phone call or two, as one invariably has friends or family who know or could reach them. As a result, the "brotherhood of the underpants" is not only about an egalitarianism bred of familiarity, the literal social ties of neighborhoods and extended families. Rather, it becomes how one imagines the community, in Benedict Anderson's well-known phrase. The community here is imagined as a form of social intimacy that after 1974 came to be concentrated in a particular territory and a particular set of institutions that embody both the experiences of victimhood and one's social ties. As a result, state and community blend together as the space where one's dirty laundry is most intimately known but where one trusts that it will not be exposed.

CHAPTER 8

An Ambiguous Domination

On the coastal road to the west of Kyrenia is a massive hotel and casino complex with the unlikely name Cratos—the word for *state* in Greek. And indeed the complex is large enough that it could almost be its own small principality, with a yacht harbor, numerous restaurants, bars and discos. It was built in a period of hopeful Turkish investment on the island, and it draws tourism primarily from a particular subclass of the Turkish elite: weekend casino gamblers during the winter months and, in the summer, men who are manicured and waxed and women with dyed blond hair who arrive already tanned and concentrate on getting tanner. They are greeted at the airport by bevies of young women in short dresses and whisked away in limousines for several days of Turkish food cooked by Turkish chefs and Turkish entertainment provided by Turkish performers, all in a Turkish hotel with Turkish staff that requires no contact with the local population.

The hotel had been open almost a decade before we finally accepted a dinner invitation to one of its restaurants, a typical Turkish grill of the sort that one finds in the better parts of Istanbul. We had heard for years that the Italian restaurant, for instance, was the best on the island, and Turkish pop stars often performed in the hotel's clubs. On the evening we arrived, however, the hotel seemed rather empty: we thought it was a midwinter slowdown, though our friends assured us that the novelty of the hotel had simply worn off.

The hotel's parking lot was strangely below the building and in front of the harbor, and as we got out of the car, Mete's high school buddy Cemal pointed up toward the semicircle of restaurants above. "You see," he said, "they were only allowed to have so much space overground. They could only have so many floors. So you see what the *garasakal* did? He built underground, as well."

Garasakal, or "blackbeard," is a rich term in the Turkish Cypriot vocabulary, a word with overlays of history and meaning. It was initially used to refer to Turkish officials and army officers who arrived secretly on the island in the 1950s to train and organize TMT. At that point, it referred to their patronizing and hierarchical attitude, which Turkish Cypriots resented and tried to chisel away. After 1974 it came to refer to Turks who arrived on the island as tourists, teachers, and technicians, who again tended to have a condescending attitude that at that time was also laced with a snide triumphalism. Stories abound of shopkeepers who refused to negotiate prices with Turkish tourists, only to be confronted with accusations of ingratitude: "We saved you, and now you won't even give us a discount?" While other words such as *fellah*, "peasant," or *çingene*, "gypsy," soon referred to the uneducated Turkish peasants who were brought in as part of a demographic engineering plan, discussed in Chapter 3, *garasakal* tended to contain elements of envy and resentment, acknowledgment that "they" were better at certain things but an unwillingness to be patronized because of it. So, if one saw a modern, well-constructed building, one could say, "*Garasakallar bu işi iyi bilir*" (The *garasakal*s really know this business). But if one saw something that was all show and no substance, such as the hotel we entered that evening, one could say, "*Garasakal işi*" (It's a *garasakal* job), meaning that it made overly exaggerated claims but could not deliver.

Rebecca had grown up with a similarly rich word: "Yankee," which for the Southerners around her who used it implied overintellectualism, condescension, and moral degradation, and which smacked of resentful admiration. Unlike foreigners, who could be assimilated, Yankees were persons who laughed at the way one spoke and seemed on a campaign to change one's values and ways of life. Turkish Cypriots similarly find themselves branded by Turkish elite as a sort of Mediterranean redneck, their dialect considered "cute" but revealing them to be country bumpkins. This has been hard for Turkish Cypriots to swallow, especially as the level of education in the island's north is higher on average than in Turkey. Some engage in code-switching, speaking in Cypriot dialect with their fellows and switching to a version of Istanbul Turkish when speaking to persons from Turkey. In an earlier period, many of the older elite abandoned the dialect altogether. Today others, especially the youth, defiantly speak only in the dialect, which has also increasingly become commodified. Popular television programs today feature speech in the dialect, and it is often used for marketing purposes.

Language is only one everyday way in which Turkish Cypriots experience the cultural, economic, and political domination of Turkey. For more than forty years, the Turkish military has kept a 25,000-strong force on the island, roughly equivalent to a fifth of the total native Turkish Cypriot population. Today, another 60,000 citizens were either born in Turkey or their parents were, while estimates using migration, labor, and education statistics indicate that there are an additional 120,000 or so persons of Turkish nationality living, studying, and working on the island. This is in contrast to a Cypriot-origin population of roughly 150,000 in the island's north (Hatay 2017). Moreover, given the perception in Turkey that north Cyprus is a type of remote province, as well as the paternalistic nature of Turkish politics, it should not be surprising that Turkish Cypriots often feel that their way of life is under threat.

This does not mean, however, that they entirely reject Turkey. Indeed, as we suggested earlier, there is a type of admiring and envious resentment in attitudes toward it. On the evening that we went to the Cratos Hotel with our friends, we ate a lavish meal in Antep style and listened to musicians playing Roma music. Somehow the conversation had turned to talking about the *garasakals*—a subject that Cemal knew very well, as his wife was one of them. He often laughed at his wife's obsession with hygiene, which he calls a "*garasakal* disease." His wife did not demur.

"When they meet each other, it's like two roosters getting ready to fight," he says, referring to the way that, in "*garasakal* culture," *garasakal*s always have to immediately establish their place in the pecking order.

At one point in the evening, however, after we had drunk much *rakı*, the musicians began playing a tune that probably for all of us conjured images of nights on the Bosphorus. Raising his glass and staring out the window at the harbor, Cemal sighed, "I could almost imagine I'm in Istanbul!"

Rebecca laughed. "You've been cursing people from Turkey all evening, but now you're longing for Istanbul!"

Cemal nodded his head and leaned forward with mock seriousness. "We love Turkey very much!" he said. "We just don't like people from Turkey" (*Türkiye'yi çok severiz, Türkiyelileri sevmeyik!*).

While his claim is a bit like saying one loves New York but hates New Yorkers, and while it produced much laughter, it also is slightly misleading.

Turkish Cypriots had long lived with an image of a "modern" Turkey that they aspired to imitate (Hatay and Bryant 2008). This was the Turkey of Turkish films, with its blond actresses and perfectly chiseled actors. This was the Turkey of the Turkish teachers who came to the island in the 1940s and 1950s and insisted that it was not against Islam for women to remove their headscarves. This was the Turkey of Turkish art music, with the likes of flamboyant singer Zeki Müren, a male who dressed in glittering women's gowns, and the Turkey of Turkish pop stars such as Ajda Pekkan, a blond diva who burst onto the music scene in the 1970s with bikinis and spiky boots. This was the Turkey of a militantly modernizing state project, implemented by persons who appeared to embody it, but it was also the Turkey of a left-wing movement that provided Turkish ways to experience the global ferment of the 1960s, including Turkish ways of growing mustaches. This was the Turkey of Istanbul *meyhane*s (taverns) and universities that Cypriot students aspired to enter, but it was also the Turkey of social hierarchies and Kemalist condescension. Given these contradictions, we have to understand Cemal as claiming that Cypriots love the image and experience of Turkey but have been frustrated in their interactions with the very persons who created that image and experience.

On another occasion, Cemal remarked to us, "The problem we have with people from Turkey is the same problem we have with the Greek Cypriots: they don't put us in the place of men/people." Being put in the place of men/people (*adam yerine konmak*) is a phrase we had discussed earlier to describe what Turkish Cypriots saw as the reason for their struggle of the 1960s. Instead, Cemal tells us, "We are under a dual siege (*çifte kuşatılmışlık*) from both the Greek Cypriots and Turkey." The idea of a "dual siege" has been common among Turkish Cypriots since at least the 1990s, sometimes expressed as being in an "open-air prison" in which both Greek Cypriots and Turkey are the guardians. Moreover, this seems to be a common problem for citizens of unrecognized states, whose "parent state" invariably tries to squeeze them but whose "patron state" often seems about to crush them. As an African phrase that has entered the Turkish lexicon has it, "When the elephants dance, the grass suffers." Behemoths, such as Turkey and Russia, may be simply going about their business, but for citizens of client states, it often seems as though they are always underfoot.

What both the complaint of not being "put in the place of men/persons" and the idea of a dual siege express is a desire but inability fully to become a political subject, to enact one's political will (*siyasi irade*), as Turkish Cypriots so often phrase it. While many Turkish Cypriots of the 1950s and 1960s understood that Greek nationalism painted them as uncivilized "barbarians" (Bryant 2004: 238–240), after 1974 they came to be portrayed by Greek Cypriot official propaganda as puppets or victims of Turkey. While in the first portrayal they are not worthy of respect, in the second, they are not even worthy of presence and have no voice. However, Turkish Cypriots were disappointed to find after 1974 that persons from Turkey (*Türkiyeliler*) similarly did not "put them in the place of men/persons," instead seeing them as passive victims who had been saved by the heroic Turkish army and had to be supported by Turkish finances. And in their encounters with the Turkish state, what they faced was a paternalism that often slid into condescension.

Here, then, we return to the idea of being "put in the place of men/persons" to discuss Turkish Cypriot agency, their ability (or lack thereof) to become subjects who enact their political will. While it would be quite easy to see Turkey's presence in the island as a hegemony against which Turkish Cypriots strategize by using what James Scott (1985) calls "weapons of the weak," our argument is somewhat different. We argue instead that the discourses of hegemony and counterhegemony so often employed by Turkish Cypriots are themselves strategies that disguise the ways in which *being a member of the category "Turkish Cypriot" has itself become a source of agency.* Because Turkish Cypriot communal victimhood legitimates the current state of affairs, it also becomes the source of action. As one of our friends always puts it, "We've made being Turkish Cypriot into a profession" (*Kıbrıslı Türk olmak meslek haline getirdik*). Or in the more vulgar colloquial, Turkish Cypriots may joke, "We both cry and fuck (them over)" (*Hem ağlarık hem sikerik*). In both of these expressions there is agency, but it is agency disguised as its lack. It is here, we argue, that the de facto subject emerges.

Patrons and the Paternal

In a novel penned in the late 1970s, Turkish Cypriot poet, writer, and one-time parliamentarian Özker Yaşın provides much unwitting insight into the concerns of the period. The novel, *Kıbrıslı Kâzım* (1977), is the humorous, semiautobiographical tale of a parliamentarian who loses an election and sulks off to Istanbul, abandoning the constituency that has rejected him. The novel begins with the disillusioned parliamentarian about to board a plane from Nicosia to Turkey. As he waits in the airport lounge, he suddenly hears a woman shrieking. Wanting everyone to hear, she is yelling loudly, "We came and saved you, our soldiers shed their blood for you, and now you have the nerve to weigh my baggage?"

Yaşın describes the woman as elderly, wearing a headscarf, and carrying several large bundles. The woman continues her tirade, calling Turkish Cypriots infidels and the bastards of Greek Cypriots. The startled airline personnel do not know what to do, but an educated Turkish Cypriot named Özkan calls calmly from his seat: "Do you know the five essential elements of Islam?"

The woman, who has gathered her bundles, is taken aback. "Of course, I do!"

"I don't believe you do," Özkan retorts calmly, proceeding to inform her that the first duty of a Muslim is not to throw a good deed in someone's face. Another duty is to be grateful for hospitality. Just as the old woman's anger seems to have shrunk, a tall Turkish officer strides over to see what is happening. Gaining strength from his presence, the old woman proceeds to shriek again about the ungratefulness of Cypriots. But the officer looks down at her from his height and says authoritatively, "Ayıp ediyorsun, teyze" (You're behaving shamefully, auntie). He proceeds to remind her that Turkish Cypriots are their brothers and that they should respect them.

There are several elements of this story that are worth unpacking. The first is obviously the sense of entitlement on the part of Turkish citizens that was widespread enough in the period that it permeated everyday transactions. Almost any Turkish Cypriot who was a teenager or adult in the late 1970s has a story of persons expecting special treatment because they were from Turkey, that is, of persons seeking to benefit from the Turkish army "saving" Turkish Cypriots. This ranged from expecting discounts to feeling that the place is one's own. One hotel manager from the period told us the story of a ship's captain staying at his hotel who one day entered the lobby and walked behind the bar as though he owned it to take a bottle of whiskey and begin to drink it. When the manager objected, the captain punched him twice and eventually had to be taken away by the police. Or in a scene that echoes the novel above but from a later period, a friend related that he and his family were at the check-in counter at Ercan Airport in the early 1990s, at a time when regulations on baggage were in any case lax, and Cyprus Turkish Air employees often allowed a bit of excess luggage. "One Turkish man had even more than the bit of excess they normally allowed, and he was told he would have to pay. He hit the roof! He was crying, 'We saved you in 1974, and how dare you demand payment for excess baggage!'"

These stories are also confirmed by some of those Turkish citizens who arrived during that period. Explaining the resentment that they later had to endure, one man who was a teenager in the 1970s remarked,

> Unfortunately, in the beginning we went through quite a bit of negativity. We were always saying to them, "We saved you." In other words, you owe us. We went through this, we said these things. These sorts of conversations happened all the time in the market, in the shops. Because the Cypriot folk don't know how to bargain, and because this is a Mediterranean country, they close the shops in the afternoon, we—that is, people coming from Turkey—found it all strange. How can you close a shop from 12:00 to 4:00 p.m.? How can one close a shop at all? They would say, "This is the way we are. We're closing." We would get angry and say things like, "We saved you. You can't behave this way toward us. In any case, we're the ones filling your stomachs." Unfortunately, these sorts of things were said. (Kurtuluş and Purkis 2014: 100)

This immigrant, then, attributes this initial attitude and reactions to it to a type of culture clash, one in which Turkish nationals confronted with a "Mediterranean country" reacted with frustrated indignation.

The attitude seems to have penetrated interactions at all levels of society, however. The hotel manager who had been slapped by the ship's captain went on to tell a story about a bet made with a member of the Turkish ambassadorial staff of the immediate post-1974 period. "The embassy staff in that period was constantly cursing Cypriots, as they always had, saying the olives are still on the trees, the carobs are still on the trees, Cypriots are lazy, and so on. I argued with a man in the embassy: 'The Cypriot Turk is not lazy. He needs leadership and administration. If you direct him, the Cypriot is hard-working. In twenty-four hours I can build a development army.' He said, 'You'll build shit!'" The former hotel manager then described with pride how he went on to collect a small army of volunteers to gather carobs and olives from orchards around the north. He was intent on proving to the embassy staffer precisely the cultural misreading that the immigrant above had described.

The old woman in Yaşın's story has her head covered, suggesting that she is religious. At the same time, she is attempting to leave the country with excess baggage, a common phenomenon during the period. It was in the first years after the war, in fact, that a postwar economy developed out of spoils, as well as a suitcase trade that took advantage of the island's more open economy to import goods not available in a then economically closed Turkey. It was primarily a grey economy that developed in the late 1970s and early 1980s out of a situation that was also prone to exploitation.

"They were all swindlers who arrived in that period," remarked the hotel manager. And indeed, there are many stories from the period of persons attempting to use the postwar confusion to sell land that did not exist, for instance. Indeed, Mete recalls seeing signs in Istanbul advertising land for sale in Cyprus only three days after the military intervention began. However, there were also stories of Turkish Cypriots collaborating with Turkish nationals in a very profitable suitcase trade. One of our friends claims that many Turkish Cypriots financed their university education in this way, filling suitcases with cartons of cigarettes, blue jeans, Pyrex, and English underwear, then selling the products privately in Turkey. According to one of Mete's friends, Uğur, who wrote an account of the period on his Facebook page, both the traders and their customers were mostly "White Turks"—a term invented in 1990s Turkey to refer to Westernized, secular Turks who primarily live in the West of the country, as opposed to "Black Turks," who were more religious, dressed traditionally, and came from the East.

> In Karşıyaka [both the name of a district in Izmir and literally "the other side of the sea"] there was an army of White Turks starved for European goods, and we were ready immediately to meet their needs. The sidewalks were suddenly filled with Mora blankets, and in the shops we were selling Pyrex with daisy designs, Kema playing cards, Pifco electric appliances, and Nescafe. Of course, here occasionally we would have Nescafe Gold Blend labels printed in the print shop and paste them on the jars at the house of a friend who was a trader. In Haspolat [a Nicosia suburb] there was a room where we would make shampoo and sell it as Alberto Balsam, etc., etc. . . . When I consider it, in that period the Turks who were settled in Girne were generally always White Turks. . . . It was a happy time for retailers.[1]

It is worth noting that in this description the traders are also swindlers, though the swindle is one in which Turkish Cypriots actively participate.

In Yaşın's novel, the shrieks of the woman with her bulging baggage are halted by the tall, handsome officer, who behaves as a gentleman but also with authority, correcting the old woman's spiteful denigration of their Turkish Cypriot "brothers." Of course, the invocation of "brotherliness" here has a different meaning than its use in the previous chapter, where it referred to egalitarian, nepotistic practices that constitute the state. One might say that this is the difference between *gardaş*, the Turkish Cypriot way of pronouncing the word, which has a distinct inflection of cultural intimacy, and *kardeş*, the "proper" Turkish form of the word that conjures the way of speaking of the *garasakals*. The officer invokes *kardeşlik*, a "brotherliness" born of being children of the same "mother," the *Anavatan*, or motherland. This becomes especially clear in the last pages of Yaşın's novel, when he travels to Ankara to visit the tomb of the first Turkish officer killed in Cyprus. There, he cries to the dead officer about what the island has become, full of swindlers and *fellah*s, peasant Turks, who have no sense of national duty and do not fit Turkish Cypriots' image of modern Turkishness.

But perhaps the most important character in Yaşın's airport story is Özkan, the proud Turkish Cypriot who demonstrates the ignorance of the woman who dares to call them *gavur*, infidel. Not only is this character more cultured and learned—seen in the way that he sits quietly reading while waiting for his plane and responds in a controlled manner—but he is also proud of his Muslim identity. One imagines that his response to the woman is the sort of response that many Turkish Cypriots had fantasized about giving to similar accusations of being *gavur*. He responds to accusations of being an infidel by demonstrating that he is more of a Muslim than his accuser.

It is important, however, that this assertion of agency is cut short by the intervention of the officer, who towers above them all and authoritatively settles the matter of Turkish Cypriots' "brotherhood." In the end, the story is one of the Kemalist officer disciplining the unruly peasant woman over the victimhood of Turkish Cypriots. While she accuses them of being ungrateful, the officer suggests that one sacrifices for family without expecting return. In both scenarios, however, Turkish Cypriots remain passive victims, either ungrateful for their salvation or victims under their "big brother's" wing. It was in this early period, then, that victimhood and questions of identity became fused in Turkish Cypriots' interactions with Turkish nationals, Turkish authorities, and the Turkish state.

We see from this story, as well, that victimhood and a rhetoric of "salvation" were in direct contradiction with Turkish Cypriots' longtime struggle to be "put in the place of men/humans." As the old woman spitefully accused Cypriots of ingratitude, Özkan rose to her challenge and made a move to correct the hierarchy. The intervention of the officer, however, once again asserted a hierarchy in which he paternalistically accepted Turkish Cypriots as "brothers." Indeed, Turkish Cypriots would soon learn that the attitude of the Turkish government and many "White Turks" toward them was paternalistic, treating them as children who had not quite grown up and were not yet prepared to handle the responsibilities of political adults. Victimhood, then, simultaneously produced them as political subjects and disempowered them as agents, ultimately making them into extras on the set of their own history.

"A Mother Who Behaves Like a Father"

Sometime in the mid-1990s, Rebecca was waiting in line at the Istanbul airport to check in for a flight to north Cyprus. She was flying with Cyprus Turkish Airways (Kıbrıs Türk Havayolları), discussed earlier as the TRNC's national airline and a source of great pride to Turkish Cypriots. She had made the trip many times before, but while stuck in the queue on this occasion, she had the time to look carefully at the departures board and scrutinize the airline codes. She noticed that although the three-letter International Civil Aviation Organization code for Turkish Airlines is THY, the abbreviation of the Turkish name (Türk Havayolları), the code for Cyprus Turkish Airways, KYV, seemed to bear no relationship to the airline's name. When her turn came to check in, she asked the young woman at the desk if she knew anything about it.

Although the ground staff members at Ercan were all Turkish Cypriot, this was an efficient young Turkish woman. "Oh, yes," she smiled coolly, "that stands for Kıbrıs Yavru Vatan."

Cyprus Baby Land. Although the idea of north Cyprus as "babyland" to the Anatolian "motherland" was widespread in Turkey, this was the first time Rebecca had seen it enshrined in something as official as an airline code. Turkish Cypriots are aware that most people on the street in Turkey think of north Cyprus as a province to which one could jet off for a weekend holiday in the sun and that many are confused to discover that flights to the island leave from the international rather than the domestic terminal. Moreover, the view of the island presented in magazine articles and television programs is of a place with good casinos, bad universities, and a wealth of brothels. These are all "industries" that developed in the 1990s, when north Cyprus began to feel the squeeze of embargoes and tried to find ways around them (see Chapter 9). As a result of these well-known "sectors," by the 1990s, the "babyland" rhetoric often had the connotation not of an innocent babe but of a spoiled, slightly degenerate juvenile.

For Turkish Cypriots, too, the implications of this familial language changed over time. While in the 1950s the rhetoric of "motherland" and "babyland" had produced a sense of security for many Turkish Cypriots, in that one expects mothers to look after their children, forty years later many Turkish Cypriots bristled at the infantilizing implications of this language. Many Turkish Cypriots describe how they shed tears of joy when Turkish troops finally landed on the island in 1974 and how they willingly gave their daughters in marriage to Turkish soldiers. In the period after that encounter, however, they became viscerally acquainted with the reality rather than the image of the Turkish state and Turkish society.

Turkey's presence in Cyprus is often described by the international community as an "occupying power" or an "invader," while Turkish Cypriots have variously called the country their "protector," "savior," and "colonizer." In the colloquial, the relationship is often expressed as "flesh and fingernail" (*et ve tırnak*), implying something natural, necessary, and inseparable. In the international relations literature, the relationship is usually described as that between a patron state and its client, and although the literature acknowledges that it is an often ambivalent relationship, there is little discussion of that ambivalence in practice.

While no single label will accurately encapsulate all the ambiguities of the Turkey–north Cyprus relationship, we refer to it as a paternal protectorate to emphasize both the familial and the foreign (see also Bryant and Yakinthou 2012). In international relations, a protectorate is a small or weak state that cedes various degrees of autonomy to a larger state in return for military protection, aid with foreign relations, and in some cases economic contributions. We find many instances of protectorates in international relations: Puerto Rico and Guam are U.S. protectorates, while Bosnia-Herzegovina may be considered a protectorate of the United Nations. However, one characteristic of the protectorate relationship between Turkey and north Cyprus is that because the latter is a de facto protectorate, the relationship is not formalized, or is so only in an ad hoc way, through economic and other protocols. Indeed, Turkey acts as a protector state for north

Cyprus while at the same time claiming to recognize its independence and autonomy.

In the past two decades an increasing strand of literature in international relations has emphasized that relations between states are usually hierarchical, that sovereignty is often partial, and that the autonomy of states is usually compromised, both politically and economically (e.g., Ashley 1988; Fowler and Bunck 1996; James 1992; Osterud 1997; Simpson 2004; Thomson 1995). Instead, one often finds a continuum of hierarchical relations, where states may cede varying degrees of authority to other powers, especially in the realms of security, economy, and international relations (Lake 2003). This continuum includes various levels of dependency, culminating in the imperial, which Lake defines as an authority relationship "in which the rule of the dominant state over both economic and security policy is accepted as more or less legitimate by the members of the subordinate polity" (2008: 294).

The relationship between north Cyprus and Turkey has clearly been defined by various degrees of dependency over time, especially in terms of security and the economy. While officially Turkey is the only state to acknowledge the TRNC's existence, in practice almost any Turkish Cypriot will remark that Turkish nationals and the Turkish government do not behave as though the TRNC is a separate state. Apart from the significant Turkish military presence, north Cyprus uses the Turkish lira and is hence directly tied to the Turkish economy in a phenomenon known as "dollarization," which is common to unrecognized states (Yeyati 2003).[2] Moreover, the present TRNC constitution puts the police under the control of the Turkish military on the island, while Turkey's yearly aid package to the island's north allows it to make certain demands regarding the funds' distribution. In addition, the TRNC's Security Council, commonly called the Coordination Committee, is composed of the president, prime minister, and both elected officials and nonelected members, including members of the military, and its decisions are to "receive priority consideration by the Council of Ministers."[3] Turkish Cypriots are also often dependent on Turkey in foreign relations, and any future solution to the island's division must satisfy Turkish Cypriots' patron state.

What we wish to suggest creates ambiguity in this particular relation of domination and authority, and makes it difficult to regulate, is the perceived *familial* nature of the relationship, which often slides between the *paternal* and the *paternalistic.* An interviewee who has been actively engaged in several negotiation teams suggested,

> In the end, an entity emerged that is not recognized but is semi-acknowledged, that is, it's partly acknowledged in the international arena, where there's no pressure on it [to dissolve] but where it can't benefit from international agreements, the international financial system or even direct flights and so is overly dependent on Turkey. . . . For instance, the Turkish military is here. One of the best ways to break the embargo is to establish universities, but when we did, most of the students came from Turkey. Because it's the closest country, the greater part of the tourist industry depends on Turkish tourism. We established an economic system based on sectors such as agriculture and tourism that depend on cheap labor, and of course the closest source of that labor is Turkey. Marriages and education are from Turkey. And maybe the most important thing: television, music, all the cultural activities are from Turkey. . . . I don't know if we should call this a daughter-in-law/mother-in-law relationship, or a daughter-mother relationship, but it's certainly a multifaceted relationship.[4]

In 2012, Rebecca conducted a series of thirty interviews with journalists and civil society representatives concerning Turkish Cypriot perceptions of their relationship with Turkey (Bryant and Yakinthou 2012). Among interviewees, even those who were most critical of Turkey's intervention on the island recognized that Turkish Cypriots perceive a "kinship" relationship and closeness with persons from Turkey and see Turkey as a protector.[5] As one left-wing journalist put it, "This relationship has a social-psychological side. That is, it has an intimate side. That intimate side is because of love." This perceived kinship relationship, then, makes it "natural" that Turkey would protect Turkish Cypriots and intervene in their affairs. And like a good mother, Turkey has for so long "taken care of" north Cyprus, protecting it, advising it, giving its allowance, and intervening to chastise. Like other parent-child relationships, Turkish Cypriots must struggle to have their autonomy recognized. Or as one businesswoman who served for many years on the Aid Commission, a group of leading Turkish Cypriots who help the Turkish embassy decide how to distribute its financial aid, remarked, "A mother-child or father-child relationship bothers me. I don't want to be a child anymore; I want to grow up."

The invocation of familial relations and the obligations entailed by those is an instance of what sociologist Pierre Bourdieu referred to as "euphemization," that is, a form of misrecognition or denial that disguises relations of domination (1977: 191). Euphemization, he notes, requires tremendous effort on the part of all involved and requires the complicity of the whole group: "The work of denial which is the source of social alchemy is, like magic, a collective undertaking" (195). It results in the transformation of "overt domination into misrecognized, 'socially recognized' domination, in other words, *legitimate authority*" (192; italics in original).

Looked at from the perspective of north Cyprus, euphemization occurs when a relation between two states—or one state and one state-like entity—is cast in the guise of family relations such that, as the left-wing journalist above remarked, Turkish Cypriots "see Turkey as their security, their support, their protector." The "legitimate authority" granted here is the one of parental domination, a relationship that in turn historically depended on Turkish Cypriots emphasizing their "helplessness" and the need of a protecting "mother," and which continues to be justified by Turkish Cypriots' transhistorical victimization, their role as "victim community." This particular form of misrecognition, however, has required constant maintenance in the form of various "proofs" that they are part of the Turkish family rather than "Greek seed" (*Rum tohumu*), as well as appropriate displays of gratitude in the form of ceremonies, speeches, and other symbolic expressions of indebtedness. In return for these expressions of "familiality," their "mother" has continued to protect and feed them.

This particular form of euphemization depends, in turn, on another form of euphemization. That euphemization is one that allows us to separate the actions of individuals from the practice of something that we abstractly refer to as "the state." There are, then, actions that we expect from representatives of that abstract, ideal "state," and normally persons who line their own pockets or engage in corrupt practices are "abusing their office." As Stephen Pierce notes, writing of the case of Nigeria, when one sees the state as an abstraction and an ideal, one "re-labels individual activity as supra-local and disinterested" (2006: 908). The maintenance of this euphemization, in turn, depends on persons who cast themselves as representatives of the abstract state and the practitioners of statecraft.

If we return to Özker Yaşın's airport story, we see this same euphemizing function in another form, when individuals come synecdochally to stand for or to see themselves as representing the state (see also Reeves 2014). The officer who intervenes in the fray does so as representative of "the state" in its militarized guise. For him, Turkish Cypriots are abstractly "brothers" of the same "mother," their common motherland. However, in this same story we see an old woman making mendacious claims on the basis of what "her" state had done for Cypriots. And in this instance the euphemizing function of the state disappears, is no longer "mystified" or "misrecognized," in the old woman's insistence that the blood of real soldiers entitled her to excess baggage. As far as Turkish Cypriots are concerned, her accusations of ingratitude demystify the state and dispel the illusion of an abstract "mother," replacing her with an elderly, headscarved woman shrieking about the weight of her bundles. Similarly, when Turkish shoppers demanded discounts or felt entitled to take bottles of whiskey because the Turkish army had "saved" Turkish Cypriots, the mystification of an abstract mother selflessly caring for helpless children was replaced with self-interested persons who behaved arrogantly toward their so-called "brothers."

However, both the justification and continuation of the relationship of dependency relied on the maintenance of the fiction of family. Turkish military intervention in the island was based on that fiction, and the continuing Turkish military presence in and economic aid to the island were based on that fiction. Moreover, it was because of that fiction that Turkish Cypriots were able to maintain a transhistorical victimhood, portraying themselves as a community on the verge of extinction if they had not been "saved" by a heroic mother who carved out a space of safety for them. Of course, as both Cemal and the journalist above made clear, most Turkish Cypriots do express an affinity with Turkey and that they feel in some sense Turkish—even if in what sense they may feel that is often not clearly defined. As a result, a contradiction emerged that is best represented by the figure of Özkan in Yaşın's story, portrayed as a cultured, learned man who defends his people's honor but also defers to the representative of the Turkish state.

If we return, then, to Cemal's initial joking remark that "we love Turkey but don't like Turks," we can see this to have another level where the mystified ideal of "family" can only be maintained by separating the state-ideal— in this case, a nurturing mother—from the persons who claim to represent the state. So even after the euphemism of a caring "mother" looking after her island "children" was demystified and revealed for what it was, the symbolic maintenance of that relationship could be retained by categorizing certain groups as *garasakal* and *fellah* rather than as "brother." The distinction between *gardaş*, with all its implications of cultural intimacy, and *kardeş*, which has the coolness of "*garasakal* language," came to encapsulate this.

We see, then, that while the relationship may retain the language of family, it also may change over time, moving on the continuum from the paternal to the paternalistic. Or to put it in more colloquial language, we could say that it moves from the "maternal" to the "paternal." For while Turkish Cypriots remain the "children" in that relationship, the continuum of dependency that we described above is expressed in the vernacular as a difference between Turkey as a loving, protective "mother" and Turkey as a harsh, disciplinary "father." At times when the relationship is strained, some people have joked, "We have a mother who plays the role of a father" (*Babalık yapan bir anamız var*). This is the point where the relationship is on the verge of demystification, of being revealed as one of symbolic domination.

As James Scott and others, including Bourdieu, have noted, one may strategize within the constraints of a formalized relationship of dependence, through such techniques as false flattery, dragging one's feet, or misweighing the harvest. In north Cyprus this has often meant, as in the case of Özkan, using the right language or making the right gestures. Excessive proclamations of Turkishness, the flying of Turkish flags, celebration of all Turkish holidays, and lavishly hosting Turkish diplomats and journalists are all ways of maintaining what Bourdieu refers to as "moral" or "affective" obligations "created and maintained by exchange"—in this case the gratitude of "children" that creates the moral and affective obligation of motherhood (1977: 191). Moreover, these expressions of indebtedness may be simultaneously affective and self-interested, both complicit in the maintenance of the system and aware of how to manipulate it.

For several decades, no one was better at the maintenance of this relationship than a man who acquired the status of a "father" in Turkey, and for certain groups in Cyprus: Rauf Denktaş, one of the most controversial figures in Cypriot history and someone who inspired both intense love and intense hatred in Turkish Cypriots, often at the same time. He was both strongly tied to Turkey, or at least to the idea of the Turkish state, and fiercely independent. He was bald, rotund, and perceived by many as "fatherly" (*babacan*), even as he ruthlessly quashed political enemies. In his position as president of the Federated State and then the TRNC from 1975 until 2005, he successfully outmaneuvered all opposition and manipulated Turkey's attempts to intervene. What we suggest he achieved more than anything else was maintenance of Turkey's role as "mother"—nurturing, protecting, aiding—even as he played the role of kindly but disciplinary father.

The Period of Father Denktaş

In 1934, the Turkish General Assembly voted in extraordinary session to give war hero and revolutionary leader Mustafa Kemal the honorific name Atatürk, or "father of the Turks." While *ata* is one of the Turkish words for *father*, it also has the meaning of *ancestor*, making Atatürk not only into a type of founding father but effectively into the originary Turk, who like Adam gave birth to a people. The fact that Rauf Raif Denktaş, the controversial former leader of the Turkish Cypriot community, was often known in Turkey as "Babatürk" (Father Turk), says much about the reverence in which he was held there.

However, this particular word for father, *baba*, is imbued with an emotional warmth and familiarity that is quite different from the reverence in which Mustafa Kemal is held. Unlike Atatürk's role of distant example for his people, Denktaş was known for his wry wit, his fondness of photography, and his refusal of any kind of security service, always mingling with people in coffee shops and restaurants. Although both men were known for a refusal to broach disagreement, Denktaş was also a keen observer of both the strengths and weaknesses of his community. Unlike Atatürk, who instituted a one-party "democracy," Denktaş threw himself into the fray of multiparty politics even at the birth of the so-called state he was instrumental in founding. And unlike Atatürk, whose cult has acquired the status of law, so that defaming him is grounds for a prison sentence, Denktaş is not only intensely hated by certain members of Turkish Cypriot society, especially on the left, but has also been the subject of mockery and vulgar condemnation.

In Turkey, the portly Turkish Cypriot president was known as a "fighting man" (*dava adamı*) and was credited both for his unrelenting resistance to Greek Cypriot aggression and for his unwavering Turkish nationalism. Indeed, one Turkish ambassador remarked in later years, "We always divided Turkish Cypriots into two categories: Mr. Denktaş and everyone else" (İnanç 2008: 57). After his death in 2012, there were expressions of grief and loss in north Cyprus, and tens of thousands filled the streets for his funeral; but there

Figure 12. The funeral of Rauf Denktaş, 2012. Women hold signs saying,
"Fatherturk Denktaş, we will never forget you," and "Father Denktaş, may you
find your place in heaven" (photo by Rebecca Bryant).

were also attempts in the media to give a more measured and balanced evaluation of his effect on the society. In Turkey, however, the expressions were
almost invariably reverent, with repeated references to his position as "father"
of Turkish Cypriots. In a special session of the Turkish parliament in honor
of the deceased, for instance, the deputy speaker of parliament remarked, "He
was a national hero, a great leader, a heroic child of this country," a "brave
leader of the Turkish world," and a leader known for his "fatherliness."[6]

In the same session, Emine Tarhan, a representative from Izmir who is
originally from a southern Aegean family of Cretan origin, recalled her own

Figure 13. Crowds swell through the streets of Nicosia carrying the former leader's photo (photo by Rebecca Bryant).

fascination with Denktaş as a child, and the closeness they felt to his cause as a family that had experienced the loss of their own island homeland:

> They would say that there was a huge man who resisted the enemy whose code name was Toros [Taurus]. He was as huge as the Taurus and the Five Finger Mountains. But he was caring, sympathetic, a real person. A real father, who cared for his children as our fathers did. . . . This enormous Turk always resisted. . . . He struggled. . . . And just as the greatest Turk [Atatürk] would always say, when asked his birthday, that it was 19 May [the date of Turkish victory against invading forces], I'm sure that Rauf Denktaş would have said that his birthday was 20 July [the date of the Turkish military intervention] to those who asked it.[7]

Tarhan implies, then, that like Atatürk, Denktaş was also "born" at the beginning of a new "world." She described this "real father" as caring for his "children" "as our fathers did," leading his children through fires of destruction to the safe harbor of a new state.

While expressions of Denktaş as the father of Turkish Cypriot citizen-children were quite common in Turkey, they found less common expression on the island itself. This seems to have been both because of the egalitarian nature of Turkish Cypriot society, where even leaders were not revered in this way, and because of the contested nature of politics in the island. Unlike other leaders who have been elevated to the stature of national father—Stalin, Atatürk, or Hafiz Asad in Syria, to name just a few—Denktaş maneuvered his way through multiparty elections to stay in power. While in other cases patriarchal symbolism has tended to elide with aspirations to totalitarianism, in the Turkish Cypriot community, Denktaş knew that he could never cling to power by openly casting himself as a national patriarch.

The impossibility of the emotional effectiveness of such symbolism in Cyprus's north also seems to derive from the unusual nature of existing patriarchal family relations there. While there is no doubt that politics are male dominated and homosociality is the norm in certain social spaces, intrafamily relations and the role of the father are considerably more relaxed than in the more traditionally patriarchal family structure in Turkey (on Turkish Cypriot family law, see Anderson 1959). Although there still tends to be a gendered division of labor within the family insofar as women take responsibility for the house and children, women have long gained higher education and worked outside the home and in the professions. Moreover, decisions within the family tend to be more democratic, often involving the children as well as parents, although all are expected to make personal sacrifices for the family unit. Patriarchal relations among Turkish Cypriots, then, seem to have more to do with men's enjoyment of male privilege within a generalized patriarchal system than with male domination by the patriarch of a family.

Indeed, the rhetoric of a paternalistic patriarch looking after his citizen-children seems to have little resonance in a society where it might be seen as "putting on airs." Peculiarly, then, the rhetoric of a "Father Denktaş" never took hold in Cyprus's north but had considerable resonance in Turkey, where it was often invoked to describe this representative of the "babyland" and its children. Similarly, after 1974, the Turkish nationalism that Denktaş came to represent sat in an awkward relation to Turkish Cypriot society. While the secular ideals of Turkish nationalism resonate on both right and left, it was nationalism as a practice—with its flags, ceremonies, and rigid ideas and language—that sat in an awkward relationship to a group that perceived itself as culturally Turkish but resented having to prove it. So, while in the enclaves Turkish Cypriots had revered the Turkish flag and had come out in the thousands for national ceremonies, celebrating them with fervor, they later resented implications that they were not "Turkish enough," which turned flag-waving and national ceremonies into rituals intended to prove their Turkishness.

The labels of *gavur* (infidel) and *Rum tohumu* (Greek seed) pointed to a perceived difference, what one of the interviewees above referred to as a culture clash, a form of cultural pollution or degeneration that needed correcting. Even Denktaş was known for insisting that Turkish Cypriots were not Turkish enough. As one former adviser recalled for us, "In a conversation I had once with Denktaş, he said to me, 'You're going to be Turkish.' And I said to him, 'Sir, we're already Turkish.' And so he said to me, 'You're going to be *more* Turkish.'"[8] While Denktaş accepted that Turkish Cypriots were in some way already Turks by virtue of birth, language, and religion, he also thought that they needed to *become* Turkish, in other words to be molded by Turkish nationalism. "Becoming Turkish," then, meant being disciplined as a national subject. This disciplining, in turn, entailed subjugation to a foreign model of power based on the patriarchal family that Turkish Cypriots resisted. And it was precisely in that space between "being Turkish" and "becoming Turkish" that the distinction between the de facto and the factitious once again emerged.

Turkish nationalism since its inception has been hierarchical, a model of "enlightenment" in which an educated, Westernized elite would bring light to the dark lives of the masses (Bryant 2004; Mardin 1991). This model of power is, in turn, paternalistic, with the Father State taking over responsibilities from the patriarchal head of household. Indeed, as numerous studies have shown, the patriarchal family structure was transferred to the new state in the birth of the Republic of Turkey (Arat 1998; Delaney 1995; Durakbaşa 1998; Kandiyoti 1991, 1997, 1998). While in the phrasing of Lynn Hunt (1992), the French Revolution supposedly overturned the rule of the father and replaced it with a fraternity of brothers under the protecting wing of the nation-mother, the Turkish model is one in which the Father State (Devlet Baba) continues to discipline his unruly citizen-children.

In the model that emerged in north Cyprus, however, the fraternity of brothers is separated from its mainland Mother (*Anavatan*, or motherland), while the disciplining Father (State) is not their own and instead becomes a stepfather, one whose authority over them in turn depends on their consent. In other words, to the extent that Turkey's presence on the island relies on a separate Turkish Cypriot state established out of Turkish Cypriot victimhood, the Turkish state must also recognize that separate entity as one over which it *should* have no control. The "Father State" is not their own, seen in the fact that, as several interviewees complained, they have no voting rights in Turkey. Not only that, but the numerous changes of government, including coups, that have deeply affected the lives of Turkish citizens since 1974 have only had faint ripples in north Cyprus. As a result, we may think of the Turkish Father State as Turkish Cypriots' "stepfather,"[9] someone who has power but whose authority depends on consent or at least compliance. Thinking of it in this way also gives another meaning to our friend's claim that "we love Turkey, we just don't like *Türkiyeliler* (Turkish nationals)," as well as to the resentment of the *garasakals*, who often put themselves forward as representatives of the stepfather who must discipline their island children.

Denktaş's funeral was crowded with Cypriots of all ages but also with persons from Turkey, a certain number of whom happened to be vacationing on the island when the funeral took place. We witnessed one such *garasakal*, a flamboyant woman in her fifties, loudly lecturing Turkish Cypriots about their funerary rituals. She had dressed in skin-tight white bellbottom pants, a voluminous white blouse, and a wide-brimmed white hat. A friend of the same age who wore a white summer dress struggled to keep up as they maneuvered their way on high heels through the crowds that pushed for a better view of the coffin. Both were heavily made up and had the carefully coiffured appearance associated with middle-class, secular women in Turkey. The woman in tight pants pulled her friend along, and while ostensibly talking to her, spoke loudly enough to make it clear that she was actually giving Turkish Cypriots a lecture: "Don't they know here," she was saying, "that black is not a Muslim color? White is the color that Muslims wear to funerals. They must have gotten this habit from the Greeks." While it was true that most Cypriots were in somber colors, it was also February, when people tend to wear darker winter clothes. Although some people stared at the woman as she passed, ranting, no one seemed especially perturbed by her. This was, after all, the paternalistic attitude that one would expect from many *garasakals*.

But these women were also among those who revered Denktaş, viewing him as a "true Turk" and a "revered child of the nation." Indeed, Denktaş was the greatest spokesperson of the "Turkish Cypriot cause" in Turkey, always able to arouse sympathy and indignation at the injustices they had suffered. Moreover, he understood that feeding the maternal relationship meant both constantly reiterating the Turkishness of his citizen-children and also showing gratefulness to the "mother." To that end, in the 1990s he converted the Martyrs' Week, the week that commemorated those lost in the conflict, into "Şükran Haftası," Thanksgiving Week, in which their losses were transformed into gratitude to Turkey for "saving" them. During that week, Turkish diplomats, politicians, and military commanders were invited to the island for various ceremonies and events. The campaign of "gratitude," however, also consisted of constant reminders to Turkish Cypriots in the media of their own death and suffering and of their rescue by Turkish troops. Denktaş also took every opportunity to visit Turkey, giving lectures and receiving honorary degrees at Turkish universities, participating in local events in Izmir and Konya, and allowing himself to be feted so that he could extol the great Turkish nation even as he ensured that Turkish Cypriot interests would remain a Turkish "national cause" (milli dava).

Ensuring that protection of the Turkish Cypriot community and its interests remained a "national cause" had two important effects with long-lasting implications for life in north Cyprus. The first was that "protection" also implied "security," and with around 25,000 troops stationed on the island, the voice with priority in matters relating to north Cyprus was always that of military commanders. And for much of Turkey's turbulent history, with its successive military coups, betting on the military was a sure win. While civilian governments may come and go, maintaining the loyalty of the military—maintaining the idea of the "national cause"—meant that Turkish Cypriot "interests" were more likely to be served.

One civil society leader with whom we spoke was also a retired bureaucrat who had worked under Denktaş for around twenty-five years. She rose through the ranks of the Ministry of Economy, where in the latter years she became a high-level bureaucrat. "For that reason," she says, "I'm someone who was able to follow the financial discussions with Turkey and economic policies from up close." In those relations, she observed, Turkish administrators would often tie Turkish monetary aid to packets of economic reform. As the Turkish economy liberalized, they expected the Turkish Cypriot economy to liberalize as well, and often demanded reform of the civil service and privatization of national industries. However, as our retired bureaucrat observed, this conflicted with the ideology of "national cause" that invoked the role of the military: "In that period, the relations between the TRNC and Turkey were mostly shaped by the military. The military always approved the requests coming from Cyprus for economic aid. In other words, we would make certain agreements with Turkey, and Turkey would place certain conditions on its aid, but when the military intervened these conditions were always soft-ened. In other words, the economic aid that we wanted was always secured by the intervention of the military."[10]

As several former bureaucrats explained to us, and as Turkish Cypriots were for the most part aware, the "thankfulness to Turkey" campaign that ensured the Turkish Cypriot community's status as a Turkish "national cause" also cemented Denktaş's relations with the real power in Turkey in that pe-riod, namely, the military, and ensured that financial aid would continue de-spite Turkish Cypriot failure to implement liberalizing "reform." Another high-level administrator remarked, "The politicians here just know how to stroke Turkey's pride in order to get money. . . . *Our people have been in power for fifty years, and they have master's degrees in lying to Turkey. . . .* They said there will be privatization, but there isn't a single institution that has been property privatized. . . . They said they would solve the employment issue, but people are still being hired in the government service in a partisan way. In other words, somehow the reforms that Turkey wants to implement here are being impeded" [authors' italics].[11] The idea that Turkish Cypriot politicians "know how to stroke Turkey's pride in order to get money" and "have mas-ter's degrees in lying to Turkey" is one that is widespread in the Turkish Cy-priot community. This seems to have presented little problem as long as Denktaş, as representative of the community, was able to maintain respect in Turkey as a "fighting man" who was invariably "put in the place of a man/human."

However, the second important effect of the "thankfulness to Turkey" campaign was that a system established via Turkish Cypriots' role as passive victims contradicted with the desire to become sovereign actors. Further-more, it made Denktaş into the sole "trustworthy" representative of Turkish Cypriot politics in Turkey, while criticism of Denktaş's politics of "thankful-ness to Turkey" became a form of treason. Indeed, it was well known that during this period one strategy that the right used to maintain its power was to convince certain Turkish bureaucrats and Turkish military commanders that without Turkey's financial support the left might come to power and that this would be a blow to the "national cause." This was one important reason that the left used a rhetoric of theft, accusing the right of monopolizing ac-cess to economic resources from Turkey in order to maintain power.

This same politics of salvation, then, simultaneously gave Turkish Cypri-ots agency *and* disempowered them, providing the motivation for the Mother's continuing care while at the same time giving the pretext for paternalistic intervention. It was also in the process of both enacting rituals and giving thanks that one "became Turkish." While one might be Turkish "in fact," that is, by birth, *becoming* Turkish entailed factitious expressions of gratitude and fealty, in other words, compliance with the (Step)Father State. The factitious nature of this emerged when even persons who fully believed that they were simply island Turks who had been separated from their mainland Mother nevertheless understood that such ceremonies were necessary in order to maintain the euphemization of a familial relationship rather than one of domination.

Moreover, this relationship of fealty and familiality depended, in turn, on Turkish Cypriots' past victimization and continuing status as victims. As a result, a contradiction emerged between their struggle to "be put in the place of men/humans," in other words, to be afforded dignity and respect as Turks, and being Turkish Cypriot, or being a group that had been victimized. In Turkey, *they came to be known as Turks to the extent that they had been "saved."* Denktaş resolved this contradiction and gained respect by simultaneously emphasizing Turkishness and an ongoing struggle—something that he was able to do as a "father" leading his citizen-children. Most Turkish Cypriots, however, were unable to sustain Denktaş's ability to maneuver between the cultural context of the island and that of the "mainland." *Becoming* Turkish entailed forms of speech and patterns of thought and behavior that Turkish Cypriots saw, understood, and often imitated, even as they were aware that the necessity to conform to these patterns was itself a form of domination. It was for this reason that resistance often took the form of refusal to speak Istanbul Turkish or to conform to hierarchical patterns of social relations.

Having rejected this way of becoming Turkish, however, what was left to Turkish Cypriots was to emphasize their struggle *as* Turks, a story that unfortunately ended with Turkey "saving" them. This precarious position of being subjects to the extent that they were "saved" made any agency dependent on their position as passive recipients of aid, extras on the set of their own history. During the reign of "Father Denktaş," the tutelage of these citizen-children could be entrusted to a paternal figure who was also a "true Turk" and a "fighting man," one who mediated between his citizen-children and the Stepfather who wrote checks but maintained a distance. However, like children of divorced parents who manipulate them to get what they want, the status of "Turkish Cypriot"—naughty stepchildren who nevertheless needed protecting as a "national cause"—soon became a role that could be played and a strategy that could be implemented for communal survival.

CHAPTER 9

The Politics of Dis/simulation

The Dome Hotel today is a worn remnant of what it once was. In the mid-1990s, when Mete was its manager, it was one of the largest and most profitable hotels in Cyprus's north. The Dome had once been considered the height of luxury, and even into the 1990s it hosted English lords and a number of well-known actresses. After the Greek Cypriots who had been held in it were expelled to the south in late 1975, it was put under a type of custodianship by the Evkaf, or Department of Religious Foundations. Evkaf similarly ran several other Greek Cypriot–owned tourist properties, though none was as well known or profitable as the Dome.

Mete came to the hotel, first as assistant manager and then as manager, as an employee of Evkaf. Because the hotel staff members were highly unionized and received good salaries, they were composed of Cypriots, as opposed to the staff of other hotels, who because of the lower wages were primarily Turkish nationals. While many of the staff members had worked in the hotel for almost twenty years by that time, managing them was still made difficult by the nepotistic system that had infiltrated all levels of political and economic life on the island.

For instance, during one especially contested parliamentary election, one of the bellboys came to Mete and informed him that until election day he would not be able to work in the evenings as he had to canvass for his party. This particular bellboy was also the *muhtar* of a village outside Girne and personally carried around thirty votes. This made him an important local member of the National Unity Party (UBP), then in power.

"I don't care if it's an election, you'll have to continue your shifts as usual," Mete replied. "If I give you that privilege, everyone else will have to make up the slack."

The bellboy smiled smugly. "Mete Bey, you know I'll get my way in the end, so you may as well give in now," he threatened.

The next morning when Mete arrived in his office, he immediately had a phone call from the chair of Evkaf's board of directors. "Mete Bey, that Hasan of yours, we think you should give him some flexibility during this time," the board chair pleaded. Mete again gave a negative answer and hung up the phone.

About an hour later the regional parliamentary representative called and also pleaded and threatened. "We need Hasan right now more than you need him," the parliamentarian tried to explain but to no avail.

Later that afternoon, the phone rang a final time. At the other end was Derviş Eroğlu, then prime minister and the head of UBP. Eroğlu's wife is also Mete's mother's cousin, a degree of kinship considered close in Cyprus. "Mete'cim," he began, using a diminutive that expresses familiarity, "what are we going to do about this Hasan problem?"

"What do you mean, *başbakanım* [my prime minister]?" Mete asked. "It would destroy all discipline and authority to let a bellboy simply decide when he works and when he won't."

"Mete, you're a good manager, so manage this," was the prime minister's reply (*Sen iyi idarecisin, idare et*).

The word that he used, *idare*, is a word of flexible connotations in Turkish, its English equivalents ranging from "thrift" and "austerity" to "administration," "conduct," "sway," and "manipulation." As a personal noun (*idareci*), it means everything from "administrator," "ruler," or "housekeeper" to "someone who is tolerant or tactful." As a verb (*idare etmek*), it means "to manage" in all of its senses, including the sense of "getting by." If you ask someone how they are doing, their reply may be *idare ediyoruz* (we're managing or we're getting by).

When the prime minister told Mete that he was a good manager so he should "manage," this invoked the form of euphemization discussed in the previous chapter, that is, the tendency to separate the ideal state and its institutions from the persons, with all their faults, who are those institutions in practice. Mete was an *idareci*, a manager or an administrator. Because of this, the prime minister suggested, he also should be able to "manage," to "get by"—something that in many ways is the opposite of the institutional sense of managing. Taking a page from Michel de Certeau (1984), we may say that being a good manager is the realm of what de Certeau calls "strategies," which are deployed by persons in institutional positions to organize the world, while managing in the sense of "getting by" is in the realm of what de Certeau calls "tactics," the ways in which persons in everyday life negotiate these structures.

However, contrary to de Certeau's assertion that tactics do not fundamentally undermine strategies, the prime minister's invocation of "getting by"—in this case, of finding a way to "get by" a manager's own management strategy—in fact has the effect of making the institutions or structures of management themselves appear factitious. What the prime minister is saying, in effect, is, "You're good at what you do, but we all know that the way things really work is this." The practice of "getting by," he implies, is the real or de facto institution, while the strategies of management become strategies for establishing order against the flow of disorder. In other words, while de Certeau assumes that strategies, being institutional, precede tactics, which respond to them, we see here that the strategies of institutions, including the state, are made to conform to the warp and weave of everyday tactics.

This chapter continues our discussion of the de facto subject's agency, the aporetic nature of which we describe here as *dis/simulation*—what in the vernacular is called "acting 'as if'" (*mış gibi yapmak*). This is an agency that is able to have real effects on the world but at the same time *should not* have those effects. We remarked earlier that to simulate was to pretend to have something one does not have, that is, to act *as if* one has a state, an illness, and so on. If to simulate is to act *as if*, to pretend, moreover, this duplicity may simultaneously require us to become complicit, particularly when the simulation is a group exercise. As Lisa Wedeen (1999) has shown in her thought-provoking work on the Hafiz Assad cult in Syria, for instance, acting *as if* one believes in the cult by displaying cult paraphernalia and participating in cult rituals makes average persons who do not want to disturb the status quo complicit in the reproduction of the cult, even if it does not signal belief. Displaying paraphernalia is a tactic for being left alone. As a result, someone who hangs a photo of Assad so that the police will not bother him acknowledges the cult's power by simulating belief. To dissimulate, in contrast, is to disguise, to actively create a fiction, such as the way advisers to the shah of Iran would reportedly erect colorful billboards around the slum areas of Tehran when the ruler would pass through in order to disguise the immiserated state of his people.

Even in the latter example, however, we already see the slippage between pretending and disguising that we show here characterizes what we call *dis/simulation*. If reports from the period are true, it points to the shah's advisers disguising the people's misery as a form of dis/simulation, a way in which the Iranian ruler attempted to fool himself, as he simultaneously knew about the misery of his people but did not wish to know. This dis/simulation, in turn, resembles the fictions invented by the Assad regime itself, which created a so-called cult around Hafiz Assad by claiming that he was the greatest ruler and national father but also that he was the nation's premier pharmacist, that he would like forever, and so on. While no one appears to have believed these claims, they did believe that not to pretend to believe them could have dire consequences. As a result, what this dissimulation actually disguised, and what made it a dis/simulation, was the brute power of Syria's president, whose smiling face on billboards *pretended to disguise* an army of civil police and a network of infamous prisons. Rather than simple dissimulation, dis/simulation in this instance is *pretending to disguise*: pretending that one euphemizes the dictator's power as that of a loving father, even though it is clear that no one actually believes this euphemization.

Similarly in Mete's case, he was not actually being asked to dissimulate, that is, to let Hasan take his hours off in the evening while pretending that this was Mete's own decision or a management strategy. After all, the prime minister surely knew that no one would believe this and that everyone would know precisely what had happened. Instead, he was being asked to dis/simulate, to pretend to protest while knowing that he would ultimately have to give in and knowing that everyone else would know that he would have to give in. "Managing" in this case asked him to become simultaneously complicit and duplicitous, finding ways to disguise his complicity as something else.

Mete's case resembles that of the dis/simulation involved in fights between men in Cyprus and many parts of the Mediterranean. When an argument between two men reaches the point of physical confrontation, the usual scenario is that the men rise to their feet and act as though they are about to come to blows but are held back from fighting by other groups of men. Some anthropologists have explained this pattern as a result of blood feuds, where an actual fight would be likely to have long-lasting repercussions in terms of reciprocal injury, whereas pretending to fight—that is, demonstrating one's willingness to fight but being held back—protects one's honor without initiating a pattern of reciprocal harm. However, the action itself is more than dissimulation, or pretending to fight. It becomes dis/simulation to the extent that men who rise to their feet as if about to come to blows do so while ensuring that they will be held back and while at the same time repeatedly crying, "Don't hold me back!"

(*Tutmayın beni!*). Mete, similarly, was expected to demonstrate a bit of resistance so that he could ultimately say that his hands were tied.

Being held back, we show below, is one of Turkish Cypriots' primary strategies for "getting by." This involves disguising agency as its lack. Turkish Cypriots do have a very real lack of agency insofar as they are under isolations and embargoes, dependent on the Turkish state, and reliant on their Greek Cypriot partners to negotiate a solution that will extricate them from this situation. However, behaving "as if" one would manage the state better, implement international treaties regarding the environment, and reform the civil service (to name only a few examples) if one did not have interference is often, we argue below, a form of dis/simulation, a way of pretending to manage while everyone knows that one is only getting by.

"A Hidden Paradise" and an "Open-Air Prison"

At more or less the same moment that Mete was battling against an intransigent bellboy, Rebecca first arrived in Cyprus. It was the late summer of 1993, still a decade before the checkpoints dividing the island would open to Cypriots and a period when it was possible for foreigners to cross the partition line to the island's north only through one checkpoint in the capital, Nicosia. At that time, the portly guards who swatted flies at the Greek Cypriot checkpoint kept close track of anyone who crossed and insisted that they return by 5:00 p.m. This was an arbitrary rule, intended to prevent tourists from staying in hotels in the island's north, as according to the RoC government all tourist facilities north of the Green Line were occupied Greek Cypriot property. In the picture painted for anyone visiting or living in the island's south, the north was an occupied danger zone where Turkish troops roamed freely, Turkish Cypriots were oppressed, and such illegal activities as arms and drug smuggling were mainstays of the economy. Many foreigners who learned of Rebecca's trips to the north would ask her to accompany them there, wary about going alone. Rebecca's Greek Cypriot neighbors would ask her, "Do they [Turkish Cypriots] have enough to eat? Is the Turkish army everywhere? Aren't you afraid of crossing?" And paradoxically, despite the perception of military rule, the north's status as global "outcast" also made it seem an "outlaw," where isolation and exceptionality appeared by definition to imply lawlessness.[1] All this gave to that long walk through the Nicosia buffer zone an air of danger and adventure.

On arrival at the "other side," one of course found similar portly border guards resting on similar cane stools, drinking the same coffee from similar cups. The name of the coffee brand written on the cups was different, just as the names on the guards' tags changed. The cars were older, the buildings a bit shabbier, and life moved at a slower pace. What was most striking, however, to many visitors was the difference between the ways that an unrecognized state was portrayed in international media and in the official propaganda of their "parent states" and the often banal realities of life on the ground.

Because of its isolation, international visitors to the north during this period often remarked that it seemed "cut off from the world," hence an exceptional space and site of "abandonment." Indeed, this political "black hole," an exceptional space excluded by the "international community," seems rather precisely to fit Agamben's definition of the camp as the space opened when the exception becomes the rule (1998, 2005). What should become clear below, however, is that it may also be possible to *enjoy one's exception*, and here we would emphasize the dual meaning of *abandonment* as both "forsaking" and "exuberance." We certainly find both of these meanings in the ways that Turkish Cypriots experienced the isolation of the period.

Living in the north at the time, one did have a sense of being cut off from the world, being in a type of protected bubble where the system and standards had developed sui generis. Indeed, the "frozen conflict" seemed to have left the north both temporally and spatially "frozen" outside the international system. As a result, visitors to the island often remarked that the north seemed "frozen in time"—an allochronicity, or what Johannes Fabian (2014: 25) calls a "denial of coevalness." Being "cut off" also left the island's north "untouched" and "pure" or "virginal."

This image of the the unspoiled and untouched, hence wild and primitive, was prime for tourism marketing. As one tourist brochure referring to the Karpassia Peninsula opines, the area's frozenness in time also makes it "wild and beautiful." At the time, what Turkish Cypriot tourism agencies and the TRNC's public relations office[2] learned to commodify was their own exceptionalism, which was what made north Cyprus truly "different." In the 1980s and 1990s, the main tourist slogans sold Cyprus's north as a "hidden paradise" that was as yet "undiscovered," an "untouched gem" that had not yet been spoiled by mass tourism. Marketing turned embargoes and isolations into "paradise" and exceptionality into enjoyment. Indeed, the commodification of exceptionalism becomes a powerful form of place-making, marking the north as a separate entity precisely because of its nonrecognition and

Figure 14. A truncated map of Cyprus showing only the main cities and tourist areas of the north (compare Figure 1).

thereby creating the paradox of a state that cannot be a state and a place that cannot be a place. Unrecognized states become a "there" because of their exceptionality—because they do not blend in or fade away but occupy stubbornly real places in geopolitical space.

Moreover, the depiction of the island's north as an exceptional space, one that can be "seen" in maps and tourist brochures, was not only one that was "sold" to the international tourist market. Rather, the more tourist agencies "bought" the idea of the north as exceptional space, the more that space was objectified for Turkish Cypriots themselves. It became more easily possible to speak of the island's north as an intimate and familiar space the more that one sold the brand of "North Cyprus" through travel agents, and the more one saw its signs and slogans represented in London and Washington.[3] As Jean and John Comaroff note regarding the commodification of culture, "The producers of culture are also its consumers, seeing and sensing and listening to themselves enact their identity—and, in the process, objectifying their own subjectivity, thus to (re)cognize its existence, to grasp it, to domesticate it, to act on and with it" (2009: loc 373). In this case, what was being sold was not the idea of a separate culture but rather the idea of "place" itself—the north as a space of wild beauty to be enjoyed because of its isolation.

During this period, Cypriot folk songs played on the radio, and Turkish Cypriots began to discover the actual wild beauty of such remote areas as the

Karpassia Peninsula. Gradually, the commodification of Cypriot identity began to take hold, with popular writers and artists using the dialect and a growing emphasis on localism—local foods, local music, the use of original place names. This localism was in part a response to Turkish labor migration, which increased in this period. However, in addition to that, the context was one in which stalled negotiations resulted in rising support for right-wing parties, and economic liberalization created a growing middle class with the buying power to enjoy their exceptionalism.

In the late 1980s, Sanayi Holding was broken apart and privatized, and by 1987, the majority of its holdings had been sold off in line with trends of neoliberal privatization in Turkey. The suitcase trade also dissipated with the opening of Turkey's markets in the 1980s. In place of both of these, however, came Asil Nadir, a London-raised Turkish Cypriot businessman who in the 1980s became one of the world's wealthiest men and funneled a significant part of his fortune back to his homeland. At the height of his wealth and power, Nadir bought up hotels and industries on the island, single-handedly expanding tourism and bringing *Telegraph*-style journalism and printing methods to the north. The "Asil effect" created new wealth, a new middle class, and a sense that the north was developing and would soon reach or even surpass the economic level of its neighbor in the south. For the first time, Turkish Cypriots left the civil service and entered Nadir's private enterprises, and this hopefulness even extended to the anticipation that Nadir would enable their state to gain recognition.

"I'll tell you, in the 1990s for the first time this community began to act as one that felt what it was like to be a community and took joy from that, and shared together," our friend Emin remarked. "You remember that period [the 1990s]. There would be crowds at art exhibitions, panels, a lot of conferences. . . . In other words, the community all together, by sharing something together, was trying to feel something in common." What Emin describes is a brief moment of what appeared to be a type of "normalization," when international pressure had eased and strategies for "getting by" enabled many people to live comfortably.

However, Emin continued, "After that, it finished. I always explain to people that we experienced such a period." Indeed, even in the period that Emin describes, when isolation produced a sense of solidarity that in many ways resembled the enclave period (see Hatay and Bryant 2008) and descriptions of a "hidden paradise" described an enjoyment of exceptionality, it was an enjoyment built on shaky ground. Already in 1990, the RoC had submitted an application for EU membership on behalf of the whole island. In 1993 the European Union approved Cyprus's eligibility, despite consistent protests from the Turkish Cypriot leadership that the RoC could not join without its constitutional partners. When in 1995 the RoC began its accession dialogue with the European Union, there was a visceral reaction in the island's north. At the time that Rebecca was conducting research, there was considerable public anger, and the right-wing political leadership of the period threatened that such a move would lead them to unite the north with Turkey. However, even then this uproar was laced with disbelief, the idea that such disenfranchisement simply could not be possible in international law.[4]

Along with this political development, it soon became increasingly apparent that the ways Turkish Cypriots in the island's north had developed of economically "getting by" the international order were on equally shaky ground. In 1991, Asil Nadir was arraigned in London on charges of stealing from his multinational company, Polly Peck, and two years later he escaped to north Cyprus, which because of its political and legal isolation was out of reach of international law. And in the mid-1990s, under pressure from its patron to become more economically independent, the north began increasing its higher-education "sector" with the opening of universities specifically aimed at Turkish students who were unable to get placement in Turkey and at students from former Soviet countries. At the same time, grey economies of casinos and brothels grew on the island: while brothels increased with the trade in women from the former Soviet Union,[5] casinos multiplied after 1998, when the Turkish government banned them in that country.

During this period, an economy developed that traded on exceptionality and turned the north into an unusual type of rentier state. The rentier state is the one that profits from its position or natural resources, usually selling these to outside buyers. The rentier state "embodies a break in the work-reward causation. . . . Rewards of income and wealth for the rentier do not come as the result of work but rather are the result of chance or situation" (Yates 1996: 21; see also Kuru 2014). Rather than resource exploitation, however, "rent" in north Cyprus was based on exploiting exceptionality—being outside the order of "normal" states. The refusal of the "international community" to *see* them meant that there was no accountability: there were no environmental treaties or trade agreements or pressure to conform to human rights norms.[6] Although the Turkish Cypriot administration has, in recent years, made great strides to implement the last of these, in part to prove its own legitimate "state-ness,"[7] the limitations of embargo and isolation, combined with north Cyprus's position outside the international order, meant that "getting by" was often about taking advantage of its interstitial position.

The shaky foundation of this economy and way of life was revealed not only by Asil Nadir's flight from the United Kingdom but also by other events in the period. The European Court of Justice issued a decision in 1994 that forbade the import to Europe of any products bearing the TRNC stamp, severely curtailing the market for Turkish Cypriot products, especially citrus. Around the same time, a displaced Greek Cypriot, Titina Loizidou, brought her property case to the European Court of Human Rights, which in 1996 issued a decision against Turkey, the respondent in the case. In 1998, the RoC received a date for its EU accession, and only two years later the north experienced a banking crisis. The banking crisis was followed a year later by a full-blown economic crisis as the Turkish economy collapsed, and the north was one of the dominoes that fell. It was in this period that their isolation ceased to be a form of enjoyment and began to seem confining.

Emin described it as a time when many Turkish Cypriots began to compare their situation with the rest of the world: "Of course, as time went on, after the initial *ganimet* flurry, people filled their stomachs, they vomited, I don't know, they got fat, and they started talking about the whole of Cyprus. . . . People started to understand. 'What's happening? The island is being taken from us!' Various things are happening, but the most important is that we're missing out on something. They realized that."

During the late 1990s, then, alongside the commodification of north Cyprus as a "hidden paradise" that indicates an enjoyment of exceptionality, there also existed an emerging, primarily left-wing political discourse of the island's north as an "open-air prison" (*açık hava hapishanesi*)—a "camp" in Agamben's sense. The metaphor of the open-air prison clearly references Turkish Cypriots' lack of mobility, the ways in which they were under what our friend quoted in Chapter 8 called a "dual siege," referring to pressure from both Turkey and Greek Cypriots. Yael Navaro, discussing this metaphor, interprets it differently, as referring to what she calls the "undeclared martial law" in north Cyprus that at the time prevented Turkish Cypriots from crossing the border to the south (Navaro-Yashin 2005). In her description, the metaphor, rather than implying abandonment, instead describes Turkish Cypriots "experiencing themselves as prisoners kept inside by administrators of the regime and by soldiers" (2005: 111) and expresses an affect resulting from "the cultivation by its fighters and administration of a spirit of terror among its subjects" (2012: loc. 1132).

As we remarked earlier, the decade of the 1990s was a period of heightened nationalism on the island, both north and south. There were skirmishes at the border that resulted in the deaths of two Greek Cypriots. In the north, there was the still unsolved murder of an opposition journalist, reaction to the RoC's EU acceptance, and the spillover effects of Turkey's low-level war against Kurdish forces in the country's southeast. However, the mid-1990s were also a period when the left came briefly to power and when the right was divided. So although the metaphor of an open-air prison was used by the left to express this sense of rising political tension, in common use it had considerably wider scope. More generally, it referred to the emerging sense that in a state of exception and isolation, they were, as Emin expressed it, "missing out on something." This was especially true for those several thousand Turkish Cypriots during this period who participated in bicommunal peace-building workshops that took place primarily in the Nicosia buffer zone but that often involved organized trips to the "other side." Then, as also happened in the 1960s, comparison with a flourishing Greek Cypriot economy and working state, well on its way to EU membership, produced a strong sense of their own entrapment, their separation from the world.

During this period, many Turkish Cypriots would take their guests to the top of the Saray Hotel, in Nicosia's center, to look out over the tiled rooftops of the north to the high-rises of the city's economically booming south, "the Greek side." Others would go to one of the walled city's bastions, a high wall surrounded by barbed wire, from where they could look down into a traffic circle below and the offices of the national telephone company just opposite. "We would look at the cars," one friend who would often go to this spot in the 1990s remembers. "All these new cars. And the clean sidewalks, and the way they had decorated the traffic circle." Navaro (Navaro-Yashin 2012) also makes reference to this spot, Zafer Burcu, and its popularity in a time of closed checkpoints. However, she makes no mention of the types of fascination and fantasy produced through such comparison and instead puzzles over the fact that her informants, while articulating a discourse of being in an "open-air prison," do not express a desire to leave.

Indeed, a focus on the material conditions of their exceptionality can give us quite a different reading of Navaro's own ethnographic material. She comments that most of the young people she met, who had grown up in the north, felt a sense of entrapment but were nevertheless hesitant about crossing to the south. One informant, Olgun, crossed for bicommunal meetings but still expressed "relief once he stepped back into the zone of the very regime, which had determined the subjection and confinement that he so complained about" (2005: 117). Navaro interprets this as a type of false consciousness: "An enduring, if manufactured, political reality leaves marks deeper than would be evident in its subjects' consciously articulated worlds" (2005: 117). In this description, it seems that the "political reality" is hegemonic all the way down and leaves no room for any other description of that emerging reality.

However, the contradictory portrayals of the island's north as an "open-air prison" and a "hidden paradise" should give clues to another way of looking at the situation. It was not only young people who had not experienced a united island who expressed discomfort with crossing to the south; even persons who grew up in the south were, by the 1990s, expressing a sense of a changed environment. One important left-wing politician who is known for his support for federation remarked to us informally at a dinner, "If you say to me, 'Let's go to Larnaca and eat fish,' I'll say, 'No, let's go to Girne.' The homeland, the space is no long Cyprus. It has been halved" (*Vatan, mekan artık Kıbrıs olmaktan çıktı. Yarımlaştı*). While this remark was made in the 2000s, even opposition journalist Şener Levent, who in the 1990s was sued multiple times by Rauf Denktaş and was the constant recipient of death threats, described a sense that he had felt since the division of Nicosia in his childhood that passing to the "Greek side" was like going to a foreign country. "No matter what, I couldn't get away from a feeling of foreignness" (*Yabancılık duyusundan kurtulamıyordum bir türlü*) (Levent 1995: 147–148). He regretted that he continued to feel this during bicommunal meetings in the 1980s.

What these older figures who have fought most of their lives for peace demonstrate is that the "enduring, if manufactured political reality" that caused what Navaro (Navaro-Yashin 2005) views as false consciousness among youth has both deeper roots and other sources than Denktaş's constant television diatribes warning against Greek Cypriots and giving lessons in nationalism and Turkishness. After all, as Navaro observes, for most people Denktaş's voice was background noise, and as we noted in the previous chapter, the portly president was often the subject of quite bawdy humor. How, then, to interpret an "open-air prison" that could also be a "hidden paradise" and expressions of a desire to leave that concealed a desire to stay?

"Nothing Will Happen in Cyprus"

The 1999 documentary *Coconut Revolution*, about the secessionist rebellion of Bougainville Island, describes the ingenuity that Bougainvilleans demonstrated under an eight-year blockade enforced by Papua New Guinea. Bougainvilleans became self-sufficient, revived traditional medicine, and recycled materials from a defunct copper mine to build a hydroelectric generator and distill coconut oil for fuel. The first leader of the revolution, Francis Ona, remarks in the film that the island's isolation had brought its benefits: "I think with the blockade still on, that would be very nice. Because then we will be learning more and more and advance into near future. So that new things will come, new ideas grow."[8]

Earlier, we described the international abandonment of north Cyprus as a geopolitical "black hole" that for those living there might be experienced like a camp or prison. More literally, we could see it as a type of enclave, what in human geographical terms is a space that is isolated or "abandoned" but may also be simultaneously chosen.[9] Or, as one woman who had fled her home in Limassol, in the island's south, remarked about her displacement, "We came here of our own free will, but because we were afraid for our lives."[10] Such "sites of confinement" (Jefferson, Turner, and Jensen 2019) have particular sociological features, one of which is precisely the paradox of isolation and solidarity, of deprivation and enjoyment, that we describe earlier.

For instance, looking back on the enclave period of the 1960s, what Turkish Cypriots tend to remember most is the sense of solidarity, today increasingly expressed as nostalgia for what most people still paradoxically remember as the most difficult period of their lives (see Hatay and Bryant 2008). In a 2009 article, veteran Turkish Cypriot journalist Ahmet Tolgay summarizes this paradox: "If they ask me, 'Is there any period of your life to which you would want to return?' I would answer without hesitation, 'The ten-year period between 1964 and 1974.' Of course, this period covers the most painful years of the Turkish Cypriot people's history. . . . What was good and magical was the social solidarity that rejected this unjust and unfeeling imprisonment." He goes on to compare the equality of the enclave period, when no one rose above anyone else and everyone received equal wages, with the period since, filled with "villas with swimming pools, expensive cars, luxurious vacations, and unlimited consumption."

We suggested above that "abandonment" can also produce enjoyment—an observation not limited to the case at hand.[11] However, the state of exceptionalism in which Turkish Cypriots found themselves is also known in north Cyprus as the Status Quo, the state of "no peace, no war" that we described earlier as a stubborn stasis—one that *should* change but *cannot*. The fact that it cannot change, however, does not alter the normative implications of the understanding that it *should* change—among those implications being that whatever one's enjoyment now, it is also an enjoyment that one *should not* enjoy. What should become clear, then, is that the enjoyment of exceptionalism described above presents a paradigmatic example of what Jacques Lacan would call *jouissance*, a "backhanded" enjoyment (Lacan 1962–63: 112), an enjoyment without pleasure, or an enjoyment that cannot be one.

Indeed, Turkish Cypriots tend to be aware that the rentier economy based on exceptionality that developed in the island's north is abnormal and that it emerges from the stubborn stasis of the Status Quo, the "facts on the ground" that can be neither removed nor resolved. Starting in the 1990s, particularly with international legal decisions condemning the north's property regime, as well as comparison with other, "normal" states, Turkish Cypriots across the political spectrum began increasingly to describe their state as one founded on *ganimet*, or spoils—in other words, on the shaky ground of "facts on the ground" that *should* be dissolved and yet cannot be.

"That culture of spoils caused our degeneration," one right-wing civil society leader tells us one day over coffee. "While people were settling here, everyone got something, everyone was eager to get his hands on something, but no one imagined this was going to continue for forty years. After all, spoils are spoils, and in the end you'll use them up. We engaged in a struggle to save ourselves but couldn't engage in a struggle to establish ourselves (*Biz kurtuluş kavgası verdik ama kuruluş kavgası veremedik*)."[12] "Establishing ourselves" appears to mean here establishing a viable, "normal" economy that is not based only on the stubborn stasis of the Status Quo and the exceptionality that it produces.

This connection emerged in an interview with Mustafa Akıncı before his election as president, quoted earlier. The interview, conducted in 2015, reflects attitudes of that period toward *ganimet* and the distribution of goods but can be used to reflect on the rentier economy that developed in the 1990s. Akıncı raised the issue when he remarked that it was very difficult to create a social energy or synergy around important questions and that there was a general cynical attitude of "long live the snake that doesn't bite me" (*beni sokmayan yılan bin yaşa*).

When we asked what might be the cause of this cynical attitude, Akıncı also tried to explain it as rooted in an exceptional economy built on spoils:

> It [the attitude] has its socioeconomic reasons. One would have to re-search it well, but with the naked eye it seems that with the structure of looting that emerged after 1974, first the depots were filled, then we started distributing. We cleaned out the depots, and we started distrib-uting immovable property. That finished, and then there was credit. That finished, and then there was distribution of jobs. . . . Wouldn't this structure degenerate a community? It would. And what happened? There is always that vision of "nothing will happen in Cyprus (*Ya, bir şey olmaz Gıbrıs'da*), and this is the way things will continue." We've seen that by living forty years, fifty years. If that's the way things are, I have to steer my own boat, I have to salvage what I can for myself. That's why this communal, unpleasant structure emerged.[13]

In our analysis, of course, this distribution has a specific meaning as a form of thymapolitical exchange that is the basis for the nepotistic state. However, its transformation into a rentier economy in the 1990s slowly created the gen-eral sense of communal degeneration reflected in this politician's analysis.

The economic system that developed in the island's north, then, emerges from exceptionality, but its strategy of "getting by" is based on the belief that "*Gıbrıs'da bir şey olmaz*" (nothing will happen in Cyprus). The "nothing will happen" here refers to positive change in the future, either recognition of their state or a negotiated solution to the island's division. It describes the stub-bornness of the Status Quo, emphasizing the stuckness (Hage 2009) of a sit-uation that should change and yet does not or cannot change. It is an expression of "realism" that says that things are out of their hands, that deci-sions are not up to them, and it can be invoked in many circumstances as a shorthand to explain why they have to "get by."

From a Turkish Cypriot standpoint, then, the hegemonic realism that James Scott described as defining "what is realistic and what is not realistic" and driving "certain goals and aspirations into the realm of the impossible" is expressed as the idea that "nothing will happen in Cyprus" (*Gıbrıs'da bir şey olmaz*). This common expression of "realism" contains the knowledge that north Cyprus will never be recognized, as well as the kernel of hope that it might be. It comprehends protests against embargoes and isolations but also the "realistic" knowledge that such punitive measures are common for "pirate states." It encompasses hopes for some form of resolution of the island's division, as well as doubts that it will ever happen. It includes desires to change the system, as well as the "realistic" knowledge that under the circumstances no change will come.

This "realism" becomes hegemonic where desire encounters the impediments of power—in this case, the power of the international system, the strength of "great power" interests, and the "state-ness" of the Turkish state for starters. Under such circumstances, the tactics of "getting by" do not attempt to subvert the "realistic" order, though they are a form of dis/simulation. The farmer who sells the Greek Cypriot land that he has gained from fighters' points may shrug his shoulders and say, "*Napayım?*" (What can I do?)—the all-encompassing question that asks, "Under isolation, what else should I do to make money?" It also simultaneously says, "This is the system, so why should I not take advantage of it? Everyone else is." Hence, the farmer accepts that the system in which he lives is one that is unlikely to be recognized, reformed, or rescued from isolations (*Gıbrıs'da bir şey olmaz*), and indeed accepts that given the way of the hegemonic world order, this is probably how things should be.

Simultaneously, however, the farmer engages in what Ernst Renan (2018) called an "everyday plebiscite," in this case one in which he votes through his actions to continue an order that he is in fact capable of destroying. As we noted in previous chapters, the sovereign exchange that has taken place in north Cyprus is one that has legitimated the state on the body and blood of Turkish Cypriots, that is, out of Turkish Cypriot victimization. Turkish Cypriots are easily able to return to their homes in the south, and they legitimate a separate state that protects them simply by remaining in the north. The Turkish Cypriot state, then, is legitimated by victimization but gains its power from refusal. Turkish Cypriots do not move; they dig in their heels. No matter how bad things get, they simply refuse to budge. When the farmer shrugs and says, "*Napayım?*" to explain why he has profited from Greek Cypriot property, he is invoking helplessness to disguise refusal.

Like the brute force that Assad's smiling face on posters pretends to disguise, *refusal* is at the core of the Turkish Cypriot state, a force that Turkish Cypriots pretend to disguise as helplessness. The young man who calls his environment an open-air prison but hesitates to leave and the farmer's "*Napayım?*" become a form of dis/simulation to the extent that everyone knows that the farmer is invoking his helplessness as a Turkish Cypriot in the world to disguise his own vested interests in the system, which he refuses to demolish.

"The line between ruler and ruled," Vaclav Havel remarked, "runs *de facto* through each person" (1986: 53). Citizens, in Havel's terms, are both subjects and agents of power, both disciplined by the regime and complicit in its re-production. Both Havel and Wedeen (1999) focus on examples in which per-sons reproduce signs that make them complicit in the reproduction of oppressive regimes. The assumption of both these authors is that average citi-zens would prefer the regime to change but see no way to change it and so engage in tactics to "get by"—in Turkish Cypriots' sense, to "manage" (*idare etmek*)—that also involve acting "as if." Acting "as if" because one has no choice in the matter in turn reproduces citizens' sense of the power of the regime. It is because people act in ways that violate their own desires that they become complicit in the regime's reproduction.

What we see in the Turkish Cypriot case, however, is that rather than act-ing "as if" because one has no choice in the matter, *one acts as if one has no choice in the matter.* The moment of refusal is disguised as helplessness, and exceptionality becomes a strategy for "getting by." The rentier economy that developed in the 1990s was based on Turkish Cypriot exceptionalism and jus-tified by invocation of the idea that "nothing will happen in Cyprus"—an invocation that was simultaneously a form of hopelessness, exceptionality, and enjoyment.

Dis/simulating Ideology

The bellboy who threatened Mete so smugly at the beginning of the chapter was not always so loyal to the party of which he became a staunch supporter. Only a couple of years earlier, he had fallen out with the party, which had refused to bring certain services to his village, embarrassing him in front of his constituency. One day two ministers who belonged to the party arrived at the hotel, and as Mete was greeting them, the bellboy suddenly appeared, shouting, "Thieves! Thieves! Don't think you'll win this election!"

Mete was shocked, but the ministers took it in stride, looking a bit sheep-ish and telling Hasan to calm down. In calling them robbers, the bellboy employed what was by then a familiar discourse of the left, one that by the 1980s had begun to center on the idea that the ruling party consisted of "thieves" (*hırsızlar*), that is, was corrupt and distributed favors and gifts to win power. In response to these accusations, the ruling party began to call its leftist rivals "traitors" and "*Rumcu*," or "Greek-lovers," referring to an increasingly vocal discourse among the left that demanded an urgent solution to the Cyprus Problem, as well as increased cooperation between the main opposition party, CTP, and the Greek Cypriot communist party, AKEL. As one former adviser of Denktaş remarked, "After 1974 a status quo emerged here. We got used to calling CTP, the leftists, Rumcu and communist. . . . On one side, there are those who swear at Denktaş, and on the other side are those who praise him. And everyone's carved out his own little space in this country (*Hepsinin de bu memlekette biraz yaşam köşecikleri oldu*). . . . The status quo here serves both the right and the left."[14] The phrase that the adviser uses, *yaşam köşecikleri*, literally means "little living corners," implying not only a certain homeliness and familiarity but also something that is out of the way, not immediately visible but tucked off in a corner. The idea of carving out such a space, moreover, suggests that the rhetoric of political division is itself one means through which that takes place, where both swearing at Denktaş and praising him become ways of marking out one's "little living corner."

This former adviser, then, suggests not only that the rhetoric of politics disguised a Status Quo that benefited everyone but also that during the period that he was in office, former president Denktaş became the foil around which much of this polarization took place. Of course, Denktaş, as we showed in Chapter 8, came to stand for the imposition of Turkish nationalism on the island, with its flags, parades, national ceremonies, and other signs of fealty to the "great Turkish nation." However, as we noted in that chapter, Denktaş both believed this rhetoric and utilized it, even as he recognized that Turkish Cypriots were not yet "Turkish enough" to believe it.

During this same period, moreover, the European Union was economically on the rise, while the Soviet Union had collapsed. As a result, CTP, the main party of the left, underwent liberalizing changes that other leftist parties throughout Europe experienced during the same period. As one friend remarked, "Of course, in this time period the Soviet Union fell apart and a party that called itself communist found a new base with the peace slogan." The "peace slogan" was the idea that only a federal solution would bring "normalization" and rescue them from exceptionality. However, as the adviser implies, this was a slogan that could simultaneously give hope in domestic political debate even as most people understood that peace was only realizable through negotiations that until then had led nowhere.

What should be clear by now is that the ideological language of both right and left in Cyprus sat in an often awkward relationship to the de facto state of affairs, the Status Quo built on "facts on the ground." Rather, as the adviser above remarks, the rhetoric of both left and right, along with displays of intense polarization, had the effect of *euphemizing* politics, in other words, of disguising the structure of the Status Quo. Indeed, our adviser above would no doubt agree with Vaclav Havel, who concluded that ideology "offers human beings the illusion of an identity, of dignity, and of morality while making it easier for them to *part* with them. . . . It is a veil behind which human beings can hide their own 'fallen existence,' their trivialization, and their adaptation to the status quo" (1986: 43).

In this rather cynical conclusion regarding ideology's social function, Havel does not entirely reject the possibility that certain persons may truly believe, for instance, that Turkey is Turkish Cypriots' motherland or that the workers of the world should unite. But he also sees that invocations of these slogans may enable people to get on with their lives in contexts where expressions of their real situation would be degrading. Havel gives the example of a greengrocer who displays the slogan "Workers of the World Unite" in his shop as an expression of obedience and a kind of talisman to ward off informers. In displaying the sign, the greengrocer also avoids the humiliation of expressing his own fear, or in Havel's words, "The sign helps the greengrocer to conceal from himself the low foundations of his obedience, at the same time concealing the low foundations of power" (1986: 42).

The greengrocer, then, has managed to carve out what the adviser above called a "little living corner" for himself, one where he feels secure behind the shield of ideology. Our adviser also seems to see the ideologies of right and left as shields that protect those "little living corners." Where our adviser and Havel would no doubt part ways, however, is in Havel's assertion that while ideology is a way of living in a lie, dissidents are those who "live in truth." For our adviser, everyone is "getting by," and "the status quo serves both the right and the left."

The Status Quo here may be understood as Turkish Cypriots' exceptionality, variously expressed as a "frozen conflict," an unrecognized state, or simply as "the Cyprus Problem." Indeed, the unsolved and seemingly unsolvable Cyprus Problem is the reason for the hegemonic realism that says that "nothing will happen in Cyprus." Or as the right-wing civil society leader quoted earlier remarked, "We became a community that's just waiting for peace" (*Bizde burada barış olacak diye bekleyen bir toplum haline geldik*). In this circumstance, the Cyprus Problem both explains and justifies Turkish Cypriots' tactics of "getting by." When Mete first began working at the Dome Hotel, for instance, he noticed that the toilets in the lobby area were filthy. When he berated the janitor for it, the man gave him a lengthy explanation for his failure that ultimately came back to the unsolved Cyprus Problem. Similarly, when Turkish Cypriots "manage" Turkey, they are able to do so because of their own exceptionality, which makes them dependent on Turkey but not a part of Turkey, and on the basis of the unsolved Cyprus Problem, which both explains and justifies Turkey's presence on the island in the first place.

What the adviser's observation reveals, then, is what we might call the surplus of the Status Quo, an enjoyment that cannot be one. This is an enjoyment that according to the "big Other"—what we have described earlier as the "recognizer" or "international community"—is impossible. The applicability of such an analysis becomes clearer in Žižek's discussion of what Alexei Yurchak (2006) refers to as authoritative discourse, the "wooden language" of ideology that people may, on occasion, feel compelled to repeat without taking it seriously. For Žižek,

> This appearance is *essential*: if it were to be destroyed—if somebody were *publicly* to pronounce the obvious truth that "the emperor is naked" (that nobody takes the ruling ideology seriously . . .)—in a sense the whole system would fall apart: why? In other words: if everybody knows that "the emperor is naked" and if everybody knows that all the others know it, what is the agency for the sake of which the appearance is to be kept at any price? There is, of course, only one consistent answer: *the big Other*—it is the big Other who should be maintained in ignorance. (1989: 198)

Adapted to our own case, one might say that a particular kind of appearance is essential to maintain the order of the Status Quo.

For his own case of late Soviet socialism, Yurchak notes that the importance of recognizing the performative meaning of authoritative discourse was that it was through a performance emptied of meaning that the community of "normal people" (*svoi*) was created. This was the community that did not take that authoritative discourse seriously but understood that one needed to go through the motions. Those who did take that language seriously, whether "activists" who believed in it or "dissidents" who opposed it, could not be *svoi,* or "normal," in this sense of ordinary citizens who are just getting by. Of course, being *svoi* "did not preclude one from feeling personal affinity to many values that were explicitly and implicitly central to the socialist system" (2006: 115).

In our case, we may see how discourses of both freedom and entrapment, both patriotism and dissidence, may be used less to *mean* than to *signal,* creating a community of persons who recognize the performance as performance. As we will see, however, the difference between the sociality of *svoi* and that of the Status Quo is that most people deny being a *statükocu,* or supporter of the Status Quo, while also knowing that they are able to deny this because changing the Status Quo is ultimately out of their hands. In such a situation, one engages in acts that appear to be nationalist fealty or anticolonial dissidence while everyone knows that "in reality" nothing will change. What results instead is a sociality of the Status Quo, where everyone knows that one is simply getting by.

"Managing" Partition

On any given day, on any street in north Cyprus, one may hear a series of greetings that represent an interesting deviation from their standard Turkish equivalent. The person initiating the greetings asks, *"Napan?"* which in the Turkish Cypriot dialect literally means "What are you doing?" and is used to ask "How are you?" The standard answer to this question is not the one that someone from Turkey would ordinarily give: for instance, "I'm well, thanks" (*İyiyim, sağol*), or even "Thankfully, I'm well" (*Çok şükür, iyiyim*). Rather, the answer is, *"Napayım?"* meaning "What can I do?" or "What should I do?" This answer is always said with a certain amount of resignation, implying that one's situation is such that there is little to do about it.

The response to this answer, in turn, is *"Napacan?"* This reply means "What can one do?"—a reply that embraces the interlocutor in the circle of *gardaşlık* by implying a whole set of circumstances that only a *gardaş* can be expected instinctively to understand. This reply says, in effect, "What can one be expected to do as a Turkish Cypriot?" This is what the mother of one party leader meant when she commented to us, regarding a particular political impasse, "In any case, no one wants to know what they should do. And that's because they know it's going to be difficult. The only thing we know is '*na-pan napayım napacan*.'" What she implies is that rather than finding a solution that might be difficult, they were "managing" or "getting by."

If we return to the contradictions of Turkish Cypriots' exceptional space, both a "hidden paradise" and an "open-air prison," it becomes clear that although both ways of describing that exceptionality disguise the Status Quo, the performative invocation of such contradictions nevertheless circumscribes what might be described as a "partition of the manageable." This is a space in which one *gardaş* recognizes another, hence defining the affective intimacy of north Cyprus as an exceptional space. As we discussed in Chapter 3, political philosopher Jacques Rancière uses the partition or distribution of the sensible to refer to the way in which we divide up who is included in the polity and who is not, who may experience its privileges and who may not, in sensory experience (2010: 502–507). Building on Rancière, we observe that in this space of exceptionality, as well, there is a particular *dispositif*, "an associative milieu of sensibilities and dispositions" (Panagia 2018: 28) that divide up the world and define who may rightfully participate in it—in other words, that define the intimacy of *gardaşlık*.

The *dispositif* of *gardaşlık* is defined, for instance, by the relaxed nature of social interaction among Turkish Cypriots, who speak to each other in the first-person singular (*sen*) in violation of all codes of Turkish politeness and who feel relaxed dealing with each other because they know the rules of the game. It is a *dispositif* that is enabled by recognition of certain performances, including the shrug of the shoulders that asks, "What should one do?" In turn, the intimacy of *gardaşlık* becomes the way that one navigates the world. This becomes especially apparent in contrast to dealings with persons from Turkey, who know the language and can navigate the formalities of bureaucracy but are excluded from participation in its privileges. One immigrant told a team of researchers, "For instance, you arrive in a government office, and there's a Turkish Cypriot there in shorts who goes in and finishes his business immediately, while you wait in front of the door dressed formally with a tie. You'll wait your turn. Because he has some relative, some uncle, some cousin, or something like that" (Kurtuluş and Purkis 2014: 97). In this instance, Turkish Cypriots enact the expected formalities of government bureaucracy when it comes to foreigners, but there are invariably ways around this system for those within it.

What we assert, however, is that this way of "getting by" is more than a tactic; indeed, "the partition of the manageable" defines what is visible, sensible, and common. One day a friend of ours, a well-known business-man, was taking his daughter to school and needed to cross the checkpoint but had forgotten his identity card. This was the period after the check-points' opening in 2003 in response to mass protests, which we discuss in the conclusion, against the refusal of the nationalist government then in power in the north adequately to negotiate with their Greek Cypriot counterparts. As Rebecca writes about elsewhere (2010), this was a period of rapid change that within a couple of years settled into a "new normal." Soon after the opening, many Turkish Cypriot parents began sending their children to the international schools in the island's south, which better prepared them for university study abroad. Many parents would simply drop their children at the Ledra Palace checkpoint and let them walk through the buffer zone to where a bus waited for them in the south. Our friend's daughter, however, was quite young, and he preferred to ac-company her through the buffer zone and make sure that she boarded the bus at the other end.

He discovered that he had forgotten his identity card but thought little about it until confronted with a young border guard who was the child of settlers who had arrived in the 1970s from the Black Sea area of Turkey. Much to his surprise, the young guard refused to let him through.

"Don't you know who I am?" our friend asked in astonishment, giving his name. "I've passed through here many times without my ID card. Who are you to tell me I can't cross?"

The young guard, however, held his ground. "Sir, this is a border," he re-plied, "and you can't just come and go as you please."

Our friend was indignant and would later complain to the young man's superiors, who would reprimand him for not "managing" the situation. What is significant about this story is not only our friend's expectation that he would be known but the indignation he experienced when someone who, as we dis-cussed in Chapter 3, was part of the group abjected from the de facto polity would frustratingly refuse to "manage" the situation. Here *idare etmek* has a different meaning than we have used before, as in this instance it becomes not a way of getting around the impediments of exceptionality but instead a way of defining a space of "manageability" within the borders of exception-ality. While the civil servant who is not qualified for her position is "manag-ing" in the sense of "getting by," those who would like to raise the standards or demand accountability are often told, "*İdare et*," where in this case the de-mand to "manage" is also a request to overlook or let slip by.

When our friend related this story to us, it reminded us of our experience at the border of another unrecognized state, the so-called Republic of Abkhazia. We had gone there on a research trip with a group of heritage Abkhaz from Turkey, most of whom had relatives in the territory. After several grueling hours of passing through the Russian checkpoint at Sochi, we were welcomed into Abkhazia by a border guard who spoke Turkish and did not even ask for our passports, instead asking how many were there to see relatives. The reactions of those in our group to the guard's magnanimous gesture were telling. One elderly man who was making his first trip to Abkhazia became disgruntled by the policeman's gesture, grumbling, "What kind of state is this?" The rest of the group, however, laughed, applauded, and rattled off family names for the border guard, who responded in kind with remarks about persons from those families.

Of course, both insisting on border formalities and waving them aside are forms of sovereign assertion, the latter demonstrating that even exceptions can implement an exception. Even the border guards of recognized states may joke and be friendly with persons they know, stamping their passports without question. Not asking for passports at all, however, caught many in the group by surprise. The guard's cavalier attitude later created worry among some who were making their first trip, as they wondered how they would explain the absence of registration when we left the country. Others in the group brushed these worries aside: "We're in Abkhazia now!" they would say, as though this should be self-explanatory.

The explanation made intuitive sense to us from our own experience in another unrecognized state where people were similarly prone to remark, as though it elucidated any irregularity, "This is the TRNC!" (*Burası KKTC!*). To say "This is Abkhazia!" or "This is the TRNC!" is to joke that it is a place where irregularity is the norm and where one should suspend one's expectations of what a state should be. But it is also, at the same time, to invoke and evoke an affective intimacy, a complicity in irregularity. It is here, then, in this joking exclamation, "We're in Abkazhia now!" that abandonment as a sovereign exception also acquires the meaning of indulgence—in other words, enjoying one's exception.

Indeed, we may see the Abkhaz guard's gesture and our friend's indignation as invocations of this affective exceptionality—as an invitation to abandonment. If their very exceptionality—the "border" that is not one—marks them out as a place in geopolitical space, "we" become those persons who understand what it is like to live with a "border" rather than a border,

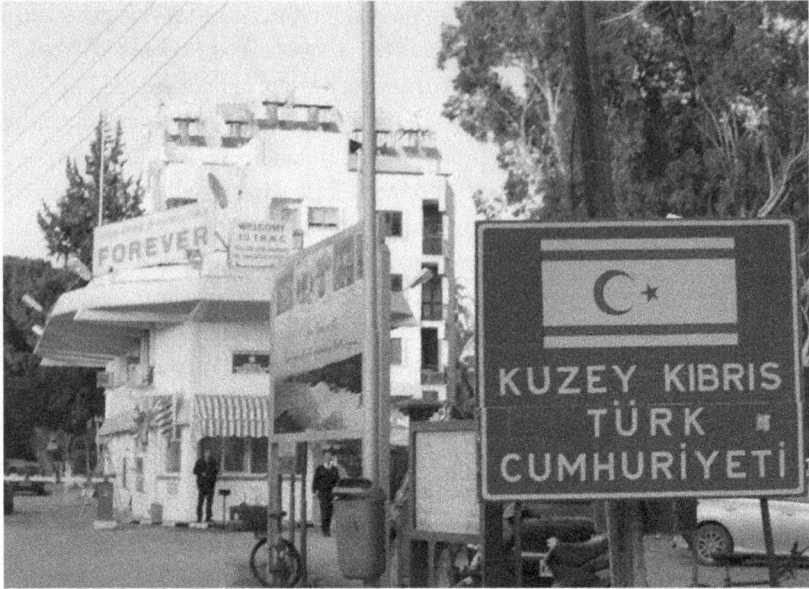

Figure 15. Insisting on sovereignty: signs at the Ledra Palace crossing point from Nicosia's south (photo by Rebecca Bryant).

a space where things such as bureaucracy might be improvisatory. Insofar as the Abkhaz guard "impersonated" the state (Reeves 2014), he simultaneously made the state personal, giving it the intimate air of complicity that invited us to abandon our expectations of what a "real" state might be.

We return, then, to the story with which we began this chapter. It should be clear now that when the prime minister told Mete, "You're a good manager, so manage," he was calling upon Mete as someone he presumed to be in possession of a particular *aisthesis*, a way of feeling that is also a common judgment, and to participate in a particular *dispositif*, or milieu of sensibilities and dispositions. In this instance, he was calling on the solidarity, or *gardaşlık*, that comes to imbue the space of exceptionality that is north Cyprus with a sense of both familiarity and collusion.

Mete, in turn, did "manage"—in this case, by forcing the bellboy to resign. "If Hasan has thirty votes," he told the prime minister, "I have a hundred. Which is more important to you?"

In one sense, Mete *rest çekti*, presented a challenge or literally put all his money on the table. At the same time, Mete's "handling" of the situation was a dis/simulation to the extent that his challenge to the prime minister was tempered by kinship. While to the outside observer, Mete told the prime minister off, he also did so knowing that the politician's hands were tied.

It is through the partition of the manageable, we wish to suggest, that de facto agency may be defined. It is a partition defined by exceptionality in which the series of greetings with which we began this section (*Napan? Napayım? Napacan?*) express the intimate familiarity of helplessness. It is in the concept of "the manageable," then, where exceptionality, statecraft, and community formation intersect to shape a particular *dispositif,* a "little living corner" in Cyprus's north. Within that space of exceptionality, helplessness becomes agency, hegemony is handcuffed, and intimacy is circumscribed by a defeated shrug of the shoulders.

The Absurdity of the Aporia

In early 2004, banners waved and music blared in the streets of northern Nicosia as tens of thousands of Cypriots converged into the square and park near the presidential palace to express their support for a United Nations–backed plan to reunify the island. The plan would soon go to a referendum on both sides of Cyprus, and in the north, people of all ages and all parties had united under slogans such as *"Yes be annem,"* a colloquial reference to Turkish Cypriots' frequent use of English loan words in everyday life and whose meaning here was "Of course, yes!" Another very popular slogan, used often throughout the campaign, was *"Bu memleketin efendisi olacağız,"* or "We will be the masters of this country," a reference to the state as status discussed in previous chapters. In this phrase, to be a master, an *efendi*, was not only to be an owner or possessor of something but also to be someone recognized as such and so worthy of respect.

The event was organized by the This Country Is Ours Platform (Bu Memleket Bizim Platformu), a group that appealed to local senses of identity against the real and perceived interference of Turkey. While the This Country Is Ours Platform emerged from parties of the left, one of their main partners in the demonstrations was Common Vision (Ortak Vizyon), a movement composed primarily of journalists and businesspeople, the participation of many of whom signaled a political about-face and was highly influential for voters. Indeed, some of those who would become the faces of the movement had in the past been staunch supporters of an independent state.

One of these was publisher and media personality Doğan Harman, who became known on the far right as "Whirligig Doğan" (Fırıldak Doğan) for his own about-face regarding reunification. His *Cypriot* (*Kıbrıslı*) newspaper consistently seasoned a populist appeal to local identity with a sprinkling of Kemalist nationalism, flavored with a bit of Leninism that sometimes spun him so far left that he ended up on the right. Amusingly, only a few months earlier, that newspaper's subtitle had been, "We Are a Small Turkey" (*Biz küçük Türkiyeyiz*). And only two years before the demonstrations, that same newspaper had published a headline calling on several leading public figures who supported reunification to state "what percentage Turkish they are" and to reveal "their real identities," a reference to accusations that they took funding from the U.S. government to support reunification.[1] But during what came to be known as the Annan Plan period, after the U.N.-backed plan and the Secretary General who sponsored it, Harman used his popular program on a private television station, his newspaper columns, and the momentum of the demonstrations to rant against the Status Quo and those who supported it. Indeed, Harman was responsible for adding a new word to the Turkish Cypriot political vocabulary: *statükocu*, or supporter of the Status Quo.

During the demonstration that we describe, a union organizer took the stage and gave a rousing speech against the Status Quo, appropriating Harman's language to argue that all those who opposed the U.N. plan were *statükocular* and so preferred things to stay as they are. One elderly man, a friend of Mete's father and former journalist, turned to Mete with a wry smile.

"Who are these Status Quo-ers he's talking about?" the older man asked. "I see the head of the Chamber of Commerce there next to him, and the head of the contractors' organization is over there with that banner. Mehmet over there next to him probably owns a thousand *dönüm*s of Greek Cypriot land."

What the older man pointed to was the irony, indeed the absurdity, that people associated very strongly with reproducing what we usually understand as the status quo, that is, the current state of affairs, would have joined forces with persons who had long supported a solution that appeared it would demolish the Status Quo. That Status Quo, Harman would write in his book of that name, might be understood—as we have argued earlier—as "the political non-solution of the Cyprus problem" (Harman 2006: 19). It is the temporal and political stuckness, the inability to move forward, that is unacceptable but preferable to war. Or as an informant quoted in the introduction phrased it, "As we were rising from people to nation, we got hung somewhere in the middle." The Status Quo, in other words, defines the experience of living with the aporia, and those who came to be labeled Status Quo-ers were persons who were accused of having an interest in this stubborn stasis.

Harman's seeming about-face, his transformation from a leftist nation-alist to a supporter of peace, becomes clearer in the 560-page collection of newspaper articles that he published as a book in 2006 with the title *Status Quo* (*Statüko*), an indication of the significance that he and his large reader-ship gave to the term. His lengthy explanations are also worth thinking about in terms of the about-face that Turkish Cypriot public opinion under-went during the period, suddenly transformed from a polity that had put nationalist politicians into office for almost thirty years to one that poured into the streets in support of a plan that politically had been associated with "traitors" and "Greek-lovers." Indeed, support for nationalist parties had only been on the rise: in the 1993 election, nationalist parties gained around 60 percent of the vote; in the 1998 election, they increased that portion to 70 percent. Although the 2000 presidential election that Denktaş again won had been contested, his rival had been another nationalist leader, Derviş Eroğlu.[2] In other words, this about-face followed a period of about a decade when nationalist politics only gained in strength.

There were conjunctural reasons for this change of allegiances, among them winds of change in the "motherlands." In August 1999, Istanbul was hit by a massive earthquake that killed more than 30,000. Greek rescue teams came to help, and Turkish rescue teams reciprocated when a smaller earth-quake hit the islands in the northern Aegean a short time later. This led to a period of "earthquake diplomacy," and newspapers filled with photographs of Foreign Ministers Ismail Cem and Yiorgos Papandreou dancing *sirtaki* on the Aegean island of Samos.

During this same period, Mete was sent to a tourism fair in Istanbul and found the conference center where the fair was held for the first time adorned with Greek and Turkish flags intertwined. Mete recalls one of his more left-ist colleagues returning to their booth with a wide grin and a pin in his lapel of those same intertwined flags. This colleague was known as a joker, and it was his way of teasing their more nationalist colleagues. One of those col-leagues immediately demanded that he remove the pin, which he feared might offend their Turkish hosts. Just as their joker friend was doing so, however, the Turkish tourism minister arrived to shake their hands and in his lapel was the same pin. It took some time for Mete's nationalist colleagues to com-prehend this change, just as at the time many Turkish Cypriots who visited the city were shocked to hear Greek bouzouki music blaring from loudspeakers on the main shopping streets and new restaurants opening that advertised

Greek food. Persons whose ancestors had arrived in Anatolia with the 1923 Greek-Turkey population exchange suddenly began to form associations and become more public about their roots. This softening was not at all visible in Cyprus, however, where the continuing "thankfulness to Turkey" campaigns necessarily entailed repeating the suffering at Greek Cypriot hands from which Turkey had "saved" them.

Moreover, in the same year as Mete's visit to Turkey, north Cyprus experienced a banking crisis that cost many people their savings. This was followed less than a year later by the extreme devaluation of the Turkish lira that accompanied the Turkish financial crisis of 2001. And out of that crisis, Turkey's Justice and Development Party (AKP), then headed by moderate Abdullah Gül, would have a sweeping victory in the November 2002 parliamentary elections. The AKP came to power with a strongly pro-European agenda and a program of wide-ranging reform.

One important development of the 1990s that had pushed some Turkish Cypriots to a more nationalist position was the insistence of their Greek Cypriot neighbors on beginning EU accession negotiations as the single legitimate government of the island and without their Turkish Cypriot partners. Despite the protest of Turkish Cypriot leaders, the relative economic strength and stability of the Republic of Cyprus, as well as the common belief that the TRNC was in any case only Turkey's puppet entity, led the European Union to proceed with accession negotiations, indeed ultimately to give the republic an accession date of 1 May 2004. Bülent Ecevit and other Turkish leaders with a leftist heritage tended to see the European Union as a tool of imperialism, while Denktaş and other Turkish Cypriot leaders declared that the RoC should not become an EU member before Turkey. With the financial crises and sudden shift in Turkish leadership, however, the winds began to blow strongly in a different direction, such that even persons who had long declared themselves staunch nationalists might suddenly wear symbols of Greek-Turkish friendship.

It was in late 2002, amid this economic and political ferment, that news first leaked that the United Nations had formulated a reunification plan that it hoped would form the basis for a federal solution to unite the island before the RoC's 2004 EU accession. Turkish Cypriots spilled into the streets at the prospect of a richer, more stable EU future, demanding that their leaders negotiate the plan. Not only this, but EU, Turkish, and Greek leaders put their full weight behind the plan. When the AKP began to put reins on the Turkish military, the traditional tactics of the Turkish Cypriot nationalist leadership—pumping up the "national cause" to win the support of the military against the civilian government—were no longer viable.

As a way of relieving the pressure, Turkish Cypriot leaders decided on 23 April 2003 to suddenly open the Cyprus "border." By that time, movement had been restricted on the island for twenty-nine years, and that opening would change the parameters of politics on both sides of the island. Rebecca explores that opening in ethnographic detail elsewhere (Bryant 2010; see also Dikomitis 2012), in particular in the context of the critical Annan Plan referendum. What concerns us here, and ends our story, is how in this context a small group of peace activists and supporters of federation who had won only 30 percent of the vote in the previous parliamentary election would suddenly find themselves at the forefront of a movement that created a swell of hope and seemed destined to change the future of the island.

That transformation is most easily understood through what that group said they wanted to change: the Status Quo, which we have referred to as the stubborn stasis. Harman, in his writings, draws together a number of the themes that we have discussed in this book, especially in his juxtaposition of the Status Quo to the state as status. As we remarked in Chapter 6, it was the lack of status that they experienced as citizens of an unrecognized state that led one commentator to complain that "the world never counted us as human" (*dünya bizi adamdan saymadı*), and for this reason they were "just a pile of stateless humans who don't know themselves what they are."[3] Another commentator in that chapter explained this through a discussion of equality: "The concrete meaning of equality is EQUALITY OF STATUS, that is, that the Cypriot Turkish Community is not a minority but is one of the main two communities of the island." It was in the refusal to accept a minority status and insistence on equality of that status that the need for institutions arose in the first place.

Harman opposes this understanding of the state as one where they would have an equal status and therefore a sovereign agency to their statusless Status Quo, one based on the territorial nation-state rather than the sovereignty they had fought for:

Why did we resist and why did we fight? Was it not to protect our physical existence and to realize all the rights given to us as humans? Were equality, sovereignty, and our right to self-determination not the fundamental goals of that struggle?

Today some self-interested persons are trying to tell us otherwise. They're shrieking that we fought for territory. We didn't fight for territory. They shouldn't confuse the goal.

We didn't fight for territory. We fought to protect our national existence and to bring to life the rights given to us by being an equal entity. The peace that we will now make is a continuation of this. (Harman 2006: 45)

What Harman expresses clearly is the desire for sovereign agency. While he writes of sovereignty, it is a sovereignty that he explicitly divorces from land. "We did not fight for land," he repeats, condemning what he calls a "conquest mentality": "In 1974 our people abandoned their lands and came to the north. Because a space of freedom had been created where we would be able to realize our equality, sovereignty, and right to self determination. The essence is not land, it is this!" (45). Harman draws a clear distinction here between a "space of freedom" (*özgürlük alanı*) and a territorial nation-state.

This suggests to us a view of sovereignty and its traps that is rather different from the traditional view. Hendrik Spruyt, for instance, while writing a genealogy of state sovereignty, at the same time takes it as teleological and so argues that "it was the concept of sovereignty that altered the structure of the international system by basing the political authority on the principle of territorial exclusivity" (1994: 3). Partly in response to this view, Jens Bartelson has recently argued that instead sovereignty may be seen as a fetish, in his view implying something inaccessible to analysis. "Perhaps the main ideological function of the concept of sovereignty," he remarks, "is not primarily to legitimize particular claims to political authority, but rather to legitimize the international system within which those claims can be understood as meaningful" (Bartelson 2014: 63).

Certainly, if we return to the Schmittian-Agambenian view of sovereignty, it is in the act of abandonment, of declaring the exception, the "rogue" or "pirate state," that we may see the sovereignty of the International Community being created. Unlike sovereign states, Bartelson argues, it is in this act that the International Community *as a sovereign* emerges. The point, as we noted earlier, is that *realizing* sovereign agency requires a *realizer*, in this case the International Community that will see and acknowledge you, recognizing you as a Legal Person. Bartelson's observation is that the International Community only gains its status through the need for its realizing function. To return to an earlier metaphor, one may feel invisible in a party where every-one ignores you, but only if you attend the party.

Of course, one may argue that for almost a century now one has had no choice but to attend the party. Not attending the party would mean a form of nonviolable isolation. But what if you want to attend the party, indeed think it is the only party in town, but the reason everyone ignores you at the party is because, by dint of circumstance, you turned up in the wrong garb? This seems to be what Harman suggests when he remarks that finally, after all these years, the Annan Plan gave Turkish Cypriots the chance to have the sovereign agency they had wanted all along. After they had all gathered in the north, Harman asks, what did they then want? "We wanted the world to recognize our sovereignty and equality," he answers.

> Now we have a such a chance. Now a chance has appeared for the world to recognize our equality and sovereignty. The Annan Plan is this op-portunity put on the negotiating table. . . . We don't want anyone to be displaced from their homes. We don't want anyone to experience the tears of refugeehood. But if we have to make concessions of territory to secure our equality and sovereignty, those concessions will be made. No one can say, "Let's keep the territory and forego sovereignty."
>
> Yes, we did not fight for territory. Territory is important in the life of a people and a state. But it is not more important than the sover-eignty of our people and state and the protection of our cultural in-tegrity and national identity. (2006: 45–46)

In this explicit contrast of territory with sovereignty, what becomes clear is that being constrained to have a territorial nation-state has stood in the way of their sovereign agency. In the context of the international system, the only way to realize their desires for sovereign agency was in a form that was not realiz-able. What they wanted was status, but what they got instead was the Status Quo, a state of affairs that derived from acquiring a state that could not be one.

The general assumption in political theory is that a state, to be a state, must be sovereign. But what if sovereignty is something that is not constitu-tive of states but rather inheres in them? What if the modern state, rather than being defined as sovereign, was instead a vehicle for the realization of sover-eignty understood as (collective) agency? The will of the people should have a form in which it can be realized, and that form has been the modern state. In this sense, we suggest, our approach to the state and sovereignty needs to disaggregate the two, to ask to what extent the nation-state can or cannot be a vehicle for sovereign agency, and what sort of agency this is that appears to be realizable through the specific institution of the modern state.

Disaggregating sovereignty from the territorial nation-state, then, allows us to see sovereignty as a capacity, a form of institutionally realized agency. De facto sovereignty is a constrained capacity, one dependent on "managing" or getting by in the international order. While there may be no state that is able to enact full sovereign agency, we have argued that what is anomalous or exceptional about de facto states is what we have called the paradox of the de facto, which acknowledges a state even as it denies one and so makes those entities aporetic from their inception. In unpacking what it means for a state to be aporetic, we have argued that the practices and orders that constitute what we call the *factum* of the de facto—what we recognize as the "real" of the state—may exist alongside or in contradiction with what we have referred to as the *factitious*, or those elements of state-ness that emphasize their own making. The factitious, we have argued, becomes visible in flags waving and churches turned into mosques, but its essential element is the embedded awareness of the potential dissolution of their state. As a result, the factitious is always on the verge of unraveling the state's "reality."

It is in the factitious, then, that we most clearly see the aporia between the real and realizable, insofar as the factitious may sometimes appear false, calling the state into question, but at other times may appear only fabricated, allowing us to believe in the state. Moreover, factitiousness is visible not only in settlers disguised as migrant laborers or appropriated property disguised as "resources." It is most clearly in the way that, to paraphrase Žižek, the de facto state-builders and citizens described here understand that what they are doing is ideological, and they do it anyway. They understand that the international community will disapprove, and so instead they search for the "work-around," a way to "get by" the international order. It is in such a way that one may disavow what one simultaneously practices, disguising agency as helplessness. "*Napayım?*" (What should I do?) becomes the all-encompassing way of "managing" in a situation where "nothing will happen in Cyprus." As we have argued, however, this is more than simply dragging one's feet in resistance to a hegemonic order. It is, instead, an acceptance of that hegemonic order, indeed a desire for that hegemonic order, that disguises one's unacceptable will as an acceptable disavowal.

Using helplessness to enable refusal and agency may appear absurd, and indeed Turkish Cypriots often remark on its absurdity. As we were completing this book, one friend, in response to a stall in the negotiations, wrote on his Facebook page,

> How can a community will and resistance be expected from the members of a community that live in luxury villas built on Greek Cypriot property, in fact buy two or three more as "investments," have one, two, even three brand new luxury cars parked in their garage, take at least two or three overseas holidays a year, never give up their weekend entertainment, and do all this with the salaries paid either directly or indirectly by Turkey? Even more absurd is that these are the same category of people who on social media hit the "like" or "love" button for calls to revolution or to demonstrations. Sorry, friends, but we won't get shit in this country with this human profile.

Although our friend refers to this as an absurd situation, his own approach is cynical, unmasking the way that ideology—"liking" revolution on social media—allows the reproduction of the Status Quo. We noted in Chapter 2 that we may see the cynic as the person out to expose the base coercive function of power, while the ironist is the one who sees even coercion as a strategy disguising something else (Žižek 1996). The ironist, for instance, might point out that much of the reaction in north Cyprus against the current Turkish government may be couched in a language of domination and oppression which in fact disguises a Kemalist secularism that allows them also to bemoan "what is happening to Turkey."

In this case described by our friend, however, we may use our analysis to see that this unmasking is not only a cynical one but is one in which everyone knows that their supposed ideology is factitious and supports the status quo, but they espouse it anyway. Like the church with the minaret or the enormous flag on the mountain, the factitious manifests and reveals the absurd. As a philosophy, Absurdism is founded on its own aporia: Albert Camus had viewed the absurd as the true philosophical attitude toward the human search for meaning, exposing a gap in understanding and the necessity of searching for something that cannot be found. Camus, and before him Søren Kierkegaard, found three ways of dealing with this fundamental aporetic position: suicide, faith, or accepting the absurd. Suicide in our case might be seen as the dissolution of the state, either into the "parent state" or through annexation to the "patron." The "faith," in this instance, is that found in a federal solution, which requires a leap of faith into an unknown future. Moreover, just as the ability to believe in God fills the gap of the existential aporia, so a federal solution acquires mystical and fetishistic elements that will make the impossible possible.

The final option is accepting the absurd, which Camus argued entails nihilism and admitting "that the absurd is the contrary of hope" (1955: 24). In contrast, then, to studies of hope for the state (esp. Jansen 2014), or to a burgeoning literature on hope and waiting (e.g., Auyero 2012; Bloch 1986; Crapanzano 2003; Hage 2009; Miyazaki 2004), we propose what Turkish Cypriots in recent years, appropriating the language of psychology, have begun to call "learned helplessness" (öğrenilmiş çaresizlik). This is the helplessness of the rat in the cage—or in Camus's example, the helplessness of Sisyphus, persistently pushing his boulder up a hill.

Unlike the laboratory rat, however, Sisyphus was a trickster, one who first put Death in chains so that no one could die and who then conned the gods into letting him return to earth after his own death. Sisyphus, then, was a master of the "work-around," and the boulder that he pushed uphill as his punishment condemned him to a life that was always on the verge of, but never quite acquiring, freedom. One can imagine him strategizing new ways to push, new torques and trajectories to try. And unlike "helplessness," the Turkish word, çaresizlik, does not have the connotation of impotence or powerlessness so much as that of irresolvability, despair, and lacking a solution. There is always the glimmer of a possibility that one extra push, one final surge, will push the boulder beyond the point of return. And one can retain that kernel of a possibility even without believing in it.

Hence, while realizing the state and its sovereignty may always be in some sense an impossible, life in de facto states shows us what it means to live with the presence of that impossibility. It shows us what it means to live in awareness of the aporia, to live in a situation that by definition both should not exist and cannot disappear. Throughout this book, however, we have seen that Turkish Cypriots have used all methods available to get by in the face of irresolvability, maintaining the possibility if not the hope that the boulder will roll to the other side. The shrug of the shoulders is never quite defeated, just as saying "nothing will happen in Cyprus" never quite rules out the possibility that something still may.

Turkish Cypriot Institutions

FOUNDING DATE	NAME
8 April 1943	Island of Cyprus Turkish Minority Institution (Kıbrıs Adası Türk Azınlığı Kurumu, KATAK)
23 April 1944	Cyprus National Turkish People's Party (Kıbrıs Milli Türk Halk Partisi, KMTHP), led by journalist and politician Dr. Fazıl Küçük
1949	KMTHP joins forces with KATAK as the Cyprus National Turkish Union (Kıbrıs Milli Türk Birliği)
8 September 1949	Federation of Turkish Cypriot Associations (Kıbrıs Türk Kurumları Federasyonu, KTKF)
16 August 1960	Turkish Cypriot Communal Chamber (Cemaat Meclisi) of the Republic of Cyprus
21 December 1963	General Committee of Cypriot Turks (Kıbrıs Türk Genel Komitesi)
27 December 1967	Temporary Turkish Administration of Cyprus (Kıbrıs Geçici Türk Yönetimi)
21 April 1971	Turkish Administration of Cyprus (Kıbrıs Türk Yönetimi)
1 October 1974	Autonomous Turkish Cypriot Administration (Otonom Kıbrıs Türk Yönetimi)
13 February 1975	Turkish Federated State of Cyprus, TFSC (Kıbrıs Türk Federe Devleti, KTFD)
15 November 1974	Turkish Republic of Northern Cyprus, TRNC (Kuzey Kıbrıs Türk Cumhuriyeti, KKTC)

NOTES

Introduction

1. "KKTC tanınmamış olsa da Kıbrıslı Türkler 'tanındı,'" *Milliyet*, 24 January 2016, http://www.milliyet.com.tr/kktc-taninmamis-olsa-da-kibrisli/dunya/detay/2183428/default.htm.

2. "Burcu: Çözümle Statümüz Yükselecek," *Gündem Kıbrıs*, 22 January 2016, https://www.gundemkibris.com/mansetler/burcu-cozumle-statumuz-yukselecek-h162485.html

3. Arman Ratip, "İki açıklama," *Halkın Sesi*, 14 February 2016.

4. On sovereign anxieties, see also Friedman (2015).

5. Other important critiques have traced the historically contingent emergence of our contemporary notions of sovereignty (Bartelson 1995; Spruyt 1994). Still others have observed that understandings of sovereignty have changed over time (Barkin and Cronin 1994; Crawford 2007; Jackson 2007); cannot be reduced to identifiable standards that apply to all states (Fowler and Bunck 1996; Freeman 1999; Østerud 1997; Thomson 1995); and contain significant contradictions (Walker 1993, 2010), such as a belief in the principle of sovereign equality that is always undermined in practice (Simpson 2004; also Ashley 1988; James 1992).

6. For a comprehensive overview of displacement in Cyprus, see the PRIO Cyprus Centre's mapping and study, "Internal Displacement in Cyprus: Mapping the Consequences of Civil and Military Strife," www.prio-cyprus-displacement.net.

7. Although eight thousand Turkish Cypriots remained outside the enclaves, Patrick reports that these villages were not given services by the government of Cyprus, as they refused to submit to government control (Patrick 1976: 463–465).

8. According to investigative journalist Makarios Droushiotis, in July 1965 "the Council of Ministers approved draft legislation extending the term of the President and House of Representatives for a year. It also approved a revision of the electoral law, abolishing the Turkish Cypriots' right separately to elect the Vice President and the members of the House of Representatives from their community." Moreover, when Turkish Cypriot parliamentarians requested protection to return to the parliament to discuss the issue, then Speaker of the House Glafcos Clerides "imposed such conditions on its acceptance as would be tantamount to an acceptance of minority status by the Turkish Cypriots." Three years later, when the Turkish Cypriot community elected Dr. Fazıl Küçük as vice president and requested that he be allowed to take the oath of office along with the elected president, Archbishop Makarios, they were told that the election itself was illegal, as elections could be conducted only by the state, not by a community (Droushiotis 2008).

9. Various sources indicate that beginning in the mid-1950s both British administrators and Turkish Cypriot leaders envisioned a division of the island (in Turkish, *taksim*) as the potential basis for a federal system. In 1956, for instance, Lord Cyril Radcliffe, one of the architects of the Partition of India, bemoaned in a report to the Cyprus government that a federation would not be possible on the island because of the lack of separate physical spaces for the communities. On the history of *taksim* and federation, see Hatay (2016).

10. This military intervention was justified through the obligations of Turkey, Greece, and the United Kingdom to maintain constitutional order in the island, as outlined in the 1960 Treaty of Guarantee.

11. Interview with Mustafa Akıncı, 27 April 2015, Nicosia.

12. Dov Lynch notes that in his own interviews with leaders in de facto states, all were convinced that rules regulating self-determination will ultimately change. "The separatist leaders," he remarks, "favor the declaratory over the constitutive approach to understanding the recognition of an entity as a state by other states. These governments maintain that recognition does not *create* a state but rather *reflects* an existing reality" (Lynch 2004: 47; emphasis in original).

13. *Kibris Postasi*: http://www.kibrispostasi.com/index.php/cat/35/news/182489 /PageName/KIBRIS_HABERLERI.

14. For a discussion of the conflict of international law and realpolitik in practices of recognition, see Kyngaert and Sobrie 2011, and for Cyprus, Nedjati 1981 (also discussed in Chapter 6).

15. Waiting itself has a growing literature exploring its practices and various affects, as well as who waits for whom (e.g., Auyero 2012; Crapanzano 1986; Hage 2009; Janeja and Bandak 2018).

16. For an excellent overview of the critical literature on sovereignty, see Kalmo and Skinner 2010.

17. Our understanding of practices and orders has been particularly influenced by Theodore Schatzki and especially his important work, *The Site of the Social* (2002).

18. Apart from the authors' works on the subject, referenced throughout the text, literature on the Cyprus conflict in English has come primarily from political science (e.g., Constantinou 2008; Hadjipavlou 2010; Ker-Lindsay 2005, 2012; Loizides 2016; Diez and Tocci 2009) and history (e.g., Asmussen 2008; Faustmann 1999; Holland 1999; Katsiaounis 1996; Markides 2001; Nevzat 2005; Rappas 2014), but with growing interest from anthropology (e.g., Dikomitis 2012; Loizos 1981, 2008; Papadakis 2005; Sant Cassia 2005) and sociology (e.g., Attalides 2009).

19. The anthropologist Sarah Ladbury (1977), along with sociologist Russell King (King and Ladbury 1982), published some of the earliest work examining the immediate postdivision period. In 1979, social psychologist Vamık Volkan published his *Cyprus: War and Adaptation*, a work that contains many useful ethnographic observations on the enclave and postwar periods. Several Ph.D. dissertations and articles examined ideological divides in the north regarding the past (Killoran 1994); intergenerational memory (Lyons 2007); tourism and land markets in an unrecognized entity (Scott 1995, 1998); and what we call here Turkish Cypriots' anxieties of perceptibility (Fosshagen 1999). Other research attempted comparison, primarily of Turkish and Greek Cypriot nationalisms and attitudes toward the Cyprus conflict (Bryant 2004; Dikomitis 2012; Papadakis 2005). While recent works from law and international relations have examined north Cyprus's exceptionality, particularly in a comparative

and EU context (Isachenko 2012; Kyris 2015; Skoutaris 2011), anthropological, sociological, or even historical work on state and politics in the island's north has been scarce.

Part I

1. Readers may notice the reference in our part title, "The Border That Is Not One," to Luce Irigaray's 1985 book, *This Sex Which Is Not One*. In that work, Irigaray argues that the Freudian and Lacanian understanding of female sexuality poses it as a lack because the position of women within patriarchy and its associated sexuality is in relation to the phallis. The phallis, in turn, is the obvious sexual organ against which women's sexual organs seem invisible, lacking. As should become clear in later chapters, our implicit reference to this argument derives from the idea that a tangible and, indeed, impassible border may be cast as its own phantom (a "border") within the hegemonic realism of the "international community."

2. *Oxford Reference Dictionary*, online (Oxford: Oxford University Press, 2019), http://www.oxfordreference.com/view/10.1093/oi/authority.20110803095433488. We should note that while there was a secret Akritas Plan for Cyprus, which was the plan developed by then President Makarios in the 1960s to force changes in the Republic of Cyprus's constitution, there was no Attila Plan. There was, however, an Operation Attila (Atilla Harekâtı), which was the name given by the Turkish military to its operation in Cyprus.

3. In his overview of uses of the term *territory*, David Storey similarly suggests three "dimensions of social life and social power are brought together in territory. There is a material component such as land, there is a functional element associated with control of, or attempts to control, space and there is also a symbolic component associated with people's social identity" (2001: 27).

Chapter 1

1. Interview conducted on 28 February 2014 in Kyrenia.

2. Several critics have called this description a "mythical" one intended to disguise the violence of founding acts (esp. Aravamudan 2005; Bosteels 2005; Surin 2005). "Historical thinking becomes mythical when this violent part of nonlaw behind the law is serenely ignored in favor of the imposition of a primordial order" (Bosteels 2005: 302). This raises the question of whether or not all founding acts may ultimately appear mythical precisely because of the way in which they transform violence into law (see Ricoeur 2010; also discussion in Chapter 5).

3. During the decolonization process in 1960, the U.K. retained two Sovereign Base Areas, Akrotiri and Dhekelia. For more information, see Constantinou and Richmond 2005.

4. According to the United Nations Guiding Principles on Internal Displacement, persons displaced from one part of Cyprus to another would technically be internally displaced persons (IDPs) (UNHCR 2004: 1). Nevertheless, "refugee" is the term that has been generally preferred by Greek Cypriots to describe their own uprooting, in large part because of the perceived affective resonance of the term (see Hadjiyanni 2002, Zetter 1999). As a result, it has become common to describe Cypriot IDPs as refugees. We should note, however, that the term "refugee" does not reflect the complexity of the Turkish *göçmen*, the word that Turkish Cypriots use to describe their own IDPs. A *göçmen* may be any kind of migrant, while the Turkish word for refugee, *mülteci*, is one that has the clear implication of being under another state's protection and is one that Turkish Cypriots never use to describe their own displacement.

5. The website of the TRNC parliament describes the change: "A transition was made to the 'Autonomous Turkish Cypriot Administration' when a need for political change emerged following the huge changes in Social Life." "Kıbrıs'ta Eski Yönetimler," Kuzey Kıbrıs Türk Cumhuriyeti Cumhuriyet Meclisi, http://www.cm.gov.nc.tr/gecmisyonetim.aspx (website of the TRNC parliament).

6. This and subsequent quotations from Hakkı Atun are taken from an interview conducted 2 March 2014 in Nicosia.

7. For a discussion of loot and looting during this period, see Bryant 2014a.

8. Although it is not the focus of our study, we should note that a similar process was happening in the island's south, though with different intent. There, Turkish Cypriots were actively prevented from fleeing to the north, as this would appear to cement division. In this process, Turkish Cypriots were also labeled as "intending evacuees," but that evacuation was actively impeded. One elderly couple from the Paphos district described to us how they and their children were stopped twice at gunpoint on the road to a crossing point about fifty kilometers from their home. Ultimately, they had to send their children to the north with smugglers, while they were only able to arrive in the north after the Vienna Agreement in 1975 (interview 25 September 2011, Morphou/ Güzelyurt). Another family from a village in the Limassol foothills described being locked in a shed for days on end, even as their fellow villagers were pillaging their orchards (interview 3 November 2011, Morphou/ Güzelyurt). Still another instance comes from a letter written to one of the assembly representatives from the Larnaca district by a villager who reported, "We can't walk freely anymore. Unfortunately, that right only belongs now to the herds of infidels. The Greek Cypriots don't ever leave our coffeehouses. They constantly harass us. We can't sleep anymore. Our children don't play on the streets anymore. In their place are armed infidel hordes in their Land Rovers. The Greek Cypriots don't leave our village for even a minute. They impede villagers trying to leave. They beat anyone they find on the roads. . . . Just yesterday the son of one of our people unfortunately got caught by the Greek Cypriots as he was trying to escape on his tractor. They took away the tractor and beat him for what was the second or third time" (TRNCPA, ATCA Legislative Assembly Minutes], 13 November 1974, 21–22). The effect was of course to make even those who wanted to stay and would have tried to stay eager to leave.

9. She uses a hyphenated word here, "ξένοι-ληστές," the two words for "stranger" or "foreigner" and "robber." She seems to use "stranger" here to indicate that they had become foreign to them, as well as that they were foreign to a town that had become hellenized, particularly during the enclave period.

10. The Turkish Cypriot psychoanalyst Vamık Volkan, who visited the island several times to assess the state of refugees during the postwar period, noted that "so widespread was the looting that a euphemistic new word was coined for it, *buluntu*, which means 'something found.' . . . The general preoccupation with *buluntu* was still evident when I visited northern Cyprus six months after the war, but it ended soon thereafter, perhaps because of steps taken by the administration, or, possibly, because there was nothing more to be 'found' readily by individuals" (1979: 121).

11. Perhaps the worst such incident was the murder of twenty-one Greek Cypriots in the village of Paliokythrea by Turkish Cypriots who were, as one later testified, on a quest for loot. See Sevgül Uludağ, "Ölümün Kıyısından Dönenler 3," *Yeraltı Notları*, 13 October 2004, https://www.stwing.upenn.edu/~durduran/hamambocu/authors/svg/svg9_13_2004.html.

12. TRNCPA, TFSC Constituent Assembly Minutes, 28 December 1975.

13. Interview conducted 10 March 2014 in Nicosia.

14. As we discuss in Chapter 3, during this period around 25,000 to 30,000 Turkish nationals arrived in Cyprus as part of a facilitated migration, and each family was granted a house and agricultural land. Since this distribution was done on the basis of families, we may estimate that around 5,000 to 6,000 houses were distributed in this way. In addition, TSFC Citizenship Law Act No. 3/1975 made families of the 498 Turkish soldiers killed in the 1974 war eligible for citizenship, as well as Turkish soldiers who had served in Cyprus until 18 August 1974. A certain number of veterans of the 1974 war returned to Cyprus and acquired citizenship under this law, though it should also be noted that of the 1,200 currently active members of the Turkish Army Veterans Association, 75 percent are married to Turkish Cypriots. It may be estimated, then, that approximately 500 additional properties may have been distributed to Turkish veterans, though many would in any case have been eligible for such properties through their spouses, in cases where those spouses were displaced persons (Hatay 2007).

15. For more ethnographic detail, see Julie Scott (1998).

16. Relatedly, Brighenti asserts, "Once a step . . . towards a radically relational conception of territory is made, territory appears precisely as what keep sovereignty and government together. The link between sovereignty and government is indeed *the* territorial relationship *par excellence*" (2006: 78).

17. Fuat Veziroğlu, TRNCPA, ATCA Legislative Assembly Minutes), 20 November 1974, 22–23.

18. Greek Cypriot anthropologist Yiannis Papadakis (2005) describes in comic detail the ways that he was watched and "minded" when he attempted fieldwork in the north in the early 1990s.

19. The phenomenon of using the parent state's currency is called "dollarization" and is common to unrecognized states. For instance, the Armenian dram is the currency of Nagorno-Karabakh and the Russian ruble the currency in Abkhazia and South Ossetia. On the phenomenon of dollarization, see Yeyati (2003). On the significance of banknotes for identity, see Penrose (2011) and Unwin and Hewitt (2001).

20. Indeed, the south continued to supply electricity for more than two decades, until a power plant with sufficient wattage could be built on the north coast. It was only in 1995 that the north acquired "independence" in the electrical supply, though that was accompanied by a new regime of blackouts and power cuts.

21. "Sağlık Bakanlığı Açıklama Yaptı: Mağusa'da görülen vaka Kolera değil Bağırsak Enfeksiyonudur," *Bozkurt Gazetesi*, 30 September 1977; "Sağlık Bakanlığı Kolera Salgınına Karşı Geniş Önlemler Aldı," *Bozkurt Gazetesi*, 26 August 1977.

Chapter 2

1. Interview with Erdal Andız, 31 August 2014, Nicosia.

2. The bust would later be replaced with a full-scale statue of Atatürk, which stands there today.

3. The English School was the island's premier school for boys—and starting in the 1960s also for girls. From its inception in the early twentieth century, graduates have gone on to top universities in the United Kingdom, and many Cypriot leaders are graduates of the school.

Although Turkish Cypriots were unable to attend the English School during the 1963–1968 period, with the lifting of the siege in 1968 some began to make the daily journey out of the enclaves for their education.

4. Fleeing Greek Cypriots were for the most part unable to take domestic and farm animals with them. While most farm animals were rounded up and distributed by the state, many people speak of the pigs and dogs that ran wild in the postwar landscape. While we were not able to discover the policy regarding dogs, we learned that some Greek Cypriot farm owners were given permission to collect their pigs and take them south, while some Turkish Cypriots collected the pigs and sold them to the south via the British bases. Pigs were obviously a polluting presence for even nominal Muslims, and many people were frightened of the hungry dogs running loose.

5. For instance, Famagusta in 1961 had a hotel bed capacity of only 324, but by 1974, tourism growth had caused that number to explode to 9,709. For the entire island, the bed capacity in 1963 was 5,249, while in 1974 it had risen to 19,192. See Ekici and Çaner 2018.

6. For more detail on the ways that people dealt with objects in the immediate postwar period and after, see Bryant (2014a).

7. "The state needs to be analyzed as such a structural effect. That is to say, it should be examined not as an actual structure, but as the powerful, metaphysical effect of practices that make such structures appear to exist" (Mitchell 1991: 94).

8. And in this sense it is in line with Finn Stepputat's use of Schmitt to analyze land conflicts in Guatemala, where he argues that the land conflict as "an occasion for the assertion and performance of sovereignty . . . frees the concept of sovereignty from the presumed association with state and territory and instead focuses on sovereignty as a set of discernible practices of exclusion, exceptional measures and use of force in the name of a particular political or moral community" (Stepputat 2008: 338). The bundle of practices on which Stepputat focuses is what we refer to here as the production of "separateness."

9. In an interesting discussion of "facts on the ground," or the material acts that secure territory after war, Nomi Stolzenberg remarks that the presence of children and grandchildren is often used to justify continuing to hold unlawfully acquired territory. Indeed, she notes, "it could well be said that children are the ultimate 'facts on the ground'" (2009: 38).

10. Uğur Karagözlü, "Cyprus: 40 years ago I was liberated," *Birmingham Press,* 14 August 2014, http://thebirminghampress.com/2014/08/cyprus-40-years-ago-i-was-liberated/

11. Commenting on this moment, Mustafa Akıncı remarked to us, "The Cypriot Turk in that period—even if we leave aside the deaths, the shooting, the destruction—experienced the humiliation, the inability to go anywhere, in other words was in a minority position in this place, a second-class citizen. For that reason, everyone greeted what happened in 1974 with joy! That is, the Cypriot Turk in such a big proportion that we could say virtually everyone wanted the operation and supported it."

12. Bryant elsewhere critically discusses the model of antagonistic tolerance that underpins Hayden's argument (see Bryant 2016).

13. SARC, SA1/ 6658/1912, 20 February 1926.

14. İsmail Bozkurt, "Bir Atatürk büstü öyküsü," *Haber Kıbrıs,* 8 October 2010, http://haberkibris.com/864cb39d-2010_10_08.html.

15. Bozkurt, "Bir Atatürk büstü öyküsü."

16. Alper Ali Riza, "The flag on the mountain," *Cyprus Mail,* 13 September 2015, https://cyprus-mail.com/2015/09/13/the-flag-on-the-mountain/.

17. TRNCPA, TFSC Constituent Assembly Minutes, 33rd Session, 23 May 1975, p. 71.

18. TRNCPA, TFSC Constituent Assembly Minutes, 33rd Session, 23 May 1975, p. 66. One example that another member, Özker Yaşın, gave was the village of Gönyeli, whose name is of uncertain origin and which in 1958 was changed first to Gönelli, then to Menderes, then to Harbiye, but which continued to be known as Gönyeli (p. 69).

19. TRNCPA, TFSC Constituent Assembly Minutes, 79th Session, 30 December 1975.

20. Representatives who had come from the island's south were quite insistent on the matter of giving their former villages' names to the places where they had settled in the north, in some cases adding "new" to the name (e.g., Agios Sergios became Yeni Boğaziçi and Gialousa became Yenierenköy) (TRNCPA, TFSC Constituent Assembly Minutes, 33rd Session, 23 May 1975, p. 69).

21. The first report outlining the principles to be used was presented in the May session as Report of the Turkish Federated State of Cyprus Management Committee Concerning the (Revised) "1975 Village Elders Committee Law" (Kıbrıs Türk Federe Devleti Kurucu Meclisi İdari İşler Komitesinin, "1975 Köy İhtiyar Heyet'leri (Değişiklik) Yasası" ile İlgili Raporudur) TRNCPA, TFSC Constituent Assembly Minutes, 33rd Session, 23 May 1975, p. 64. The law under question passed unanimously in the same session. When the committee later submitted its list of names to the Constituent Assembly in December, members of the assembly voted on each name individually. Of the 200 names that were voted in the assembly, 122 were already in use by Turkish Cypriots; 33 were places in the north with Turkish names dating from the Ottoman period; 64 were villages and towns in the north whose names had already been changed in 1958; and an additional 23 were the names of villages from the south whose displaced villagers insisted on transporting those names to their new places. This breakdown of names approved in the north is taken from our comprehensive mapping of Cypriot displacement, in which we analyzed displacement to and from every village in Cyprus. That research is available at www.prio-cyprus-displacement.net.

22. TRNCPA, TFSC Constituent Assembly Minutes, 79th Session, 30 December 1975.

23. TRNCPA, TFSC Constituent Assembly Minutes, 79th Session, 30 December 1975, p. 25.

24. TRNCPA, TFSC Constituent Assembly Minutes, 79th Session, 30 December 1975, p. 10.

25. Interview with a left-wing bureaucrat (anonymized), 2 April 2014, Nicosia.

26. Navaro-Yashin (2012) observes that Turkish Cypriots often code-switch between the names as a form of "local knowledge" against persons from Turkey, but this is only one in a a larger set of differentiating practices.

27. The fact that in recent years many international mapping systems such as Google Maps have begun to use the new names has produced its own anxiety, which Rebecca discusses in her book in progress, *Faking the State*.

28. "Eroğlu: Bu eser KKTC'ye vurulan bir mühür," *Haber7com*, 14 April 2012, http://www.haber7.com/kibris/haber/868928-eroglu-bu-eser-kktcye-vurulan-bir-muhur.

29. These observations apply to the period covered by this book but not to the post-2003 period, the subject of Rebecca's ethnography *Faking the State* (in progress). Until 2002, only nine mosques were built, while in the period of Turkey's Justice and Development Party (AKP) after 2002, forty-five were built. While the AKP has encouraged the building of mosques and other religious sites since coming to power in Turkey and has funded such sites in Cyprus, we

should note that this new mosque building has been also a result of the 2003 opening of the checkpoints and visits by Greek Cypriots, who were disturbed to find churches converted to mosques. In numerous cases, Turkish Cypriot villages requested new mosques to replace those that had been converted. Nevertheless, there has also been a backlash against this mosque building, in part because the Evkaf Office copied mosque designs from Turkey that were not indigenous to the island. Subsequent mosque-building that takes account of indigenous architecture has encountered less reaction (Constantinou, Demetriou, and Hatay 2012).

30. Of the remaining churches, a handful of churches would later be turned into museums or put to other uses, such as music schools and art galleries. Most, however, were left to ruin, a few even converted into barns. The small chapels surrounded by cemeteries have suffered the most, as both the cemeteries and the chapels themselves are invariably devastated.

31. Interview conducted on 17 June 2009, Nicosia.

Chapter 3

1. Interview conducted by Rebecca Bryant on 17 September 2004, location not given to preserve anonymity.

2. There are many reports in Cyprus of the Turkish army taking its own *ganimet* (loot), particularly removing parts of factories and shipping them to Turkey. However, what Zehra refers to is most likely the army's removal of goods discussed in Chapter 1, where items were placed in "loot depots" at the request of the Turkish Cypriot administration.

3. The first article of the Montevideo Convention of 1933 lists the general requirements of statehood as having a permanent population, a defined territory, a government, and the ability to enter into relations with other states. See also Crawford (2007: 48ff), Fowler and Bunck (1996), Østerud (1997), and Paul (1999).

4. While this was the government estimate in 2010, a Crisis Group report for the same period asserts that a more reasonable estimate would be around 30,000. See International Crisis Group (2010: 2).

5. Although a 2004 census put the population at around 670,000 (International Crisis Group 2004), a more recent estimate suggests that it may have declined to around 400,000 (Popescu 2011: 39).

6. Interview in Sukhumi, September 2012.

7. TFSC Constituent Assembly Minutes, 3 March 1975

8. By 1981, their number had dropped to around a thousand, according to RoC government reports because of harassment and discrimination. See the Embassy of the Republic of Cyprus, Washington, D.C., web page, "Enclaved Persons," http://www.cyprusembassy.net /home/index.php?module=page&pid=21.

9. TRNCPA, TFSC Constituent Assembly Minutes, 28 February 1975.

10. See also Mamdani (2015) and Wolfe (2006) for reflections on practices of exception that enable the eradication of indigenous populations.

11. Interview with Nuri Çevikel, then president of the Turkish Immigrants Association, September 2003.

12. One interviewee, Yusuf, had arrived in Cyprus as a young man and told us how in a number of cases where a village was to be transferred, a small group of the village's leading men went to Cyprus first to see what the place was like. They returned to the village with reports of houses that could be spun around and televisions on offer. We speculate that the

spinning house myth was probably because in some areas of the island, as a result of building restrictions, people would first build their house on supports and later build the lower floor. Or the mayor of one town told us that his father had said to him, "We'll go with empty suitcases and return with full ones," indicating that they initially had no intention of remaining. The mayor commented to us, "Instead, we haven't been able to return, we haven't even been able to fill our suitcases, and we still haven't been able to understand what our position is here" (interview, October 2005).

13. Interview conducted 2 March 2014 in Nicosia.

14. Baggy pants traditional to Turkish villages, worn by both men and women.

15. Fazıl Küçük, "Geri Gönderilmeli" [They Must Be Sent Back], *Halkın Sesi*, 25 May 1978, quoted in Ramm (2009: 225).

16. In almost all of these eighteen villages, Turkish nationals were a minority. There were, additionally, twenty-eight villages that had previously been entirely Greek Cypriot where only Turkish nationals were settled. A small number of transferees were also settled in the towns of Kyrenia and Morphou and larger numbers in the city of Famagusta.

17. Law for Housing, Allocation of Land, and Property of Equal Value (Iskan, Topraklandırma, ve Eşdeğer Mal Yasası [İTEM law], No. 41/1977). In July 1982, an amendment to this law ended the distribution of properties to Turkish nationals. Turkish nationals immigrating to Cyprus after implementation of this law received no properties from the state and had to buy or rent properties on the local market.

18. It should be noted, however, that not everyone who applied under this amendment was granted citizenship. For instance, some of the Kurdish origin immigrants interviewed by Hatay claimed that because of tensions between Kurdish militant organizations and the Turkish state, many Kurdish immigrants to the north had been unable to acquire TRNC citizenship. It should also be noted that many Kurds who did receive TRNC citizenship in the early 1980s used TRNC travel documents to travel to the United Kingdom, where they applied for political asylum.

19. During that period there were two opposition groups in the assembly: the first, known as the Freedom Group (Özgürlük Grubu) consisted of older members of the previous Autonomous Assembly (Fuat Veziroğlu, İsmail Bozkurt, Dr. Burhan Nalbantoğlu); the second, known as the Group of Six (Alpay Durduran, Özker Özgür, Mustafa Akıncı, Ekrem Ural, Turgut Mustafa, Fatma Sezer), had been chosen by various civil society organizations to represent them in the Constituent Assembly. The only woman in the assembly, Fatma Sezer, would later recall that these two groups would soon merge, forming a single opposition voice on such issues as the constitution and fundamental laws, and doing so within a framework of "freedom, democracy, and social justice." Fatma Azgın, "Takva Filmi ve Siyasi Kirlenme," *Yenidüzen*, 4 September 2016.

20. Veziroğlu was reporting on a visit that he made to a Famagusta hostel with fellow MPs Ziya Rızkı and Mustafa Akıncı.

21. As Mete shows elsewhere (Hatay 2005), persons transferred from Turkey, though mainly conservative, came from all political persuasions and so gravitated to the parties emerging in the island's north that most closely resembled the ones with which they associated in Turkey. By the 1980s, however, their exclusion from political processes led to the formation of their own political party, uniting politically and ethnically divided groups around that exclusion. One Kurdish man living in the Karpassia whom we interviewed (5 April 2008, Nicosia)

said of this period, "In Turkey we were discriminated against as Kurds, but here we are discriminated against as Türkiyeli [persons from Turkey]."

22. Kristeva notes, "The abject has only one quality of the object—that of being opposed to I. . . . What is abject . . . the jettisoned object, is radically excluded and draws me toward the place where meaning collapses (1982: 1–2).

23. TRNCPA, TFSC Constituent Assembly Minutes, August 1975.

24. TRNCPA, TFSC Constituent Assembly Minutes, 17 September 1975.

25. Alfonso Cuco, "The Demographic Structure of Cyprus, Report of the Committee on Migration, Refugees, and Demography, Parliamentary Assembly," doc. 6589, 27 April 1992. The full report can be found at http://www.moi.gov.cy/moi/pio/pio.nsf/All/20C7614D06858E 9FC2256DC200380113/$file/cuco%20report.pdf?OpenElement.

26. U.N. Document A10310, S/11859, 24 October 1975, cited in Ioannides (1991: 3).

27. Cuco, "Demographic Structure of Cyprus."

Part II

1. It is worth noting that Hikmet Bil was a journalist for *Hürriyet* newspaper and was engaged with the Cyprus Problem from the early 1950s. At that time, he was one of the journalists responsible for whipping up public opinion and turning Cyprus into a "national cause" in Turkey. Speros Vryonis (2005) charges him with responsibility in the attacks on Greek properties during the Istanbul pogroms of 6–7 September 1955.

2. Piracy has also been attributed with both historical-legal and discursive significance in the emergence of our contemporary understanding of sovereignty. See esp. Benton (2010), Mills (2014), and Thomson (1994).

Chapter 4

1. "It is the tactics of government which make possible the continual definition and redefinition of what is within the competence of the state and what is not, the public versus the private, and so on" (Foucault 1991: 103).

2. Interview with Fatma Azgın (Sezer), 2 April 2014, Nicosia.

3. TRNCPA, TFSC Constituent Assembly Minutes, 59th Session, 15 September 1975, p. 60.

4. TRNCPA, ATCA Legislative Assembly Minutes, 9th Session, 20 November 1974, p. 10.

5. TRNCPA, ATCA Legislative Assembly Minutes, 8th Session, Larnaka Milletvekili Sayın İsmail Bozkurt'un Otonom Kıbrıs Türk Yönetimi Başkanlığına, 13 November 1974, Tarihli Sorusu (Larnaka Member of Parliament Mr. İsmail Bozkurt's Question Dated 13 November 1974, Addressed to the Presidency of the Autonomous Turkish Cypriot Administration), p. 42. It is worth noting here that this question is addressed to the ATCA's presidency. However, at this time, the so-called president of the ATCA, Rauf Raif Denktaş, also retained the title of Vice President of the Republic of Cyprus, a post to which he had been elected in 1973.

6. Schatzki describes a teleoaffective structure as comprising "acceptable or prescribed ends, acceptable or enjoined projects to carry out those ends, acceptable or prescribed actions to perform as part of those projects—thus acceptable or enjoined end-project-action combinations—as well as, possibly, accepted or prescribed emotions and even moods" (2010: loc. 1343).

7. TRNCPA, ATCA Legislative Assembly Minutes, 10th Session, 27 November 1974.

8. Interview with Fatma Azgın (Sezer), 2 April 2014, Nicosia.

9. TRNCPA, ATCA Legislative Assembly Minutes, 22nd Session, 7 September 1974, p. 7.

10. TRNCPA, TFSC Constituent Assembly Minutes, 59th Session, 15 September 1975.

11. The other five principles were nationalism (*milliyetçilik*), secularism (*laiklik*), reformism (*inkilapçılık*), populism (*halkçılık*), and republicanism (*cumhuriyetçilik*). The last of these was in response to the previous monarchic system, while reformism refers to the perceived need for radical modernization.

12. Kıbrıs Türk Federe Devleti Anayasası (Constitution of the Turkish Federated State of Cyprus), available at www.mahkemeler.net/cgi-bin/anayasa/ktfdana.doc.

13. TRNCPA, ATCA Legislative Assembly Minutes, 10th Session, 27 November 1974, p. 15.

14. TRNCPA, TFSC Constituent Assembly Minutes, 59th Session, 15 September 1975, p. 60.

15. Interview with Mustafa Akıncı, 27 April 2015, Nicosia.

16. TRNCPA, TFSC Constituent Assembly Minutes, 13th Session, 6 April 1975, p. 13.

17. TRNCPA, TFSC Constituent Assembly Minutes, 13th Session, 6 April 1975, p. 24.

18. TRNCPA, TFSC Constituent Assembly Minutes, 13th Session, 6 April 1975, p. 28.

19. For more on the temporality of this distinction, see Bryant (in progress).

Chapter 5

1. Interview with Erdal Andız, 31 August 2014, Nicosia.

2. In the minutes of the TFSC Constituent Assembly, however, representative Turgut Mustafa claimed that Sanayi Holding "had taken over the responsibility for 250 factories" (TRNCPA, TFSC Constituent Assembly Minutes, 12th Session, 5 April 1975, p. 76.

3. *Sanayi Holding* documentary (Nicosia: Baraka Kültür Merkezi, 2014), produced by Mine Balman, Firuzan Nalbantoğlu, Mustafa Batak, and Besim Baysal; Ergün Vudalı quoted.

4. *Sanayi Holding* documentary, Mehmet Seyis quoted.

5. Discussing the necessity of the state for leftist politics, Philip Abrams remarks that Marx and Marxists have been "hypnotised by the brilliant effect of . . . discovering the state as the political concentration of class relationships." Marxism, he continues, "knowing the state to be unreal 'for the purposes of theory' needs it to be real 'for purposes of practice'" (Abrams 1988: 72).

6. As tends to be the case in postconflict societies, nationalist authors have themselves produced a considerable amount of this material. And as is also the case in many postconflict societies, critiques of nationalist politics and nationalist scholarship occupy a proportionately large place in the literature. For the latter, see, e.g., An (2006), Kızılyürek (2002, 2016), and Sonan (2014). While there has been some focus on the left, it has primarily been either documentary of the community's leftist movements or descriptive of its suppression by the right.

7. Sara Friedman (2015, 2020) argues that de facto states are often highly invested in demonstrating the strength of their democracies and support for human rights as a way to show that they are a "real" state. Nina Caspersen has argued that "unrecognized states attempt to disassociate themselves from images of lawlessness, violence, and ethno-national radicalism, and instead convey an image of democratic, effective entities that are deemed acceptable by the international community and therefore—it is believed—'worthy' of recognition'" (2011: 78). Indeed, Caspersen notes that this investment in multi-party democracies makes some de facto entities, such as Somaliland, at least claim to be more democratic than their "parent

states," or those states from which they have broken away (2012: 57). Certainly, Donnacha Ó Beacháin's observations (2012) regarding the competitiveness, even cacophony, of Abkhazia's multi-party system apply also in north Cyprus, which Freedom House rates as "Free," as opposed to, e.g., Turkey's "Not Free" status (Freedom House 2019). For an overview of discussions regarding South Caucasus de facto states, see Broers 2013.

8. The film was made in the wake of a spat with then Turkish prime minister Recep Tayyip Erdoğan regarding Turkish demands that the Turkish Cypriot government undertake austerity measures and Turkish Cypriot resistance to those demands. This resulted in accusations by Erdoğan that Turkish Cypriots were *besleme*, or foster children, a word with the negative connotations of freeloaders and scroungers.

9. *Sanayi Holding* documentary, Sümer Kaya, mechanical engineer, quoted.

10. *Sanayi Holding* documentary, Sümer Kaya quoted.

11. *Sanayi Holding* documentary, Zeki Erkut quoted.

12. *Sanayi Holding* documentary, İnci Yaşamsal, factory worker and Dev-İş Famagusta regional representative, quoted.

13. *Sanayi Holding* documentary, Ergün Vudalı quoted.

14. *Sanayi Holding* documentary, Enver Yazgın, production planning and quality control engineer, quoted.

15. "Sanayi Holding Belgeseli Mağusa'da Gösterildi," 1 April 2014, Baraka Kültür Merkezi website, https://www.ankaradegillefkosa.org/sanayi-holding-belgeseli-magusada-gosterildi/

16. Serkan Soyalan, "Sanayi Holding Belgeseli," *Yenidüzen*, 26 February 2014, http://www.yeniduzen.com/sanayi-holding-belgeseli-81181h.htm.

17. Presentation by Symeon Matsis at the conference "Reviving Famagusta: From Ghost Town to Eco-City?" London School of Economics, 21 February 2014.

18. TRNCNA, TSFC Constituent Assembly Minutes, 60th Session, 17 September 1975.

19. Interview with Öntaç Düzgün, Turhan Kuran, and Eşref Vaiz, 26 August 2016, Nicosia.

20. Interview with Öntaç Düzgün, 29 March 2013, Nicosia.

21. This observation emerged during a number of our interviews and discussions with persons who had been members of leftist movements in Turkey.

22. The oldest was CTP, which had begun gathering many young university graduates and would come third in the election with 13 percent of the vote. One party with an explicitly social democratic platform and a direct association with Ecevit's CHP, Halkçı Parti, would receive close to 12 percent, while the main opposition contender was a party newly formed in advance of the election, the Communal Liberation Party (Toplumcu Kurtuluş Partisi, or TKP). The founders of the latter party were some of the main opposition leaders in the Founding Assembly, including Mustafa Akıncı, Fatma Sezer, and İsmail Bozkurt, all quoted earlier. Some of these, such as Bozkurt, were also respected veterans of TMT.

23. TRNCPA, ATCA Legislative Assembly Minutes, 22nd Session, 7 February 1975, p. 24.

24. TRNCPA, ATCA Legislative Assembly Minutes, 22nd Session, 7 February 1975, p. 58.

25. Hasan Hastürer, "Yanarım yanarım, neye yanarım bilir misiniz?" *Kıbrıs Postası*, 20 August 2010, http://www.kibrispostasi.com/print.php?col=98&art=8860.

26. TRNCPA, TFSC Constituent Assembly, 59th Session, 15 September 1975, p. 11.

27. TRNCPA, TFSC Constituent Assembly Minutes, 57th Session, 5 September 1975.

28. Although the word *bourgeois* has been translated into Turkish as *burjuva*, Özgür was insistent on finding "pure Turkish" (*öz Türkçe*) words that corresponded in meaning, rather than transliterating from foreign languages. TRNCPA, TFSC Constituent Assembly Minutes, 13th Session, 6 April 1975, p. 94.

29. TRNCPA, TFSC Constituent Assembly Minutes, 12th Session, 4 April 1975, p. 98.

30. Interview with former prime minister, Ferdi Sabit Soyer, 4 April 2014. He used this phrase to explain how the left in the post-1974 period used new democratic opportunities to overcome the antidemocratic BEY regime.

Chapter 6

1. In 2007, it was superseded by a Philippine-sponsored Israeli flag in the desert near Masada (Ken Jennings, "You Can See Northern Cyprus's Flag from Space," *Condé Nast Traveler*, 26 March 2018, https://www.cntraveler.com/story/you-can-see-northern-cyprus-flag-from -space).

2. KKTC Beşparmak Dağları Bayrağı Işıklandırma Derneği website, http://www .kktcbayrak.org.

3. Alper Ali Riza, "The Flag on the Mountain," *Cyprus Mail*, 13 September 2015, https:// cyprus-mail.com/2015/09/13/the-flag-on-the-mountain/.

4. "KKTC Bayrak/TRNC Flag," https://www.youtube.com/watch?v=AgB_oJ_D4as.}

5. Alper Ali Riza, "The Flat on the Mountain," *Cyprus Mail*, 13 September 2015, https:// cyprus-mail.com/2015/09/13/the-flag-on-the-mountain/.

6. We capitalize Status Quo throughout the rest of this book to distinguish the meaning that it acquires in conflict contexts from its meaning in everyday use.

7. "Status quo," https://en.wikipedia.org/wiki/Status_quo.

8. Kudret Özersay, Facebook page, 29 December 2016.

9. UNSC Resolution 541 (18 November 1983, paragraph 4; UNSC Resolution 550 (11 May 1984), paragraph 6; available online at http://www.un.org/en/ga/search/view_doc.asp ?symbol=S/RES/541(1983).

10. "Mr. R. R. Denktash Addressing the U.N. Security Council on Nov/1983," https://www .youtube.com/watch?v=Couo4LeSP88

11. "Mr. R. R. Denktash Addressing the U.N. Security Council on Nov/1983."

12. "Mr. R. R. Denktash Addressing the U.N. Security Council on Nov/1983."

13. Keith Kyle, "The Economic Consequences of 1974," Archived on https://web.archive .org/web/20130529113801/http://www.cyprus-conflict.net:80/economic_conseq_of _1974%20-%20kyle.html, accessed 6 May 2017.

14. The headline ran in full: "Günaydın Kuzey Kıbrıs Cumhuriyet! uzun ömürler diler ve de Kıbrıs Cumhuriyetleri birliğinin habercisi olarak seni karşılıyoruz! Merhaba Güney Kıbrıs, Küçük kardeşin dün gece dünya'ya geldi, seni saygıyla selamlıyor! Merhaba dünya emekçi halkları bizi aranıza alır mısınız? Emekçi Rum halkı uzat elini de elimiz havada kalmasın!" (Good morning North Cyprus Republic! We wish you long life and greet you as the precursor of a union of Cyprus Republics! Hello South Cyprus, your little brother came into the world last night and greets you with respect! Hello workers of the world, will you welcome us among you? Working Greek Cypriot people, extend your hand so that our hand is not left in the air!), *Söz*, 15 November 1983.

15. "Dün Bir Bildiri Yayınlayan KTÖS: Rumlar Duygusallığı Bir Kenara İtip Kurulan Cumhuriyeti Tanımalıdırlar," *Söz*, 15 November 1983, pp. 1 and 3.

16. "Denktaş Döndü! Mitinge Katılım Düşük Düzeyde Oldu," *Söz*, 15 October 1983, p. 3.

17. Erdal Andız, "Oyalanmaya Gerek Yok!" *Söz*, 15 November 1983.

18. "Denktaş Döndü! Mitinge Katılım Düşük Düzeyde Oldu," *Söz*, 15 October 1983, p. 1.

19. See the letter from Rauf Denktaş to U.N. secretary general, 15 November 1983, enclosed in A38/586/S/16148, Proceedings of the General Assembly 38th Session, 1983–84, available at https://library.un.org/sites/library.un.org/files/itp/a38-parti_1.pdf.

20. "Denktaş: 'Kişiliğimizi koruma kararımız değiştirilemez,'" *Bozkurt*, 19 November 1983, p. 1.

21. "Alpay Durduran Türk Politikasının Tartışılmasını İstedi," *Yenidüzen*, 31 May 1983, p. 2.

22. "Alpay Durduran Türk Politikasının Tartışılmasını İstedi."

23. Sabahattin İsmail, "Özgür'ün Değerlendirmesi Üzerine," *Söz*, 15 November 1983. Interestingly, there appear to have been two versions of *Söz* newspaper for this same date, one with a headline announcing the declaration of independence. This may indicate that the parliamentary vote was, indeed, a surprise even to the newspapers following events closely.

24. B. Mahmudoğlu, "Gerçeğe Sığınarak: Önce Türkiye Onaylamalı," *Söz*, 15 October 1983, p. 3.

25. Sabahattin İsmail, "Nasıl bir eşitlik," *Söz*, 8 October 1983. It is worth noting that İsmail during this time was a leftist but in the period of heightened nationalism of the 1990s moved towards the right and later became a columnist for the ultranationalist *Volkan* newspaper.

26. Raif Denktaş, "Sadede Gelelim Beyler," *Söz*, 19 August 1983, pp. 1–2.

27. Erol Erinçer, "Yine Bağımsızlık," *Söz*, 15 October 1983.

28. Charlotte Epstein notes, "Recognition is the act, both necessary and conclusive, which establishes the international personality of an entity that governs a population inhabiting a territory" (2018: 867).

29. In his early work, Jens Bartelson argued that the research agenda for political knowledge should be to understand how we "distinguish between what is inside the state from what is outside the state" (1995: 51). In later work, he takes this even further to assert, "Perhaps the main ideological function of the concept of sovereignty is not primarily to legitimize particular claims to political authority, but rather to legitimize the international system within which those claims can be understood to be meaningful" (2014: 63; see also Biersteker and Weber 1996).

30. Parliamentary questions E-5053/2009, 22 October 2009, written question by Antigoni Papadopoulou (S&D) to the Commission , Subject: Turkish flag on Mount Pentadaktylos, http://www.europarl.europa.eu/sides/getDoc.do?type=WQ&reference=E-2009-5053& language=EN.

31. Parliamentary questions E5053/2009, 27 January 2010, Answer given by Mr. Rehn on behalf of the Commission, http://www.europarl.europa.eu/sides/getAllAnswers.do?reference =E-2009-5053&language=EN.

32. "'Çıkar ilişkileri geleceği kurmayı olumsuz etkiledi,'" *Haber Kıbrıs*, 11 June 2012, https://haberkibris.com/-cikar-iliskileri-gelecegi-kurmayi-olumsuz-etkiledi-2012-06-11.html

33. Interview with right-wing civil society leader, 17 May 2012, Nicosia, Cyprus.

34. This is what Wendy Brown refers to as "the 'I know—but still . . .' structure of the fetish" (2010: 114).

Part III

1. Although we make no claims to systematic representation in such a survey, the pool of almost five thousand persons represents about 3.5 percent of the north's citizen population. In addition, the more than two hundred responses that we received in less than two hours were gender balanced and came from a good distribution of age groups, socioeconomic backgrounds, and political affiliations.

Chapter 7

1. The amount of aid and its parameters have changed over time, particularly in the balance between grant and loan. The amounts have also appeared to change at times when the Turkish Lira lost value against other currencies. As an indication, in 2009 the Turkish government gave 270 million TRY in grants and 658 million in credit for a total of 928 million TRY ($600 million). In 2010, this amount increased to 421 million TRY in grants and 636 million TRY in credit, and 37 million in incentive credit for a total of 1 billion 96 million TRY ($720 million) ("Türkiye 12 Yılda 6 Katrılyon Verdi," *Star Kıbrıs*, 12 September 2010, http://www.starkibris.net/index.asp?haberID=70087). The protocol signed between the Turkish and north Cyprus governments in 2018 put the figure at 2.187 billion Turkish lira ($390 million), 1.05 billion ($187 million) of which was grant-in-aid and the rest loans (Sefa Karahasan, "Türkiye'den KKTC'ye 2 milyar 187 milyon TL'lik yardım," *T24*, 4 June 2018, https://t24.com .tr/haber/turkiyeden-kktcye-2-milyar-187-milyon-tllik-yardim,643549).

2. Article 111 of the TRNC constitution puts the police under the control of the Turkish military on the island. In addition, the TRNC's Security Council, commonly called the Coordination Committee, is composed of the president, prime minister, and both elected officials and nonelected members, including members of the military, and its decisions are to "receive priority consideration by the Council of Ministers."

3. We should note that although Cypriots are usually able to use personal ties and networks to acquire privileges and exceptions, this does not mean that there is no police violence in north Cyprus. That violence, however, is almost without exception practiced on immigrants. See the Turkish Cypriot Human Rights Association's report, *İşkence İddiaları ile İlgili Rapor* (Report Concerning Torture Claims), available at http://www.ktihv.org.

4. Businessman interviewed 30 August 2014, Kyrenia. All subsequent quotations in this section are from this interview.

5. A *dönüm* is a local land measurement equivalent to approximately one-quarter of an acre.

6. Interview with Hakkı Atun, 2 March 2014, Nicosia.

7. Nicos Sampson was a young leader of EOKA B, the Greek Cypriot paramilitary offspring of the original EOKA, which was responsible for the attempted coup against President Makarios that prompted the Turkish military intervention in 1974. He was known as an erratic and violent character who often made anti-Turkish pronouncements, and he is considered responsible for certain incidents of violence against Turkish Cypriots in 1974.

8. "Maaşlara yüzde 12,11 artış gelecek," *Kıbrıs Gazetesi*, 9 July 2018, https://www .kibrisgazetesi.com/haber/maaslara-yuzde-1211-artis-gelecek/45594.

9. For further explanation, see Barışsever (2007). For a humorous, English-language introduction to the system, see the program of Turkish Cypriot filmmaker and comedian Mehmet Ekin Vaiz, in which he attempts to explain the *müşavir* system to foreign students in north Cyprus: "Everybody wants to be a müşavir!" *Neydi Olacağı* online program, produced by

Mehmet Ekin Vaiz, https://www.facebook.com/neydiolacagi/videos/everybody-wants-to-be
-müşavir-/1580296825567629/.

10. Interview with former bureaucrat and government adviser, 14 May 2012, Nicosia, Cyprus.

11. Interview with retired schoolteacher active in civil society, 27 April 2012, Nicosia, Cyprus.

12. Tufan Erhürman, "Don Kardeşliği ve Haset," first published in *Adres*, 24 August 2014, available on the author's blog, http://www.tufanerhurman.com/don-kardesligi-ve-haset/.

13. "Kemal: Hakkımı istiyorum," Duygu Alan, *Havadis*, 7 September 2014, p. 5.

14. Navaro-Yashin (2012) discusses the "spirit of TMT" as one that was hegemonic in the late 1990s. This was a period when Denktaş's collusion with the Turkish military aimed at marginalizing the left and resulted in a particular discursive framing of that collusion, reflected in Navaro-Yashin's descriptions. As should become clear in Chapter 8, however, claims of hegemony need to be examined rather than taken onboard wholesale.

Chapter 8

1. Uğur Karagözlü, "Girne Çarşısı," 4 February 2014, Facebook, https://www.facebook
.com/search/top/?q=Ugur%20Karagozlu%20girne%20çarşısı&epa=SEARCH_BOX.

2. For instance, the use of the Armenian dram in Nagorno-Karabakh and the Russian ruble in Abkhazia and South Ossetia.

3. TRNC Constitution, Article 111, available at Kuzey Kıbrıs Türk Cumhuriyeti Mahkemeleri, http://www.mahkemeler.net/cgi-bin/anayasa.aspx

4. Interview with businessman who has participated in committees on various subjects during negotiations, 8 August 2012, Nicosia, Cyprus.

5. In repeated polling over decades, Turkish Cypriots continue to support Turkish troops and guarantees on the island. According to a 2016 poll conducted by independent polling agencies, 89.4 percent of respondees supported a continuing Turkish troop presence, while 88.8 percent wanted Turkish guarantees to continue (Evie Andreou, "Polls Highlight Extent of Opposite Views on Guarantees, Settlers, and Troops," *Cyprus Mail*, 28 December 2016, https://cyprus-mail.com/old/2016/12/28/polls-highlight-extent-opposite-views-guarantees
-settlers-troops/). Surveys conducted over several years by the bicommunal Cyprus 2015 project generally show that under certain circumstances Turkish Cypriots could support the withdrawal of Turkish troops and no guarantees, but at the time of a 2010 survey support still remained at about 31 percent and 25 percent, respectively ("Poll Findings: Cyprus," 10 December 2010, https://www.interpeace.org/2010/12/poll-findings-cyprus/).

6. Türkiye Büyük Millet Meclisi Genel Kurul Tutanağı, 24th Period, 2nd Legislative Year, 52nd Session, 17 January 2012, https://www.tbmm.gov.tr/develop/owa/tutanak_g_sd.birlesim
_baslangic?P4=21103&P5=B&page1=7&page2=7.

7. Ibid.

8. Interview with former presidential adviser, 23 April 2012, Nicosia, Cyprus.

9. Relatedly, poet Mehmet Yaşın (2000) develops the idea of the "stepmother-tongue" to describe Turkish Cypriots' (and other marginal speakers') relations to the preferred, Istanbul form of Turkish. The idea of the "stepmother" is also used to evoke the disciplining in a language that does not have the affective intimacy of one's "mother tongue."

10. Interview with retired TRNC bureaucrat and financial adviser, 10 May 2012, Nicosia, Cyprus.

11. Interview with retired TRNC administrator, 3 May 2012, Nicosia, Cyprus.

Chapter 9

1. Indeed, much of the literature on unrecognized states has until very recently viewed these entities as "black holes," "predicated on criminal or quasi-criminal organisations" (Kolossov and O'Loughlin 1999: 152). In these presumably inaccessible entities, elites allegedly secure status and money through sales of drugs and weapons (e.g., King 2001) or through forms of racketeering in which they exploit the conflict to extort privileges from a dependent population (Lynch 2007). Other work (e.g., Caspersen 2012) has begun to complicate this picture and to show how such states, once they emerge from the conflict period, instead develop grey economies because of isolations that make trade and travel difficult.

2. This office is called the Tanıtma Dairesi, *tanıtma* being a word that means both "to introduce" and "to get recognized."

3. The brand "North Cyprus" became so widespread that when one tourism magazine asked Mete to write an article on coffeehouses, they proceeded to change all references to Cyprus in the article to "North Cyprus." As a result, the article in its published form referred, for instance, to "the Ottoman conquest of north Cyprus." This example also demonstrates the way in which tourist and state propaganda blended during the period.

4. On the RoC's accession process and its effects on intercommunal relations, see Tocci (2002).

5. On the phenomenon in Turkey, see Gülçür and İlkkaracan (2002).

6. "Irresponsibility is part of my invisibility," remarked Ralph Ellison. "But to whom can I be responsible, and why should I be, when you refuse to see me? . . . Responsibility rests on recognition, and recognition is a form of agreement" ([1947] 1995: 14).

7. It is a common strategy of unrecognized states to attempt to demonstrate their legitimacy through multiparty democracy and implementation of international human rights norms. Much of this research tends to argue that the use of democracy and human rights is opportunistic, aimed primarily at the international community and intended to secure recognition. "By implementing international standards domestically and—at least rhetorically—promoting democracy and human rights, they have hoped to be rewarded by *de jure* recognition in due course" (Blakkisrud and Kolstø 2011: 182; also Blakkisrud and Kolstø 2012; Ó Beacháin, Comai, and Tsurtsumia-Zurabashvili 2016). One author has even argued that Transnistrian state-building "could be seen as a product of the international community just as much as an expression of local desires" (Isachenko 2009a: 100). In this literature, attempts to enact the state and produce stateness do not stem on their own from desires for the state effect but rather from a more functional attempt to gain legitimacy in the eyes of the international community. In contrast, Sara Friedman's recent analysis (2020) is more consonant with our own, as she argues that unilateral implementation of human rights norms constitutes a form of aspirational sovereignty, one in which unrecognized administrations attempt to make their states "recognizable" as such.

8. Dom Rotheroe, dir., *The Coconut Revolution* (Stampede Films, 2000).

9. We discuss the sociology of enclaves in more detail in Bryant and Hatay (2011) and Bryant (2014b). For early studies of enclaves, see Gringauz (1949, 1950) and Douglas (1993). A collection that appeared as this book was in production addresses such spaces through the trope of "stuckness" (Jefferson, Turner, and Jensen 2019).

10. In a study that Rebecca conducted on Turkish Cypriot displacement and attitudes towards a settlement, interviewees consistently made similar remarks about the perceived necessity of something that was also a choice. See Bryant 2012; the quote is taken from p. 51.

11. Some authors have even argued that "many post-modern unrecognized states often find the ambiguous political and economic space provided by their anomalous status to be more attractive than the other highly romanticized option . . . of independent statehood" (Harvey and Stansfield 2010: 16).

12. Interview with right-wing civil society leader, 15 September 2014, Nicosia.

13. Interview with Mustafa Akıncı, 27 April 2015, Nicosia.

14. Interview with former adviser to President Denktaş, Erdal Andız, 15 May 2012, Nicosia.

Conclusion

1. Sabahattin İsmail, "İşbirlikçilerin parçalanması ve sonuçları," *Türk Solu*, 24 November 2003, http://www.turksolu.com.tr/44/ismail44.html.

2. The main parties of the left, then struggling for votes, accused Turkey of interfering, using Turkish nationals who had gained citizenship in the island as a Trojan horse. Mete's study of voting patterns of the period, however, shows that the 25 percent of the citizen population that was of Turkish origin voted in very similar ways to their Cypriot-origin counterparts and so could not have been responsible for the increasing support of nationalist parties (Hatay 2007).

3. B. Mahmudoğlu, "Gerçeğe Sığınarak: Önce Türkiye Onaylamalı," *Söz*, 15 October 1983, p. 3.

BIBLIOGRAPHY

ARCHIVES

National Archive and Research Center (Milli Arşiv ve Araştırma Merkezi), NARC
State Archive of the Republic of Cyprus, SARC
Turkish Republic of North Cyprus Parliamentary Archives (TRNCPA)
    Otonom Kıbrıs Türk Yönetimi Yasama Meclisi Zabıtları (Autonomous Turkish Cypriot Administration Legislative Assembly Minutes), referenced as ATCA Legislative Assembly Minutes.
    Kıbrıs Türk Federe Devleti Kurucu Meclisi Zabıtları (Turkish Federated State of Cyprus Constituent Assembly Minutes), referenced as TFSC Constituent Assembly Minutes.

SECONDARY SOURCES

Aalberts, Tanja. 2018. "Misrecognition in Legal Practice: The Aporia of the Family of Nations." *Review of International Studies* 44(5): 863–881.

Abdo, Nahla, and Nira Yuval-Davis. 1995. "Palestine, Israel and the Zionist Settler Project." In *Unsettling Settler Societies*, edited by D. Stasiulis and N. Yuval-Davis, 291–322. London: Sage.

Abrams, Philip. 1988. "Notes on the Difficulty of Studying the State (1977)." *Journal of Historical Sociology* 1(1): 58–89.

Adamides, Constantinos, and Costas Constantinou. 2012. "Comfortable Conflict and (Il)liberal Peace in Cyprus." In *Hybrid Forms of Peace: From Everyday Agency to Post-Liberalism*, edited by O. Richmond and M. Mitchell, 242–259. New York: Palgrave Macmillan.

Adil, Mehmet. 2007. "Visibility 600 Metres: Reflections on the National Monument of the Turkish Republic of Northern Cyprus." Unpublished PhD diss., Faculty of Creative Arts, University of Wollongong, Australia.

Agamben, Giorgio. 1998. *Homo Sacer: Sovereign Power and Bare Life*. Translated by Daniel Heller-Roazen. Stanford: Stanford University Press.

———. 2005. *State of Exception*. Translated by Kevin Attell. Chicago: University of Chicago Press.

Aggarwal, Ravina. 2004. *Beyond Lines of Control: Performance and Politics on the Disputed Borders of Ladakh, India*. Durham, NC: Duke University Press.

Ahmed, Sara. 2014. *Willful Subjects*. Durham, NC: Duke University Press.

Akçalı, Emel. 2007. "The Other Cypriots and Their Cyprus Questions." *Cyprus Review* 19(2): 57–82.

———. 2011. "Getting Real on Fluctuating National Identities: Insights from Northern Cyprus." *Antipode* 43(5): 1725–1747.

Althusser, Louis. 1971. "Ideology and Ideological State Apparatuses: Notes Towards an Investigation." In *Lenin and Philosophy and Other Essays*, trans. Ben Brewster. New York: Monthly Review Press, 127–188.

Alvarez, Robert Jr. 1995. "The Mexican-U.S. Border: The Making of an Anthropology of Borderlands." *Annual Review of Anthropology* 24: 447–470.

An, Ahmet. 2006. *Kıbrıslı Türklerin Siyasal Tarihi (1930–1960)*. Nicosia: Özyay Matbaacılık.

Anand, Nikhil. 2015. "Leaky States: Water Audits, Ignorance, and the Politics of Infrastructure." *Public Culture* 27(2): 305–330.

Anders, Gerhard. 2010. *In the Shadow of Good Governance: An Ethnography of Civil Service Reform in Africa*. Leiden: Brill.

Anderson, J. N. D. 1959. "The Family Law of Turkish Cypriots." *Die Welt des Islams* 5: 161–187.

Arat, Zehra F. 1998. "Educating the Daughters of the Republic." In *Deconstructing Images of "The Turkish Woman,"* edited by Z. F. Arat, 157–180. New York: St. Martin's.

Aravamudan, Srinivas. 2005. "Carl Schmitt's *The Nomos of the Earth*: Four Corollaries." *South Atlantic Quarterly* 104(2): 227–236.

Arendt, Hannah. 1958. *The Human Condition*. Chicago: University of Chicago Press.

———. 1968. *The Origins of Totalitarianism*. New York: Harcourt Brace.

———. 1969. "On Violence." In *Crises of the Republic*, 83–163. Harmondsworth: Penguin.

Aretxaga, Begoña. 2000. "A Fictional Reality: Paramilitary Death Squads and the Construction of State Terror in Spain." In *Death Squad: The Anthropology of State Terror*, edited by J. A. Sluka, pp. 46–69. Philadelphia: University of Pennsylvania Press.

Ashley, Richard K. 1988. "Untying the Sovereign State: A Double Reading of the Anarchy Problematique." *Millennium—Journal of International Studies* 17(2): 227–262.

Asmussen, Jan. 2008. *Cyprus at War: Diplomacy and Conflict During the 1974 Crisis*. London: I. B. Tauris.

Attalides, Michael. 2009. *Cyprus: Nationalism and International Politics*. Mannheim: Peleus.

Austin, J. L. 1962. *How to Do Things with Words: The William James Lectures Delivered at Harvard University in 1955*. Oxford: Oxford University Press.

Auyero, Javier. 2012. *Patients of the State: The Politics of Waiting in Argentina*. Durham, NC: Duke University Press.

Babuş, Fikret. 2006. *Osmanlı'dan Günümüze Etnik-Sosyal Politikalar Çerçevesinde Göç ve İskan Siyaseti ve Uygulamaları*. Istanbul: Ozan Yayıncılık.

Ballinger, Pamela. 2003. *History in Exile: Memory and Identity at the Borders of the Balkans*. Princeton: Princeton University Press.

Barkin, J. Samuel, and Bruce Cronin. 1994. "The State and the Nation: Changing Norms and the Rules of Sovereignty in International Relations." *International Organization* 48(1): 107–130.

Barışsever, Mehmet. 2007. *Müşavirin Not Defteri*. Nicosia: Mavi Basın Yayın.

Bartelson, Jens. 1995. *A Genealogy of Sovereignty*. Cambridge: Cambridge University Press.

———. 2013. "Three Concepts of Recognition." *International Theory* 5: 107–129.

———. 2014. *Sovereignty as Symbolic Form*. London: Routledge.

Bassiouni, M. Cherif. 1996. "International Crimes: *Jus Cogens* and *Obligatio Erga Omnes*." *Law and Contemporary Problems* 59(4): 63–74.

Baudrillard, Jean. 1981. *Simulacra and Simulation*. Translated by Sheila Faria Glaser. Ann Arbor: University of Michigan Press.

Baudrillard, J., and E. Noailles. 2007. *Exiles from Dialogue*. Cambridge: Polity.

Baybars, Taner. (1970) 2006. *Plucked in a Far-Off Land: Images in Self Biography*. Nicosia: Moufflon.

Beck, Martin, and Johannes Gerschewski. 2009. "On the Fringes of the International Community: The Making and Survival of 'Rogue States.'" *Security and Peace* 27(2): 84–90.

Beckingham, C. F. 1957. "The Turks of Cyprus." *Journal of the Royal Anthropological Institute of Great Britain and Ireland* 87(2): 167–174.

Bello, Walter. 2002. "Battling Barbarism." *Foreign Policy* 132: 41–42.

Benjamin, Walter. 1996. "Critique of Violence." In *Walter Benjamin: Selected Writings, Volume 1: 1913–1926*, edited by M. Bullock and M. W. Jennings, 236–252. Cambridge, MA: Harvard University Press.

Benton, Lauren. 2010. *A Search for Sovereignty: Law and Geography in European Empires, 1400–1900*. Cambridge: Cambridge University Press.

Biersteker, Thomas J., and Cynthia Weber. 1996. "The Social Construction of State Sovereignty." In *State Sovereignty as Social Construct*, edited by T. J. Biersteker and C. Weber, 1–21. Cambridge: Cambridge University Press.

Bigo, Didier, and Elspeth Guild. 2005. *Controlling Frontiers: Free Movement into and Within Europe*. Farnham, UK: Ashgate.

Bil, Hikmet. 1976. *Kıbrıs Olayı ve İçyüzü*. Istanbul: İtimat Kitabevi.

Billig, Michael. 1995. *Banal Nationalism*. London: Sage.

Billuroğlu, Ahmet. 2012. *KKTC'nin İlanının Perde Gerisi: Kripto Geldi Mi?* Nicosia: Söylem Yayınları.

Birand, Mehmet Ali. 1979. *Diyet: Türkiye ve Kıbrıs üzerine pazarlıklar*. Istanbul: Milliyet Yayınları.

Blakkisrud, Helge, and Pål Kolstø. 2011. "From Secessionist Conflict Toward a Functioning State: Processes of State- and Nation-Building in Transnistria." *Post-Soviet Affairs* 27(2): 178–210.

———. 2012. "Dynamics of de Facto Statehood: The South Caucasian de Facto States Between Secession and Sovereignty." *Southeast European and Black Sea Studies* 12(2): 281–298.

Bloch, Ernst. 1986. *The Principle of Hope*. London: Blackwell.

Bosteels, Bruno. 2005. "The Obscure Subject: Sovereignty and Geopolitics in Carl Schmitt's *The* Nomos *of the Earth*." *South Atlantic Quarterly* 104(2): 295–304.

Bourdieu, Pierre. 1999 (1977). *Outline of a Theory of Practice*. Cambridge: Cambridge University Press.

———. 1979. *Distinction: A Social Critique of the Judgement of Taste*. Translated by Richard Nice. Cambridge, MA: Harvard University Press.

Branch, Jordan. 2013. *The Cartographic State: Maps, Territory, and the Origins of Sovereignty*. Cambridge: Cambridge University Press.

Brighenti, Andrea. 2006. "On Territory as Relationship and Law as Territory." *Canadian Journal of Law and Society* 21(2): 65–86.

Broers, Laurence. 2013. "Recognising Politics in Unrecognised States: 20 Years of Enquiry into the *De Facto* States of the South Caucasus." *Caucasus Survey* 1(1): 59–74.

Brown, Chris. 2001. "Moral Agency and International Society." *Ethics and International Affairs* 15(2): 87–98.

Brown, Wendy. 2010. *Walled States, Waning Sovereignty*. New York: Zone.

Bryant, Rebecca. 2004. *Imagining the Modern: The Cultures of Nationalism in Cyprus*. London: I. B. Tauris.

———. 2010. *The Past in Pieces: Belonging in the New Cyprus*. Philadelphia: University of Pennsylvania Press.

———. 2012. *Displacement in Cyprus—Consequences of Civil and Military Strife. Report 2: Life Stories: Turkish Cypriot Community*. Nicosia: PRIO Cyprus Centre.

———. 2014a. "History's Remainders: Time and Objects After Conflict." *American Ethnologist* 41(4): 681–697.

———. 2014b. "Living with Liminality: De Facto States on the Threshold of the Global." *Brown Journal of World Affairs* 20(2): 125–143.

———. 2016. "Introduction: Everyday Coexistence in the Post-Ottoman Space," in *Post-Ottoman Coexistence: Sharing Space in the Shadow of Conflict*, ed. R. Bryant (Oxford: Berghahn Books), 1–38.

———. In progress. *Faking the State: On Pirates, Puppets, and Other Unbecoming Subjects*.

Bryant, Rebecca, and Mete Hatay. 2011. "Guns and Guitars: Simulating Sovereignty in a State of Siege." *American Ethnologist* 38(4): 631–649.

———. In progress a. "Simulating the State: Mimicry and Proto-State Formation."

———. In progress b. "The Leftover Community: Demography and Anxiety in a Society Under Siege."

Bryant, Rebecca, and Madeleine Reeves. 2020. "Introduction: Enacting Sovereign Agency." In *Sovereignty Beyond the State: Political Desires in Exceptional Places*, edited by R. Bryant and M. Reeves. Ithaca, NY: Cornell University Press.

Bryant, Rebecca, and Christalla Yakinthou. 2012. *Cypriot Perceptions of Turkey*. Istanbul: Turkish Economic and Social Studies Foundation.

Butler, Judith. 1990. *Gender Trouble: Feminism and the Subversion of Identity*. New York: Routledge.

———. 1997a. *Excitable Speech: A Politics of the Performative*. New York: Routledge.

———. 1997b. *The Psychic Life of Power: Theories in Subjection*. Stanford, CA: Stanford University Press.

Byman, Daniel, and Charles King. 2012. "The Mystery of Phantom States." *The Washington Quarterly* 35(3): 43–57.

Camus, Albert. (1955) 2012. *The Myth of Sisyphus: And Other Essays*. Translated by Justin O'Brien. New York: Random House.

Caspersen, Nina. 2011. "States Without Sovereignty: Imitating Democratic Statehood." In *Unrecognized States in the International System*, edited by N. Caspersen and G. Stansfield, 73–89. Abingdon, OX: Routledge.

———. 2012. *Unrecognized States*. Cambridge: Polity.

Catselli, Rina. 1974. *Kyrenia: A Historical Study*. Kyrenia: Kyrenia Flower Show.

Cattelino, Jessica R. 2008. *High Stakes: Florida Seminole Gaming and Sovereignty*. Durham, NC: Duke University Press.

Chaflin, Brenda. 2014. "Public Things, Excremental Politics, and the Infrastructure of Bare Life in Ghana's City of Tema." *American Ethnologist* 41(1): 92–109.

Chatterjee, Partha. 2004. *The Politics of the Governed: Reflections on Popular Politics in Most of the World*. New York: Columbia University Press.

Chatty, Dawn. 2010. *Displacement and Dispossession in the Modern Middle East*. Cambridge: Cambridge University Press.

Chu, Julie Y. 2014. "When Infrastructures Attack: The Workings of Disrepair in China." *American Ethnologist* 41(2): 351–367.

Ciddi, Sinan. 2009. *Kemalism in Turkish Politics: The Republican People's Party, Secularism and Nationalism*. New York: Routledge.

Clark, Bruce. 2007. *Twice a Stranger: How Mass Expulsion Forged Modern Greece and Turkey*. London: Granta.

Clastres, Pierre. 1977. *Society Against the State: The Leader as Servant and the Human Uses of Power Among the Indians of the Americas*. New York: Urizen.

Coleman, Leo. 2014. "Infrastructure and Interpretation: Meters, Dams, and State Imagination in Scotland and India." *American Ethnologist* 41(3): 457–472.

Comaroff, Jean, and John L. Comaroff. 1991. *Of Revelation and Revolution, Volume 1: Christianity, Colonialism, and Consciousness in South Africa*. Chicago: University of Chicago Press.

———. 2009. *Ethnicity, Inc.* Chicago: University of Chicago Press (Kindle edition).

Conklin, William E. 2012. "The Exclusionary Boundary of the Early Modern International Community." *Nordic Journal of International Law* 81: 133–173.

Constantinou, Costas M. 2004. *States of Political Discourse: Words, Regimes, Seditions*. New York: Routledge.

———. 2008. "On the Cypriot States of Exception." *International Political Sociology* 2(2): 145–164.

Constantinou, Costas M., Olga Demetriou, and Mete Hatay. 2012. "Conflicts and Uses of Cultural Heritage in Cyprus." *Journal of Balkan and Near Eastern Studies* 14(2): 177–198.

Constantinou, Costas M., and Oliver P. Richmond. 2005. "The Long Mile of Empire: Power, Legitimation and the U.K. Bases in Cyprus." *Mediterranean Politics* 10(1): 65–84.

Constantinou, Costas M., and Giorgos Kykkou Skordis. 2011. *The Third Motherland* (documentary). Nicosia.

Corbridge, Stuart, Glyn Williams, Manoj Srivastava, and René Veron, editors. 2009. *Seeing the State: Governance and Governmentality in India*. Cambridge: Cambridge University Press.

Cornell, Svante E. 2002a. *Autonomy and Conflict: Extraterritoriality and Separatism in the South Caucasus—Cases in Georgia*. Uppsala, Sweden: Uppsala University Department of Peace and Conflict Research.

———. 2002b. "Autonomy as a Source of Conflict: Caucasian Conflicts in Theoretical Perspective." *World Politics* 54(2): 245–276.

Crapanzano, Vincent. 2003. "Reflections on Hope as a Category of Social and Psychological Analysis." *Cultural Anthropology* 18(1): 3–32.

Crawford, James R. 2007. 2nd edition. *The Creation of States in International Law*. New York: Oxford University Press.

Darian-Smith, Eve. 1999. *Bridging Divides: The Channel Tunnel and English Legal Identity in the New Europe.* Berkeley: University of California Press.

Dayıoğlu, Ali. 2014. *Kuzey Kıbrıs'ın Ötekileri: Rumlar, Marunîler, Romanlar, Aleviler, Kürtler.* İstanbul: İstanbul Bilgi Üniversitesi Yayınları.

Dean, Mitchell. 2010. *Governmentality: Power and Rule in Modern Society,* 2nd edition. New York: Sage.

De Certeau, Michel. 1984. *The Practice of Everyday Life.* Translated by Steven Randall. Berkeley: University of California Press.

De Guevara, Berit Bliesemann, and Florian P. Kuhn. 2011. "'The International Community Needs to Act': Loose Use and Empty Signalling of a Hackneyed Concept." *International Peacekeeping* 18(2): 135–151.

Delaney, Carol. 1995. "Father State, Motherland, and the Birth of Modern Turkey." In *Naturalizing Power: Essays in Feminist Cultural Analysis,* edited by S. Yanagisako and C. Delaney, 177–199. New York: Routledge.

Deleuze, Gilles, and Félix Guattari. 1987. *A Thousand Plateaus: Capitalism and Schizophrenia,* translated and with an introduction by Brian Massumi. Minneapolis: University of Minnesota Press.

Derrida, Jacques. 1993. *Aporias.* Translated by Thomas Dutoit. Stanford: Stanford University Press.

———. 1994. *Spectres of Marx: The State of Debt, the Work of Mourning, and the New International.* Translated by Peggy Kamuf. New York: Routledge.

Diez, Thomas, and Nathalie Tocci, eds. 2009. *Cyprus at the Crossroads.* Manchester: Manchester University Press.

Dikeç, Mustafa. 2012. "Space as a Mode of Political Thinking." *Geoforum* 43: 669–676.

Dikomitis, Lisa. 2012. *Cyprus and Its Places of Desire: Cultures of Displacement Among Greek and Turkish Cypriot Refugees.* London: I. B. Tauris.

Donnan, Hastings, and Thomas M. Wilson, eds. 1994. *Border Approaches: Anthropological Perspectives on Frontiers.* Lanham, MD: Rowman and Littlefield.

———. 1999. *Borders: Frontiers of Identity, Nation, and State.* Oxford: Berg.

Douglas, Mary. 1993. *In the Wilderness: The Doctrine of Defilement in the Book of Numbers.* New York: Oxford University Press.

Droushiotis, Makarios. 2008. "Zurich: From Curse to Blessing in Disguise." *Cyprus Mail,* 1 October.

Dunn, Elizabeth Cullen. 2008. "Postsocialist Spores: Disease, Bodies, and the State in the Republic of Georgia." *American Ethnologist* 35(2): 243–258.

———. 2018. *No Path Home: Humanitarian Camps and the Grief of Displacement.* Ithaca, NY: Cornell University Press.

Dunn, Kevin C. 2009. "Environmental Security, Spatial Preservation, and State Sovereignty in Central Africa." In *The State of Sovereignty: Territories, Laws, Populations,* edited by D. Howland and L. White, 222–242. Bloomington: Indiana University Press.

Durakbaşa, Ayşe. 1998. "Kemalism as Identity Politics in Turkey." In *Deconstructing Images of "The Turkish Woman,"* edited by Z. F. Arat, 139–155. New York: St. Martin's.

Dzenovska, Dace, and Iván Arenas. 2012. "Don't Fence Me In: Barricade Sociality and Political Struggles in Mexico and Latvia." *Comparative Studies in Society and History* 54(3): 644–578.

Ekici, Tufan, and Gizem Caner. 2018. *Sector Analysis in North Cyprus: Tourism*. PRIO Cyprus Centre Report 4. Nicosia: PRIO Cyprus Centre.

Ellis, David C. 2009. "On the Possibility of 'International Community'." *International Studies Review* 11(1): 1–26.

Ellison, Ralph. 1995 (1947). *Invisible Man*. New York: Vintage.

Epstein, Charlotte. 2018. "The Productive Force of the Negative and the Desire for Recognition: Lessons from Hegel and Lacan." *Review of International Studies* 44(5): 805–828.

Epstein, Charlotte, Thomas Lindemann, and Ole Jacob Sending. 2018. "Frustrated Sovereigns: The Agency That Makes the World Go Around." *Review of International Studies* 44(5): 787–804.

Erdoğan, Yılmaz. 2001. *Vizontele*. Istanbul: BKM.

Ertürk, Yakın. 2006. "Turkey's Modern Paradoxes: Identity Politics, Women's Agency, and Universal Rights." In *Global Feminism: Transnational Women's Activism, Organizing, and Human Rights*, edited by M. M. Ferre and A. M. Tripp, 79–109. New York: New York University Press.

Fabian, Johannes. 1983. *Time and the Other*. New York: Columbia University Press.

Faustmann, Hubert. 1999. *Divide and Quit? British Colonial Policy in Cyprus 1878–1960*. MATEO (Ebook).

Fehérváry, Krisztina. 2002. "American Kitchens, Luxury Bathrooms, and the Search for a 'Normal' Life in Postsocialist Hungary." *Ethnos* 67(3): 369–400.

Feld, Steven. 2005. "Places Sensed, Senses Placed: Toward a Sensuous Epistemology of Environments." In *Empire of the Senses: The Sensual Culture Reader*, edited by D. Howes, 179–191. Oxford: Berg.

Ferguson, James and Akhil Gupta. 2002. "Spatializing States: Toward an Ethnography of Neoliberal Governmentality." *American Ethnologist* 29(4): 981–1002.

Fosshagen, Kjetil. 1999. "'We Don't Exist': Negotiations of History and Identity in a Turkish Cypriot Town." M.A. thesis submitted to the Department of Anthropology, University of Bergen.

Foucault, Michel. 1991. "Governmentality." In *The Foucault Effect: Studies in Governmentality*, edited by Graham Burchell, Colin Gordon, and Peter Miller, 87–104. Chicago: University of Chicago Press.

———. 2007. *Security, Territory, Population: Lectures at the Collège de France, 1977–1978*. Edited by Michel Senellart. Translated by Graham Burchell. New York: Picador.

Fowler, Michael Ross, and Julie Maria Bunck. 1996. "What Constitutes the Sovereign State?" *Review of International Studies* 22(4): 381–404.

Freedom House. 2019. *Democracy in Retreat: Freedom in the World 2019*. Washington, DC: Freedom House. Available at https://freedomhouse.org/sites/default/files/Feb2019_FH _FITW_2019_Report_ForWeb-compressed.pdf.

Freeman, Michael. 1999. "The Right to Self-Determination in International Politics: Six Theories in Search of a Policy." *Review of International Studies* 25(3): 355–370.

Friedman, Sara L. 2015. *Exceptional States: Chinese Immigrants and Taiwanese Sovereignty*. Berkeley: University of California Press.

———. 2020. "Aspirational Sovereignty and Human Rights Advocacy: Audience, Recognition, and the Reach of the Taiwan State." In *Sovereign Beyond the State: Political Desires in Exceptional Places*, edited by Rebecca Bryant and Madeleine Reeves. Ithaca, NY: Cornell University Press.

Gellner, Ernest. 1983. *Nations and Nationalism*. Ithaca, NY: Cornell University Press.

Gingeras, Ryan. 2011. *Sorrowful Shores: Violence, Ethnicity, and the End of the Ottoman Empire, 1912–1923*. Oxford: Oxford University Press.

Grant, Bruce. 2009. *The Captive and the Gift: Cultural Histories of Sovereignty in Russia and the Caucasus*. Ithaca, NY: Cornell University Press.

Green, Sarah F. 2010. "Performing Border in the Aegean." *Journal of Cultural Economy* 3(2): 261–278.

Greenberg, Jessica. 2011. "On the Road to Normal: Negotiating Agency and State Sovereignty in Postsocialist Serbia." *American Anthropologist* 113(1): 88–100.

Gringauz, Samuel. 1949. "The Ghetto as an Experiment of Jewish Social Organization (Three Years of Kovno Ghetto)." *Jewish Social Studies* 11(1): 3–20.

———. 1950. "Some Methodological Problems in the Study of the Ghetto." *Jewish Social Studies* 12(1): 65–72.

Gülcür, Leyla, and Pınar İlkkaracan. 2002. "The 'Natasha' Experience: Migrant Sex Workers from the Former Soviet Union and Eastern Europe in Turkey." *Women's Studies International Forum* 25(4): 411–421.

Günsev, Mesud. 2004. *20 Temmuz 1974: Şafak Vakti Kıbrıs*. Istanbul: Alfa.

Gupta, Akhil. 1995. "Blurred Boundaries: The Discourse of Corruption, the Culture of Politics, and the Imagined State." *American Ethnologist* 22(2): 375–402.

Gürel, Ayla, and Kudret Özersay. 2006. *The Politics of Property in Cyprus: Conflicting Appeals to "Bizonality" and "Human Rights" by the Two Cypriot Communities*. PRIO Cyprus Centre Report, 3. Nicosia: PRIO Cyprus Centre.

Gürel, Ayla, Fiona Mullen, and Harry Tzimitras. 2013. *The Cyprus Hydrocarbons Issue: Context, Positions and Future Scenarios*. PRIO Report 1. Nicosia: PRIO Cyprus Centre.

Hadjipavlou, Maria. 2010. *Women and Change in Cyprus: Feminism, Gender and Conflict*. London: I. B. Tauris.

Hadjiyanni, Tasoula. 2002. *The Making of a Refugee: Children Adopting Refugee Identity in Cyprus*. Westport, CT: Praeger.

Hage, Ghassan. 2009. "Waiting Out the Crisis: On Stuckness and Governmentality." In *Waiting*, edited by Ghassan Hage, 97–106. Carlton, Australia: University of Melbourne Press.

Harman, Doğan. 2006. *Statüko*. Nicosia: Kıbrıslı Yayınları.

Harvey, James, and Gareth Stansfield. 2010. "Theorizing Unrecognized States: Sovereignty, Secessionism, and Political Economy." In *Unrecognized States in the International System*, edited by N. Caspersen and G. Stansfield, 11–26. London: Routledge.

Harvey, Penelope. 2005. "The Materiality of State Effects: An Ethnography of a Road in the Peruvian Andes." In *State Formation: Anthropological Explorations*, edited by C. Krohn-Hansen and K. Nustad, 216–247. Cambridge: Pluto.

Harvey, Penelope, and Hannah Knox. 2012. "The Enchantments of Infrastructure." *Mobilities* 7(4): 521–536.

Hatay, Mete. 2005. *Beyond Numbers: An Inquiry into the Political Integration of the Turkish "Settlers" in Northern Cyprus*. PRIO Report 4/2005. Oslo: International Peace Research Institute.

———. 2007. *Is the Turkish Cypriot Population Shrinking? An Overview of the Ethno- Demography of Cyprus in the Light of the Preliminary Results of the 2006 Turkish-Cypriot Census*. PRIO Report 2/2007. Oslo: International Peace Research Institute.

———. 2008. "The Problem of Pigeons: Orientalism, Xenophobia, and a Rhetoric of the 'Local' in North Cyprus." *Cyprus Review* 20(2): 145–172.

———. 2011. "Coexistence or Domination? The Minaret and Belltower in Historical Perspective." Paper presented at the conference "Shared Spaces and Their Dissolution: Practices of Coexistence in Cyprus and Elsewhere," Nicosia, Cyprus.

———. 2015a. "'Kısın Yahu bu Hoparlörlerin Sesini': Kıbrıs'ta Geçmişten Günümüze Ezan Meselesi." *Poli/Havadis,* 13 September.

———. 2015b. "Gökyüzündeki Rekabet: Çan Kuleleri ve Minareler." *Poli/Havadis,* 20 September.

———. 2016. "Federal Kıbrıs'taki 'Kripto Taksim' Paradoksu." *Poli/Havadis,* 18 September.

———. 2017. *Population and Politics in North Cyprus: An Overview of the Ethno-Demography of North Cyprus in the Light of the 2011 Census.* PRIO Cyprus Centre Report 2/2017. Nicosia: PRIO/Friedrich Ebert Stiftung.

Hatay, Mete, and Rebecca Bryant. 2008. "The Jasmine Scent of Nicosia: On Returns, Revolutions, and the Longing for Forbidden Pasts." *Journal of Modern Greek Studies* 26(2): 423–449.

Havel, Václav. 1986. "The Power of the Powerless," trans. P. Wilson. In *Living in Truth: Twenty-Two Essays Published on the Occasion of the Award of the Erasmus Prize to Václav Havel.* Edited by Jan Vladislav. London: Faber & Faber.

Hayden, Robert. 2016. "Intersecting Religioscapes in Post-Ottoman Spaces: Trajectories of Change, Competition and Sharing of Religious Spaces." In *Shared Spaces and Their Dissolution: Practices of Coexistence in the Post-Ottoman Sphere,* edited by Rebecca Bryant. Philadelphia: University of Pennsylvania Press.

Hayden, Robert M., and Timothy D. Walker. 2013. "Intersecting Religioscapes: A Comparative Approach to Trajectories of Change, Scale, and Competitive Sharing of Religious Spaces." *Journal of the American Academy of Religion* 81(2): 399–426.

Heper, Metin. 1976. "Political Modernization as Reflected in Bureaucratic Change: The Turkish Bureaucracy and a 'Historical Bureaucratic Empire' Tradition." *International Journal of Middle East Studies* 7: 507–21.

———. 1985. *The State Tradition in Turkey.* Ann Arbor: University of Michigan Press.

Herzfeld, Michael. 1985. *The Poetics of Manhood: Contest and Identity in a Cretan Mountain Village.* Princeton: Princeton University Press.

———. 1997. *Cultural Intimacy: Social Poetics in the Nation-State.* New York: Routledge.

Hirschon, Renée. 2003. "'Unmixing' Peoples in the Aegean Region." In *Crossing the Aegean: An Appraisal of the 1923 Compulsory Population Exchange Between Greece and Turkey,* edited by R. Hirschon, 3–12. Oxford: Berghahn.

Holland, Robert. 1999. *Britain and the Revolt in Cyprus, 1955–1959.* Oxford: Clarendon.

Howes, David, and Constance Classen. 2014. *Ways of Sensing: Understanding the Senses in Society.* New York: Routledge.

Howland, Douglas, and Luise White. 2009. "Introduction: Sovereignty and the Study of States." In *The State of Sovereignty: Territories, Laws, Populations,* edited by D. Howland and L. White, 1–19. Bloomington: Indiana University Press.

Hunt, Lynn. 1992. *The Family Romance of the French Revolution.* Berkeley: University of California Press.

İnanç, Gül. 2008. *Türk Diplomasisinde Kıbrıs, 1970–1991: Büyükelçiler Anlatıyor.* Istanbul: Türkiye İş Bankası Kültür Yayınları.

International Crisis Group. 2004. *Moldova: Regional Tensions over Transnistria.* Europe Report No. 157.

———. 2010. *South Ossetia: The Burden of Recognition.* Europe Report No. 205.

Ioannides, P. Christos. 1991. *In Turkey's Image: The Transformation of Occupied Cyprus into a Turkish Province.* New York: Aristide D. Caratsas.

Irigaray, Luce. 1985. *This Sex Which Is Not One.* Translated by Catherine Porter. Ithaca, NY: Cornell University Press.

Isachenko, Daria. 2012. *The Making of Informal States: Statebuilding in Northern Cyprus and Transdniestria.* New York: Palgrave Macmillan.

Ismail, Salwa. 2006. *Political Life in Cairo's New Quarters: Encountering the Everyday State.* Minneapolis: University of Minnesota Press.

Jackson, Robert. 1990. *Quasi-States: Sovereignty, International Relations, and the Third World.* Cambridge: Cambridge University Press.

———. 2007. *Sovereignty: Evolution of an Idea.* Cambridge: Polity Press.

James, Alan. 1992. "The Equality of States: Contemporary Manifestations of an Ancient Doctrine." *Review of International Studies* 18(4): 377–391.

Janeja, Manpreet K., and Andreas Bandak, editors. 2018. *Ethnographies of Waiting: Doubt, Hope and Uncertainty.* London: Bloomsbury.

Jansen, Stef. 2009. "After the Red Passport: Towards an Anthropology of the Everyday Geopolitics of Entrapment in the EU's 'Immediate Outside.'" *Journal of the Royal Anthropological Institute* 15(4): 815–832.

———. 2014. "Hope For/Against the State: Gridding in a Besieged Sarajevo Suburb." *Ethnos* 79(2): 238–260.

———. 2015. *Yearnings in the Meantime: "Normal Lives" and the State in a Sarajevo Apartment Complex.* Oxford: Berghahn.

Jauregui, Beatrice. 2014. "Provisional Agency in India: *Jugaad* and Legitimation of Corruption." *American Ethnologist* 41(1): 76–91.

Jefferson, Andrew, Simon Turner, and Steffen Jensen. 2019. "Introduction: On Stuckness and Sites of Confinement." *Ethnos* 84(1): 1–13.

Kalmo, Hent, and Quentin Skinner, editors. 2010. *Sovereignty in Fragments: The Past, Present and Future of a Contested Concept.* Cambridge: Cambridge University Press.

Kandiyoti, Deniz. 1991. "End of Empire: Islam, Nationalism, and Women in Turkey." In *Women, Islam, and the State*, edited by D. Kandiyoti, 22–47. Philadelphia: Temple University Press.

———. 1997. "Gendering the Modern: On Missing Dimensions in the Study of Turkish Modernity." In *Rethinking Modernity and National Identity in Turkey*, edited by S. Bozdoğan and R. Kasaba, 113–132. Seattle: University of Washington Press.

———. 1998. "Some Awkward Questions on Women and Modernity in Turkey." In *Remaking Women: Feminism and Modernity in the Middle East*, edited by L. Abu-Lughod, 270–287. Cairo: American University in Cairo Press.

Kapferer, Bruce, ed. 2004. *State, Sovereignty, War: Civil Violence in Emerging Global Realities.* Oxford: Berghahn.

Kapferer, Bruce, and Bjørn Enge Bertelson, eds. 2009. *Crisis of the State: War and Social Upheaval.* Oxford: Berghahn.

Katsellis, Rina. 2017. *Kyrenia's Legend: The Life and Times of Costas Catsellis.* Translated by Irena Joannides. Nicosia: Armida.

Katsiaounis, Rolandos. 1996. *Labour, Society and Politics in Cyprus During the Second Half of the Nineteenth Century*. Nicosia: Cyprus Research Centre.

Ker-Lindsay, James. 2005. *EU Accession and UN Peacemaking in Cyprus*. London: Palgrave Macmillan.

———. 2012. *The Foreign Policy of Counter Secession: Preventing the Recognition of Contested States*. Oxford: Oxford University Press.

Keser, Ulvi. 2007. *Kıbrıs'ta Yeraltı Faaliyetleri ve Türk Mukavemet Teşkilatı (1950-1963)*. Istanbul: IQ Kültür Sanat Yayıncılık.

———. 2012. "1958-1963 Mücadele Sürecinde Kıbrıs'ta Basın ve Nacak Gazetesi." *Çağdaş Türkiye Tarihi Araştırmaları Dergisi* XII 24: 305–348.

Kıbrıs Türk Federe Devleti. 1977. *Özgürlüğün III. Yılında KTFD*. Nicosia: KTFD Devlet Matbaası.

Killoran, Moira. 1994. "Pirate State, Poet Nation: The Poetic Struggle over 'the Past' in North Cyprus." Unpublished PhD diss., Department of Anthropology, University of Texas, Austin.

King, Charles. 2001. "The Benefits of Ethnic War: Understanding Eurasia's Unrecognized States." *World Politics* 53 (July): 524–552.

King, Russell, and Sarah Ladbury. 1982. "The Cultural Construction of Political Reality: Greek and Turkish Cyprus Since 1974." *Anthropological Quarterly* 55(1): 1–16.

Kızılyürek, Niyazi. 2002. *Milliyetçilik Kıskacında Kıbrıs*. Istanbul: İletişim Yayınları.

———. 2005. *Doğmamış bir Devletin Tarihi: Birleşik Kıbrıs Cumhuriyeti*. Istanbul: İletişim Yayınları.

———. 2016. *Bir Hınç ve Şiddet Tarihi: Kıbrıs'ta Statü Kavgası ve Etnik Çatışma*. Istanbul: İstanbul Bilgi Üniversitesi Yayınları.

Kohn, Hans. 2008. (1944) *The Idea of Nationalism: A Study in Its Origins and Background*. With a new introduction by Craig Calhoun. New Brunswick, NJ: Transaction Publishers.

Köklüçınar, Engin. 1976. *Ağlayan ve Gülen Kıbrıs*. Istanbul: Yenigün.

Kolossov, Vladimir, and John O'Loughlin. 1999. "Pseudo-States as Harbingers of a New Geopolitics: The Example of the Transdniestr Moldovan Republic (TMR)." In *Boundaries, Territory and Postmodernity*, edited by D. Newman, 151–176. London: Frank Cass.

Kolstø, Pål. 2000. *Political Construction Sites: Nation-Building in Russia and the Post-Soviet States*. Boulder, CO: Westview.

———. 2006. "The Sustainability and Future of Unrecognized Quasi-States." *Journal of Peace Research* 43(6): 723–740.

Kolstø, Pål, and Helge Blakkisrud. 2008. "Living with Non-Recognition: State- and Nation-Building in South Caucasian Quasi-States." *Europe-Asia Studies* 60(3): 483–509.

Kovach, Karen. 2003. "The International Community as Moral Agent." *Journal of Military Ethics* 2(2): 99–106.

Krasner, Stephen D. 1999. *Sovereignty: Organized Hypocrisy*. Princeton: Princeton University Press.

Kristeva, Julia. 1982. *The Powers of Horror: An Essay on Abjection*. Translated by Leon S. Roudiez. New York: Columbia University Press.

Kurtuluş, Hatice, and Semra Purkis. 2008. "Türkiye'den Kuzey Kıbrıs'a göç dalgaları: Lefkoşa'nın dışlanmış göçmen-enformel emekçileri" *Toplum ve Bilim* 112: 60–101.

———. 2014. *Kuzey Kıbrıs'ta Türkiyeli Göçmenler*. Istanbul: Türkiye İş Bankası Yayınları.

Kuru, Ahmet T. 2014. "Authoritarianism and Democracy in Muslim Countries: Rentier States and Regional Diffusion." *Political Science Quarterly* 129(3): 399–427.

Kuzey Kıbrıs Türk Cumhuriyeti Cumhuriyet Meclisi. N.d. Kıbrıs'ta eski yönetimler. http://www.cm.gov.nc.tr/GecmisYonetim.aspx, accessed January 19, 2011.

Kyle, Keith. 1997. *Cyprus: In Search of Peace*. Minority Rights Group International Report 97/3. London: Minority Rights Group.

Kyngaert, Cedric, and Sven Sobrie. 2011. "Recognition of States: International Law or Realpolitik? The Practice of Recognition in the Wake of Kosovo, South Ossetia, and Abkhazia." *Leiden Journal of International Law* 24: 467–490.

Kyris, George. 2015. *The Europeanisation of Contested Statehood: The EU in Northern Cyprus*. Farnham, UK: Ashgate.

Ladbury, Sarah. 1977. "The Turkish Cypriots: Ethnic Relations in London and Cyprus." In *Between Two Cultures: Migrants and Minorities in Britain*, edited by J. L. Watson, 301–331. Oxford: Blackwell.

Lacan, Jacques. 1962–53. *The Seminar of Jacques Lacan: Book X: Anxiety*. Translated by Cormac Gallagher from unedited French transcripts. Unpublished manuscript, available at http://www.lacaninireland.com/web/translations/seminars/.

Lake, David. 2003. "The New Sovereignty in International Relations." *International Studies Review* 5(3): 303–323.

———. 2008. "The New American Empire?" *International Studies Perspectives* 9(3): 281–289.

Levent, Şener. 1995. *Mersin 10 Turkey*. Nicosia: Işık Kitabevi.

Lloyd, David. 2012. "Settler Colonialism and the State of Exception: The Case of Palestine/Israel." *Settler Colonial Studies* 2(1): 59–80.

Lodge, Martin, Lindsay Stirton, and Kim Moloney. 2015. "Whitehall in the Caribbean? The Legacy of Colonial Administration for Post-Colonial Democratic Development." *Commonwealth & Comparative Politics* 53(1): 8–28.

Loizides, Neophytos. 2016. *Designing Peace: Cyprus and Institutional Innovations in Divided Societies*. Philadelphia: University of Pennsylvania Press.

Loizos, Peter. 1981. *The Heart Grown Bitter*. Cambridge: Cambridge University Press.

———. 2008. *Iron in the Soul: Displacement, Livelihood, and Health in Cyprus*. New York: Berghahn.

Lombard, Luisa Nicolaysen. 2012. "Raiding Sovereignty in Central African Borderlands." PhD diss., Department of Anthropology, Duke University, Durham, NC.

Lowenthal, David. 1985. *The Past Is a Foreign Country*. Cambridge: Cambridge University Press.

Lubkemann, Stephen C. 2008a. *Culture in Chaos: An Anthropology of the Social Condition in War*. Chicago: University of Chicago Press.

———. 2008b. "Involuntary Immobility: On a Theoretical Invisibility in Forced Migration Studies." *Journal of Refugee Studies* 21(4): 454–475.

Lynch, Dov. 2004. *Engaging Eurasia's Separatist States: Unresolved Conflicts and de Facto States*. Washington, DC: U.S. Institute of Peace Press.

———. 2007. "De Facto 'States' Around the Black Sea: The Importance of Fear." *Southeast European and Black Sea Studies* 7(3): 483–496.

Lyons, Bayard. 2007. "Narratives of Suffering, Dynamics of Space and Practices of Intergenerational Memory in Turkish Cyprus." Unpublished PhD diss., University of California, Los Angeles.

Malkki, Liisa. 1995. *Purity and Exile: Violence, Memory and Cosmology Among Hutu Refugees in Tanzania*. Chicago: University of Chicago Press.

Mamdani, Mahmood. 2015. "Settler Colonialism: Then and Now." *Critical Inquiry* 41(3): 596–614.

Mani, Lata. 2008. "The Phantom of Globality and the Delirium of Excess." *Economic and Political Weekly* 43(39): 41–47.

Mardin, Şerif. 1991. *Din ve ideoloji.* Istanbul: İletişim Yayınları.

Markell, Patchen. 2003. *Bound by Recognition.* Princeton, NJ: Princeton University Press.

Markides, Diana Weston. 2001. *Cyprus 1957–1963—From Colonial Conflict to Constitutional Crisis: The Key Role of the Municipal Issue.* Minneapolis: University of Minnesota Press.

May, Joseph A. 1973. *Kant's Concept of Geography and Its Relation to Geographical Thought.* Toronto: University of Toronto Press.

Mbembe, Achille. 2003. "Necropolitics." Translated by L. Meintjes. *Public Culture* 15(1): 1–40.

McConnell, Fiona. 2009. "De Facto, Displaced, Tacit: The Sovereign Articulations of the Tibetan Government-in-Exile." *Political Geography* 28: 343–352.

———. 2016. *Rehearsing the State: The Political Practices of the Tibetan Government-in-Exile.* Oxford: John Wiley & Sons.

McGranahan, Carole. 2016. "Theorizing Refusal: An Introduction." *Cultural Anthropology* 31(3): 319–325.

Meadwell, Hudson. 1999. "Secession, States and International Society." *Review of International Studies* 25(3): 371–387.

Mehta, Uday S. 2007. "Indian Constitutionalism: The Articulation of a Political Vision." In *From the Colonial to the Postcolonial: India and Pakistan in Transition*, edited by D. Chakrabarty, R. Majumdar, and A. Sartori, 13–30. Oxford: Oxford University Press.

Mills, Robert Elliott. 2014. "The Pirate and the Sovereign: Negative Identification and the Constitutive Rhetoric of the Nation-State." *Rhetoric and Public Affairs* 17(1): 105–136.

Mitchell, Timothy. 1990. "Everyday Metaphors of Power." *Theory and Society* 19(5): 545–577.

———. 1991. "The Limits of the State: Beyond Statist Approaches and Their Critics." *American Political Science Review* 85(1): 77–96.

Miyazaki, Hirokazu. 2004. *The Method of Hope: Anthropology, Philosophy and Fijian Knowledge.* Stanford: Stanford University Press.

Mongia, Radhika Viyas. 1999. "Race, Nationality, Mobility: A History of the Passport." *Public Culture* 11(3): 527–556.

Moran, Anthony. 2002. "As Australia Decolonizes: Indigenizing Settler Nationalism and the Challenges of Settler/Indigenous Relations." *Ethnic and Racial Studies* 25(6): 1013–1042.

Muehlebach, Andrea. 2012. *The Moral Neoliberal: Welfare and Citizenship in Italy.* Chicago: University of Chicago Press.

Murray, Stuart J. 2006. "Thanatopolitics: On the Use of Death for Mobilizing Political Life." *Polygraph* 18: 191–215.

Navaro-Yashin, Yael. 2006. "De-Ethnicizing the Ethnography of Cyprus: Political and Social Conflict Between Turkish-Cypriots and Settlers from Turkey." In *Divided Cyprus: Modernity and an Island in Conflict*, edited by Y. Papadakis, N. Peristianis, and G. Welz, 84–99. Bloomington: Indiana University Press.

———. 2012. *The Make-Believe Space: Affective Geography in a Postwar Polity.* Durham, NC: Duke University Press.

Nedjati, Zaim M. 1981. "Acts of Unrecognised Governments." *International and Comparative Law Review* 30(2): 388–415.

Nevzat, Altay. 2005. Nationalism Amongst the Turks of Cyprus: The First Wave. PhD diss., Faculty of Humanities, Department of History, University of Oulu, Finland.

Ó Beacháin, Donnacha. 2012. "The Dynamics of Electoral Politics in Abkhazia." *Communist and Post-Communist Studies* 45: 165–74.

Ó Beacháin, Donnacha, Giorgio Comai, and Ann Tsurtsumia-Zurabashvili. 2016. "The Secret Lives of Unrecognised States: Internal Dynamics, External Relations, and Counterrecognition Strategies." *Small Wars and Insurgencies* 27(3): 440–466.

Öktem, Kerem. 2005. "Reconstructing Geographies of Nationalism: Nation, Space and Discourse in Twentieth Century Turkey." Unpublished PhD diss., School of Geography, University of Oxford.

———. 2009. "The Nation's Imprint: Demographic Engineering and the Change of Toponyms in Republican Turkey." *European Journal of Turkish Studies*, Thematic Issue 7(7).

Öncül, Tamer, and Öntaç Düzgün. 1999. *Kıbrıs Türk Yüksek Öğrenim Hareketleri 1960–1981*. Nicosia: Naci Talat Vakfı Yayınları.

Orr, Graeme. 2010. "A Fetishised Gift: The Legal Status of Flags." *Griffith Law Review* 19(3): 504–526.

Østerud, Øyrind. 1997. "The Narrow Gate: Entry to the Club of Sovereign States." *Review of International Studies* 23: 167–184.

Özsağlam, Muhittin Tolga. 2003. "Kuzey Kıbrıs'ta Milliyetçi Akımlar Üzerine Düşünceler." In *Kıbrıs'ın Turuncusu*, edited by M. Hasgüler and Ü. İnatçı, 219–228. Ankara: Anka Yayınları.

Paasi, Anssi. 1996. *Territories, Boundaries and Consciousness: The Changing Geographies of the Finnish-Russian Border*. New York: J. Wiley & Sons.

———. 1998. "Boundaries as Social Processes: Territoriality in the World of Flows." *Geopolitics* 3(1): 69–88.

———. 1999. "Nationalizing Everyday Life: Individual and Collective Identities as Practice and Discourse." *Geography Research Forum* 19: 4–21.

———. 2009. "Bounded Spaces in a 'Borderless World'? Border Studies, Power, and the Anatomy of Territory." *Journal of Power* 2(2): 213–234.

Painter, Joe. 2006. "Prosaic Geographies of Stateness." *Political Geography* 25: 752–774.

Panagia, Davide. 2018. *Rancière's Sentiments*. Durham, NC: Duke University Press.

Pancyprian Bar Association (Πανκύπριος Δικηγόρικος Σύλλογος). 2013. Ο περί της Διαδικασίας Τυποποίησης των Γεωγραφικών Τοπωνυμίων της Κυπριακής Δημοκρατίας Νόμος του 1998 (66(I)/1998) (The Procedure for the Standardization of Geographical Names of the Republic of Cyprus Law 1998 (66(I)/1998). http://www.cylaw.org/nomoi/enop/non-ind/1998_1_66/full.html.

Papadakis, Yiannis. 2005. *Echoes from the Dead Zone: Across the Cyprus Divide*. London: I. B. Tauris.

Parla, Taha, and Andrew Davison. 2004. *Corporatist Ideology in Kemalist Turkey: Progress or Order?* Syracuse, NY: Syracuse University Press.

Patrick, Richard A. 1976. *Political Geography and the Cyprus Conflict: 1963–1971*. Edited by James H. Bater and Richard Preston. Waterloo: University of Waterloo (Department of Geography, Publication Series No. 4).

Paul, Darel. 1999. "Sovereignty, Survival and the Westphalian Blind Alley in International Relations." *Review of International Studies* 25(2): 217–231.

Pegg, Scott. 1998. *International Society and the de Facto State.* Aldershot, UK: Ashgate.

Pelkmans, Mathijs. 2006. *Defending the Border: Identity, Religion and Modernity in the Republic of Georgia.* Ithaca, NY: Cornell University Press.

———. 2013. "The Affect Effect." *Anthropology of This Century* 7 (May 2013). http://aotcpress .com/articles/affect-effect/.

Penrose, Jan. 2002. "Nations, States and Homelands: Territory and Territoriality in Nationalist Thought." *Nations and Nationalism* 8(3): 277–297.

———. 2011. "Designing the Nation: Banknotes, Banal Nationalism and Alternative Conceptions of the State." *Political Geography* 30: 429–440.

Pierce, Steven. 2006. "Looking Like a State: Colonialism and the Discourse of Corruption in Nigeria." *Comparative Studies in Society and History* 48(4): 887–914.

Pietz, William. 1985. "The Problem of the Fetish I." *RES: Anthropology and Aesthetics* 9: 5–17.

Plümer, Aytuğ. 2008. *Kıbrıs Ekonomi Tarihi: Sarsıntılı bir Devrin Anatomisi (1960–1974).* Nicosia: Rüstem Kitabevi.

Pomper, Philip. 2012. "The Evolution of the Russian Tradition of State Power." *History and Theory* 51: 60–88.

Popescu, Nicu. 2011. *EU Foreign Policy and Post-Soviet Conflicts: Stealth Intervention.* New York: Routledge.

Rabinowitz, Dan. 2001. "The Palestinian Citizens of Israel, the Concept of Trapped Minority and the Discourse of Transnationalism in Anthropology." *Ethnic and Racial Studies* 24(1): 64–85.

Ram, Moriel. 2015. "Colonial Conquests and the Politics of Normalization: The Case of the Golan Heights and Northern Cyprus." *Political Geography* 47(1): 21–32.

Ramm, Christoph. 2006. "Assessing Transnational Renegotiation in the Post-1974 Cypriot Community: 'Cyprus Donkeys,' 'Black Beards,' and the 'EU Carrot.'" *Southeast European and Black Sea Studies* 6(4): 523–542.

———. 2009. Turkish Cypriots, Turkish "Settlers" and (Trans)National Identities Between Turkish Nationalism, Cypriotism and Europe. Unpublished PhD thesis, Faculty of Social Sciences, Ruhr-Universität Bochum.

Rancière, Jacques. 2004. *The Politics of Aesthetics: The Distribution of the Sensible.* Translated and introduced by Gabriel Rockhill. New York: Continuum.

Rappas, Alexis. 2014. *Cyprus in the 1930s: British Colonial Rule and the Roots of the Cyprus Conflict.* London: I. B. Tauris.

Reeves, Madeleine. 2014. *Border Work: Spatial Lives of the State in Rural Central Asia.* Ithaca, NY: Cornell University Press.

Reeves, Madeleine, Johan Rasanayagam, and Judith Beier, editors. 2014. *Ethnographies of the State in Central Asia: Performing Politics.* Bloomington: Indiana University Press.

Renan, Ernst. 2018. "What is a Nation? (Qu'est-ce qu'une nation? 1882)." In *What Is a Nation? and Other Political Writings,* translated and edited by M. F. N. Giglioli, 247–263. New York: Columbia University Press.

Richmond, Oliver P. 2002. "States of Sovereignty, Sovereign States, and Ethnic Claims for International Status." *Review of International Studies* 28(2): 381–402.

Ricoeur, Paul. 2005. *The Course of Recognition.* Translated by David Pellauer. Cambridge, MA: Harvard University Press.

———. 2010. "Power and Violence." Translated by L. Jones. *Theory, Culture and Society* 27(5): 18–36.

Ronen, Yael. 2011. *Transition from Illegal Regimes under International Law*. Cambridge: Cambridge University Press.

Roschin, Evgeny. 2016. "The Hague Conferences and 'International Community': A Politics of Conceptual Innovation." *Review of International Studies* 43(1): 177–198.

Rutherford, Danilyn. 2012. *Laughing at Leviathan: Sovereignty and Audience in West Papua*. Chicago: University of Chicago Press (Kindle edition).

Sadrazam, Halil. 1990. *Kıbrıs'ta Varoluş Mücadelemiz, Şehitlerimiz ve Anıtlarımız*. Ankara: Türkiye Şehitlikleri İmar Vakfı Yayınları.

Şafaklı, Okan. 2003. "KKTC' de Kooperatiflerin Finansman Üzerine Bir Çalışma." *Yönetim ve Ekonomi* 10(2): 175–189.

Sant Cassia, Paul. 2005. *Bodies of Evidence: Burial, Memory and the Recovery of Missing Persons in Cyprus*. Oxford: Berghahn.

Schatzki, Theodore R. 2002. *The Site of the Social: A Philosophical Account of the Constitution of Social Life and Change*. University Park: Pennsylvania State University Press.

———. 2010. *The Timespace of Human Activity: On Performance, Society, and History as Indeterminate Teleological Events*. Lanham, MD: Lexington Books (Kindle edition).

Schmidt, Dennis R. 2016. "Peremptory Law, Global Order, and the Normative Boundaries of a Pluralistic World." *International Theory* 8(2): 262–296.

Schmitt, Carl. 2006. *The Nomos of the Earth, in the International Law of the Jus Publicum Europeaum*. New York: Telos.

Schnitzler, Antina von. 2013. "Traveling Technologies: Infrastructure, Ethical Regimes, and the Materiality of Politics in South Africa." *Cultural Anthropology* 28(4): 670–693.

Schöpflin, George. 1997. "The Function of Myths and a Taxonomy of Myths." In *Myths and Nationhood*, edited by G. Hosking and G. Schöpflin, 19–35. London: Hurst & Co.

Schwenkel, Christina. 2017. "Spectacular Infrastructure and Its Breakdown in Socialist Vietnam." *American Ethnologist* 42(3): 520–534.

Scott, James C. 1976. *The Moral Economy of the Peasant: Subsistence and Rebellion in Southeast Asia*. New Haven: Yale University Press.

———. 1985. *Weapons of the Weak: Everyday Forms of Peasant Resistance*. New Haven: Yale University Press.

Scott, Julie. 1995. "Identity, Visibility, and Legitimacy in Tourism Development in North Cyprus." Unpublished PhD diss., University of Kent, Canterbury.

———. 1998. "Property Values: Ownership, Legitimacy and Land Markets in Northern Cyprus." In *Property Relations: Renewing the Anthropological Tradition*, edited by C. Hann, 142–159. Cambridge: Cambridge University Press.

Simpson, Audra. 2014. *Mohawk Interruptus: Political Life Across the Borders of Settler States*. Durham, NC: Duke University Press.

Simpson, Gerry. 2004. *Great Powers and Outlaw States: Unequal Sovereigns in the International Legal Order*. Cambridge: Cambridge University Press.

Skoutaris, Nikos. 2011. *The Cyprus Issue: The Four Freedoms in a Member State Under Siege*. Oxford: Hart.

Sloane, Robert D. 2002. "The Changing Face of Recognition in International Law: A Case Study of Tibet." *Emory International Law Review* 16(1): 107–186.

Smith, Daniel Jordan. 2007. *A Culture of Corruption: Everyday Deception and Popular Discontent in Nigeria*. Princeton: Princeton University Press (Kindle edition).

Soguk, Nevzat. 1999. *States and Strangers: Refugees and Displacements of Statecraft*. Minneapolis: University of Minnesota Press.

Sonan, Sertaç. 2014. "In the Grip of Political Clientelism: The Post-1974 Turkish Cypriot Politics and the Politico-Economic Foundations of Pro-*Taksim* Consensus." Unpublished PhD diss., Faculty of Social Sciences, University of Duisberg-Essen, Germany.

Spruyt, Hendrik. 1994. *The Sovereign State and Its Competitors*. Princeton: Princeton University Press.

Spyrou, Stella. 2004. Ἐγκλειστοι στο "Dome" στην Κερύνεια, ο πατέρας μου και άλλοι, 1974–75." In *Η Κερύνεια Μας*, 211–224. Nicosia: Kyrenia Municipality.

Stepputat, Finn. 2008. "Forced Migration, Land, and Sovereignty." *Government and Opposition* 43(2): 337–357.

Stolzenberg, Nomi M. 2009. *Facts on the Ground*. University of Southern California Law School Legal Working Paper Series, Paper 45.

Storey, David. 2001. *Territories: The Claiming of Space*. Harlow: Prentice-Hall/Pearson Education.

Strange, Susan. 1999. "The Westfailure System." *Review of International Studies* 25(3): 345–354.

Strong, Paul. 1999. "The Economic Consequences of Ethno-Nationalism in Cyprus: The Development of Two Siege Economies After 1963 and 1974." Unpublished PhD diss., Economic History, London School of Economics, University of London.

Surin, Kenneth. 2005. "World Ordering." *South Atlantic Quarterly* 104(2): 185–197.

Talat, Ayşenur. 2015. "Multi-Dimensionality of Migration: The Case of Post-1974 Immigrants in the Bahçeli Village in the Northern Part of Cyprus." Unpublished PhD diss., submitted to the Social Sciences Institute, Middle East Technical University, Ankara, Turkey.

Taussig, Michael. 1992. *The Nervous System*. New York: Routledge.

Thomson, Janice E. 1994. *Mercenaries, Pirates, and Sovereigns: State-Building and Extraterritorial Violence in Early Modern Europe*. Princeton: Princeton University Press.

———. 1995. "State Sovereignty in International Relations: Bridging the Gap Between Theory and Empirical Research." *International Studies Quarterly* 39: 213–33.

Thrift, Nigel J. 2000. "It's the Little Things." In *Geopolitical Traditions: A Century of Geopolitical Thought*, edited by D. Atkinson and K. Dodds, 380–387. New York: Routledge.

Tocci, Natalie. 2002. "Cyprus and the European Union Accession Process: Inspiration for Peace or Incentive for Crisis." *Turkish Studies* 3(2): 104–138.

Tolgay, Ahmet. 2009. "Unutulmayan Yıllar." *Kıbrıs Gazetesı*, 31 May.

Torpey, John. 1998. "Coming and Going: On the State Monopolization of the Legitimate 'Means of Movement.'" *Sociological Theory* 16:3: 239–259.

———. 1999. *The Invention of the Passport: Surveillance, Citizenship and the State*. Cambridge: Cambridge University Press.

Trimikliniotis, Nicos, and Corina Demetriou. 2011. "Labour Integration of Migrant Workers in Cyprus: A Critical Appraisal." In *Precarious Migrant Labour Across Europe*, edited by M. Pajnik and G. Campani, 73–96. Ljubljana: Mirovni Institut.

Tuan, Yi-Fu. 1975. "Geopiety: A Theme in Man's Attachment to Nature and to Place." In *Geographies of the Mind*, edited by D. Lowenthal and M. Bowden, 11–39. New York: Oxford University Press.

Turner, Victor. 1987. *Betwixt and Between: Patterns of Masculine and Feminine Initiation*. La Salle, IL: Open Court.

United Nations. 1975. United Nations Resolution 367 (1974). Adopted by the Security Council on 12 March 1975. Available at http://www.un.int/cyprus/scr367.htm.

———. 1983. United Nations Resolution 541 (1983). Adopted by the Security Council on 18 November 1983. Available at http://www.un.int/cyprus/scr541.htm.

United Nations Humanitarian Relief Agency. 2004. *Guiding Principles on Internal Displacement.* Available at https://cms.emergency.unhcr.org/documents/11982/44794/UN%2C+G uiding+Principles+on+Internal+Displacement%2C+1998/47806967-dd92-4d67-ad47 -578aa8b5d11f

United States Department of State. 2019. *2018 Country Report on Human Rights Practices: Cyprus.* https://www.state.gov/reports/2018-country-reports-on-human-rights-practi ces/cyprus/.

Unwin, T., and V. Hewitt. 2001. "Banknotes and National Identity in Central and Eastern Europe." *Political Geography* 20: 1005–1028.

Varnava, Andrekos, Nicholas Coureas, and Marina Elia, editors. 2009. *The Minorities of Cyprus: Development Patterns and the Identity of the Internal-Exclusion.* Cambridge: Cambridge Scholars Publishing.

Vincent, Joan. 1978. "Political Anthropology: Manipulative Strategies." *Annual Review of Anthropology* 7: 175–194.

Vismann, Cornelia. 1997. "Starting from Scratch: Concepts of Order in No Man's Land." In *War, Violence and the Modern Condition*, edited by Bernd Hüppauf, 46–64. Berlin: Walter de Gruyter.

Volkan, Vamık D. 1979. *Cyprus—War and Adaptation: A Psychoanalytic History of Two Ethnic Groups in Conflict.* Charlottesville: University of Virginia Press.

Vryonis, Speros. 2005. *The Mechanism of Catastrophe: The Turkish Pogrom of September 6–7, 1955, and the Destruction of the Greek Community of Istanbul.* New York: Greekworks.

Wahba, Jacklin. 2002. "Labor Mobility in Egypt: Are the 1990s any Different from the 1980s?" In *The Egyptian Labor Market in an Era of Reform*, edited by R. Assaad, 258–286. Cairo: American University in Cairo Press.

Walker, R. B. J. 1993. *Inside/Outside: International Relations as Political Theory.* New York: Cambridge University Press.

———. 1996. "Space/Time/Sovereignty," in Mark E. Denham and Mark Owen Lombardi (editors) *Perspectives on Third-World Sovereignty: The Postmodern Paradox.* New York: St Martin's Press.

———. 2010. *After the Globe, Before the World.* New York: Routledge.

Weber, Cynthia. 1992. "Reconsidering Statehood: Examining the Sovereignty/Intervention Boundary." *Review of International Studies* 18(3): 199–216.

———. 1995. *Simulating Sovereignty: Intervention, the State, and Symbolic Exchange.* Cambridge: Cambridge University Press.

———. 1998. "Performative States." *Millennium—Journal of International Studies* 27(1): 77–95.

Weber, Lynn, and Lori Peek, editors. 2012. *Displaced: Life in the Katrina Diaspora.* Austin, TX: University of Texas Press.

Wedeen, Lisa. 1999. *Ambiguities of Domination: Politics, Rhetoric, and Symbols in Contemporary Syria.* Chicago: University of Chicago Press.

Wilson, Alice. 2016. *Sovereignty in Exile: A Saharan Liberation Movement Governs.* Philadelphia: University of Pennsylvania Press.

Wilson, Alice, and Fiona McConnell. 2015. "Constructing Legitimacy without Legality in Long Term Exile: Comparing Western Sahara and Tibet." *Geoforum* 66: 203–214.

Wilson, Thomas M., and Hastings Donnan, eds. 2010. *Border Identities: Nation and State at International Frontiers.* Cambridge: Cambridge University Press.

Witsoe, Jeffrey. 2011. "Corruption as Power: Caste and the Political Imagination of the Postcolonial State." *American Ethnologist* 38(1): 73–85.

Wolfe, Patrick. 2006. "Settler Colonialism and the Elimination of the Native." *Journal of Genocide Research* 8(4): 387–409.

Yarrington, Landon. 2015. "The Paved and the Unpaved: Toward a Political Economy of Infrastructure, Mobility, and Urbanization in Haiti." *Economic Anthropology* 2: 185–204.

Yaşın, Mehmet, ed. 2000. *Step-Mothertongue: From Nationalism to Multiculturalism—Literatures of Cyprus, Greece and Turkey.* London: Middlesex University Press.

Yaşın, Özker. 1976. *Girne'den Yol Bağladık.* Istanbul: İtimat Kitabevi.

———. 1977. *Kıbrıslı Kâzım.* Istanbul: Yücel.

Yates, Douglas A. 1996. *The Rentier State in Africa: Oil Rent Dependency and Neocolonialism in the Republic of Gabon.* Asmara, Eritrea: Africa World Press.

Yeyati, Eduardo. 2003. *Dollarization.* Cambridge, MA: MIT Press.

Yiftachel, Oren. 2002. "Territory as the Kernel of the Nation: Space, Time and Nationalism in Israel/Palestine." *Geopolitics* 7(2): 215–248.

Yurchak, Alexei. 2006. *Everything Was Forever, Until It Was No More.* Princeton: Princeton University Press.

Zamindar, Vazira Fazila-Yacoobali. 2007. *The Long Partition and the Making of Modern South Asia: Refugees, Boundaries, Histories.* New York: Columbia University Press.

Zetter, Roger. 1985. "Rehousing the Greek-Cypriot Refugees from 1974: Dependency, Assimilation, Politicisation." In *Cyprus in Transition: 1960–1985,* edited by John T. A. Koumoulides, 106–125. London: Trigraph.

———. 1999. "Reconceptualizing the Myth of Return: Continuity and Transition Amongst the Greek-Cypriot Refugees of 1974." *Journal of Refugee Studies* 12(1): 1–22.

Žižek, Slavoj. 1989. *The Sublime Object of Ideology.* London: Verso.

———. 1996. *The Indivisible Remainder: On Schelling and Related Matters.* London: Verso.

ACKNOWLEDGMENTS

As always happens with works whose research and writing spans such an extended period, we have accumulated many debts. Rebecca's primary debt is to the European Institute of the London School of Economics, and specifically to the Hellenic Observatory, which provided her with the A. N. Hadjiyannis Associate Professorial Research Fellowship, under which the writing of much of this book took place. Rebecca was also a research associate of the Peace Research Institute Oslo (PRIO) between 2012 and 2016, when she was an investigator on a Norwegian Research Council–funded project, "Imagined Sovereignties." This and Rebecca's forthcoming book are both results of that funding, and she thanks Åshild Kolås of PRIO for engaging her in that collaboration.

In addition, the Friedrich Ebert Stiftung and the Turkish Economic and Social Studies Foundation (TESEV) supported Rebecca's coauthored report (with Christalla Yakinthou) on Cypriot perceptions of Turkey, for which she conducted a set of thirty interviews on Turkish Cypriots' relations with their patron state. Both Mete and Rebecca were engaged in different parts of a European Union–funded project, run by PRIO's Cyprus Centre, "Internal Displacement in Cyprus: Mapping the Consequences of Civil and Military Strife." For that project, Mete undertook a comprehensive mapping of Cypriot displacement, both locating and narrating routes of displacement for every village and town on the island. Rebecca conducted a series of oral history interviews that resulted in a report and several short documentary films on Turkish Cypriot experiences of displacement. We thank Greg Reichberg of PRIO for his facilitation of that project. Mete also thanks Harry Tzimitras, director of the PRIO Cyprus Centre, for his support during the final writing stages, which went on longer than expected. In addition, Hubert

Faustmann of the Friedrich Ebert Foundation has funded parts of Mete's PRIO Cyprus Centre research that have fed into this project.

Along with these debts, however, are the personal and intellectual debts that one accumulates over a decade. Our thanks go first and foremost to our friends and interlocutors in Cyprus. Among these, we wish to acknowledge by name Kudret Akay, Mustafa Akıncı, Erdal Andız, Hakkı Atun, Fatma Azgın, Mutlu Azgın, Umut Bozkurt, Emin Çizenel, Taner Derviş, Öntaç Düzgün, Erhan Erçin, Tufan Erhürman, İsmet Ersoy, Oğuz Etçi, Tamer Gazioğlu, Halil Giray, Ayla Gürel, Müzeyyen Hatay, Serden Hoca, Turhan Korun, Nahide Merlen, Layik Mesutoğlu, Cenk Mutluyakalı, Zaim Necatigil, Münür Rahvancıoğlu, Sami Saygun, Sertaç Sonan, Ferdi Sabit Soyer, Hürrem Tulga, Eşref Vaiz, and Hakkı Yücel. We owe many thanks to Gökhan Şengör for making available previously unaccessed materials in the Turkish Cypriot National Archive and to Sibel Siber for facilitating our access to the TRNC Parliament's achive. We are also grateful to the many persons whose anonymous stories and observations are incorporated here.

Because this book has become entangled with Rebecca's other projects, and with presentations and discussions that emerged from those, much of the book was theoretically shaped in conversation with colleagues spread across the world. Among those, she would like to single out Madeleine Reeves, whose ever-sharp mind and intellectual energy helped in refining concepts, even if she was not aware of it. Discussions with Jens Bartelson, Cynthia Weber, and Lisa Wedeen aided in identifying the contribution that a work of historical ethnography can make to political theory. To that end, Rebecca would particularly like to thank the Lund University Department of Political Science for an invitation to participate in a workshop on state-building where, as the only anthropologist, she was challenged to think through these questions. Similarly, discussions with Elizabeth Davis and Carol Greenhouse challenged her to hone the work and its contribution to anthropology. Long talks with Gyan Pandey, as well as briefer discussions with Ted Svensson, helped in thinking through how to write about partition. We are very grateful to Tom de Waal, our travel partner in Abkhazia, for inviting us on the journey and sharing with us his knowledge of other sovereignty conflicts and the lives of other unrecognized citizens.

In the course of completing this work, we lost two friends who had an influence on both of us. Rebecca became friends with historian Rolandos Katsiaounis during her very earliest days on the island, when they worked for months on end in the same archives together. Rolandos had a sweeping knowledge of the island's history that helped ground our own work. Poet Filiz Naldöven was Rebecca's close friend, with whom she had many long conversations about precisely the absurdities that we describe in this book. Filiz had said for years that she could not wait to read the book, and we regret that the time it took to complete it outstripped her own.

As we were still in the process of thinking about how to write this book, we lost Mete's father, Özer Hatay, a journalist with a passion for Cypriot history. We would have wanted more time to discuss the work with him, and we always felt his gentle spirit hovering over the project. His wit, principles, and ironic way of viewing Cypriot politics have guided this work even in his absence.